Masculinities in Polish, Czech and Slovak Cinema

Masculinities in Polish, Czech and Slovak Cinema

Black Peters and Men of Marble

Ewa Mazierska

Berghahn Books

New York • Oxford

First published in 2008 by
Berghahn Books
www.berghahnbooks.com

First paperback edition published in 2010

Library of Congress Cataloging-in-Publication Data
A C.I.P. record for this book is available
from the Library of Congress

British Library Cataloguing in Publication Data
A catalogue record for this book is available from the British Library

Printed in the United States on acid-free paper

ISBN: 978-1-84545-540-8 (hardback)
ISBN: 978-1-84545-239-1 (paperback)

Contents

List of Illustrations

Acknowledgements

I wish to express my gratitude to Peter Hames, Petra Hanáková, Dina Iordanova, Monika Kęska, Kevin Moss, Jonathan Owen, Sylva Polaková, Robert B. Pynsent, Laura Rascaroli, Katerina Svatonová, Grażyna Świętochowska, Dorota Tubielewicz Mattson, Jan Uhde and Bartosz Żurawiecki for reading the whole or parts of this manuscript and their insightful comments.

I am also indebted to my sister, Małgorzata Mazierska, my mother, Daniela Mazierska, Grzegorz Balski, Grażyna Grabowska, Anna Gugulska, Peter Hames, Petra Hanáková, Dina Iordanova, Ivan Klimeš, Anna Kozanecka, Krzysztof Loska, Ewa Modrzejewska, Jonathan Owen, Waldemar Piątek, Andrzej Pitrus, Małgorzata Radkiewicz, Věra Sokolová, Katerina Svatonová, Michał Szczubiałka, Josef Škvorecký, Grażyna Świętochowska, Jan Uhde, Błażej Warkocki, Adam Wyżyński, Piotr Zwierzchowski and Bartosz Żurawiecki, who helped me to find the films, journals, books and stills used in the book and allowed me the access to their work. I am also grateful to all institutions and individuals who granted me permission to use the stills, especially to the 'Perspektywa' Film Studio for allowing me to use a still from Janusz Morgenstern's film, *To Kill this Love*, on the book cover. All efforts have been made to clear the copyright for all pictures.

My special thanks goes to my husband, Gifford Kerr, who helped me with editing the manuscript.

I am also grateful to the University of Central Lancashire and Arts and Humanities Research Councils whose grants allowed me to embark on this project and finish it on time.

Introduction

Until the early 1990s the term 'gender studies' was immediately associated with the studies of women. Women were typically compared and contrasted with an 'eternal man', whose essence did not change over time and who remained the same in different cultures. However, due to a number of factors – such as the rise of feminism and a male backlash against this ideology, the development of queer theory, as well as some significant social and economic changes in the developed world – the male condition has been discovered as an object of serious academic discourses, a topic of a popular discussion in the media and a problem to be tackled by specific policies, institutions and movements. Michael Messner lists such diverse symptoms of this interest in men in the United States as a conservative Christian movement whose purpose is to help Christian men to reclaim the spiritual leadership of their families and communities, the mushrooming of pro-feminist and gay men's organisations to confront sexual harassment and homophobia in society, and the 'men's rights' movement that argues that men are victims of laws and traditions that privilege women (Messner 1997: 1–2). Other authors add to these signs the debate about why men have high incidence of suicide and lower life expectancies, and the issue of why boys are failing at school (Segal 1997: ix). Although some of these movements and debates, particularly those conducted from conservative positions, proclaim the existence of true, pure or proper masculinity, their very efforts to distinguish this from any impure or problematic masculinity points to the fact that masculinity is a sociocultural construct, not a natural and stable reality. Lynne Segal perfectly captures this paradox by saying: 'The closer we come to uncovering some form of exemplary masculinity, a masculinity which is solid and sure of itself, the clearer it becomes that masculinity is structured through contradiction: the more it asserts itself, the more it calls itself into question' (ibid.: 123).

Whilst the need to make masculinity visible, and analyse and deconstruct it, is now taken for granted by Western scholars, the most visible signs of which are the numerous shelves in university libraries filled with books on this subject[1], including a growing body about representation of men in film (see, for example, Krutnik 1991; Cohan and Rae Hark 1993; Studlar 1996), this field is still underdeveloped in Eastern Europe (or Central Europe, East-Central Europe or Other Europe, as the region comprising countries of the previous Soviet bloc is now named). Jitka

Malečkova in an essay published in 1996 goes as far as saying that: 'Research on specific men's views, experiences or problems seems to be completely nonexistent in the Czech human and social sciences' (Malečková 1996: 108). Consequently, often the only avenue to acquire some knowledge about a particular aspect of East European men's lives, for example, their participation in politics or rearing children, is by learning about this aspect of women's lives or society as a whole. Of course, the knowledge acquired this way is unsatisfactory for all sorts of reasons. This deficit of sources refers also to men as represented in film. There are no books in the Polish, Czech or Slovak language devoted to this issue and even articles on this subject are uncommon, which largely reflects a lack of interest in East-Central Europe as such. There has also been little work done comparing cinemas of these countries. Even in publications that tackle films from the whole of the Soviet bloc, authors typically use a country-by-country approach (see Liehm and Liehm 1977; Slater 1992), rather that comparing films from different countries using a particular criterion.[2] The lack of sources about men from this part of Europe is reflected in Western thinking about men. Books on this subject focus on Western (typically British and American) constructions of masculinity. Even in publications that explicitly refer to European men, the specificity of East European men is ignored. For example, in the recently published book, *The Trouble With Men: Masculinities in European and Hollywood Cinema* (Powrie 2004), we do not find a single chapter devoted to the cinematic portrayal of men in East European cinema. Similarly, publications devoted to specific categories of men, such as gay men, either openly or conspicuously ignore the existence of this category in Eastern Europe or give it only a token recognition (Dyer 1990; Murray 1998; Benshoff and Griffin 2004).

This book attempts to tackle this omission by providing a study of Polish and Czechoslovak men in Polish and Czechoslovak films.[3] My primary task here is thus to analyse what divides and what links Polish and Czechoslovak men in film and the ideologies concerning their representation. In line with contemporary thinking on gender, my assumption is that masculinity should be considered in the plural. There are different masculinities, depending on the different cultural and historical circumstances in which men are brought up, on the different stages in men's lives and even on the different roles men play in any given moment of their lives. They are also affected by men's personal idiosyncrasies. On the other hand, certain similarities such as sharing the same nationality or living under the same political and economic system, account for certain similarities between men and the ideologies of masculinity that surround them.

Why do I compare Polish and Czechoslovak cinema, rather than Polish and East German or Czechoslovak and Romanian? The main reason is my initial assumption (which this book is meant to test) that Polish and Czechoslovak cinemas have an adequate amount of similarity and difference to afford fruitful comparison. In particular, Poland and the lands currently comprising the Czech Republic and Slovakia were always neighbours and at certain periods were even part of the same state. Moreover, for over forty years following the end of the Second World War Poland and Czechoslovakia endured a similar political and economic system, that of state socialism, and at a similar moment abandoned it, choosing democracy and a market economy. On the other hand, many authors point out that the Czechoslovak version of socialism was different to the Polish one and provoked a different reaction among its citizens, and the manner in which Poland and Czechoslovakia changed their system was somehow dissimilar. Furthermore, after the Second World War, Czechoslovak and Polish cinemas developed under similar conditions, namely a nationalised film industry, and after the fall of communism they started to be privatised. Film specialists also maintain that Poland and Czechoslovakia boasted distinctive cinemas, having predilections for different characters, emotional tone and visual style (see Chapter 1).

I also chose these two cinemas because emotionally they are closest to me. I was born and lived in Poland most of my life, therefore know Polish cinema intimately. Equally, from an early age I was enchanted by the films of Poland's southern neighbour. Indeed, Czechoslovak films were the only films from the old Soviet bloc that I always watched with pleasure and this has not changed since 1989. I was especially drawn to their male characters. Somehow I found myself more attuned to the world of Black Peter, Miloš Hrma or Lemonade Joe than to Maciek Chełmicki, Maciek Tomczyk or Franz Maurer.

By examining Polish, Czech and Slovak cinematic men I also hope to engage with a number of larger discourses. One of them concerns 'real' men and their countries' histories, cultures and national ideologies. Secondly, I would like to contribute to the debate as to whether and to what extent it is justified to talk about 'East European man' as a homogenous entity – a product of living under the same set of political circumstances, variably described as communism or state socialism and, after 1989, as postcommunism. Furthermore, I would like to explore what Polish and Czechoslovak men share with, and what differentiate them from, their Western counterparts, or from a 'universal man' distilled from Western discourses on men. Rather than focusing on the types of men that appeared exclusively in Polish and Czechoslovak culture, such as the 'little Czech' and the 'Polish romantic', or are specific only to the political system under which the men lived, such as the socialist 'new man' or the shock worker, I will attempt to map them onto some categories familiar from Western male studies, such as the soldier, the father, the heterosexual lover and the man who does not conform to the heterosexual norm. Each category, ascribed to a specific role men play in their lives or a specific identity they employ, will be analysed in a separate chapter. The division of men into these categories is heuristic, not ontological. I assume that these roles are not mutually exclusive; we can even imagine some men playing all these roles in their lives. Consequently, I will also look at the connections between these various roles, the problems that arise from men's need to fulfil more than one role or apply more than one identity, frequently returning to the same films in different chapters. As some of these roles, if not all of them, involve the cooperation of women with men (most importantly that of the heterosexual lover), and the position of men in society reflects and is influenced by the position of women, women cannot be ignored in my study. My investigation should also contribute to a discussion of nations and nationalisms, again in the plural, because there is no nationalism in general (Bhabha 1990). The reason is that nationalisms assume specific constructions of gender and sexuality, in the most blatant sense requiring men and women to behave in a certain way, and punishing them for transgressing the norms specific to each gender (Mosse 1985; Parker et al. 1992).

My approach will be both diachronic and synchronic. I will discuss certain traits pertaining to men living in different moments of history, but represented in films made at a similar time, and men of one epoch but depicted in films made in different periods, for example men living under Stalinism in the films of the 1950s and 1970s. By 'accompanying' Polish and Czechoslovak screen men through the history of their countries and their cinemas, I will explore what links them and what divides them. I will also look at the sociopolitical systems and cultural traditions in which they functioned. My assumption is that the systems and the traditions were patriarchal but there was no single model of patriarchy in the countries I am discussing.

Film offers an excellent lens through which to look at masculinities and nations because, to use Lenin's phrase, 'film is the most important art', or at least it had been for a considerable time in the countries and cultures which I examine here, until it was dislodged from its privileged position by such media as television and later perhaps the internet. It was used as a mirror, to capture the present situation of the country and reflect its history, and as a chisel, to mould society in a particular way by instilling in it specific ideas and values, and offering citizens models to follow. In the crudest sense, the political authorities used cinema as propaganda. More subtly, at certain periods, especially when the ruling elite lacked the power to impose a particular lifestyle on citizens or was uncertain which lifestyle it wanted to promulgate, cinema was offered as a 'sleeping pill', diverting citizens' attention from the daily problems or mistakes made by the authorities. Equally, in Poland and Czechoslovakia cinema served as a way to challenge and resist the official version of national history. It could be argued that in the second role Polish and Czechoslovak cinema was at its most successful. The films and directors who offered the society counter-narratives and alternative models to those officially propagated even received a privileged place in national cinemas. The figures of men fulfilled an important function in promoting specific attitudes and behaviour, therefore male actors had a crucial role to play in larger cultural discourses. Although I do not devote a specific chapter to male stars, their significance is discussed on numerous occasions in this book.

The comparative character of my study inevitably leads to situating it in a number of contexts. They include the political histories of Poland and Czechoslovakia, cultural traditions of the respective countries and the histories of their cinemas. For this reason, before I analyse the different roles men play in films, I will outline the histories of Poland and Czechoslovakia, and the histories of their cinemas, focusing on the similarities and differences between these countries. It must be emphasised, however, that my objective here is not to provide a comprehensive account of the lives of Polish, Czech and Slovak people over the centuries, but only to sketch what appears to me as the prevailing historical discourses on the respective nations. Similarly, I will not offer here a comprehensive study of the national cinemas but only present the main schools and their most distinguished representatives. What interests me especially are the moments when Poland's and Czechoslovakia's histories took different turns and how this might affect the lives and identities of men living in these countries. Another ramification of my investigation is the Western study of men, from which I will borrow terminology and hypotheses to test in my investigation. It should be mentioned here that the premise of a large part of the recent studies on men is that masculinity is in crisis or even that men, despite their apparent or real dominance, constitute the less happy and more suffering half of the population (Horrocks 1994; Segal 1997; MacKinnon 2003). I will try to check if the 'crisis theory' is also valid in regard to Polish, Czech and Slovak men.

Almost all Polish and Czechoslovak films contain male characters and the vast majority of films cast men in the roles which I intend to examine in this book. Yet, it is impossible to cover the whole range of film production in these two, and since 1993, three, countries, even superficially. One has to limit oneself to 'important examples' of films. But which examples do I consider important? Firstly, those which include typical representation of men and those which most affected the viewers' imagination. The second feature can be assessed by critical acclaim, box office success, as well as the film's longevity, measured by its afterlife in academic discourse, 'cult status', repeated broadcasting and DVD editions. I try to take all these factors into account. I also attempt to balance discussion of films well known to readers with those which were omitted or marginalised in previous analyses; those regarded as high-brow and artistic with those which are low-brow and popular. Ultimately, however, despite watching over three hundred films for this study, I have no pretence to base my research on any 'representative sample' of Polish and Czechoslovak films. Rather I admit that it is a product of a particular discourse, in this case, of me writing a study of men in these films, not a preexisting entity which such a study attempts to uncover (on arbitrary character of discourse see Foucault 1986: 284). However, I will regard it a success if my 'men in Polish, Czech and Slovak cinema' both resemble the men known to readers and have some freshness about them. I want to emphasise that although this book is meant to contribute to the history of cinema of these countries, it has no ambition to replace it. Accordingly, many films important for artistic or political reasons are omitted from my discussion, because the issues around masculinity are not foregrounded in them as they are in other, perhaps less artistically accomplished films. On the other hand, some should be considered because they offer an interesting insight into the lives of men but are excluded simply because of the limited space I have at my disposal. I should also mention that in this book I focus on men as seen by men, so to speak. Renditions of male characters created by female, and especially feminist, directors hardly feature in my book because I feel that they deserve a separate study. Similarly, I am excluding films made by Polish, Czech and Slovak filmmakers abroad, as I feel their nationality is problematic.

Czechoslovakia and Poland are for me equal partners in my comparison. If at any point of my investigation I devote more space to one country than the other, it is because a particular phenomenon turns out to be more pervasive or visible to me in one country than in the other. Similarly, when discussing postcommunist cinema, I attempt to account for the fact that after 1993 the subject of my study consists of films made in three countries rather than two: Poland, the Czech Republic and Slovakia. However, I must admit that I found it difficult to balance the number of Czech and Slovak films, especially when regarding the nationality of the director as the main criterion of the nationality of the film.

In an interview given in 1992, Jiří Menzel said that after the Velvet Revolution the citizens of Czechoslovakia lost interest in Poland as, indeed, in any other country that belonged to the Eastern bloc, adding that even under communism his countrymen hardly found that Poland captivated their imagination. This was because Czechs, Slovaks, as well as Poles found the capitalist West more attractive than the socialist East. Yet, he also added that this lack of interest was largely due to ignorance, particularly in relation to the cultures of the neighbouring countries (Trzaska 1992: 10–1). I hope that *Masculinities in Polish, Czech and Slovak Cinema: Black Peters and Men of Marble* (apart from providing Western readers with some knowledge of Eastern men on screen), will encourage such an interest among the citizens of these countries in the cultures of their neighbours.

Notes

1. Lynne Segal in the 1997 edition of her book, *Slow Motion*, counts four hundred new texts in the last ten years alone devoted to the subject of men (Segal 1997: xii).
2. Notable exceptions are an essay by Yvette Biró, 'Pathos and Irony in East European Films' (Biró 1983) and a recent book by Dina Iordanova, *Cinema of the Other Europe* (Iordanova 2003).
3. I use 'Czechoslovak cinema' as a shorthand for 'Czechoslovak, Czech and Slovak cinema'. In the next chapter I will subject the term 'Czechoslovak' to a more detailed analysis.

Chapter 1

Polish and Czechoslovak Histories, Cultures and Cinemas

One is a Czech, a Pole or a Belgian because of the lack of better opportunities.
(Král 1983: 46)

Poland, the Czech Republic and Slovakia (Czechoslovakia before 1993) are situated in Central Europe. Such a location has allowed their citizens to perceive themselves as belonging to Europe, understood as a particular system of values which include tolerance, democracy and multiculturalism, or even as being at the heart of Europe, spreading the best European traditions and bridging the gap between the Slavic East and German and Roman West (Holý 1996; Černý 2001; Kroutvor 2001; Davies 2005).[1] On the other hand, during the course of history it brought significant limitations, resulting from being squeezed between its more powerful neighbours, Germany and Russia, which were not shy to enlarge their territories by invading them. As a consequence of these factors, the Czech, Polish and Slovak nations were involved in many wars and their territories served as other countries' battlefields. Czechoslovakia was even described as an 'unfortunate country, more frequently subjugated or "liberated" than any other European nation' (Vogel 1974: 140). There are also important differences between these countries and their nations. Poland is a much larger country than Czechoslovakia ever was, both in terms of its population and surface area. Poland's current population is over 38 million people, the Czech Republic's 10 million, Slovakia's 5.4 million. While Poland is a middle-sized European country, the Czech Republic, Slovakia and their predecessor, Czechoslovakia, could be described as demographically and geographically small. J.F.N. Bradley argues that size influenced the history of the Czech and Slovak nations immensely, imposing on them additional limitations to those resulting from their geographical position. 'The most basic limitation was that neither of these nations could dare to challenge power hegemonies in Central Europe. They either had to join them more or less voluntarily and derive whatever benefits they could, or they were crushed and integrated in the hegemonies against their will' (Bradley 1971: 197). The power in which Czechs invested their greatest hope was Austria. The view that the Austrian empire would assure them a large degree of political autonomy and cultural influence in Europe gave rise to the concept of austroslavism, created by the historian and politician František Palacký (1798–1876) (Kroutvor 2001: 255–6).

By contrast to Czechs and Slovaks, at certain periods of its history, principally during the reign of the Jagiellonian dynasty in the fifteenth and sixteenth centuries, Poland possessed economic and military power to be reckoned with in the whole of Europe. However, its grandiose ambitions, demonstrated by engaging in costly wars, were in due course punished by the loss of political might and later independence. On the whole, both Poland and Czechoslovakia experienced long periods of political decline and nonexistence as separate states. Hence, Polish, Czech and Slovak histories are typically perceived as discontinuous. Ladislav Holý claims that the 'meaning of Czech history is distilled not from what actually happened in the past but from the imagination of what would have happened if, as it were, Czechs had been left to their own devices' (Holý 1996: 120). Poles also like to select from the flow of past events only those which adhere to a certain vision of Polish national character, principally eliminating the periods when Poland was not 'free'. As a result of such an attitude, some right-wing politicians recently proposed changing the name of the Polish state into 'IV Rzeczpospolita' (the Fourth Republic of Poland), as opposed to III Rzeczpospolita, as Poland was renamed after the fall of communism. In this way they want to emphasise Polish discontinuity even in the period after 1989 by completely discarding the time when postcommunist parties governed Poland, as if this period existed somehow outside Polish history in the proper sense.

Czech and Slovak Histories and National Characters

In the dominant discourse on Czech and Slovak history the permanent discontinuity began when the Great Moravian empire, regarded as the first common state of Czechs and Slovaks, collapsed at the beginning of the tenth century. After that Czechs and Slovaks had to struggle to preserve their autonomy against the colonising attempts of more powerful neighbours: Germans in the case of Czechs, Hungarians in the case of Slovaks. For Czechs the most tragic moment was the Battle on the White Mountain in 1620 (Bradley 1971: 84–102; Holý 1996: 120), which ended the uprising of the Protestant Bohemian nobility against the absolutist rule of the Catholic Habsburgs established on the Czech throne since 1526. The rebellious Czech nobility was destroyed and could not be replaced by the handful of Catholic nobles who had returned with the Ferdinand's armies and who in popular perception were Germans. German imperial officials took over the administration of the kingdom and introduced other repressive measures that 'decapitated the Czech nation: its elite, the nobility, was either destroyed, and its estates expropriated, or exiled; or alienated from the Czech nation and absorbed into the Habsburg system' (Bradley 1971: 86). The defeat on the White Mountain was followed by what is widely seen as three centuries of 'darkness' that eclipsed all aspects of Czech culture and social life. During these dark centuries the Czech kingdom was almost continuously an arena of political and religious conflict and it became marginalised within the Habsburg empire; its role reduced to paying heavy taxes to the Emperors and providing soldiers to fight in wars in which they had no interest. The Czech language almost disappeared from the streets of towns and was only used by the lowest classes: peasantry and later, the proletariat. Consequently, 'the peasant creations such as songs, poems and proverbs became the culture of the Czechs, for they were written and composed in the Czech language, while other cultural manifestations in the Czech kingdom were written in Latin or German' (ibid.: 97). The view that darkness followed the Battle on the White Mountain is most strongly espoused by Palacký, who, being a Protestant, approached Czech history from a Protestant perspective. However, it is also possible to see the period of Germanisation and re-Catholisation as a time of Czech economic and cultural prosperity. Such a view is promulgated by the Catholic historian Josef Pekař and his followers (Pynsent 1994: 182; Holý 1996: 124). They point out that during the eighteenth century industrialisation began, gradually changing Bohemia into one of the most industrialised and modern parts of Europe. It solved the Czech kingdom's balance of payments problem, created population surpluses and led to a relative prosperity of the kingdom in years to come. Moreover, the country created its own architectural/artistic style known as Czech Baroque (Pynsent 1994: 184) that today attracts millions of tourists to Prague and other Czech towns.

Proponents of the idea of darkness following the year 1620 claim that at the end of the eighteenth century the process of rebuilding Czech culture and identity began. This 'Czech revival' was assisted by widening access to education that led to the spread of literacy and the creation of the new Czech elite of intellectuals, consisting of teachers, engineers and scientists. This rebuilding was carried through largely by rediscovering, codifying and researching the Czech language. A chair of the Czech language was established at Prague University, elevating it from the humble position of a means of communication for peasants to that of an academic discipline and literary instrument. Father Josef Dobrovský, an enlightened former Jesuit, compiled the first comprehensive Czech grammar, in 1809. The revival of the Czech language was accompanied by a new interest in history. Czech nobles sponsored research into their own family archives and financed historical publications (Bradley 1971: 115). Simultaneously, the nineteenth century saw the development of Czech nationalism, which was predominantly cultural, but punctuated by military revolts. The most famous took part in Prague in 1848, when crowds of people, including some Slavonic guests who came from all parts of the Habsburg Empire to discuss philology and history, clashed with troops picketing the streets to maintain public order. The apparent suffering of Czechs under foreign domination ended in 1918, with the establishment of the Czechoslovak Republic, principally due to the collapse of the Austro-Hungarian Empire and thanks to the diplomatic efforts of some Czechs, especially Tomáš G. Masaryk, to whom I return in due course.

The concept of 'revival', used in reference to Czech culture, points to such a deep crisis preceding it, that it equated with near death (Kundera 1981: 21). As previously mentioned, its apparent main cause was the absorption of the Czech upper classes into

German society and culture. Thus, in the nineteenth century they were faced with the choice of adopting either a German identity or a Czech one which was new to them. As Bradley argues: 'It would have been much easier and more rewarding to slip aside, into the mainstream of German culture' (Bradley 1971: 121). Milan Kundera uses the term 'the Czech wager' (to highlight its similarity with Pascal's wager) to describe the decision Czech people faced. Their consideration featured such dilemmas and questions as: whether it is worth expending intellectual energy in creating a new culture for a small nation, rather than enjoying the privilege of being part of a large nation with a well-established and sophisticated culture; will this new culture be distinctive enough to compete effectively with the cultures of other European nations (see Kundera 1981: 21)? Kundera gives a positive answers to these questions, arguing that Czech culture and especially literature, as exemplified by the works of Franz Kafka, Max Brod, Jaroslav Hašek and Karel Čapek, has a universal appeal and even became a paradigm of modern world literature. This opinion is based on his observation that this literature does not proclaim the superiority of Czechness over other national countries but rather rejects nationalism. Moreover, it offers a vision of the world in which history is cruel and mad, which is also the vision of history prevailing today, especially after the experiences of the Holocaust and Stalinism. Such a vision, argues Kundera, could be conceived only by a small nation that went through many defeats and humiliations unknown to large nations of imperialistic ambitions (ibid: 21–2). Petr Král goes even further that Kundera by suggesting that the value of Czech literature lies in its rejection of and scorn for all things Czech. He himself admits that when he was growing up in Prague the word 'Czech' for him and his friends had only negative connotations (Král 1983: 46). Gilles Deleuze and Felix Guattari reach a similar conclusion about the specificity and value of Czech literature in their analysis of the work and life of Franz Kafka (who is widely regarded as the greatest writer to be born on Czech soil). They represent Kafka, like the protagonists of his works, such as the hero of the autobiographical *Letter to the Father*, as someone who suffers 'an exaggerated Oedipus [complex]'. He dreams of escaping his father and everything he stands for: his culture and history, Jews, Czechs and Germans, in extreme cases by entering a completely different level of existence, for example through becoming an animal (Deleuze and Guattari 2000: 9–15).

Kundera and others, such as Josef Kroutvor, emphasise that Czechs chose their existence as a separate nation more by intellectual efforts than by military struggle (Kundera 1981: 21; Kroutvor 2001: 255). Bradley points out that the leaders of the Czech nationalist movement in the eighteenth and nineteenth century were members of the intelligentsia (often of German origin), who were practical, intelligent citizens who went about their business, not officers or any self-proclaimed insurrections wanting to change the political status quo (Bradley 1971: 112). This had an impact on the character of Czech culture, in which the importance of military struggle is underplayed and even has bad connotations, as a sign of madness or self-indulgence. Conversely, culture, particularly literature, has a special meaning for Czechs. It can be regarded as their main weapon against foreign invasion, taking the place of conventional politics (Kroutvor 2001: 231).

The construction of Czech history in the various discourses, and especially the one proposed by Palacký and his followers, influenced the way Czechs imagine themselves as a nation. They ascribe to themselves such features and traditions as possessing a dove-like mentality (thanks to never starting a war), a propensity to egalitarianism and democracy (due to the lack of indigenous gentry following the destruction of the Czech gentry after the Battle on the White Mountain) and being well educated and cultured or *kulturní* (thanks to the exceptional role literature played in Czech history and Czech standing in the international arena). However, as Ladislav Holý observes, the carrier of these traditions is the nation as a whole, rather than any of its particular members. This means that the ideals can persist even if most people do not live up to them (Holý 1996: 85), being used, for example, as standards with which the nation's leaders are compared. The first President of Czechoslovakia, Tomáš Garrigue Masaryk (1850–1937), excellently embodies the qualities Czechs ascribe to their nation, thanks to being an intellectual, even a philosopher, a friend of Karel Čapek, a modest and modern man with feminist views (Filipowicz 2005), who worked for the creation of Czechoslovakia through diplomatic rather than military efforts. Masaryk also encapsulates Czechs' respect for democratic institutions, such as parliament and government. The citizens of Czechoslovakia and Czechs especially took great pride in the fact that in the interwar period Czechoslovakia was the only country in Central Europe to enjoy democracy, surrounded by fascist or semi-fascist states such as Germany, Hungary and Poland. Although today various authors point to its authoritarian character, particularly in relation to Masaryk who was able to use the institutions of democracy for his own purposes, as captured in the phrase 'Masaryk's republic' (Holý 1996: 165), Czechoslovakia still stands out as more democratic against the background of its neighbours. Similarly, Masaryk comes across as more committed to the principles of democracy than Józef Piłsudski, the most important politician in interwar Poland.

The greatest challenge for Czechoslovakia's interwar government and the most serious threat to the country's democracy derived from its being a multiethnic state, which largely resulted from its constitution within the historical borders of the Bohemian kingdom. Numerically, the strongest ethnic group was the Czechs, followed by Germans and Slovaks. Effectively Czechoslovakia remained a democracy till March 1939, when, following the Munich agreement in September 1938 between Hitler and the French and British Prime Ministers, the Sudeten districts, with a predominantly German population, were separated from Czechoslovakia, and the government was forced to allow Germany to occupy its land and demobilise its armed forces. As Bradley puts it, 'Munich turned the wheel of history by returning Czechs under the German hegemony' (Bradley 1971: 159). At the same time, it can be seen as a final blow to Palacký's dream of a federal Central Europe with Western Slavs living peacefully together under benevolent Austrian leadership. By and large, the Second World War destroyed Central Europe by dividing it into West and East (on Central Europe, see Kroutvor 2001).

Let us now turn to Slovakia. After the collapse of the Great Moravian Empire, Slovakia became part of the Hungarian state, in which it remained without any autonomy as an integral part of St. Stephen's crown until the end of the First World War. Yet, it should also be mentioned that Bratislava retained its position as the capital city of Hungary until 1848, when the capital moved to Budapest. Moreover, as in Czech lands, in Slovakia late in the eighteenth century a national renaissance began, consisting largely of creating institutions promoting Slovak literature and language. Some of the leading figures of this renaissance, such as Ján Kollár (1793–1852), Pavel Jozef Šafařík (1795–1861) and Palacký, were active in both Bohemia and Slovakia or at least familiar with the culture, history and contemporary political situations of both of these countries (Holý 1996: 93). One of the questions which was hotly debated during the national revival was whether Czechs and Slovaks were one nation or two closely related but separate nations. The view that they were one nation was expressed, for example, by Dobrovský. Its inhabitants began to be referred to first as Czechoslavs and later as Czechoslovaks–a nation bound together by common history, tradition and culture. However, efforts to create a common Czechoslovak national identity were paralleled by efforts to assert a separate Slovak identity. They were motivated by two considerations. The first was Slovak anxiety that in a common Czechoslovak tree Slovaks were merely branches while Czechs were the trunks and the roots. The second was the strong Czech Protestant tradition, viewed as alien to the deep-rooted Catholic faith of most ordinary Slovaks. The decisive act in establishing a separate Slovak identity in relation to the Czechs was the creation of a Slovak literary language at the end of the eighteenth century (ibid.: 93–6).

Nevertheless, faced with continuous Magyar oppression, shortly before the First World War and particularly during the war, Slovak politicians joined forces with Czechs in order to create one state following the defeat of the Austro-Hungarian Empire. In 1916 Milan Štefánik (1880–1919), a Slovak astronomer and war hero, together with Masaryk and Edvard Beneš (who after Masaryk's death would be Czechoslovakia's second President) created the Czechoslovak National Council as an embryo of a future Czechoslovak government. Their efforts led to the creation of Czechoslovakia.

As previously mentioned, one of the most serious problems of prewar Czechoslovakia pertained to the relation between Czechs and the minorities, including Slovaks. Czechs were not only numerically dominant but also occupied most of the positions of power in public administration, education and health services, and not only in Czech lands but in Slovakia as well. Initially this was due to the shortage of qualified Slovak personnel but later mainly due to Czechs' unwillingness to free up positions of power for Slovaks. Such a situation exacerbated Slovak aversion to a Czech presence in Slovakia and strengthened the separatist tendencies among Slovaks. These tendencies were also fuelled by the Protestant overtones of the symbols of the new country. Separatist aspirations were politically articulated by the Slovak People's Party, under the leadership of Andrej Hlinka, who, apart from his interest in politics, was a high-ranking Catholic priest. After the Munich agreement, Hlinka's party formed an autonomous Slovak government and Slovakia began to function as an autonomous part of the country, renamed Czecho-Slovakia. In 1939 the Slovak leader Jozef Tiso declared Slovakia an independent state under the official protection of Nazi Germany. The Slovak government pursued

Nazi-inspired policies including the forced transfer of Slovak Jews to Nazi concentration camps. Slovak opposition to Nazi rule culminated in 1944 in a national uprising which aimed to free Slovaks from Nazi control and to reunite them with Czechs in a single Czechoslovak Republic. The uprising was eventually crushed by German military forces but it laid the basis for the autonomous role of Slovakia in postwar Czechoslovakia (Holý 1996: 97–101).

Slovaks share some important traits with their neighbours or 'older brothers', as Czechs used to like to see themselves in relation to Slovaks. In particular, according to the dominant discourse on Slovak national character, they are also egalitarian. There are also differences. Slovaks appear to be somehow less dove-like and 'cultured' than Czechs. The prevailing stereotype of a Slovak is that of a wild, plain-spoken mountaineer with a penchant for strong alcohol rather than beer. Slovaks are also more religious and emotional than Czechs (Paul 1979: 219). It is telling that while the Czech character is seen as embodied by such figures as Švejk and Father Kondelík (discussed in due course), both phlegmatic and passive, the favourite Slovak hero is Juraj Jánošik, a Robin Hood-like highwayman from the eighteenth century operating on both sides (Slovak and Polish) of the Tatra mountains, who stole from the wealthy to give to the poor. Needless to say, Jánošik is everything but passive; he connotes bravura, passion and commitment (ibid.). Jánošik is not an exclusively Slovak hero; Slovaks share his legend with Poles (who call him Janosik). He was the main character in a number of films produced on the Polish side of the Tatra, including a Slovak–Polish co-production, to be directed by Agnieszka Holland and her daughter, half-Czech Kasia Adamik, which was abandoned in 2004. This strong presence of Jánošik/Janosik in Slovak and Polish popular culture might be interpreted as a sign that Slovaks are at least as similar to Poles as they are to Czechs.

After the Nazi defeat and liberation (or 'liberation') by the Red Army, Czechoslovakia was resurrected with Edward Beneš as its President and a coalition government, headed by a communist Klement Gottwald. In 1948 Gottwald led a successful coup d'état which resulted in communist control of every aspect of politics and the economy, and Beneš's abdication. As Bradley mentions, the communist coup was remarkable for its smoothness: only one minor clash occurred in Prague and no blood was shed (Bradley 1971: 178), thus confirming the opinion about the dove-like character of the Czech nation. In the late 1940s and 1950s Czechoslovakia implemented Stalinist policies and experienced the same distressing phenomena as many other socialist countries of this period, including political purges, show trials and forced labour camps for political opponents, immortalised in such films as *Žert* (*The Joke*, 1969), directed by Jaromil Jireš and *Skřivánci na niti* (*Larks on a String*, 1969–1990), directed by Jiři Menzel (which will be discussed in the following chapters), as well as in an acclaimed compilation documentary, *Papierové hlavy* (*Paper Heads*, 1996), directed by Dušan Hanák. Political terror was coupled with the nationalisation of industry, collectivisation of agriculture and the ruthless subjugation of Slovakia to the political centre in Prague. At the same time, after the Second World War, Czechoslovakia, together with East Germany, enjoyed the highest living standards and the smallest social inequalities in the whole Soviet bloc

(Wolchik 1991: 20–6), thus confirming the egalitarian stereotype of Czechs and Slovaks. It is argued that thanks to the relative prosperity and equality of Czechoslovak society, as well as the ruthlessness with which the authorities dealt with political dissidents, which included punishing their children by denying them university education, social protests were relatively infrequent and rarely attracted the masses, unlike in neighbouring Poland and Hungary (Bradley 1971: 187–93; Wolchik 1991: 25–6; Holý 1996: 142–3). The exception to this rule was the Prague Spring of 1968, which followed the fall of Gottwald's successor, President and first secretary, Antonín Novotný. Novotný, who inherited a host of problems from the Gottwald era, attempted in the 1960s to introduce some reforms. They predominantly concerned the economy and consisted of limited decentralisation. Moreover, victims of the 1950s purges were partially rehabilitated and some degree of freedom of expression was granted. Yet the limited nature of these reforms, combined with the attempt to stifle any dissent, only enraged and emboldened citizens. A consequence was students and intellectuals' protest and a power struggle within the Party, where supporters of Novotný clashed with 'liberals', made up of economists and other experts as well as disaffected Slovaks. Due to the growing power of the 'liberals', as well as the lack of support for Novotnýites by Leonid Brezhnev, who visited Prague in December 1967, the President had to resign in early 1968 (Dowling 2002: 104–6).

The man who replaced Novotný, the young Slovak leader, Alexander Dubček (1921–92), was in favour of reforming the state by easing censorship, institutionalising guarantees of civil liberties for all citizens, economic reform, accommodating Slovak desires for a greater role in the state and a general broadening of participation in the debate about change in Czechoslovakia beyond the elite level (Wolchik 1991: 31–5; Dowling 2002: 107–12). However, such an attempt to create 'socialism with a human face' was regarded by the Soviet Union as a threat to its hegemony within the Eastern bloc and political stability in the region. The logical conclusion to this assessment was the military intervention which took place on 20 August 1968. The Soviet army and four other Warsaw pact allies effectively invaded Czechoslovakia. The country reacted mostly with passive resistance which was punctuated by cases of more dramatic opposition, principally the act of self-immolation of a young Czech student, Jan Palach, in January 1969, who became the last Czech martyr (Pynsent 1994: 209–10). The invasion marked the end of the new leadership and a return to one of the harshest political regimes in the Soviet bloc, known as 'normalisation' and led by Dubček's successor, Gustáv Husák. The political situation again changed dramatically in November 1989, when, following the Polish and East German example, Czechs and Slovaks rejected communism in a series of strikes and demonstrations. The consequence of these events, known as the Velvet Revolution thanks to its smoothness and lack of fatalities, was that Czechoslovakia embraced democracy and a market economy, choosing as its President a leading dissident and famous playwright, Václav Havel. The last important event in the history of Czechoslovakia is the so called Velvet Divorce, namely the equally smooth separation of Czechs and Slovaks in 1993, paving the way to the creation of the

Czech Republic and Slovakia. The Velvet Divorce is depicted as an event brought about and negotiated by politicians, chiefly Czech Vaclav Klaus and Slovak Vladimir Meciar. As Maria Dowling put it, 'Meciar threatened Klaus with secession and Klaus called his bluff' (Dowling 2002: 167). Nevertheless, it also demonstrates that, left to their own devices, Slovaks choose independence rather than cohabitation with their Czech 'brothers'.

The discontinuity and fragility of Czechoslovak history is reflected in the bad feelings the term 'Czechoslovakia' evoked even before 1993. Milan Kundera perfectly summarises the reasons for this negative attitude, as well as embracing it:

> I never use the word in my novels, even though the action is generally set there. This composite word is too young (born in 1918), with no roots in time, no beauty, and it exposes the very nature of the thing it names: composite and too young (untested by time). It may be possible in a pinch to found a state on so frail a word, but not a novel. That is why, to designate my characters' country, I always use the old world 'Bohemia'. From the standpoint of political geography, it is incorrect, but from the standpoint of poetry, it is the only possible name. (Kundera 1990: 126)

Polish History and National Character

The year of 966 is regarded as the beginning of the Polish state, when Mieszko, the chief of the Polanie accepted Christianity for himself and his people. In the following centuries Poland alternately grew in power and declined, endured foreign invasions including those of Teutonic Order, Tartars and Swedes, and invaded the lands of their neighbours. Similarly, it disintegrated and unified, as well as built unions with other countries, such as Hungary, Lithuania, Saxony and Sweden. The union with Lithuania was most successful, creating a state which dominated East-Central Europe until the seventeenth century – the Polish–Lithuanian Commonwealth. In the eighteenth century it lost its statehood in the partitions between its neighbours: Russia, Prussia and Austro-Hungary. The third partition in 1795 led to Poland's disappearance from the European map for over 120 years. The causes of the partitions are complex, including some costly wars in which the country was engaged in the seventeenth and eighteenth century, regressive policies towards its peasantry and the abuse by a large proportion of its nobility (*szlachta*) of the democratic system it enjoyed. These political roots are often linked to some vices in the Polish national character, such as quarrelsomeness, backwardness, self-indulgence and unwillingness to change. Although the long period of partitions mortally weakened Poland politically and militarily, it did not destroy many of the traditions and values of the *szlachta*, out of whose ranks was to emerge the modern Polish intelligentsia, nor the Roman Catholicism which distinguished most Polish-speakers from Protestant Prussians and Orthodox Russians, if not Catholic Austrians (Lukowski and Zawadzki 2001: 109). The largest part of the pre-partitioned Poland was annexed by

Russia. This fact explains why Polish culture defines itself more in relation (typically in opposition) to Russian culture than to any other culture, such as German or Austro-Hungarian. Paradoxically, Russian colonisation of the largest chunk of Poland ensured that Poland survived culturally. As Jerzy Lukowski and Hubert Zawadzki put it, 'Although in her propaganda Catherine II had claimed that she was recovering the lost lands of old Kievan Rus, Russia lacked the more sophisticated bureaucratic machinery of her Germanic neighbours to embark on a thorough policy of russification' (ibid: 110). Consequently, Polish schools continued to function and during the reign of Tsar Alexander I (1801–25) the University of Wilno (Vilnius) even became a beacon of Polish academic life and by far the largest university in the Russian Empire (ibid.: 114).

During the nineteenth century Poles, or more exactly, the Polish upper classes, tried to challenge the loss of statehood in two contrasting ways. One, which discerns Poles from Czechs, consisted of military action. Polish post-partition history is thus punctuated by wars and uprisings whose purpose was to regain the lost territories. Polish forces assisted Napoleon in his wars against Prussia and Russia, and stood against the Russian administration, most famously in the November Uprising of 1830 and January Uprising of 1863. The uprisings were crushed, leading to a worsening of the situation of many Poles and mass emigration. Although unsuccessful, their memory was cherished in literature and oral traditions. The continuous fighting was for Poles proof that the nation was still alive and did not lose its aspiration of political independence. The second means of challenging the partition, not unlike in the Czech kingdom during the second half of the eighteenth and the nineteenth century, consisted of legal, economic and cultural activity. We should list here the publication in the early nineteenth century of the first modern Polish-language dictionary by Samuel Bogumił Linde, and the founding in Puławy of a museum devoted to the glorification of Poland's past by Princess Izabela Czartoryska. During the times of Polish political nonexistence two important literary paradigms were also created: Romanticism and Positivism. The first , represented by Adam Mickiewicz (1798–1855),[2] regarded as the greatest Polish poet, as well as Juliusz Słowacki and Zygmunt Krasiński, authors who spent a large part of their lives as émigrés, has been regarded until now as the greatest influence on Polish self-perception. It proclaimed the primacy of the country over other values, expecting the individual to sacrifice his personal happiness and even his own life in the combat for the country's liberation. Although Polish Romanticism drew on folk traditions such as legends, myths and folk music, it was a distinctively elitist current thanks to being created by and addressed principally to the leaders of the nation. Positivism, whose main representatives are Bolesław Prus, Henryk Sienkiewicz and Eliza Orzeszkowa, did not exalt military action but instead promoted humble work (*praca u podstaw, praca organiczna*) as a means to resist the occupier and paid greater attention to the ordinary members of the Polish community: peasants and later also the urban proletariat. Nevertheless, it also declared the supremacy of the country over the individual. It could be argued that literature played for Poles as important a role as for Czechs, but while it helped Czechs to see themselves as 'citizens of the world', for

Poles it was more an instrument to assert their national identity and the legitimacy of their aspirations for statehood. The preoccupation with the Patria made Polish Romantic literature appear inward-looking and parochial, despite or because of the pronouncement in many Romantic works that Poland plays a privileged role in world history, as conveyed by Mickiewicz naming Poland the 'Christ of the nations'. The opinion about the provincialism of Polish Romanticism is espoused by probably the most internationally renowned Polish writer, Witold Gombrowicz (see, for example, Gombrowicz 1997: 11–6; 352–62). This parochialism was the more dangerous as Romanticism is regarded as the highest point in Polish literature; an opinion encapsulated by saying that Mickiewicz's epic poem *Pan Tadeusz* (1834) is the 'Polish Bible'.[3]

In 1918, Poles, in common with Czechs and Slovaks, regained their statehood, following the collapse of the three empires that partitioned Poland and the Allies recognition of Polish aspirations for independence. After the war the Polish state was in a difficult position, founded on the unification of three parts, each with a different level of economic development, as well as ethnic composition. Ethnic minorities (including Jews) comprised over 30 per cent of the total population and in Eastern regions Poles made up less than 40 per cent. Moreover, Poland had suffered serious devastation during the war, subsequently causing high unemployment, poverty and hyperinflation. This situation led to widespread mistrust of democratic structures and to strong popular support for ultra right-wing, nationalistic movements. During the interwar period Poland experienced, amongst other events, the murder of its first President, Gabriel Narutowicz in 1922 by a right-wing fanatic and in 1926 a coup, led by Józef Piłsudski (1867–1935), a major figure in the Polish fight for independence during the First World War and a military leader of the rank of Field Marshal. The power of parliament was first limited, then dissolved in 1930 and the most prominent members of the opposition arrested. The political situation in the 1920s and 1930s also affected national culture. The first half of the 1930s was marked by a substantial restriction in freedom of speech, manifesting itself in censorship of the press and cinema. Piłsudski's coup was carried out in the name of Sanacja, a term used in the sense of restoring 'health' to the body politic, and which gave the name to the political regime that lasted beyond Piłsudski's death, virtually till 1939. With its emphasis on discipline, anti-corruption and loyalty to the state, Sanacja appealed to a wide cross-section of the population, both on the right and on the left. The ideology Piłsudski treated with greatest distrust was communism and understandably so – the secret clauses of the Ribbentrop–Molotov Pact of August 1939, revealed only in 1946 but denied by the USSR until 1989, provided for the joint division of Eastern-Central Europe and the new partition of Poland. Consequently, when the Second World War broke out, in parallel with the Nazi attack from the West which began on 1 September 1939, Poland suffered Soviet aggression and colonisation from the East, starting in the middle of September 1939. A symbol of its ruthlessness was the Russian execution in 1940 of several thousands of Polish officers at Katyń in Byelorussia, which virtually wiped out the whole Polish officer class.

Against the Nazi armies Poland fought a regular, although short war, known as the September campaign. It was an uneven struggle. The bitter resistance of the Polish armed forces could not deter the superiority of the Nazis in terms of men and modern equipment. Defeat was followed by the Nazi occupation which was ended by the liberation of Polish territory by the Soviet Army in 1945. Although occupation was a time of hardship, with death being inflicted on anyone who engaged in resistance or harboured Jews, in many parts of the country underground political and cultural life flourished, including armed forces, universities and publications. Most Poles involved with the resistance joined Armia Krajowa (the Home Army), an underground organisation that considered the Polish government-in-exile in London (which was a continuation of the Polish prewar government) to be the only legitimate Polish authority, and wanted any future Poland to be independent from the Soviet Union. The Home Army played a crucial role in the 1944 Warsaw Uprising, the goal of which was to liberate Warsaw from the weakened Nazi occupiers. But it did not succeed, partly due to the strong resistance of the German army, which consolidated its forces in Warsaw, and partly due to its isolation. The Russian army that was approaching Warsaw from the East decided not to intervene, so as not to help an organisation whose ultimate objective was opposed to its own. There was also very little assistance from the Western allies. After the war, the members of the Home Army and organisations affiliated to it were considered the main enemy of socialist Poland; many were imprisoned for years and many died in the fight against the new communist authorities (Lukowski and Zawadzki 2001: 190–249; Davies 2005: 190–398).

After the war Stalin imposed a communist government on Poland, known as PKWN (Polish Committee of National Liberation). Thus Poland joined the group of European socialist countries and formed close political, military and economic links with its eastern neighbour. This was as much the result of the Soviet victory over Germany as of Western indifference toward its future. (Davies 2005: 365). The unfortunate political outcome of the war was compounded by the enormous human loss. In total, about six million Poles died during the war, including practically the entire Jewish population of about three million. Poland had just under twenty-four million inhabitants in 1946, as opposed to thirty-five in 1939, and it was the most devastated country in Europe (Lukowski and Zawadzki 2001: 241–49; Davies 2005: 364–6).

As with Czechoslovakia, in the late 1940s and the first half of the 1950s, when Bolesław Bierut was first the President and then Prime Minister, Poland was forced into Stalinisation. This consisted of the nationalisation of industry, the rejection of political pluralism by rigging elections and suppressing political opponents (mostly from the reconstituted peasant party), the creation of a vast and repressive security apparatus and politically motivated executions. However, it was still not as complete or ruthless as in Czechoslovakia. Much economic activity, notably in agriculture and trade, remained in private hands. The communist authorities also failed to suppress the Catholic Church that retained its position as spiritual centre of postwar Poland and the pillar of anti-communist resistance. Thanks to the Stalinists' failure to destroy opposition and the ordinary citizens' continuous dissatisfaction with the standard of living and the lack of democracy, postwar Poland was punctuated by social protests, not unlike Poland during partitions. Moreover, in due course they became more and more frequent. The first large one took place in June 1956, when scores of demonstrators, protesting against the lack of democracy and deteriorating living conditions, were killed by government troops during street riots in Poznań. These events paved the way for Władysław Gomułka (1905–82), who envisaged a more independent, less totalitarian Poland, to become the new Party leader. Gomułka himself, who not unlike Dubček proclaimed a 'Polish road to socialism', lost his position as a result of his inability to keep his promises and the consequent new wave of protests in 1970 and 1971, this time in the shipyards of Gdańsk and Gdynia. The new Party leader became Edward Gierek, who introduced a programme of rapid expansion of the economy, fuelled by Western credits. However, despite an improvement in living conditions, Westernisation and general democratisation in the 1970s, the decade was marred by further protests, including in Radom and Ursus in 1976. Electing Karol Wojtyła as the Pope in 1978, and his pilgrimage to Poland in 1979, encouraged Poles to oppose the government. In July 1980 new waves of strikes swept across the country. The creation of an interfactory strike committee in Gdańsk under the chairmanship of Lech Wałęsa, a 37-year-old electrician, proved to be a turning point; the floundering authorities capitulated over the central demand for an independent trade union, 'Solidarity'. Under Wałęsa's leadership Solidarity became a focus for a wide range of protest groups and a mass social movement. Consequently, an effective state of 'dual power' was emerging in Poland, which also posed a threat to the Soviet empire in Eastern Europe (Lukowski and Zawadzki 2001: 250–75; Davies 2005: 413–91).

Solidarity's rise to power was halted by the introduction of martial law in December 1981 by the new Party leader, General Wojciech Jaruzelski. It was followed by the internment of the leaders of the opposition, including Wałęsa. However, martial law was only a temporary halt on the Polish road to democratisation, helped by the political changes in the USSR, especially Gorbachev's announcement that Poland was free to determine its fate. In 1989 semi-free elections took place which can be now regarded as the first key move in dismantling the communist system in East-Central Europe. In 1990 Wałęsa won the presidential election, to be replaced five years later by the postcommunist politician, Aleksander Kwaśniewski, who remained Poland's President for ten years, ironically being the most popular politician in the postcommunist Republic of Poland (Lukowski and Zawadzki 2001: 275–89; Davies 2005: 496–518). By contrast, Wałęsa failed to retain the immense respect he had amassed during his time as Solidarity leader and in due course became regarded as epitomising Polish political weaknesses and almost a national joke. Among the many 'sins' attributed to the first Solidarity leader we should list his idea of 'war at the top' articulated for the first time in 1990 when he said: 'We need a war at the top in order to maintain peace at the bottom [of political life]. Therefore I encourage you to fight'. In due course this 'war at the top' was associated with the acrimonious relations between Wałęsa and other Solidarity leaders, principally Tadeusz Mazowiecki, the disintegration of the Solidarity camp and the major fragmentation of the political scene in which, paradoxically, the postcommunists constituted the most stable element. Wałęsa and the political style he used during his career are also regarded as partly responsible for the rise of populism in the late 1990s and the early 2000s, epitomised by the peasants' party 'Samoobrona' (Self-defence), led by Andrzej Lepper, and the more moderate 'Prawo i sprawiedliwość' (Law and Justice), and the neverending discussion about how to solve the problem of communist agents (so-called *lustracja*). It is worth adding here that even the names of these political groupings can serve as confirmation of the Polish penchant for grandiose ideas and inability to be in solidarity with each other in peaceful times.

The history of Wałęsa's rise to power and his fall, the history of Solidarity and the political developments in Poland after 1989, support the idea that the Polish history of continuous fighting for independence created a particular national character that thrives during times of conflict but is less able to adjust to periods of political stability. Patriotic, courageous, proud, honourable and idealistic romantics who are happy to die for their country, during times of peace transform into their own caricatures. Their patriotism changes into xenophobia, idealism into fanaticism and quarrelsomeness, courage becomes stupidity. The last decade of Polish history demonstrates that a romantic mindset in times of peace becomes self-destructive and ridiculous, which, besides, was already discovered some decades earlier by authors such as Gombrowicz and Sławomir Mrożek (Piwińska 1973: 338–48).

Part of the Polish and Czechoslovak (or Czech and Slovak) histories is the history of their mutual relations and these are regarded as not convivial. On the other hand, they were never as bad as relations with Germany and Russia, simply because neither Poles, Czechs nor Slovaks were really ever in a position to threaten the existence of a neighbouring nation, unlike their more powerful neighbours. František Daniel explains the lack of warm feelings by the politics of the Habsburgs, who cultivated animosities between their subjugated nations, and later by the Soviet Union who used a similar strategy of 'divide and rule' (Daniel 1983: 50). The best known example of the implementation of this strategy is the invasion of Czechoslovakia in 1968 in which Polish troops were used. Antoni Kroh, in a book devoted to Polish–Czech relations, claims that their animosities began in the nineteenth century, when a large number of Czechs moved to Galicia, the part of Poland that was taken by Austro-Hungary in the partitions. Many of them were clerks, tax collectors and policemen; on this territory they created the first modern administration. Although their role can be regarded as positive, they were deeply disliked by the Polish noblemen who were hostile to any form of bureaucracy and, especially, to any control of their finances. Other Czech immigrants in Galicia included railwaymen, engineers, brewers, doctors, foresters and teachers: in short, people who possessed the skills Poles living there lacked. The noblemen, claims Kroh, showed the Czech newcomers, whom they regarded as a mixture of servants and occupiers, contempt that concealed fear and a sense of inferiority. Symbolic of this attitude were the numerous nicknames given to Czechs such as 'bohmaki', 'wencliczki', 'precliczki' and most commonly used, even till now, 'pepiczki' (Kroh

1992: 6–7). These terms, referring to the food with which Czechs were associated and to some common Czech names, are not particularly derogatory, as none of them refers to any real vice of Czechs, but they are all diminutive, suggesting that Poles regard their neighbours as 'small people', which is also the way Czechs represent themselves in cinema, literature and culture at large (Kroutvor 2001). It is worth adding in passing that the role Czechs played in partitioned Poland can be compared to one they played in Slovakia after 1918: they modernised a backward society, but at the same time made their hosts realise how backward they were and consequently humiliated them. Kroh also notes that Czechs were easily assimilated into Polish society, which points to the similarity of Polish and Czech languages and traditions. Many first-generation Poles of Czech origin became very successful, for example the poet Leopold Staff and the painter Jan Styka (Kroh 1992: 7–8).

The stereotype of the Czech is also expressed in the only Polish film known to me that discusses Polish–Czechoslovak relations (although in the context of relations within the whole Soviet bloc), Filip Bajon's *Sauna* (1992). In this film a brave, charismatic, although in the end beaten Pole, Janek, played by Bogusław Linda, is compared to a Czech Miloš, who is less charismatic but more successful and content. Just as the image of a Czech in Polish culture does not differ much from the Czech's self-image, so the image of Poles in Czechoslovak culture does not diverge much from the way Poles tend to see themselves: as admirable but irrational hotheads and losers. For example, *Pupendo* (2003), directed by Jan Hřebejk, alludes to such a perception.

What Poland and Czechoslovakia also have in common is the domination of their histories and cultures, or at least the discourses on their political and cultural histories, by male figures. In this respect they are, however, not unique against the backdrop of other nations in Europe and in the world, whose histories are written in such a way as if women, if not for their role of bringing men into this world, would not exist at all. Yet, paradoxically, the absence of women (in politics, social life, etc.) renders men invisible, as it equates their specific problems with universal problems. It will be my task in the following chapters to change this impression.

The Histories and Specificities of Polish, Czechoslovak, Czech and Slovak Cinemas

Political and cultural histories of Czechoslovakia and Poland had a major impact on the histories of their respective cinemas. In particular, Polish, Czech and Slovak film critics argue that the histories of their cinemas are discontinuous. For example, Jiří Voráč claims that 'the history of Czech cinema has frequently been marked and stigmatised, more than the non-industrial and more individual art disciplines, by large historical social upheavals which the Czech lands experienced in this century' (Voráč 1997: 5). In a similar vein Petra Hanáková argues that 'Czech cinematography is defined by radical breaks' (Hanáková 2005a: 154). Undoubtedly one such gap coincided with the 'normalisation' after 1968, described as 'a frontal attack threatening the very spiritual, cultural, and thus also national identity of the Czechoslovak society' (Hames 1989:

107). As a consequence of the systematic suppression of artistic creativity at this time many of the leading directors emigrated, including Miloš Forman, Ivan Passer, Ján Kadár, Jan Němec, Vojtěch Jasný and Jiří Weiss. Some directing stars of the 1960s, such as Jiří Menzel, Věra Chytilová and Evald Schorm, ceased to work for a longer period of time and when they eventually returned to filmmaking, their artistic output did not match their previous achievements. Others, such as Ladislav Helge and Pavel Juráček, did not make any more films. The work of the directors who left the country was largely disowned and banned, and their names eliminated from the history of Czechoslovak cinema. At this period film production dropped to a very low level (ibid.). Ladislav Holý claims that 'hardly a novel, film or drama of any significance had been published or performed in Czechoslovakia since 1968' and quotes Heinrich Böll who said that Czechoslovakia had become a 'cultural Biafra' (Holý 1996: 143). The extreme policies of the 'normalisation' and its fruits have encouraged some authors to claim that Czechoslovak postwar cinema can be reduced to two periods: the golden age in the 1960s and the period of the Czech New New Wave after 1989 (Vorác̆ 1997). As I believe that a large proportion of what is associated with Czechoslovak cinema in the minds of fellow East Europeans are films made between these two golden periods, and some of my favourite Czechoslovak films were made in the 1970s, I find these opinions too extreme. A similar view was recently expressed by Petra Hanáková in her perceptive analysis of Czech crazy comedies and spoofs from the 1970s and 1980s. Not only does she argue that the 1970s and 1980s brought some valuable films, but demonstrates that there is a strong link between their hybrid character and Czech culture at large. Moreover, Hanáková shows that in an important sense they accurately reflected and dealt with the social and political conditions of the citizens of Czechoslovakia, especially the cultural isolation of the region, through using the strategy of self-hybridisation and self-colonisation (Hanáková 2007). Nevertheless, the year 1968 tore Czechoslovak cinema in a way which has no parallel in any other East European cinema, including Polish. Another radical rupture in Czechoslovak cinema took place in 1993 when Czechoslovakia broke into the Czech Republic and Slovakia.[4]

I would like to make a digression here. The likely terminal divorce between Czechs and Slovaks not only makes it incorrect to classify films made after 1993 in Prague or Bratislava as 'Czechoslovak', but also encourages critics to regard films made before 1993 as either solely Czech or solely Slovak, rather than Czechoslovak. It is worth adding that such an approach was tacitly or openly taken by some film historians before 1993. Josef Škvorecký wrote his history of Czech cinema only, excluding a Slovak dimension (Škvorecký 1971), and Mira and Antonín Liehm in their book on Soviet and Eastern European postwar film discussed Czech and Slovak cinema separately (Liehm and Liehm 1977). However, while it makes sense in some situations to treat the films made before 1993 as Czech or Slovak, for example on account on the nationality of their directors, the language spoken by the characters and even the national traditions they depicted, in another sense many of them were Czechoslovak because they were shot by Czech and Slovak crews, tackled problems experienced by the whole country and addressed the whole spectrum of viewers living in Czechoslovakia, irrespective of whether they were Czechs or Slovaks. For me, even the films of Miloš Forman and Jiří Menzel are, from this perspective, Czechoslovak rather than Czech. Moreover, as Andrew Horton demonstrates by presenting the life, post-Velvet Divorce, of *Obchod na korze* (*A Shop on the High Street*, 1965), a film directed by Ján Kadár, a Budapest-born Slovak with Jewish roots, and Czech Elmar Klos, such an attempt to ascribe a current national identity to an historical film is both methodologically problematic and politically dangerous (Horton 2000-1; see also Iordanova 2005). Accordingly, rather than attempting to determine the nationality of each film discussed in this book once and for all, I will allow myself the liberty to describe some of them in more ways than one, for example variably Czechoslovak and Slovak. The advantage of this approach is its sensitivity to any future cultural changes which might bring about new readings of old films.

As a result of the oppressive regime of 'normalisation', as well as other factors, such as the shorter lives of leading Czechoslovak directors in comparison with their Polish colleagues, Czechoslovak postwar cinema lacks film authors whose work bears witness to every important moment in the country's postwar history. The closest to this model are Otakar Vávra (b. 1911), Věra Chytilová (b. 1929) and Jiří Menzel (b. 1938). However, the gaps in Chytilová and Menzel's working lives were so long and in the case of Menzel his artistic output so uneven, that they are still largely associated with the 'Czech miracle' of the 1960s. At the same time, the negative consequences of these various discontinuities were assuaged by such factors as the relatively high average film production in Czechoslovakia, reaching 35–40 feature films per year (Daniel 1983: 50) and the close connections between Czech cinema and other disciplines of art such as theatre, literature and painting.

The ruptures in Polish cinema appear less dramatic and postwar Polish cinema strikes me as rather more continuous than discontinuous. The most potent symbol of its continuity is the career of Andrzej Wajda (b. 1926), who has worked as a film director for over fifty years and during this time directed over forty films, thus becoming one of the most productive filmmakers in the history of world cinema. Moreover, Wajda's films belong to the most important schools and paradigms of Polish cinema, including socialist realism, the Polish School, Cinema of Moral Concern and postcommunist cinema, and almost all genres which were ever tried in Poland (perhaps with an exception of science fiction and fantasy). Although a large proportion of Wajda's films were critical of the socialist regime, he was never forced to publicly recant his views. Moreover, with the exception of *Człowiek z marmuru* (*Man of Marble*, 1977), none of Wajda's films were shelved. Other directors such as Wanda Jakubowska, Aleksander Ford, Jerzy Kawalerowicz, Janusz Morgenstern and Krzysztof Zanussi also maintained their careers for many decades. Although there were periods when Polish filmmakers' creative freedom was limited, either through censorship or self-censorship, it was never suppressed to the extent that a large proportion of filmmakers of any given generation had to emigrate or abandon filmmaking altogether. Polish emigrant directors such as Roman Polański, Walerian Borowczyk, Jan Lenica, Jerzy Skolimowski, Andrzej Żuławski and Agnieszka Holland chose living and working abroad not so much because they were not allowed to make films in Poland, as because their artistic sensitivity was such that they felt they could achieve greater success working abroad. I will also dare to say that their absence was less discernible in Polish cinema than the absence of Forman and Passer was for Czechoslovak film.

Polish New Wave, named the Polish School, appeared earlier than in Czechoslovakia, in the middle of the 1950s, which largely resulted from the fact that the political thaw started in Poland earlier than in its southern neighbour. Moreover, unlike in Czechoslovak cinema, which experienced a profound crisis in the 1970s, in Poland this decade is regarded as very successful, culminating in the Cinema of Moral Concern, when a whole new echelon of filmmakers emerged offering fresh insights into Polish reality, including Krzysztof Zanussi and Agnieszka Holland. Perhaps the closest to Czechoslovak cinema of 'normalisation' was in Poland the period following the year 1981, when martial law was introduced. As in Czechoslovakia in the early 1970s, this event was followed by a large drop-off in overall film production, the emigration of filmmakers, such as Agnieszka Holland and Jerzy Domaradzki, as well as a lowering of overall artistic standards. Andrzej Wajda famously said that due to martial law he lost his talent, by which he meant mostly his ability to communicate with his viewers (Sobolewski 1993: 6). Nevertheless, all these events were on a smaller scale than in Czechoslovakia in the 1970s, not least because after martial law Poland returned relatively quickly to the previous level of artistic freedom.

Apart from the political, institutional and 'human' discontinuities suffered by Czechoslovak cinema, there are also continuities that pertain to such aspects of film as prevailing types of characters, mise-en-scène and rhetoric, or at least a mode of addressing the viewer. In some ways Czechoslovak cinema even comes across as more consistent than Polish. Vratislav Effenberger and Petra Hanáková claim that we can discern in Czech cinema an underlying framework of popular tradition and the relative permanence of the myth of petty Czechness (Effenberger 1996; Hanáková 2005a), which also can be found in Czech literature (Král 1983: 47; Kroutvor 2001). Czech filmmakers typically choose as their protagonist the 'small Czech' (*Čecháček*), Clueless Hans/Johnny (*Hloupý Honza*): small men, both in terms of class background/education and mental profile. The leading characters in Czech films are compliant, servile clerks, servants, labourers, docile, conformist, unambitious and provincial, even if they live in a large city. The stereotype of the 'small Czech' has not changed much over the last hundred years, not least because the art of adaptability is his greatest asset (Effenberger 1996: 171–2; Hanáková 2005a: 152–5). From the dominance and persistence of the 'small Czechs' Hanáková concludes that Czech cinema lacks real heroes; if they appear in cinema at all, they come across as imported, out of place. The incompatibility of 'proper heroes' with Czech culture is signified by casting foreign actors, including Polish, in heroic roles (Hanáková 2005a: 157) or modelling them on foreign characters.

In Czech cinema we find examples both of acceptance and rejection of the lack of true heroes. The strategy of acceptance consists of representing Čecháček's passivity as shrewdness, his slow-wittedness as cleverness or cunning (ibid.: 152–3). We find this strategy, most famously, in the adaptations of Hašek's *The Good Soldier Švejk*. Recently the passive and slow-witted but in reality intelligent and sensitive 'simple Czech' reappeared in films such as *Návrat idiota* (*Return of the Idiot*, 1999), directed by Saša Gedeon, *Příběhy obyčejného šílentsví* (*Wrong Side Up*, 2005), directed by Petr Zelenka and *Obsluhoval jsem anglického krále* (*I Served the King of England*, 2006), directed by Jiři Menzel. Yet, in the most distinguished school in Czechoslovak cinema, the New Wave of the 1960s, filmmakers treat the opportunist and cowardly survivor with derision (Effenberger 1996: 174; Hanáková 2005a: 155). Take, for example, the fathers in Forman's films (who will be discussed in detail in Chapter 3) or in *Ecce homo Homolka* (1969) by Jaroslav Papoušek. In Papoušek's film a typical Czech family, who are enjoying a picnic in the wood, run away and return home after hearing a woman calling for help. Josef Škvorecký, commenting sarcastically on their behaviour, writes:, 'They don't want to get involved with anything like that…The Homolkas live encased in their ultra-humble world, self-sufficient in their stupidity, conceited in their ignorance, profound in their emptiness. They are ideal objects for dictators and manipulators' (Škvorecký 1971: 98–9).

Slovak cinema also has a penchant for characters recruited from the lower classes: peasants and labourers. Yet, although they are as provincial as their Czech counterparts, if not more so, in terms of their geographical and class roots, they are certainly less provincial in their mindset. Rather than observing in Slovak cinema docile servants and happy conformists, we find people who cross the boundaries of the mundane, often becoming various types of outsiders: tramps, itinerant artists, madmen, deserters, preachers. The leading Slovak directors, Juraj Jakubisko, Juraj Herz and Elo Havetta, all favour such characters. Their choice can be linked to the

Fig. 1.1 *The Firemen's Ball* (1967), directed by Miloš Forman.

more extreme living circumstances of Slovak people, their closeness to death, and the stronger influence of folklore imagery (in which the theme of death is constantly present) on Slovak films.

The typical, one would like to say, iconic, iconography of a Czechoslovak film, consists of ballrooms (especially in films of Czech directors), funfairs and circus performances (particularly in Slovak films). It is difficult to find a Czechoslovak film of which a part is not set in such places, the most memorable in Forman's *Lásky jedné plavovlásky* (*A Blonde in Love*, 1965) and *Hoří, má panenko* (*The Firemen's Ball*, 1967); Juraj Herz's *Spalovač mrtvol* (*The Cremator*, 1968); Evald Schorm's *Farářův konec* (*End of a Priest*, 1968); *Lalje polné* (*Wild Lilies*, 1972) by Elo Havetta and, after 1989, in *Return of the Idiot* by Saša Gedeon. Not only are these settings frequent but Czech and Slovak filmmakers managed to develop a distinctive visual style, choreography and symbolism for them. The long shots and long takes, in which the various parties and balls are shot, juxtaposed with close-ups of a number of their participants, unfold the lives of ordinary members of a community as full of unforeseen events and dramas. They subtly point to the individuality of Petrs and Honzas, and the measure of freedom these small people enjoy despite the authorities' unrelenting attempts to control it. The preference for folk festivals, funfairs and religious ceremonies, characteristic particularly of Slovak filmmakers, also underscores the folk roots of the protagonists and accentuates the huge appetite of the ordinary people for magic, despite the communist attempts to impose a rational ideology on its citizens. It must be emphasised that despite their roots in the folk traditions, the characters in Slovak films do not give the impression of being 'folksy' or archaic. On the contrary, they come across as modern or at least appealing to modern sensibilities. Elo Havetta, speaking in the 1970s of the new Slovak films, remarked that they are bonded by folklore but dared to say: 'We [Slovak directors] are perhaps the first who knew how to recreate folklore as something modern' (Havetta, quoted in Hames 2005: 220).

The narratives of Czechoslovak films tend to be loose, with much vital information about the characters withdrawn from the viewer and instead, many apparently unimportant details inserted. Such a mode of narration reflects the way history was created in Czech and Slovak lands, namely as an assemble of semi-private, tiny anecdotes, rather than history with a capital H (Kroutvor 2001), similar to the way it was recreated in literature, a seminal example being the work of Bohumil Hrabal. Often the events unfold slowly, as if the camera was indiscriminately catching the flood of life, rather than the director selecting its most poignant moments. In the New Wave films this gives the impression that Czechoslovak films are amateur or home cinema.[5] In addition, some scenes might be included purely for their formal qualities, rather than to advance the narrative. This feature likens Czechoslovak cinema to the avant-garde, distancing it from mainstream, narrative films. Moreover, realistic events are often blended with subjective and imaginary scenes, as in a dream or daydream, and means such as camerawork, use of colour, even music underscore the subjective and idiosyncratic vision of the characters. This quality can be linked to the influence of surrealism on

Czechoslovak cinema (Owen 2007), which began in the films made before the Second World War and peaked in the New Wave films and the work of Jan Švankmajer, but can still be discerned in postcommunist films, although perhaps in less imaginative ways. Together with folklore, surrealism constituted the strongest inspiration for Czechoslovak film and these two influences are interconnected, as surrealism has an affinity to folklore and folklore in its large part consists of the society's unconscious. Finally and perhaps most importantly, Czechoslovak and especially Czech cinema has a predilection to humour and irony rather than pathos (Daniel 1983; Hames 2000). As František Daniel claims:

> In irony the objective of the art determines the types of the characters, their cast, the means of expression, the style of storytelling. To ridicule something, the ironic writer uses characters who convey the appropriate image: people who are weak, who are almost imperceptible, who seemingly are dumb – but only seemingly; who are average from all points of view except in their spirit; and who can effectively ridicule those who pretend to be powerful, those who pretend to be wise and pretend to have all the answers. (Daniel 1983: 55)

Daniel suggests that irony and humour in general are the weapon of the powerless, and this connection largely explains why irony and comedy are so common in Czech film and culture at large. Devoid of political power, the inhabitants of Czech lands and, as Josef Kroutvor argues, in Central Europe as a whole, used it as a way to come to terms with their diminutive position (Kroutvor 2001). Various authors argue that the presence of irony distinguishes Czech cinema from cinemas of other countries of the region, most importantly Polish and Hungarian (Daniel 1983; Hames 2000).

While there is a broad agreement that in Czechoslovak cinema 'small people' dominate, it is more difficult to say what characters prevail in Polish cinema. Certainly it owes a large part of its renown to the charismatic heroes from Andrzej Wajda's films, such as Maciek Chełmicki in *Popiół i diament* (*Ashes and Diamonds*, 1958) or Tadeusz in *Krajobraz po bitwie* (*Landscape after the Battle*, 1970), but we also find them among the characters of *Westerplatte* (1967), directed by Stanisław Różewicz and in many films by Kazimierz Kutz (on Kutz, see Mazierska 2000). Maciek Chełmicki, played by the charismatic Zbigniew Cybulski, especially captured the viewer's imagination and until now has been widely regarded as the most memorable character in Polish cinema (Kurz 2005: 187–218). For him and his cinematic 'brothers' their relationship with their country overshadows other dimensions of their lives, especially their private pursuits such as finding love or making a career. Usually these people fight and die for their country knowing that they would lose and die. The filmmakers edify the doomed heroes by suggesting that their defeat was a kind of victory, because it set an example for the younger generation that might be more lucky, or because any alternative course of action would be indefensible from a moral perspective. We find the roots of 'honourable losers', especially those created by Wajda, in Polish Romanticism: the works of Adam

Mickiewicz, Juliusz Słowacki, Zygmunt Krasiński and Cyprian Kamil Norwid. For example, the idea that defeat contains a seed of victory, which is conveyed by the title of Wajda's *Ashes and Diamonds*, is borrowed from the poem by Norwid. To this list of writers who might inspire Wajda and his followers, the distinguished Polish literary critic Maria Janion adds Joseph Conrad, whom she regards as a very Polish writer because he conveyed in his work the essentially Polish experience of defeat, although also able to transform it into an universal experience (Janion 1998: 264–5). Although defeated heroes and martyrs are in fact not very numerous in Polish cinema, they overshadow characters of other types thanks to the compassion with which they are treated by their creators and, consequently, their attractiveness to the viewers who find it easy to identify with them.

Figure 1.2 Zbigniew Cybulski and Adam Pawlikowski in *Ashes and Diamonds*.

The romantic heroes have their 'shadows' in the shape of various anti-heroes: opportunistic survivors and buffoons. They include Jan Piszczyk (Bogumił Kobiela) in *Zezowate szczęście* (*Bad Luck*, 1960), directed by Andrzej Munk; Wiktor Rawicz (Zbigniew Cybulski) in *Jak być kochaną* (*How to Be Loved*, 1962), directed by Wojciech Has (see Chapter 2); Kowalski-Malinowski (Zbigniew Cybulski) in *Salto* (1965) by Tadeusz Konwicki, as well as, in the later period, protagonists of the films of Stanisław Bareja, Jerzy Gruza and Marek Koterski. I describe them as the 'shadows' of Chełmickis and Zadras, because they typically compare themselves with Romantic heroes or are contrasted with them by filmmakers. Moreover, heroes and their shadows were often played by the same actors, principally Cybulski. As a result of these factors, rather than offering a viable alternative to the doomed patriots in the films of Wajda and even Kutz, the anti-heroes reaffirm the validity of the values the romantics embody. Interesting but neglected in critical discourse are the characters in the films by Wojciech Has, particularly those played by Gustaw Holoubek. They are neither 'mad patriots' nor anti-heroes but rather intellectuals who, in a way that brings them close to existentialism, question the meaning of life, faced with the inevitability of passing time and death. I also mention them because Has-like characters resurface in the films of other directors, most recently in *Wojaczek* (1999) by Lech Majewski. The closer we come to the contemporary day, the more difficult it is to establish the values and behaviour of a typical character in a Polish film, or even to discern the main types of protagonists (see, for example, Janowska 2005).

The axis honourable loser vs. anti-hero is accompanied by another division: pathetic vs. ironic mode. The pathetic mode was used by filmmakers choosing charismatic heroes and favouring history with a capital 'H', dramatic events such as wars and uprisings (Biró 1983); the ironic by those focused on anti-heroes and ordinary life. By and large, however, Polish cinema, not unlike Hungarian cinema, is identified with pathos rather than irony.

The mise-en-scène associated with Polish cinema is that of the upper classes: the manor house, the officers' headquarters or the study of an intellectual filled with books and family mementoes. Often the image of idyllic country life or battle is adorned with the figure of a perfectly shaped white horse – symbol of the Polish fight for independence. Such a mise-en-scène that harks back to Polish Romantic vocabulary, particularly in Wajda's films but also to a certain extent in Zanussi's, Has's and even Jan Jakub Kolski's works, points to a world that is forever lost, to lost home and lost country (on landscape in Wajda's films see Ostrowska 2004). Another type of mise-en-scène, perhaps less identified with Polish film but equally common and no less distinctive, can be described as the mise-en-scène of 'real socialism'. Introduced to Polish cinema in the 1960s, it consists of high-rise block estates (in the 1990s known as *blokowiska*), with ugly, poor quality buildings, roads with potholes and puddles of water, and never-ending construction/reconstruction works which gives the estates the aura of temporariness. The most famous Polish cinematic housing estate is that of Ursynów in Warsaw, featured in Krzysztof Kieślowski's *Dekalog* (*Decalogue*, 1988). We can also find estates of this kind in the films of Stanisław Bareja and Marek Koterski.

Unlike in Czech and Slovak cinema, surrealism and other types of unrealistic artistic currents have not influenced Polish cinema in a major way. In this respect, Polish cinema is not dissimilar to Polish culture at large. Maria Janion claims that a large deficiency in Polish culture is its unfamiliarity with or rejection of psychoanalysis (Janion, quoted in Krzemiński 1991: 17). It could be suggested that, obsessed with the fate of their country, the creators of culture neglected the individual, his/her inner life and especially unconscious. Perhaps the pressure to talk in the name of the whole tormented nation, or at least one's generation, was so great, that those directors who were more interested in the individual as an individual, in his/her uniqueness, felt marginalised within the boundaries of national cinema, the seminal example being Wojciech Has. Others chose to emigrate. Almost all Polish emigrant filmmakers, including Walerian Borowczyk, Jan

Lenica, Roman Polański and Andrzej Żuławski are, broadly speaking, non-realists. In the films of other Polish filmmakers such as Krzysztof Kieślowski and Agnieszka Holland, the unrealistic element emerged or was strengthened when they worked abroad, as if their imagination was set free when they left Poland. The rejection of surrealism and subjectivism is connected with Polish filmmakers' predilection for a tight narrative. Those filmmakers who favoured fragmented narrative were regarded as outsiders, especially, again, Has. In comparison with its southern neighbours, Polish cinema also reveals a weaker connection with folk traditions. If folklore is utilised, it is usually represented as either the lifestyle of past generations, as in Jan Jakub Kolski's films, or something of a local character, belonging to a specific ethnic group, such as the inhabitants of Silesia in Kazimierz Kutz' films. Polish cinema has no equivalent of Havetta or Jakubisko, namely directors who represent folklore as modern, as a living force.

I am mentioning these differences not only to circumscribe (however simplified) the characteristics of the lineage of Polish, Czech and Slovak cinema, but also to draw attention to the difficulty encountered by a researcher who attempts to compare them from a particular perspective, in my case masculinity. Such comparison often requires comparing films that come across as very different from the perspective of style or artistic quality, and forces the use of different methods of interpretation for different films, for example searching for hidden meanings in one film, while reading its comparator more literally. Obviously, such comparison is to an extent flawed but I dare to say that no comparison is free from problems of this kind. Moreover, limiting oneself to comparing films belonging to the same genre or aesthetic tradition inevitably would lead to using a very limited number of examples and, consequently, to very limited conclusions. In this study, as I already indicated, I want to account as much as possible for the versatility and breadth of Polish, Czech and Slovak films.

Notes

1. For example, Carlos Fuentes quotes Milan Kundera protesting when he located Prague in Eastern Europe: 'No, not Eastern Europe, certainly not. Prague is in the centre, not in the east of Europe; the European east is Russia, Byzantium, in Moscovy, Caesaropopism, tsarism and orthodoxy' (Kundera, quoted in Fuentes 1988: 161).
2. It is an interesting coincidence that Adam Mickiewicz and Jan Palacký, both regarded as the leading figures in creating the languages and cultures of their nations, shared the year of their birth – 1798.
3. While Polish Romantic literature has problems in crossing national borders, the music of the most accomplished Polish Romantic composer, Fryderyk (Frédéric) Chopin, is universally applauded.
4. In reality, the separation of Czech and Slovak cinema in 1993 was much less radical than the political divorce that happened at the same time. A majority of films included in the catalogue of Slovak films made in the years 1993–2007 are Slovak-Czech co-productions. Similarly, a large proportion of Czech films are made with Slovak capital and personnel.
5. The discontinuous and quasi-amateurish character of Czechoslovak cinema entered Polish colloquial speech in the saying, 'This is like a Czech film – nobody has a clue what is going on'.

CHAPTER 2

Madmen, Martyrs, Dodgers: Men and War

In Polish patriotism there exists a dark zone, bordering on madness and suicide. When an enemy threatens the country, mad Polish patriots come to light.
(Janion 1989: 7)

'There have to be crooks in this world too', said Švejk, lying down on his straw mattress. 'If everyone were honest with each other, they'd soon start punching each other's noses.'
(Jaroslav Hašek, *The Good Soldier Švejk*)

War, Masculinity, Nation

Although fewer men were ever soldiers than fathers or lovers, it is widely accepted that there is a particularly strong connection between masculinity and partaking in a war. Graham Dawson argues that the soldier or, more precisely, the soldier hero, constitutes a hegemonic form of masculinity. Military virtues such as aggression, strength, courage and endurance have repeatedly been defined as the inherent qualities of manhood, whose apogee is attainable only in battle. Accordingly, they constitute a model which men are asked to emulate and a norm against which they are assessed (Dawson 1994: 1). In a similar vein George Mosse writes that 'War was an invitation to manliness' and refers to Christopher Isherwood and George Orwell's claim that during the late 1920s English writers suffered from a sense of shame that they had missed the war (Mosse 1985: 114).

We already observe the working of this hegemonic, 'military' masculinity at an early age when boys are given toy soldiers, tanks and guns to play with, in contrast to girls who have to amuse themselves with dolls and miniature pots and pans (Dawson 1994: 233). Similarly, the cruel and dramatic initiation rites, practised in many 'primitive' cultures, which include the separation of boys from their mothers, long-term isolation, beatings, hunger and confrontation with death, are meant to 'transform sweet little boys into terrible warriors' (Badinter 1995: 72), hence, into men. Dawson suggests that the soldier hero enjoys a privileged position as a quintessential figure of masculinity largely due to its link with the concepts of nation and the nation state. 'Intimately bound up with the foundation and preservation of a national territory, the deeds of military heroes were invested with the new significance of serving the country and glorifying its name. Their stories became myths of nationhood itself, providing a cultural focus around which the national community could cohere' (Dawson 1994: 1). To put it bluntly, soldier heroes are glorified and offered as role models because the states and national communities desperately need them. Another reason why soldiers epitomise masculinity results from the fact that the space of military combat used to constitute a distinctive masculine zone not contaminated by any female presence, although significantly affecting women's lives. Until the Second World War most wars took place away from civilian areas and it was almost impossible to be soldiers during the day and fathers and lovers at night. Of course, privileging the soldier as a paradigm of masculinity serves patriarchy, therefore in patriarchal discourses women are denied the right to fight in wars, usually on the grounds that nature gave them a different social role to men. Exhortation of the war and army life as the ultimate masculine experience does not mean that men take part in wars enthusiastically or even willingly (Mosse 1985: 115). After all war, despite its apparent gratification, such as the thrill of combat, the pleasure of victories (if there are victories) and comradeship with fellow soldiers, is a dangerous and traumatic event. A soldier risks imprisonment, injury, even torture and death, and suffers long periods of physical discomfort and separation from his relatives and friends. It could be suggested that the nationalist ideologies of soldiering, emphasising its nobility, alongside more coarse methods, such as conscription and execution for desertion, are the means to obliterate or play down the obvious perils and discomforts of being a soldier.

Mainstream cinema, both in the West and in the East, tends to go along with the idea that it is a duty and privilege of a man to be a soldier, bravely defending his country. It even plays a crucial role, as war propaganda, in disseminating the cult of the soldier. This can be explained by the strong connection between film (mainstream film especially) and the dominant ideology (Comolli and Narboni 1992). A sign of the importance of promoting war heroism for national culture is the fact that directors who fulfil this requirement often occupy a privileged position in the national cinema. This is certainly true about Andrzej Wajda who is the ultimate 'Polish director' largely because a significant part of his artistic output consists of war films, including his so-called 'war trilogy'. The interest vested by dominant ideology in the positive representation of fighting in the war, especially defending one's country with arms, does not mean that we do not find films which question war efforts and propose subversive images of soldiers. However, typically the strand of films promoting the heroic myth is stronger and receives more critical recognition than the subversive strand. Moreover, there is a time lag between these two types of movies; subversive films gain momentum only after the memory of a particular war fades and the audiences becomes tired with movies glorifying the war. Andrew Spicer observes that in British cinema the 'myth of the Blitz' as a heroic story of courage, endurance and pulling together which obliterated class divisions and political allegiances was strongest in the 1950s, whilst the majority of films challenging it were made in the later part of this decade and the early 1960s (Spicer 2004: 167–8). In a similar vein John Haynes notes that the most remarkable Russian film offering a revisionist view of the Second World War (the Great Patriotic War, as it was called in Soviet Russia), Sergei Bondarchuk's *Sud'ba cheloveka* (*The Fate of a Man*, 1959) was made after numerous films extolling the heroic achievements of Russian soldiers were completed (see Haynes 2003: 157–8).

War in Polish and Czechoslovak Cultures

War is a popular topic in practically every national cinema but there are national variations in its representation. These differences derive from different national histories and ideologies surrounding particular wars, cultural and artistic traditions of representing them (which themselves, to an extent, reflect the specific national experiences of the war but adding a layer of critical reflection), as well as from specific attitudes to the war of the filmmakers dealing with this subject. Some of these factors account for the similarity between the way Polish and Czechoslovak cinemas depict wars, especially the Second World War on which I will focus in this chapter, some explain the differences in their respective representations. In countries of the Soviet bloc, especially during the period of Stalinism, certain opinions about the war were not allowed. We can list here the unwritten prohibition of glorifying the soldiers fighting the Nazis on the side of Britain or supporting the prewar governments, or representing Russian soldiers in a negative way. The differences pertain to the fact that Poland fought a proper, albeit short, war against the Nazis in September 1939 (the so called September Campaign), whilst Czechoslovakia surrendered to Germany after the Munich agreement of 1938 (see Chapter 1). The issue is further complicated by creating a Slovak state in 1939, which although dependant on Berlin, was and still is regarded by many Slovaks as enjoying more autonomy than Slovaks had in prewar Czechoslovakia (Holý 1996: 109–10). Not surprisingly, Poland is full of monuments commemorating military leaders and battles, while in 'Kundera's Bohemia' and Slovakia there are hardly any. Czech efforts to construct images of war heroes have never been successful, a notable exception being Jan Žižka (to whom I return in due course). Heroic images did not last long or had not been unambiguously accepted by the whole nation (ibid.: 130). Czechs celebrate their suffering rather than their victories (Pynsent 1994: 190–6; Holý 1996: 130): the true heroes of the Czech nation are its martyrs. Robert Pynsent and Petra Hanáková argue that such an identification has a negative consequence in that it absolves or even encourages passivity, self-denigration and masochism (Pynsent 1994: 147–210; Hanáková 2005a: 151).

For most of the postwar period the main problems preoccupying Polish war historians, writers and filmmakers was the gap between the immense economic, military and human cost on the part of Poland during the Second World War, as well as earlier wars and uprisings, and the small rewards resulting from the country's efforts. As various authors suggest, Polish filmmakers developed two principal strategies to deal with this gap (see, for example, Nurczyńska-Fidelska 1982: 59–116). One consisted of extolling Polish heroism, showing it as an achievement and value in itself, more important than measurable consequences of heroic action, such as winning or losing a battle. A paradigmatic example of such strategy is the romantic strand of the Polish School, equated with the films of Andrzej Wajda of this period (mid 1950s to mid 1960s). The second strategy somehow amplifies the fissure between the war effort and its results by deriding Polish heroism and underscoring the scale of Polish defeat, as in the so called rational strand of the Polish School, whose main representative is Andrzej Munk. Paradoxically, sometimes these two strategies go hand in hand or at least some war films were open to both interpretations, heroic and ironic, such as *Krzyż Walecznych* (*Cross of Valour*, 1958), directed by Kazimierz Kutz or Munk's *Eroica* (1957).

The minor resistance of Czechs to the Nazi invasion and subsequent occupation, and the largely positive attitude of Slovaks to the creation of the pro-Nazi Slovak state, was treated in Czechoslovak cinema in two principal ways. One illuminates the attitudes that testified to Czech and Slovak resistance to Nazism, especially among ordinary people. This strategy is conveyed in films such as *Ostře sledované vlaky* (*Closely Observed Trains*, 1966), directed by Jiři Menzel and *...a pozdravuji vlaštovky* (*And Give My Love to the Swallows*, 1972), directed by Jaromil Jireš. The second approach consists of focusing on Czech and Slovaks' war 'sins': collaboration with the enemy, cowardice, conformism and indifference to the plight of the war's main victims, the Jews. We find the principal examples of this trend in *Démanty noci* (*Diamonds of the Night*, 1964), directed by Jan Němec, and Juraj Herz's *Spalovač mrtvol* (*The Cremator*, 1968). Not infrequently, these two approaches coincide, as in *Obchod na korze* (*A Shop on the High Street*, 1965), directed by Ján Kadár and Elmar Klos. It could even be argued that combining collaboration with resistance in one film became a Czech speciality.

Another factor affecting the representation of war in film is the way military conflicts are portrayed in literature, because some books on this subject hold a strong grip on people's ideas in this area. For the inhabitants of Czechoslovakia and for Czechs especially *The Good Soldier Švejk* by Jaroslav Hašek is such a book, although its fame spread beyond Czechoslovakia and Europe. Stern describes its protagonist as the 'only genuine popular creation of modern European literature' (Stern 1992: 109).[1] *The Good Soldier Švejk*, first published in instalments from 1921 till 1923, is set during the First World War and casts as its main character Josef Švejk, a private in the Austro-Hungarian army, who in civilian life used to sell mongrel dogs, passing them as pedigrees, and dwelled in a working class district of Prague. Although Hašek's novel concerns a war, he describes it not as an adventure but as a bureaucratic machine (Kundera 1990: 48–9; Kroutvor 2001: 258–62). There are hardly any combat scenes included in it and little attention is paid to weapons and military training. Instead, its focus is on the army as an organisation with a complex chain of command and complicated procedures. Moreover, the army command does not have any illusions that the soldiers will volunteer to fight and happily die for the Kaiser or their country but assumes that they will rather employ all possible means to avoid fulfilling their military duties. Consequently, a significant part of the army machine is used to prevent it happening. A perfect example is the military hospital, where all patients are presumed to be malingerers simulating illness to avoid combat, therefore they are treated by their doctors in such a cruel way that they either choose to go to the front or die as a result of their treatment.

Hašek's book (as is the case with many other masterpieces) is open to various or even contrasting interpretations. The most contentious issues include its attitude to war and the state of mind of its protagonist. It is clear that Hašek is against the war in which Švejk and other Czechs are forced to take part, but is he against any war? The next crucial question is whether Švejk is a genuine idiot or only plays an idiot; whether he is 'plain bloody hopeless' or is 'hopeless with intent', as he is described in the book. Or, perhaps, as Peter Steiner persuasively argues, he transcends these categories and 'an overall, totalising interpretation of the good soldier is impossible' (Steiner 2000: 46). The closest we can approach the nature of Švejk, in Steiner's opinion, is to treat him as a 'homo ludens', the descendant of Diogenes (ibid: 25–68). However, what is beyond dispute is that Hašek's novel includes 'vulgar language, bawdy humour and thorough debunking of all lofty ideals (whether heroism, loyalty or justice)'(ibid.: 26) and that, rightly or wrongly, Švejk came to be regarded as an embodiment of the Czech national character that encompasses all the aforementioned traits, as well as a peaceful demeanour, incompetence and extreme adaptability (Sayer 2000: 160; Roberts 2005: 167). As Stern maintains, 'the popularity of Hašek's book is attested to by the vocabulary (name, abstract noun, verb, adjective) that has sprouted from its hero's name: "švejkovina" (on the analogy of "oblomovshchina") has connotations of cunning and scrounging, of cutting corners and choosing an easy way out, of talking oneself out of difficulty and then lying low' (Stern 1992: 120–1). 'Švejkism' (a term coined by the communist writer and Hašek's friend, Ivan Olbracht), has become a concept which characterises the passive form of Czech resistance against a superior power, which involves conformism, moral laxity and unheroic 'realism'.

Some historians have traced the 'Švejkian' attitude to the defeat of the Protestant Czechs on the White Mountain in 1620 and see it as:

> characteristic of 'the leeward life of the nation' under the Habsburgs throughout the next three centuries, and offer it as an explanation for a host of more recent events: the Munich surrender of 1938, the relative weakness of the Czech resistance throughout the Second World War, the passivity of the country's liberal majority during the communist coup d'etat of February 1948 and the four decades of subservience to Moscow, including first the Slánský trials of 1952 and then the suppression of the 'Prague Spring' and another capitulation in the summer of 1968. Seen in this cheerless perspective, the 'velvet revolution' of November 1989, too, appears as a spontaneous but prudently delayed reaction to a series of events initiated in Moscow, Gdynia and Warsaw, Budapest and (who'd have thought it?) Dresden, Leipzig and East Berlin. (Stern 1992: 121)

Figure 2.1 Rudolf Hrušínský as Švejk in *Dobrý voják Švejk* (*The Good Soldier Švejk*, 1956), directed by Karel Steklý.

The most obvious sign of the significance of Švejk for Czech cinema is the fact that Hašek's novel was adapted several times for cinema and television. The best-known version of Švejk's adventures, the two-part *Dobrý voják Švejk* (*The Good Soldier Švejk*, 1956) and *Poslušně hlásím* (*Humbly Report*, 1957), by some critics regarded as best, by other as the worst adaptation of Hašek's book, was directed by Karel Steklý, with Rudolf Hrušínský playing Švejk. Steklý's adaptation owes its lasting charm mostly to its humble desire not to impose an authorial voice on the novel, particularly in relation to the main character. And yet, due to the change of medium, the cinematic Švejk is less ambiguous than its literary predecessor by coming across as idiotic. A more important sign of Švejk's presence in Czechoslovak cinema is the fact that what is widely regarded as 'Švejkian spirit' pervades a large proportion of war films produced in Czechoslovakia. They do not take the war for granted but question its morality and sanity, usually by applying comedy. Moreover, the nationalistic discourse which typically prevails in war films, in Czechoslovak productions is situated in the background. There is also little emphasis on combat itself. Film authors tend to ask what the war means for a particular individual or a family, rather than for the nation, and choose ordinary civilians as protagonists rather than soldier heroes. They also reject a Manichean, black and white vision of the war conflicts by showing that what from one perspective looks like heroism or bravery, from another reveals less appealing qualities.

I will also regard Franz Kafka as an important influence on Czechoslovak war cinema. Kafka did not write war novels but his work deals with the experiences of people in an extremely hostile human environment, which can be compared to the life of a civilian under military occupation or under a totalitarian system, such as fascism or Stalinist communism, or even to a Jew persecuted by the Nazis. Kafka describes emotions such as extreme fear, shame and 'the bewilderment of accused unaware of what crime they could have committed, and feeling the more guilty on that account' (French 1982: 84). His characters are utterly objectified by a mysterious system and devoid of individuality, therefore also humanity, which is often conveyed by the motif of people changing into animals or simply of making animals the main characters in the story. Not surprising, many authors compare Kafka to Hašek (French 1982: 84; Steiner 2000: 25–68). Karel Kosík and Milan Kundera render Josef Švejk and Kafka's most famous creation, Josef K., as kind of twins. Both men are alone in their confrontation with the bureaucratised universe which renders them not as real men but merely shadows of their existence in a file kept in some kind of archive (Kosík, quoted in Steiner 2000: 34–6, Kundera 1990: 48–9). Kosík even observes that Švejk is escorted by two soldiers from Hradčany garrison jail to Karlin and two guards lead the bank clerk Josef K. to the Strahov quarries. Both groups pass through the same places but meeting each other is impossible (Kosík, quoted in Steiner 2000: 25). Josef K. is executed while Josef Švejk survives, not least because his papers had been placed in files relating to a certain Josef Koudela. Although Hašek and Kafka depict the same world, the first sees in it a chance for the individual to preserve his physical existence and integrity, largely by 'matching the illogic of the system with his own idiosyncrasies' (ibid.: 47), while for the second such a chance does not exist. To put it crudely, Hašek is an optimist, while Kafka is a pessimist. Similarly, I will argue that while the majority of Czech war films conform to the vision of the world depicted by Hašek and Kafka, the fate of their characters differ.

Finally, I will argue that Czechoslovak war cinema, at least during socialist realism, was inspired by Julius Fučík (1903–43), the author and protagonist of *Reportage: Written from the Gallows*. Fučík was a journalist, a literary critic, a devoted communist and a member of an anti-Nazi conspiracy who was imprisoned, interrogated and executed by the Gestapo. He wrote his main work on 167 scraps of paper smuggled from the Pankrac prison during his internment there. The fact that he encapsulates communism and the resistance to the Nazis, as well as being able to articulate and elaborate the connection between these two attitudes, made him a very useful character for the communist propaganda machine: the ultimate communist martyr. For these reasons, a cult was imposed with great force on him in the 1940s and 1950s with numerous accolades bestowed on the martyr, including the honorific 'National Hero' used regularly in front of his name since 1946, being posthumously decorated with the highest Czechoslovak military medal, the Order of the White Lion. In addition, the Czechoslovak Youth Union (the Czechoslovak version of the Soviet Komsomol) instituted in the early 1950s a new tool of indoctrination, aptly called the 'Fučík Badge' (Steiner 2000: 99). Although Fučík, the real man and the literary persona, is a patriot willingly risking his life for his ideals, he is a martyr rather than ordinary hero, because he demonstrates his patriotism not by fighting with arms, but through enduring torture.

Czechoslovakia thus lacks 'forthright soldier heroes' or they are marginalised in national traditions, as if to confirm the opinion that Czechs and Slovaks (although to a lesser extent) are peaceful nations that never started a war (Paul 1979: 253–6; Holý 1996: 136). The lack of indigenous heroes and the scepticism about them is excellently conveyed by frequent parodies of Western films with heroes, examples being Oldřich Lipský's Czech western *Limonádovy Joe aneb koňská opera* (*Lemonade Joe, or a Horse Opera*, 1964) or *Konec agenta W4C prostrednictvím psa pana Foustky* (*The End of Agent W4C*, 1967), directed by Václav Vorlíček, which is a James Bond spoof. It should be added that this type of film has no Polish equivalent, perhaps because if Poles wanted to mock heroes and supermen, they had many of their own to choose from.

It will be difficult to find a Polish equivalent of *The Good Soldier Švejk*, namely a book that concerns war (or any fighting with arms) and occupies a comparable position in Polish culture as Hašek's does in Czech. Probably the closest analogue is Adam Mickiewicz's Part III of *Dziady* (*The Forefathers's Eve*, 1832). I will argue that more useful is to compare *The Good Soldier Švejk* with a larger body of Polish romantic and neoromantic literature or even the romantic tradition in a wider sense (that also includes orally transmitted legends). As Maria Janion argues, for Polish romantics 'the motherland is god' (Janion 1989: 10). However, she is not a gentle and merciful goddess but rather a ruthless and demonic entity that does not allow a man to have any other objects of affection. A person who gives in to such a concept of motherland could easily cross the borders of rationality, becoming mad. Polish literature, oral tradition and art is awash with mad patriots. The archetypal example is Tadeusz Rejtan (1742–80), a member of the Polish parliament during the first partition of Poland who tried to prevent it happening by extreme means, including throwing himself at the entrance of the house of parliament. Rejtan's extreme form of patriotism became immortalised in a picture by Jan Matejko and in Mickiewicz's *Pan Tadeusz* (1834), the most popular Polish romantic work. Janion finds the newest incarnation of a mad patriot in Jerzy Krzysztoń's novel *Obłęd* (*Madness*, 1980) whose main character after December 1970 finds himself in a psychiatric ward. She describes him as the 'successor of a society in which the perception of historical greatness is intertwined with the despair caused by a mean present' (ibid.: 22). His madness has its source in the very gap between the apparently deserved greatness of his country and its real insignificance. Such a perception of a breach between the postulated greatness of a nation and its actual mediocrity, as Ladislav Holý observes, also pertains to the dominant discourse on Czech history (Holý 1996: 120–5). Yet Poles appear to react more extremely than their neighbours to this gap between what is deserved and what exists, or so one can guess comparing Janion's and Holý's analysis of the respective national cultures.

Janion does not talk about patriotic madness as a homogenous condition, but discerns its three main types:

1) real madness – a psychiatric condition caused by the misfortunes and defeats of one's country;
2) lack of political sobriety and responsibility, leading to crazy political action, as epitomised by the Polish proverb 'to attack the sun with a hoe';
3) political idealism that forces one to follow moral rules whatever the costs, rejecting pragmatism, political calculation and diplomacy.

Unlike the first two types, that are regarded as unwelcome and dangerous, the third type is cherished and encouraged. It is suggested (and Janion herself appears to endorse this view) that it is better to be mad in the third sense and lose a war than reject this madness and win it (Janion 1989: 12). Moreover, she suggests that Poland is a great nation precisely because it is capable of this type of madness (ibid.: 32). On the other hand, she admits that 'positive madness' frequently leads to the first and second types. People illuminated by high patriotic ideals often act irresponsibly and are at great danger of losing their sanity. Tadeusz Rejtan is a case in point as he literally went mad and committed suicide. On the whole, there is a close link between patriotic madness *alla pollacca* and suicide. Polish patriots either take their own life or enter a situation in which they have no chance to survive, such as the Polish cavalrymen who, according to a legend, attacked German tanks with sabres in the campaign of September 1939, an image immortalised in Andrzej Wajda's *Lotna* (1959). However, their suicide does not equal an ultimate death because it benefits their countrymen and future generations. This idea is conveyed by the motif of the resurrection of the romantic protagonist, used, for example, in Mickiewicz's *Forefathers' Eve*. Although Janion does not state it explicitly, from the examples she uses we can conclude that mad patriotism is a male preserve. Polish men serve their country by losing their senses and taking their own lives, women by producing men who happily die for their country.

The closer we approach contemporary times, the more ambivalent the attitudes we discern to Polish mad patriotism. After the Second World War this ambivalence was encapsulated by a new term that entered the Polish vocabulary, *bohaterszczyzna*. It derives from *bohater* (*hero*) and is closely related to *bohaterstwo* (*heroism*), but refers to the degenerate form of heroism – heroism that is superfluous and mannered. Such a type of heroism, as Andrzej Werner notes, was ascribed to the participants of the Warsaw Uprising of 1944 by its opponents who after the war embraced the communist regime in Poland (Werner 1987: 56–7).

Along with mad patriots, who commit acts of extreme bravery, in Polish romantic literature we can also identify characters who manifest love for their country by 'moral war' or a 'war of imagination' but in reality are unable to act. A model example is Kordian in Juliusz Słowacki's poem of the same title (1834). Kordian is a (fictitious) nineteenth century conspirator who attempted to assassinate Russian Tsar Nicolai I when in 1829 he came to Warsaw to be crowned a Polish king. Kordian failed to kill his enemy, paralysed by fear and distaste for murder. Subsequently Kordian was sentenced to death but saved himself by a circus act of jumping over the bayonets on a horse. However, he was probably shot in the end because the courier with the news of his acquittal did not come on time. It is easy to dismiss Kordian and others of his kind as fantasists and cowards but it is also possible to view them positively as bearers of more individualistic values to those espoused by mad patriots, even prototypes of 'existential men'. A well-known twentieth-century Polish writer, Zofia Nałkowska, says 'Kordian was able to withdraw from the planned act because he put his loathing of murder and disgust of brutality higher than heroic exaltation' (Nałkowska, quoted in Siwicka 2002: 110). A number of authors, including an influential film critic Aleksander Jackiewicz, have argued that romantic ideology was disastrous for Poland. It weakened the country politically and economically, and rendered Polish men unable to fulfil their grandiose ambitions, therefore neurotic and ultimately weak and impotent (Jackiewicz 1968; 64–72; 1989: 353–61).[2] However, my argument in this chapter is that Polish war cinema failed to create a viable alternative to the romantic hero: a man who is not romantic, but still deserves admiration and respect, and with whom the audience can identify.

Whilst the problem of war was always present in Polish and Czechoslovakian cinema, there were periods when this subject was particularly fashionable. The first such period follows the end of the war, namely the late 1940s when the scars of war were fresh. The second coincides with the Polish and Czechoslovak New Waves. In Poland the New Wave, named the 'Polish School', is almost synonymous with films about the Second World War. Their production can be attributed predominantly to the political thaw following Stalin's death, which allowed certain previously taboo issues to be addressed. The third period follows the collapse of communism in Poland and Czechoslovakia. The upsurge of war films after 1989 can be explained by the directors' desire to reevaluate the war in the light of a new political situation, as well as their awareness of the usefulness of this topic as a prism to look at the new times. Accordingly, the focus of this chapter will be on examining these three periods. Although the films discussed here represent the past, they are also anchored in the times of their production,[3] therefore they should tell us something of importance about men who lived then.

Inspired by the War, Moulded by Stalinism

Mira and Antonín Liehm observe that 'the first postwar films in Eastern Europe sought their inspiration for the most part from wartime experiences and the Nazi occupation' (Liehm and Liehm 1977: 228). Indeed, films about the Second World War were shot in Poland and Czechoslovakia almost immediately after the combat finished. Typically, their directors made their debut before the war, such as Leonard Buczkowski and Martin Frič. They brought to the films their prewar experience and methods, which in due course became criticised for not adhering to socialist realistic orthodoxy. However, gradually a distinctive, socialist realistic style of representing the war was established. As the Liehms argue, this style was characterised by a clear demarcation between good and bad: 'good was white and ultimately victorious, evil was black and safely vanquished, and the audience's identification with the "good guys" was ensured. These war films resembled westerns, even in their abundance of action' (ibid: 228). Yet, in my opinion, it is difficult to find films that fully adhere to this description. Moreover, the most popular and critically acclaimed films were somehow flawed attempts at inscribing the war into the precepts of socialist realism.

The first Polish film to be completed after the war was Leonard Buczkowski's *Zakazane piosenki* (*Forbidden Songs*, 1946). It tells the story of several Warsawians inhabiting the same tenement block from the beginning of the war till its liberation. Buczkowski's work is typically dismissed as an anthology of songs popular in Warsaw during the Nazi occupation, barely joined together by a thin narrative (Michałek and Turaj 1988: 4; Haltof 2002: 50). Consequently, despite being the first film ever made in People's Poland, *Forbidden Songs* receives little critical attention and when it does, it is construed as an unideological work whose ideological dimension was inserted into it during its remaking, following criticism by the communist authorities. While it is true that the film was remade and rereleased in 1948, to ensure a positive representation of the Red Army as the liberator of Warsaw, some ideas were present in it from the very beginning. This concerns the representation of the war roles of men and women. The film opens with a sequence of singing a popular war song, 'Tę piosenkę, tę jedyną, śpiewam dla ciebie dziewczyno' (This song, this only song, I sing for you, my girl) to the accompaniment of a piano. The song is obviously addressed to a woman but is sung by a group of men only, including the main character in the film, Roman Tokarski (Jerzy Duszyński). The very content of the song construes women as passive and excluded from the war zone. Roman presents the war experiences of his family, friends and himself to a Polish soldier who spent the war years in Scotland. From his story we learn that in fact women played an important role during the war. Roman's sister Halina (Danuta Szaflarska) was an active member of an anti-Nazi resistance, smuggling forbidden literature and weapons to Warsaw. The siblings also helped to hide a Jew and were involved in the assassination of a Volksdeutsch (Polish-born German) woman who collaborated with the enemy. The overall message is that while women were equal with men in fighting the enemy, they were later excluded from the memory of the war.

Forbidden Songs concerns the everyday heroism of the Warsawians. Buczkowski shows that almost everybody was involved in fighting the Nazis, even people from whom normally one would not expect heroic acts such as old people and children. However, the highest type of heroism, consisting of the direct fight with the German oppressor, is reserved for men. Tacitly Buczkowski also refers to the immense moral pressure the heroic norm exerted on those who by nature were less courageous or on heroes in a moment of weakness. One example is Mr Cieślak, Roman and Halina's neighbour, who is derided by his countrymen for being afraid to keep illegal leaflets in his flat or refusing to listen to forbidden songs in public. However, even he in the end gives in to the overall patriotic atmosphere and takes part in the Warsaw Uprising. Another example is the behaviour of Halina when she learns that her boyfriend was killed in battle. Although she suffers immensely, she hides her tears and her feelings, in this way admitting that during the war private pleasures and sufferings must give way to public ones. *Forbidden Songs* was an immensely popular

Figure 2.2 A scene from *Za wami pójdą inni…* (*You Will Be Followed by Others…*, 1949), directed by Antoni Bohdziewicz.

film, having 10.8 million viewers within the first three years of its release (Haltof 2002: 50). Its popularity can be partly explained by its subject – the war. When, in 1947, the popular Polish film magazine, *Film*, conducted a survey amongst its readers, asking them what themes they favoured in cinema, the most common answer was the Second World War (Lubelski 1992a: 76). Buczkowski conformed to the dominant Polish ideology of war by presenting it as something which Poles partake of united and in good spirits.

Unlike *Forbidden Songs*, *Za wami pójdą inni…* (*You Will Be Followed by Others…*, 1949), directed by Antoni Bohdziewicz, was tailored to the socialist realist standard by making the members of the Polish left (Gwardia Ludowa, Polska Partia Robotnicza) the main characters in the story and using the narrative as a means to disgrace the Polish prewar bourgeoisie as selfish, snobbish and unpatriotic, and denounce the loyal to the Polish government-in-exile Home Army (Armia Krajowa), which was the dominant movement fighting the Nazis in Poland, as timid and lacking in initiative. The film revolves around the budding romance between a young communist, Władek (Adam Hanuszkiewicz) and a young woman from a rich home, Anna (Ewa Krasnodębska) who, influenced by his attitude, agrees to shelter a Jew in her home and eventually pays with her life for joining the resistance. However, despite its 'right' attitude, Bohdziewicz's film also had problems with censorship and had to be partly changed because during its shooting, the film's heroes and the organisations they represented lost their position in the governing elite and had to fight for their political survival.

While in Polish films from the 1940s and early 1950s the emphasis is on the conflict between Poles and Germans, in Czechoslovak films we more often find an attempt to represent the Second World War as a class war. Its cause is presented as a double betrayal of the Czech people by the external enemy of Germany and internal of the Czech bourgeoisie. The Second World War is represented thus, among other films, in *Uluopená hranice* (*Stolen Frontier*, 1947) by Jiří Weiss, which I will discuss in detail and *Bíila tma* (*White Darkness*, 1948) by František Čap.

Stolen Frontier tells the story of the inhabitants of a Czech frontier region during the autumn of 1938, when Czech workers were forced to leave their houses by their German neighbours. Weiss proposes the idea that previously Czechs and Germans were united by a common fight for workers' rights. Their unity was destroyed by the poisonous concept of a Greater Germany that would include the Sudetenland and the promise of a better life for Germans thanks to the expulsion of Czechs from any positions of power. Some Germans joined the Nazi militia because they bought into the nationalistic slogans, others for pragmatic reasons. Together, however, the new ideas changed the outlook on life of almost all Germans. This dramatic change is epitomised by the story of a mixed family, father being German, mother Czech. While the parents try to keep away from politics, their children take a clear stance; the son Honzik or German Hans (Josef Maršálek) joins a Nazi organisation, a member of which kills his mother; the daughter Anna Marie feels Czech. Such a division of loyalties might be explained by the rules of inheritance; the son follows, if not his father's views, at least his blood, the daughter by choosing Czechness follows her mother. Yet, it can also be seen as symbolic for the way Czechs and Germans were construed in the discourse on war even in Czech culture; the Czechs being the weak, feminine side, the Germans strong and masculine. Hans identifies with this idea by accusing his father of giving up on his masculinity and becoming nobody by marrying a Czech. This opinion is, perhaps against Weiss's intentions, confirmed through visual means. Hans's father looks old and unkempt and sports a pipe, which symbolises his phlegm and lack of energy. He is everything but a model for his ambitious son who strives to get a gun, a symbol of the phallic power his father rejected. Although Weiss is at pains to demonstrate the heroism of Czechs, it transpires that they lack the courage and commitment the Germans display. Their laid-back attitude is encapsulated by one of the Czech border guards, who in the middle of the conflict is reading a British detective novel, wishing he was able to display the same manners as its protagonist. The Czech servicemen also lack leadership, therefore when the order comes from Prague to stop fighting, it comes across as a rational decision because the Czechs will certainly lose, only at a greater human cost, if they continue. However, in the last scene the Czech fighters express their sense of being betrayed by the (bourgeois) government and hope that the wrongs will be repaired, as obviously they were, thanks to the liberation by the Soviet troops.

Návrat domů (*Return Home*, 1948), directed by Martin Frič, offers an even more ambivalent image of a Czech soldier than *Stolen Frontier*. The film's protagonist, lieutenant Kliment Mareš (Karel Höger), returns home after the war where he fought in the Red Army. He hopes to reunite with his family and friends but learns that his fiancée married another man, his mother and sister were arrested and executed, and most of his old friends perished. He is very disappointed, if not in despair, but he cannot ponder on the war's devastation for ever, because he has to leave his home again, this time to protect Czechoslovakia's border. On his journey Mareš is to be accompanied by his female colleague, sergeant Stáňa, who is secretly in love with him. Thus, paradoxically, the remedy for the despair caused by the war is another military service. Although from a socialist-realistic perspective *Return Home* has the perfect protagonist, a man who fought for his country in the 'right' army and is prepared to defend the borders of a socialist Czechoslovakia, authors adopting socialist-realist ideology were critical of the way he was constructed. For example, Irena Merz described Mareš as a 'weak and lost individual suffering war wounds and problems typical for the intelligentsia' and the whole film as a 'bourgeois drama detached from the sociopolitical situation of the people's democracy, that could be made everywhere' (Merz 1954: 16).

Daleká cesta (*Distant Journey*, 1950) by Alfréd Radok attracted even more criticism from socialist-realistic-minded reviewers, mostly due to the expressionistic style of the film (Cieslar 2004: 48). Putting this aside, what strikes one is the rather unflattering representation of Czech society facing the persecution of their Jewish neighbours and friends. One observes little compassion for their plight; their desperate situation raises in most cases indifference or a desire to profit from their misery, for example by buying cheaply the property they had to leave when moving to the Terezín ghetto (Theresienstadt). Only the stance taken by the main character, doctor Toník, is very different to that of the majority. Instead of abandoning his hospital colleague with whom he is in love, he marries her and endures all the discomforts and problems resulting from becoming a 'white Jew', such as losing his job in the hospital, being ostracised by his own family and eventually being sent to Terezín. Tonik's behaviour is noble and courageous but he comes across as a martyr, not a soldier hero. Moreover, he is motivated more by his private interests, namely his love for his wife, than concern for the whole Jewish community. Or at least, at the root of his care for the community is his care for his family. As Katerina Clark observes, such an attitude did not conform to the socialist-realistic idea that the community was prior and the family was valuable only insofar as it served the community (Clark 2000: 115).

The Second World War and its political outcome also inspired a group of films that represented earlier wars, principally the Hussite wars of the fifteenth century. They include Otakar Vávra's Hussite trilogy: *Jan Hus* (1954), *Jan Žižka* (1955) and *Proti všem* (*Against Everybody*, 1956), and Vladimír Borský's *Jan Roháč z Dube* (*Jan Roháč of Duba*, 1947).

With the exception of Borský's film they were made several years after *Stolen Border*, *Distant Journey* and *Return Home*, which appears to impact on the way they construct the characters, rendering them more socialist-realistic. As their very titles suggest, each focuses on an individual who is a political and spiritual leader of the masses. Although the man lived several hundreds years previously, the film author projects on him a socialist mindset. He is a friend of ordinary people, an enemy of the rich and has a 'Robin Hood' mentality, believing that where there is a large gap between the rich and the poor, the poor have the right to deprive the rich of their wealth. These leaders in the films are typically constructed as martyrs rather than victorious soldiers, in accordance with the rule that Czechs celebrate their suffering rather than their victories. Two of the leaders, Jan Hus and Jan Roháč of Duba, are sentenced to death and executed: Hus dies by being burnt at the stake, Roháč is hanged. Their historical significance consists thus not in the number of battles won but in the moral example they set for their followers, for paving the way to a future utopia, which can be identified with the time after the victory of socialism. Such a construction of the narrative pertains to a socialist-realistic novel (Clark 2000: 39–40) and, by extension, to any socialist-realistic work. The exception is Jan Žižka who is victorious in Vávra's film, as he was in historical reality. His special benefit to socialist realism resulted from the fact that he is remembered as a man who burnt churches and monasteries, and unlike Hus, was not an intellectual (Holý 1996: 135). Needless to add that these qualities are underscored by Vávra. The wars are usually represented as conflicts between the Czechs and the Germans, who try to deprive ordinary Czech folk of their country with the assistance of the Czech upper classes. In *Jan Roháč of Duba* the defeat of the German King of Bohemia, Emperor Sigismund, paves the way for a closer collaboration between the Czechs and the Poles when the Czech people turn to the Polish king to take the Czech crown for himself or his son. We can see a parallel in this solution to the outcome of the Second World War, when the defeat of Germany led to Poland and Czechoslovakia's collaboration within the bloc of socialist countries.

The Czech films of distant wars do not have their counterpart in Polish cinema of the first half of the 1950s. We should regard *Krzyżacy* (*Knights of the Teutonic Order*, 1960) by Aleksander Ford as the work closest to the model offered by Vávra and Borský. This film, not unlike its Czech counterparts, also represents the Polish nation as threatened in the fifteenth century by German invasion and the power of Church. However, it underscores military action and heroism rather than martyrdom; decisive victory rather than the noble defeat that led to the future utopia.

Mad Patriots in the Films of the Polish School

Although some of the films described in the previous section are of high artistic quality, it was only in the period of the New Waves that the two cinemas developed unique styles of representing the war. The principal Polish films representing the war from the years 1955–65 belong to the Polish School. This paradigm largely modelled itself on romantic art in terms of visual representation, choice of characters and, most importantly, ideology (see Ozimek 1980: 205; Jackiewicz 1968: 64–89; Nurczyńska-Fidelska 1995: 7–19; Coates 2005: 116–54). We find in the Polish School films an idea that the war was worth fighting even when the fighters were doomed (which was

Figure 2.3 Tadeusz Janczar as Jasio Krone in *Pokolenie* (*A Generation*, 1954), directed by Andrzej Wajda.

typically the case). What mattered was not the outcome of the struggle but the moral impulse behind the act. Yet, in order to enter the hopeless situation the fighter must typically be somehow divorced from reality, irrational, even mad in the sense elucidated by Maria Janion.

In this section I want to discuss the story of this Polish patriotic madness in Andrzej Wajda's 'war trilogy' of *Pokolenie* (*A Generation*, 1954), *Kanał* (*Kanal*, 1956) and *Popiół i diament* (*Ashes and Diamonds*, 1958), regarded as the centrepiece of the Polish School, and its criticism in *Jak być kochaną* (*How to Be Loved*, 1962) by Wojciech Has. Unlike Wajda or Andrzej Munk, whose *Eroica* (1957)[4] is the fourth most celebrated example of the Polish School, Has's allegiance to the Polish School is weaker. He was always regarded as an outsider, a filmmaker more immersed in his own style than in Polish history and national identity (Kornatowska 1995: 41; Michałek 2002: 132–3), but in my opinion this position allowed him to look at the war from perspectives neglected by his colleagues.

A Generation[5], Wajda's debut film based on a novel by Bogdan Czeszko, is justly regarded as a transitional work between socialist realism and the Polish School. Its very title captures the socialist-realistic requirement of telling the stories of masses of people bound by a common fate and class consciousness, the proletariat, and Wajda's own ambition, rooted in the ethos of Polish Romanticism, of speaking on behalf of the whole tormented nation. Set in 1943, the film casts as the main characters two young factory workers: Stach Mazur (Tadeusz Łomnicki) and Jasio Krone (Tadeusz Janczar), who belong to the so called 'generation of Columbuses', a term borrowed from the book by Roman Bratny, *Columbuses Born in 1920* (1957). Bratny wrote that for these people the Second World War was a crucial experience and that they lost most as a result of the war: their youth, innocence, even life itself. Wajda depicts here their ideological maturation understood in terms of joining an anti-Nazi conspiracy and the communist movement. Stach, who is the main character and the narrator of the film, is an uncomplicated young man. He is guided into adulthood by an older foreman, Mr Sekuła, who advises him less on how to be a good craftsman as on how to understand capitalism in Marxist terms, emphasising the exploitation of workers. Jasio, on the other hand, in his long white coat, reminiscent of 1950s Western intellectuals, comes across as mysterious, complicated and irrational.

He describes himself as a communist but does not want to join the organisation. He is the first one in the group to kill a German but later insists on being treated as a civilian, and shows an existential distaste for killing, which also bears similarity to Kordian. Despite that, he agrees to help the Jews during the Ghetto Uprising. Moreover, his suicide when cornered by the Nazis is at odds with the optimistic world of socialist realism. Although Stach's role is greater than that of Jasio, the impression is that the latter character is more significant to the director. This was noted by a number of critics, including Andrzej Werner (Werner 1987: 46–7) and Bolesław Michałek, who wrote: 'The inner world to which Wajda personally felt most attuned was that of Jasio Krone – edgy, troubled, bewildered, switching from one extreme to the other, and not with Stach, the dour proletarian' (Michałek 1973: 20). Thanks to his death Jasio also proves more heroic and patriotic than Stach because, as Janion points out, self-inflicted death is the ultimate proof of one's patriotism. Another character in the film is Dorota, a young female communist who inspires Stach to join the anti-Nazi organisation. Highly energetic and idealistic, she is a familiar stereotype from the 1950s, but her tragic end separates her from the heroines of socialistic realistic films. Through Dorota, Wajda includes in his film the motif of love, which is desired by the characters but rendered impossible, because of their sense of duty toward their motherland–their ultimate love. In Wajda's subsequent war films it will be a norm that an erotic kiss is followed by a 'kiss of death'.

While in *A Generation* only Jasio betrays symptoms of patriotic madness, in *Kanal*, scripted by Jerzy Stefan Stawiński, madness is an epidemic affecting virtually all Poles. One factor allowing Wajda such a representation is his focus on a particular historical period – September 1944, the final part of the Warsaw Uprising, when it became clear that the insurrectionists, recruited predominantly from the Home Army, had been defeated. Wajda thwarts any hope on the part of the viewer that his characters might be an exception to the rule by informing us through the voice of the narrator: 'Look at them carefully, these are the last hours of their lives.' If we obey his request, we might notice that among the members of the decimated battalion is somebody nicknamed Korab with the familiar face of Tadeusz Janczar, who played Jasio Krone in *A Generation*. Looking at Wajda's characters makes one wonder: 'What made these people go to an almost certain death?' Perhaps it was faith in their victory. Yet the director denies the viewers any information about the political background of the Uprising, such as reference to the Soviet Army's encampment on the other side of the Vistula and its unwillingness to help Polish soldiers (Werner 1987: 53–9; Coates 2005: 120). Whatever the reasons for Wajda's withholding such information, it adds to the impression that the insurrectionists are madmen who chose certain death rather than patiently waiting for the end of the war. Another factor adding to the impression that the people portrayed in the film are crazy is the setting most of the film in Warsaw's sewers. Although in reality this route saved the lives of a significant number of insurrectionists, the obvious connotation of a sewer is a place where only vermin lives, or a hell. Wajda exploits such associations through the use of mise-en-scène and music (Ozimek 1980: 27). Most of the time the sewer is full of mist, apparently due to Germans putting a poisonous gas into it. The mist makes it look like a pot with boiling tar in which the sinners suffer for their crimes. Moreover, it is full of spooky sounds, repeated by echo, as if devils were mocking the efforts of the insurrectionists to escape. The cross, shown shortly before the characters descend to the kanał, is another potent symbol of their inevitable demise.

All Wajda's characters are victims of patriotic madness, but he discerns several types of this condition, in line with the typology offered by Janion. All of them are mad because they are idealists inspired by a higher moral aim and act selflessly, neglecting their own life. Wajda also points to patriotic madness as lack of realism and responsibility in political action. Of such a madness, which is much less noble, stand accused the leaders of the Uprising, represented in the film by the commander of the battalion, nicknamed Zadra (Wieńczysław Gliński), because his more responsible superiors are never shown. Significantly older than his subordinates,

Zadra should predict what will happen but fails to do so. He is well aware of his mistake and bitterly comments on the small size of the Polish pistols and grenades, used against German tanks and cannons, asking rhetorically 'When will we Poles learn our lesson?' As Andrzej Werner notes, the division of the insurrectionists into the irresponsible and careless command and the ordinary soldiers who fell victims to their command, conveyed a distinctive political position which is, broadly speaking, pro-communist (see Werner 1987: 54–5). In *Kanal* we also find men who literally go mad. This condition befalls a musician who leaves his comrades in a sewer and goes alone in the opposite direction into death, oblivious to the people whom he meets; the wounded Korab who hallucinates that he is walking through a forest; and Zadra, who returns to a sewer upon discovering that he is the only person who managed to escape. The group presented in *Kanal* consists of over twenty men and two women, named Halinka and Daisy. Such a gender composition approximately conforms to the norm that mad patriotism is a male feature. This opinion is also confirmed by Wajda highlighting the different behaviour of men and women. Although Daisy is a political idealist, as proved by her joining the Uprising, she never loses her sanity in the sewers. She even turns out to be more stoical and mature than men of her age, tending to their wounds and keeping them in the sweet delusion that they will soon reach freedom. We can regard her as a 'sister' of Dorota in *A Generation*. Observing her unwavering strength and sanity one cannot help but think that the Uprising might have been a more successful affair if women have been in charge of the strategic decisions. Inevitably *Kanal* offers a more pessimistic and darker rendering of the war than *A Generation*, as if in this film the director takes the role of a patron of all those to whom the war brought only defeat and misery (Janion 1998: 261–72). One of the insurrectionists says, 'Future generations will honour us', as if expecting that their sacrifice will not be forgotten, while simultaneously acknowledging its absurdity.

In *Ashes and Diamonds*, based on the novel by Jerzy Andrzejewski, Wajda also casts as the main character a member of the Home Army, Maciek Chełmicki (Zbigniew Cybulski). Maciek is less enthusiastic about fighting than his predecessors from Wajda's films; he would rather return to normality. The period when the film is set, 8 May 1945, explains his attitude. This is a time when 'normality' starts again after six years of suffering and the majority of people celebrate the new times. Moreover, Maciek falls in love with a beautiful barwoman Krystyna (Ewa Krzyżewska) which opens new avenues which he did not consider before: a chance to study, perhaps to have a family. Yet, he continues killing on the orders of his superiors from the Home Army. First he kills two men working in a cement factory, instead of the new district Party Secretary, Szczuka (Wacław Zastrzeżyński) and his associate. When this botched job is revealed, he shoots Szczuka. Shortly after this act Maciek is fatally wounded by a Polish army patrol, from which he runs away to catch a train, and dies on a rubbish heap. This is not a straightforward suicide but Maciek's death has a suicidal dimension, as he could easily have avoided it if he had acted rationally. Maciek thus conforms to the stereotype of a mad patriot, as described by Janion. From the information provided within the film we also learn that he is, or at least was, a political idealist; his joining the Home Army is ultimate proof of that. He also fought in the Warsaw Uprising and spent long periods in the sewers. We can also regard him as short of political sobriety, as he fights the new political order, despite having no chance of winning. Finally, we can see him as a man who, after killing Szczuka, verges on real madness, as testified by the absurd way he dies.

Irrespective of the assessment of Maciek's political stance, critics and ordinary viewers agree that his demise is very moving. As Janina Falkowska put it, 'With his doubts and almost hysterical reactions, with his uncertainty and strong desire to live and love Maciek is a deeply human figure. His death on the heap of rubbish symbolises the senselessness and pointlessness of his sacrifice and thus of similar sacrifices of countless other young people' (Falkowska 2004: 73). Maciek is so moving because he is both ordinary, as Falkowska notes, and extraordinary, thanks to the charismatic performance of Zbigniew Cybulski, widely regarded as the most memorable role in the history of Polish cinema. It appears as if the actor overshadowed the character he was given to play by his own personality. In *Ashes and Diamonds* Cybulski impersonates not only a Home Army fighter, but also a man of his own generation, with his political and moral dilemmas (to support the communist regime or to oppose it) and his contemporary clothes, dark glasses and 'waiting mood' typical of bored youth (Lubelski 1992b: 22); hence his linking with James Dean (see Coates 2005: 31). Cybulski's Maciek is also so unique and enduring because he combines two apparently irreconcilable characteristics of a male (or indeed any) film character. On the one hand, he is a typical active male hero who, as was already said, shoots, even more than is necessary or desirable. On the other hand, his behaviour suggests that he enjoys being looked at, by both men and women. He even invites gazes and in this sense he appropriates a position normally ascribed to women in film (in a way which today is associated in the West with such male stars as David Beckham). Wajda appeared to sense this quality in his most famous actor and facilitated Cybulski's 'to-be-lookedness' by presenting him in close-ups, making him the object of Krystyna's loving gaze, as well as situating Maciek against Pawlikowski's ascetic, asexual and secretive Andrzej.

The subsequent story of Cybulski, including his untimely death in 1967 in circumstances not very different from those of Maciek, as he lost his life while hurrying to catch a train, reinforces the perception of Maciek's tragedy and the viewers' almost unconditional acceptance of this character. His death was therefore like the death of an ultimate Polish male (Kurz 2005: 187–218). Not surprisingly, after 1967 the search began to find his replacement: an actor who would embody masculinity 'Polish style' for the next generations of Poles. It could be argued that this role was first taken by Daniel Olbrychski, as acknowledged in Wajda's later film, *Wszystko na sprzedaż* (*Everything on Sale*, 1968), then by Bogusław Linda, the star of Kieślowski's *Przypadek* (*Blind Chance*, 1981) and popular police films of the 1990s, beginning with Władysław Pasikowski's *Psy* (*Dogs*, 1992), and even later by Michał Żebrowski, who played the main parts in *Ogniem i mieczem* (*With Fire and Sword*, 1999), directed by Jerzy Hoffman, and *Pan Tadeusz* (1999), directed by Andrzej Wajda. However, none of these actors ever revealed such pleasure in being looked at as did Cybulski. They are both regarded as very masculine, macho actors, excelling in action films where they tauten they bodies, demonstrating their hard muscles, while Cybulski is remembered as a somehow 'softer' man, who in one film carried a gun, in another used washing powder.[6]

The voices of admiration for Maciek were hardly balanced by those critical of him. The most persuasive opprobrium belongs to Aleksander Jackiewicz[7], who was also, as previously mentioned, an ardent critic of Polish romantic ideology. Jackiewicz compares Maciek to Kordian from Słowacki's poem because Maciek is also given the task of killing a man who, in the opinion of his superiors, was sent by a foreign power. However, unlike Kordian, who fails his assignment to kill Tsar Nikolai, Maciek kills his adversary and even kills him twice, so to speak. Another difference between the two characters derives from the fact that Maciek's victim, Szczuka, is a Polish patriot who does not want to subjugate Poland to a foreign rule but to rebuild it. Therefore, Jackiewicz suggests, Maciek's assassination is an attack on his own country (Jackiewicz 1975: 239–43; 1983: 28; 1989: 365–6). It can also be viewed as an Oedipal killing because Szczuka has a son of Maciek's age who also belongs to an anti-communist conspiracy and from whom he is estranged (Jackiewicz 1975: 241). Thus, Wajda presents the birth of 'People's Poland' as starting with the loss of the best men in the opposing camps of the supporters and opponents of the prewar order, and the archetypal Polish father and son. Jackiewicz describes Kordian as an 'impressive character who is nevertheless a buffoon, making literature from his life, Poland and war' (Jackiewicz 1983: 26). The critic does not develop the motif of Maciek's buffoonery, perhaps because he regards him as less of a poser than Kordian, as testified by his ability to kill Szczuka. For me, however, Maciek is no less a buffoon than Słowacki's character and his ability to kill is the ultimate sign of this trait. He kills not because of any strong political views against the communists (indeed, he appears to have no political views at all), nor due to the loyalty to his comrades, because he has no comrades left to be loyal to. Most of them died and the two who survived the war later abandoned him: Andrzej literally, by moving to another town, Drewnowski metaphorically, by joining the communists. The reason for Maciek's killing is his wish to show that such an act is within his means, that he is a perfect actor who does not shrink from any role. He even says it openly, angering the serious Andrzej, who finds such justification for killing people blasphemous.

In the role of the fiancée of one of the workers killed by Maciek, in his mistaken attack on Szczuka, Wajda cast Barbara Krafftówna. As we might guess, it is a minor role; Krafftówna is on screen for less than a minute, lamenting her Staszek's death. We look at her through the eyes of Maciek, who by chance notes her presence, while opening his hotel room window to get some fresh air. Maciek quickly closes the window again, perhaps the woman's mourning reminds him of his killing or, more likely, because he finds her behaviour a poor spectacle. Indeed, Krafftówna's character, Stefka, is constructed in such a way as to distance the viewer. One minute she hysterically laments Staszek, next she allows herself to be thrown onto a bed by a coarse, obviously working-class fellow, who promises her a pair of stockings for sexual services.[8] I suggest that the significance of Stefka's character is to undermine

Figure 2.4 Zbigniew Cybulski as Wiktor and Barbara Krafftówna as Felicja in *Jak być kochaną* (*How to Be Loved*, 1962) by Wojciech Has.

Staszek's death by showing that nobody, even his own fiancée, truly regrets it, and to question the suffering of women who lost their men folk in the war by depicting their memory as flimsy. One day a woman mourns her fiancé or husband, the next she goes to bed with another man.

Four years after *Ashes and Diamonds*, Krafftówna returned to the role of a grieving 'war widow' in *How to Be Loved*, based on the story of Kazimierz Brandys, and the man whose death she mourns is played by Zbigniew Cybulski. Yet, unlike Wajda, who in his films undermines female suffering, Has puts it in the centre of the discourse, allowing Krafftówna's Felicja to present her version of the story in a series of flashbacks. Felicja, the star of a popular radio series, reminisces on a plane to Paris on the German occupation. As a young actress she was in an anti-Nazi conspiracy and was in love with her colleague, Wiktor Rawicz (Zbigniew Cybulski). When Rawicz became suspected of killing a Nazi collaborator, she agreed to shelter him in her flat. This position required many sacrifices from her, including working in a German theatre and enduring rape by a German policeman. Rawicz, however, instead of being grateful to Felicja, hated her. His hatred stemmed from his awareness that Felicja knew about his injured masculinity due to his inability to fulfil the roles of a soldier and defender of a woman. When the war was over, Rawicz abandoned her, while she had to suffer further humiliations, this time due to being accused of collaborating with the Nazis. Eventually Rawicz, lonely and destroyed by alcoholism, returned to Felicja but only to commit suicide.

Giving the voice to a woman, whose war experiences are very different to those of men, throws a new light on Polish heroic masculinity. In particular, the character of Rawicz provides a useful prism through which to look at Maciek Chełmicki. It allows one to see what initially perhaps only Jackiewicz noted: that Maciek is essentially a buffoon who lives his life not so much in order to achieve particular objectives, such as winning the war, but to impress other people and himself. War for him is ultimately a theatre where he can show off. For somebody like him a peaceful life, with its small victories, joys and disappointments, might not be a viable option, as it gives little chance for tragic performance. Hence, paradoxically, in the light of Rawicz's pathetic end, Maciek's suicide might have been a rational step for him. On the other hand, it is possible that Maciek and others of his kind would eventually adjust to postwar 'small stabilisation' (as did Cybulski by playing in the 1960s in a string of contemporary films). Such a scenario is suggested by casting as Felicja's neighbour on the plane Wieńczysław Gliński, who played Zadra in *Kanal*. In their short conversation he admits that war also deeply hurt him – he lost his son, not unlike Zadra, who lost his 'sons' from the batallion in the sewers. The meeting of Felicja and Gliński's character thus testifies to the war's destructiveness but also to human resilience, as conveyed by their ability to live, have polite conversation and even be successful. Has also hints that it is not only the fault of Chełmickis and Rawiczs that they die stupidly or lie about their heroic acts. Equally guilty is the atmosphere of patriotic madness that forces men to engage in an unequal fight with an enemy or to risk being treated as cowards.

How to Be Loved is regarded as a centrepiece of the existentialist strand of the Polish School (see Ozimek 1980: 206) and justly so. Its existentialism consists in privileging the situation of an individual over that of a group, and perceiving this situation as ultimately absurd. As Konrad Eberhardt notes, Felicja suffers 'because in life we cannot expect that good deeds will be rewarded and bad punished' (Eberhardt 1982: 82). In the same essay Eberhardt also quotes Camus who wrote that, 'When I was young, I demanded from people more than they were able to give me. Now I am able to expect less from them. I am just grateful for their silent presence and their noble gestures have for me the value of a revelation', claiming that these words could serve as an epitaph to Has's films (ibid.: 83). For me these words also offer a useful standpoint from which to assess the romantic characters of the Polish School. If Poles demanded less from each other, they would all be happier. Would, however, their country suffer more as a result of such minimalism? Unfortunately, neither cinema nor history has an answer to this question.

All Colours of Suffering, All Shades of Betrayal: War in Czechoslovak New Wave Films

While the Polish School films tend to represent soldiers, Czechoslovak New Wave films focus on civilians. By 'civilian' I mean not so much the official status of a person as his approach to war. A civilian does not join an army or an underground organisation spontaneously and wholeheartedly but either rejects the military life or enters it reluctantly. Similarly, a civilian is excused for being less concerned with his country, more with his own personal problems, especially preserving his life. We also expect that collaboration with the enemy is more widespread among civilians than soldiers, not least because soldiers have fewer opportunities to move to the enemy's side and find it more risky. Accordingly, in Czechoslovak films we encounter a different set of problems than in Polish films, less social and political, more personal and moral. Czechoslovak films also differ in emotional tone to their Polish counterparts. A large proportion of them, including the Oscar-winning *Obchod na korze* (*A Shop on the High Street*, 1965), directed by Ján Kadár and Elmar Klos and *Ostře sledované vlaky* (*Closely Observed Trains*, 1966), directed by Jiři Menzel, are tragicomedies. They are also adaptations of literary works, including the two mentioned above, respectively of Ladislav Grosman and Bohumil Hrabal, and typically we also find the mixture of comedy and tragedy in the literary sources. This blending of comedy and tragedy attests not only to the national character of Czechs as 'laughing beasts' but also to the more versatile and less extreme nature of civilian life during the war. The focus on civilians is also linked to the fact that many films cast Jews as the main characters: examples are *Démanty noci* (*Diamonds of the Night*, 1964), directed by Jan Němec, *A Shop on the High Street* and *Transport z ráje* (*Transport from Paradise*, 1962) by Zbyněk Brynych.

We observe the privileging of the personal and moral perspective even in *Smrt si říká Engelchen* (*Death Is Called Engelchen*, 1963), directed by Ján Kadár and Elmar Klos, although its protagonist, a Slovak named Pavel (Jan Kačer) is a military man: a member of an underground anti-Nazi organisation. However, by questioning the ruthless 'logic of war' that assumes that during the war mistakes are made and individual people must be sacrificed for a 'greater good' (the phenomenon described today as 'collateral damage'), he comes across more as a civilian than a soldier. The film is set shortly after the war and takes the form of a series of flashbacks in which the injured Pavel reminisces on a number of incidents in which he took part since he joined the Slovak partisans. Although most belong to the partisans' mythology, none are presented as a source of pride or joy for Jan. On the contrary, each proves traumatic for him. One such event is the killing of a captured German. Jan, who was given this task by his Russian commander, fulfils it with a sense of guilt, recognising that the German, who proves to be a gentle and cultured man, is a fellow human being, who perhaps took part in the war as reluctantly as he. The viewer watching his growing affinity to the German hopes he will spare his life and when it does not happen, feels disappointment. Killing the German undermines Jan's moral superiority over the occupiers and introduces a discord into his self.

Another morally ambiguous assignment that later torments Jan is finding the collaborators within one's own community. The ambiguity results from the fact that one is never sure who is a collaborator and in this way risks punishing innocent people. By recalling a village burnt by the Nazi troops as punishment for their inhabitants' collaboration with the partisans, Pavel also has to reflect on the price a larger population has to pay for the activities of their 'liberators' and the partisans' moral right to usurp such a role. In his memories Pavel sees women crying and cursing the guerrillas for the loss of their children and houses. The loss feels

Figure 2.5 Jan Kačer as Pavel in *Smrt si říká Engelchen* (*Death Is Called Engelchen*, 1963), directed by Ján Kadár and Elmar Klos.

particularly great and unnecessary in the light of his later knowledge that at the time of this accident the outcome of the war was already decided – the Nazis would lose the war. Jan's Russian commander (in line with the way Russian soldiers were represented in Eastern European films during the period of communism), comes across as a paternalistic figure who teaches Jan how to be a good soldier and communist. Nevertheless, he orders Jan to perform acts which cause him inner turmoil such as the killing of the German. Moreover, his continuous background presence alludes to the subservient role Slovak people played in the anti-Nazi resistance on their own territory and even to the idea, conveyed unambiguously in *The Good Soldier Švejk*, that the wars in which Czechs and Slovaks participated were not 'their' wars but vehicles in the political affairs of their distant superiors.

It is obvious that Jan uses introspection not to indulge in his heroism but to rebuild his inner unity that was shattered by the war. However, by pondering on his past, he transforms what is already a history into an everlasting nightmare. His masochistic attitude is noted and criticised by Jan's doctor who tells him to pull himself together and move on: literally, by working on his injured body and metaphorically, by coming to terms with the past and starting to think about the future. Yet Jan treats this advice with suspicion and even hostility. Similarly, he gets upset when a group of children visit him in hospital to thank him for his effort to liberate their country. In one scene he breaks a small mirror, offered to him by the doctor, as if he was rejecting the image of him other people know. In a deeper sense, it might signal his refusal to pass the mirror stage and grow up. Although in Jan's introspection he is everything but a hero, for the wider public, as signified by the visit of adulating school children, he is a model to emulate. The visit testifies to the need to find war heroes in postwar Czechoslovakia that explains the subsequent cult of Julius Fučík which I previously discussed. Kadár and Klos suggest that such a status is bestowed only on men. The fate of Jan's lover Marta (Eva Poláková) is a case in point. She had worked as a secretary for senior Nazis, becoming also their mistress, and at the same time acted as a secret agent of the Slovak and Russian underground. She had enjoyed the respect of the Russian high command but people who did not know her involvement in the underground and some of her fellow conspirators regarded her as a German whore. Even Jan could not reconcile himself with her double role, not least because allowing her to carry on with her tasks meant sharing her with other men and not being able to defend her against other men's abuse. Marta's work as a spy thus was a blow to his male ego, laying bare his weakness as a lover and a soldier. This double blow is most visible in an episode in a hotel where Marta prepares herself to meet with her German lover, causing jealous Pavel immense suffering. In this episode traditional gender roles are reversed: Pavel is passive, helpless and waiting, while Marta is active and in charge of her life. Marta herself is well aware of her ambiguous status within the Slovak community and realises that her actions, although justified in the context of war, are a source of humiliation for Pavel. Therefore, when the war is over, she decides to leave her village, telling Pavel that there would be no future for them. Thus although Marta achieved at least as much as Pavel for the conspiracy, she is not rewarded but punished. We observe the different treatment of male and female veterans in the hospital where Jan is greeted as a hero, while Marta must hide her true identity behind a veil to avoid being recognised. Another female character is a peasant girl whose main role in war, not unlike Marta, is to provide sex, albeit not for the Nazi officers but for the Slovak partisans. Her lovers show her no gratitude for her service but slap her and make fun of her; their debasing jokes being a means to strengthen their male bond. Pavel is often among the men who make fun of the woman and, although he seems to be distanced from his sexist colleagues (as indeed, from all actions in which he takes part), he never protests at their attitude. The girl is not reconciled with her role as a booster of the soldiers' egos and she asks the partisans to take her on their military actions. Her wish is greeted with a mocking laugh; the men assume that her presence will desecrate their efforts. The woman herself, not unlike Marta, seems to accept the shame and guilt attached to her life during the occupation, as suggested by her becoming a nurse in the hospital where Pavel is treated for his wounds after the war. As Sister Alzbeta, in her white attire, with the veil hiding part of her head, she strikes a contrasting figure to her old self during the war. Pavel, who confides in her his war experiences also does not notice the similarity between these two women. The trajectory of the peasant girl from an object of sexual entertainment to a nurse, suggests that the choices for women are very limited: they can either be whores or Madonnas, and in both capacities they have no lives of their own but are condemned to serving men. Thus war, as represented by Kadár and

Figure 2.6 Jozef Kroner as Tóno Brtko in *Obchod na korze* (*A Shop on the High Street*, 1965), directed by Ján Kadár and Elmar Klos.

Klos, is a masculine endeavour that helps men to consolidate their grasp on power in society, while keeping women in 'their place'.

In the next film by Kadár and Klos, *A Shop on the High Street*, war is rendered as physically distant, but greatly influencing the characters. The film is set in a small Slovak town in 1942, during the time of the fascist Slovak State that adopted the anti-Semitic Nuremberg Laws. Its main character, Tóno Brtko (Jozef Kroner), a man making a modest living as a carpenter, becomes a beneficiary of the new situation, when he is offered the title of Aryan controller of a small button shop belonging to an elderly Jewish widow, Mrs Lautmannová (Ida Kamińska). This title is a gift from his brother-in-law, one of the first people in town who joined the fascist Militia. Tóno accepts this gift reluctantly, largely because of pressure exerted on him by his wife who aspires to the life led by her newly rich sister and brother-in-law. Soon it turns out that the shop makes no profit and its owner is supported by the Jewish community. Moreover, Tóno is too kind-hearted to explain to the deaf Mrs Lautmannová what her real position is. Instead, on the advice of the main Aryan helper of Jews in the town, he agrees to play the role of her shop assistant. As time passes, he becomes increasingly immersed in the poor widow's life, wearing the suits of her dead husband, mending her furniture and keeping her company. In her presence he practically takes a new identity. At the same time, at home he conceals his tender attachment to the Jewish woman.

Tóno 'has accepted a double game: he is not capable of refusing a tempting offer to profit from the bitter fate of the Jews and attempts, at the same time, to ease his conscience by helping them. Both his worlds are threatened and then begin to approach each other until they actually come together directly in front of his "shop" on the high street, where another deportation of Jews is being organised' (Mistríková 2004: 100). His reaction to the clash of these two orders is schizophrenic. Frightened that they will both be deported to the death camp, he locks Mrs Lautmannová in a wardrobe that causes her death and then commits suicide by hanging himself. In this way he becomes Mrs Lautmannová's ultimate saviour and oppressor, or hero and traitor in one body. Tóno's schizophrenic attitude proves more disastrous than if he was consistent in his behaviour. If he was a hero, he could perhaps save the Jewess. If he was a traitor, he would save himself. While Konrad Eberhardt regrets Polish maximalism in matters referring to the fate of their country, especially the demand to show extreme bravery even when one has no chance of winning, the Slovak critic Lubica Mistríková mourns the Slovak lack of courage and their excessive concern for their own well-being. She writes about Tóno Brtko, 'Alone he has no chance of winning, but if there were many Brtkos and they found greater courage within themselves, perhaps the world would be different' (ibid.: 101). A lack of courage as the root of the demise of Jews is also pointed out by the film's authors who said, 'Violence is caused not only by men equipped with revolvers but also by the good, orderly, insignificant people who collaborate with the criminals because they are afraid of them' (Kadár and Klos, quoted in L.K. 1965: 53).

In *Closely Observed Trains*, based on the novella by Bohumil Hrabal and directed by Jiři Menzel,[9] not unlike in the two works by Kadár and Klos, experiencing war is combined with the male protagonist's quest for identity. Miloš Hrma (Václav Neckář) begins his screen existence as a shy and self-doubting character. He tells us off-screen about himself and his family, whilst we see photographs of his ancestors and of Miloš looking straight into the camera. This creates the impression of him looking at himself in a mirror or even of a divided self and, hence, of his search for identity. From his story we gather that Miloš would rather distance himself from his ancestors than follow in their footsteps. His very name, Hrma, is funny, meaning mons veneris. More importantly, his male ancestors, although they worked on the railway and wore uniforms, which signifies service to their country, were exemplary loafers and charlatans. They include Miloš's father, who has drawn his pension from the age of forty-eight, to the envy of the whole village, and Miloš's grandfather, who was killed by a German tank when he attempted to hypnotise German troops as they headed to Prague. Although war is talked about by Miloš's superiors on a daily basis, his life is overshadowed by his private affairs, namely his desire to lose his virginity and his shame when he fails as a lover due to premature ejaculation, which leads to his suicide attempt. Miloš reacts so extremely because he identifies masculinity solely with sexual prowess. He tells the doctor that because he failed as a lover he is not a man, and later he looks for a woman to teach him about sex in order to become a man. Such a stance might be understandable in a time of peace, but during a war it is regarded as highly inappropriate; soldiers are expected to be morally pure, meaning 'cleansed of sexuality' (Mosse 1985: 116–24). Menzel, of course, is well aware of the

Figure 2.7 Václav Neckář as Miloš Hrma in *Ostře sledované vlaky* (*Closely Observed Trains*, 1966), directed by Jiři Menzel.

'correct' meaning of maleness during the war, but rejects it by portraying the military men as pompous hypocrites, for whom ideas are more important than people. This refers particularly to the local Nazi official Zedníček, who upon his visit to the station tries to convince the railwaymen that German military retreats are tactical manoeuvres that will ultimately bring the Nazis decisive victory, and describes Miloš's suicide attempt as 'sabotage' of German efforts to liberate the whole of Europe. At the same time, the director suggests that a healthy interest in sex, combined with a fair degree of laziness and disregard for authority (the last two features being regarded as quintessentially Švejkian) can go hand in hand with true bravery. This is true about Hubička, the station employee and an utter loafer who seemingly spends all his time at work seducing women, but is also involved in anti-Nazi resistance. Similarly, Miloš's decision to blow up a 'closely observed train' with ammunition for the German army, and his subsequent death, are precipitated by the night of sexual bliss he spends with Viktoria Freie, a woman who brings him a bomb to be used in the act of sabotage. Although Miloš commits an act of utter bravery, his death comes across not as heroic but absurd. Its absurdity results from the disparity between his preoccupation with his private problems and the heavy price he has to pay for participating in the action, the importance of which he appears not even to grasp. Moreover, his death comes as a surprise because its gravity contrasts with the overall humorous tone of the film. By showing an 'accidental hero' who is more interested in sex than in Patria, Menzel rejects the traditional image of the war hero (Škvorecký 1971: 169–70; Žalman, quoted in Hames 2004: 126; Owen 2007). Peter Hames observes that the 'association of sex with the theme of national liberation was one of the most politically "subversive" qualities of the film, undercutting the traditional (and inhuman) convention of the noble Resistance fighter' (Hames 2005: 155–6). By representing Miloš's death as absurd, as well as saturating the film with the humorous, almost surreal episodes, such as Zedníček's going on his car on the railway track (which mirrors the 'tactical retreat' of the Nazi army he talks about), *Closely Observed Trains* renders the war as absurd. At the same time as opposing the heroic tradition, Menzel adheres to the very Czech custom of seeing national heroes as martyrs rather than fighters. We see it specially in a scene, when, carried away from a room where he tried to take his life, wrapped in sheets, Miloš looks like Christ on a pietà.

To a greater extent than the two films previously discussed, *Closely Observed Trains* blurs the boundary between private space and the war zone. It reflects the previously mentioned fact that most Czechs did not fight the Second World War on the battlefield but also conveys Menzel's desire to undermine (or simply reposition) the war from a solely male and military affair, to one deriving from other places and zones, and affecting the whole spectrum of human activities and circumstances. To start with, the main setting of the film is the railway station. It is represented as a borderline space between the war zone and domestic space. The closeness to the war zone is signified by the frequent visits of military-minded Zedníček, as well as by German soldiers and nurses working for the Red Cross, and the passing of ammunition trains heading for the front. As bordering on the war zone, the railway station is a dangerous place, as we can see when Miloš is approached by a group of German soldiers and almost loses his life. On the other hand, it is close to the homes of its workers and is almost like a home for them. The stationmaster is seen tending his pigeons there and helping his wife rear geese. Hubička uses it as place to seduce women.

The Nazis deeply disapprove of the proximity of the railway station to home. They shame the stationmaster when he arrives for an important meeting in a uniform covered with pigeon feathers and when they see the female telegraphist's bottom covered with stamps. The blurred division between home and war zone does not mean that Menzel grants his female characters a more prominent role in the war effort than in the films set entirely at the front. Women in this film have no lives of their own, they live only to serve their men, either by sleeping with them, such as the telegraphist, the conductress or prostitutes in a brothel, or by feeding them, such as the stationmaster's wife and Miloš's own mother. The idea that women are for sex is conveyed by frequent verbal and visual comparing them to horses. The stationmaster is aroused by the sight of the Baroness's aristocratic bottom and that of her splendid horse, whom he clumsily tries to mount – this being a substitute for seducing the Baroness. Even Viktoria Freie's main function is to help Miloš overcome his sexual problems and in this way embolden him to blow up the train. The reduction of women's war service to serving the men who participate in the war bears similarities with *Death Is Called Engelchen*. However, whilst Kadár and Klos depict it as a tragedy for women, Menzel's female characters appear to be reconciled to their meagre position, even happy to be treated as purely sexual objects.

Not only does Menzel reject a neat division of space into domestic and military zones but also the dichotomy of good Czechs and bad Germans. His film includes a bad Czech, the Nazi Zedníček who (rather than any German) encapsulates the Nazi ideology, simultaneously bringing association with Stalinism, with its putting ideas over people, puritanism and self-discipline. Menzel also shows that even in the extreme situation of war, some Germans were able to show some humanity to their enemies, as in the episode when Miloš is taken to a train by some suspicious Nazi soldiers, most likely to execute him, but is spared his life when one of the Germans notices the scars on his hand. As Jonathan Owen notes, 'the scars resulting from Miloš's "irresponsible" suicide attempt are mirrored in the scars of the Nazi soldier, who quickly discerns a kinship of transgressive humanity over and above national or political differences' (Owen 2007).

The film *Transport from Paradise* is based on a collection of short stories, *Night and Hope*, by Arnošt Lustig, an Auschwitz survivor and one of the most renowned Czech writers and authors of Holocaust novels, who left Czechoslovakia after the Soviet-led invasion of 1968. Lustig himself praised the film, claiming that it 'sometimes goes beyond the book' (Kostková 2001). It is set in the ghetto of Terezín and practically includes only Jews incarcerated there and their Nazi overseers. However, rather than neatly divide the social universe into the oppressors and their victims, Brynych focuses on the ways the Nazis implicated the Jews in their compatriots, and their own annihilation, thus creating many categories of victims and oppressors. That such an implication was a well-thought out policy is announced early in the film when the leader of the camp explains to a Nazi General, visiting the ghetto, that he pursues in

Terezín a policy of 'collaboration'. This 'collaboration' includes allowing the Jewish council to decide who will go to the death camps in the next transport and taking responsibility for strict discipline in the blocks. Perhaps the most perfidious act on the part of the Germans is forcing the Jews to make a pro-Nazi propaganda film that states that Terezín is for Jews a kind of holiday camp, where they enjoy themselves, taking advantage of the Germans who look after all their needs. This perception of the ghetto as near-paradise provides the title of the film that is, of course, ironic. Brynych shows that the policy of 'collaboration' indeed corrupted many Jews, such as the vice-chairman of the council, Marmulstaub, who used his position of power to ensure a comfortable life for himself, including the sexual services of desperate women to whom he promised to delete their names from the transport lists.

On the other hand, Brynych balances the images of betrayal with scenes of heroism, such as the illegal printing of anti-Nazi posters and leaflets by the prisoners, and a young man taking the place of another man on the transport, thus condemning himself to certain death. Neither does the director deprive the oppressors of a basic humanity. Such a humanity is granted to the Czech-speaking Binde, a translator in the camp, who kills an old woman involved in anti-Nazi resistance on her request, rather than sentencing her to prolonged tortures. All these acts of betrayal, mercy and heroism are represented in the same, matter-of-fact way. Neither the victims, the heroes nor the oppressors receive a detailed psychological portrayal. Our contact with them is short and partial, as that of a visitor to the concentration camp, which alludes to the fact that the film is set shortly before the Red Cross's visit to Terezín. Yet enough is shown to get an insight into day-to-day life in the camp and the ordeal of its inmates. Such an approach, that can be described as egalitarian, poignantly contrasts with that offered in Wanda Jakubowska's *Ostatni etap* (*The Last Stage*, 1947) or Steven Spielberg's *Schindler's List* (1993), where the focus is on 'special cases': heroes who appear to deserve to be saved more than the masses who drowned. The idea that the main institutions of the Holocaust, the ghetto and the concentration camp, from a moral point of view constituted a very complex universe, with the roles of the oppressors and victims overlapping, was transferred to Brynych's film from Lustig's *Night and Hope*, based on the author's own memories of the Terezín ghetto. We also find it in the work of such Holocaust survivors as Primo Levi and Tadeusz Borowski (Levi 1988; Borowski 1992). All of them objected to construing the Holocaust as a 'Hollywood narrative' with individual heroes and a happy ending. We can also discern in *Transport from Paradise* a Kafkaesque dimension, because Brynych presents Terezín as an extremely bureaucratised universe, where 'real' life is merely a shadow of one's life in a file. Similarly, in Kafka's *The Trial* and in *Transport from Paradise* people die not because of what they did but because of their name being placed on a certain list. The issues pertaining to gender are never discussed in the film but, to a much larger extend than Radok in *Distant Journey*, Brynych points to the masculine order of the ghetto. The Nazi overseers are all men, as are the Jewish councillors determining the composition of the transports to the gas chambers, kapos responsible for discipline in the ghetto and the director of the propaganda film to be shown to the outside world. Similarly, the leaders of the anti-Nazi resistance are men, although they rely on the help of women to conduct their illegal work. The utter patriarchalism of the various structures of power, German and Jewish, legal and illegal, has an adverse impact on the position of the weakest inhabitants of Terezín, the women, the elderly and the children, making them the most neglected, exploited and tormented section of the ghetto population. On the whole, *Transport from Paradise* shows that war is an utterly male affair in the sense that it strengthens and multiplies male structures, institutions and traditions, disadvantaging all those who find themselves outside them.

The focus on the civilian's perspective inevitably leads to undermining the political/military dimension of the war, including such issues as who started the war and whether it was a just conflict. Juraj Jakubisko in *Zbehovia a pútnici* (*Deserters and Pilgrims*, 1968) goes the furthest in stripping the war of any national politics and instead representing it as a universal experience. Although the film consists of three parts, each depicting a different war, respectively the First and Second World War and a future nuclear disaster, its author tries to obliterate the specificity of each conflict by avoiding such devices as establishing shots or even a dialogue to map out the conflict and explain the motifs of the characters. It feels like we are placed in the middle of the event of which we must make sense. Only costumes and weaponry allow us to situate the narrative in any historical and cultural context, although they also are at times confusing. Moreover, the same actors are used in each part of the film, often in similar roles, to create the impression that we watch the same war over and over again like a nightmare that does not want to go away. This impression is strengthened by the 'dreamy' style of the film that includes unusual camera positions, shots from a hand-held camera, distorted images and many episodes that do not forward the action and appear to be included purely for their symbolic meaning. As the title of the film suggests, Jakubisko's work focuses on those who try to disentangle themselves from the war. The main character in the first part is a young deserter who during the First World War flees from the battlefield and returns to his village. His return, however, does not allow him any respite from the combat but sparks off new conflicts. He disrupts a wedding, is betrayed to the Hussars and eventually the whole village becomes a scene of brutal killing and carnage. In one of the most disturbing scenes we see small children being thrown from their potties by other children, and boys no older than seven using guns. The message of Jakubisko in this episode is that war is highly infectious: it contaminates younger generations and spreads in space. Moreover, it is a highly destructive force that ultimately destroys all parts of the conflict and changes Earth into a wasteland. This idea is conveyed most strongly by a character who introduces himself as 'Death' – his presence marks the demise of other characters. He reappears in all episodes, showing that death is the ultimate outcome of military conflicts. It is worth emphasising that although in Slavic folklore Death is typically symbolised by a feminine character, in Jakubisko's film it is distinctively male. From such representation we can infer that Jakubisko regards war as a distinctively male and deadly affair.

From the Ruins of Romanticism: Polish Postcommunist War Films

The collapse of communism allowed the assessment of the war experiences of Polish, Czech and Slovak men from a new perspective. Filmmakers tackling this subject after 1989 were unencumbered by such factors as the requirement to present the Soviet Union as the sole liberator of their country and did not need to avoid referring to the fates of the soldiers fighting the Nazis in the 'wrong armies'. Equally important was the fact that the introduction of democracy and market economy brought about the decline of certain attitudes and values that previously strongly informed the representation of the war, such as, in Poland, Romanticism (Krzemiński 1991). When we talk about Poland we should also mention an event preceding the fall of communism, namely the martial law of 1981 because, paradoxically, as Maria Janion observes, 'it unmasked the pro-combatant rhetoric' that dominated Polish discussions about the war (Janion 1998: 298). Another factor that cannot be underestimated when assessing the shift in depicting war after 1989 is the changing attitude to male heroism that has taken place in the West since the 1970s or perhaps even the 1960s. David Cohen, in a book published in 1990, writes: 'Today, it's hard to admire a hero without ambivalence. Heroes almost parody themselves. Even films which appear to glorify the macho hero of old tend to undermine him. James Bond cuts a slightly ludicrous figure. Rambo, wild man of the techno-West, has a name that sounds uncomfortably like Dumbo (the elephant) or Sambo. Can that be entirely accidental?' (Cohen 1990: 18).

In Poland the opportunity to look at the war afresh was seized by Andrzej Wajda who in the years 1989–2008 made four films on this subject; war cinema in Poland is still by and large associated with his name. It should be said that Wajda continued to make films about the Second World War throughout his entire career, and his preoccupation with this subject after 1989 can be seen as a sign of the continuity of his career. However, his take on the war changed substantially over the almost half a century that divides *A Generation* on the one hand and *Pierścionek z orłem w koronie* (*The Ring with a Crowned Eagle*, 1992), *Wielki Tydzień* (*Holy Week*, 1995) and most importantly *Wyrok na Franciszka Kłosa* (*The Sentence on Franciszek Kłos*, 2000) on the other. The main shift is towards choosing more ordinary and rational characters, which can be interpreted as a confirmation of the previously mentioned opinion that after 1989 Romanticism lost its privileged status in Polish culture. *The Ring with a Crowned Eagle* and *Holy Week* still represent characters who fight for their country but more reluctantly than their cinematic predecessors. Life instinct is stronger in them than death wish; they feel more civilians than soldiers. This attitude is encapsulated by the answer Marcin (Rafał Królikowski), the protagonist of *The Ring with a Crowned Eagle*,[10] gives to a question that a teenage insurrectionist asks him after the defeat of the Warsaw Uprising: 'Why don't you want to go to prison?' – 'Because it is stupid.' After the uprising, Marcin, a member of the Home Army who was in charge of a platoon, decides to establish contact with the new communist powers. He claims that he does so because of the responsibility for 'his boys' (in this way bearing association with Zadra from *Kanal*), but one guesses that he uses it as a moral alibi obscuring his true motif which is to live and be successful in the new Poland (Janicka 1993: 13). In due course his collaboration with the communists deepens, requiring new compromises and excuses. At the same time Marcin continues to meet his superior from the Home Army, passing him information about the actions of the communists such as the deportation of a large group of the Home Army members to Siberia. His position can be likened to a 'double agent', played also by Drewnowski in *Ashes and Diamonds* but, unlike Drewnowski, Marcin's spying proves more useful to the communists than to those attached to the Polish government in London. At one point the authorities use Marcin as bait to identify members of the Home Army who in due course are exterminated. His eventual suicide that ends the film is tantamount to his recognition that by flirting with the new authorities he made the wrong choice. It appears as if in Wajda's eyes, juxtaposing collaboration with resistance cannot produce healthy fruits; fighting and wooing the enemy is the worst possible choice.[11] As I will argue in due course, other postcommunist films, principally those made by Czech directors, dare to contradict this opinion. The critics regarded the ending of *The Ring with a Crowned Eagle* as unconvincing, because after rationalising his first collaboration with the new authorities the viewer expects Marcin to continue such rationalisations till the end of his life, or at least till the victory of Solidarity in 1981 (Woroszylski 1993).

Marcin encourages comparison with Maciek Chełmicki who after the war also faced the choice between continuing fighting against the new regime or becoming a civilian. However, he is not just 'Maciek who chose a different option' but a man who chooses in a different way – faster, with less soul-searching and instead relying more on the persuasion of others, including people of dubious moral credentials. Unlike Maciek, who never loses his poise and dignity, Marcin can suffer a mortal humiliation by somebody and still stick to his tormentor, even follow him like a faithful dog. Kosior, the Polish secret service agent, mocks Marcin on a daily basis, metaphorically castrates him by removing the crown from the eagle on the ring Marcin wears, yet still Marcin repays him with obedience. Even Marcin's love life does not have the intensity of Maciek's encounter with Krystyna because it seems as if Marcin simply follows the women who are available and willing to help him. After he loses his first girlfriend Wiśka, who agrees to be raped by a Russian soldier in order to save his life, he moves in with the fellow insurrectionist Janina and forgets Wiśka. Such a lack of care for Wiśka not only distances him from the archetypal Polish 'knight' who will die to protect a woman but also undermines his credibility as a man who puts the welfare of 'his people' first. On the whole, Marcin is rather a melodramatic than tragic character and his eventual downfall makes a lesser impact on the viewer than Maciek's death. I will suggest that despite nominally being the same age as Maciek, Marcin represents a different generation: those born in the 1960s and 1970s, who are pragmatic in their actions and care more about their own advancement than about their nation or their friends. At the same time, they cannot shed the romantic legacy completely, and therefore they try to look for justification of their actions in higher ideals, which makes them look somehow disoriented, even schizophrenic. The later fame of Rafał Królikowski, who became one of the leading actors in the 1990s and 2000s, playing young men who are nice but weak and lacking in charisma, suggests that the audience of Wajda's film saw in him one of them, rather than the 'new Maciek'.

Jan Małecki (Wojciech Malajkat) in *Holy Week*, based on the story by Jerzy Andrzejewski, is even more of a civilian than Marcin. There is no sign of him belonging to any resistance movement and he has a pregnant wife with whom he shares a dream about peaceful times when they can enjoy normal family life. This dream would be fulfilled if not for being at the wrong place at the wrong time, where he accidentally meets Irena Lilien, his Jewish ex-girlfriend who avoided being locked in the ghetto. This meeting forces him to provide shelter for her. He does it reluctantly, aware that Irena's presence jeopardises the safety of his family and people living in his tenement block. Indeed, Jan dies when trying to retrieve Irena's suitcase from her old hiding place. Wajda juxtaposes his death with his wife's labour. This parallel points not only to the ruthless economy of life and death but also underscores that Jan's fate matters most to his wife and child and, ultimately, that he belongs to the private sphere of the family, rather than to the public zone of the army, as was the case of men in Wajda's Polish School films. Again, as with Marcin, his death does not awake strong emotions in the viewer. This reaction might have something to do with the fact that Wojciech Malajkat, not unlike Rafał Królikowski, represents a different, more 'earthly' type than Cybulski and Janczar. Consequently, one feels a distance between the director and the characters, as if they were not really his creations. This distance is also signified by the scarce use of close-ups of male faces, which were one of Wajda's trademarks in his Polish School period. In *The Ring with a Crowned Eagle* and *Holy Week* men are usually shown from a distance, which renders identification with them difficult. Moreover, the national and religious symbols with which Wajda saturated his films of the 1950s, are used here infrequently. They are not absent altogether, as demonstrated by the titles: *The Ring with a Crowned Eagle* referring to the symbol of Poland as a free and proud country and *Holy Week* to the celebration of Christ's death and resurrection, but the bearers and transmitters of these symbols are women. It is Wiśka who gives Marcin a ring with a crowned eagle, presumably to remind him never to give up his dream of a free Poland, and Jan's wife Anna who gives birth whilst in church. This 'feminisation of symbolism' reinforces gender positions in both films; whilst men come across as somehow hesitant, thwarted, even crooked, women prove more charismatic and virtuous. The overall visual style of *The Ring with a Crowned Eagle* and *Holy Week*, unlike Wajda's Polish School films, is realistic and their realism is reminiscent of television productions of the 1980s. The change of style underscores the fact that Wajda's characters prefer an ordinary life than a honourable death – that they are not romantic.

Wajda's more recent war protagonist, Franciszek Kłos (Mirosław Baka), is different from all his characters because he is a Nazi collaborator: a policeman who serves his German masters by brutally killing Jews and Poles. He is also different in being of working-class or perhaps peasant origin, as conveyed by his crude manner of speaking and his simple house adorned only with his wedding photograph. Although during the war Kłos fights on the opposite side to Marcin and Jan, he shares with them some important features. He lacks romanticism and is essentially a civilian who joins the German police not because of his political convictions but to ensure a better life for himself and his family. Paradoxically, these 'family feelings' do not bring him closer to his mother, wife and children. His mother and wife are so ashamed of his actions, that include killing a small child from the neighbourhood, that in the end they abandon him. His own children hide from him when he appears in their bedroom drunk and threatening to kill them, apparently to save them the future stigma of having a Nazi collaborator father. Like Marcin, although in a more transparent way, Kłos attempts to work for two masters and he easily absolves himself from any wrongdoing. For example, after telling his wife that he tried to receive the documents of a Volksdeutsche for his good service to the German police, he says that 'I might be a Volksdeutsche on the outside but a true Pole inside'. Similarly, during his church confession, he forgives himself by saying that he killed mostly Jews who are 'enemies of the Catholic Church'. There is never any true remorse on his part. He treats both his German masters and God equally: as an insurance policy against any harm from the Polish conspirators who sentenced him to death. His lack of any morals is even noticed by the Germans who mock and humiliate him, calling him a drunken *polnische Schwein*. Needless to add that Wajda treats Kłos with utter disdain. His character's eventual death comes as a relief, even to Kłos's own mother. If there is any message *The Sentence on Franciszek Kłos* contains for men in war, it is to put country first and not to retreat into the private sphere. 'Privatisation' means betrayal of one's country and does not guarantee happiness in private life; there is no middle way for a man between being a soldier and a traitor.

The visual style of *The Sentence on Franciszek Kłos* is even more different from Wajda's Polish School films than the style of *The Ring with a Crowned Eagl*e and *Holy Week*. It comes across as a mixture of Dogme 95 conventions with that of a theatre (Piotrowska 2001: 20). The entire film is shot in digital video, the setting is minimal, most action takes place in interiors and the camera is very close to the actors who sometimes appear to address the audience directly. There is little attempt to recreate the war setting; the small town where the action takes place looks like a sleepy town during the communist period. Such a style encourages us to regard *The Sentence on Franciszek Kłos* not only as a film about the Second World War but also about Polish life in the postwar period. This interpretation is further facilitated by certain expressions uttered by the characters that sound like communist jargon. Moreover, Mirosław Baka was cast in *The Ring with a Crowned Eagle* as Tatar, who helped Marcin join the communists and ultimately corrupted him. Consequently, it feels like Tatar and Kłos are two versions of the same man: one collaborating with Russians, the other with Germans. If we compare representations of men in Wajda's Polish School films and his war films made after 1989, we would notice that for this director nobility of blood and heroic behaviour go hand in hand, whilst lowly background is linked to treason and corruption. Thus, as I argued earlier, positively marked masculinity, as represented by Wajda, can be achieved only by men of a higher social class.

Wajda functions in Polish cinema and culture at large as a 'national director' and even 'the essential Pole' who transmits in his films the values and ideals of the Polish nation understood as a homogenous whole. Jan Jakub Kolski, probably the most important Polish filmmaker to make his debut after the fall of communism, questions this unity in his films, using the Second World War as a litmus test of Polish harmony. Moreover, unlike Wajda, Kolski treats the war not as an external calamity but as a situation which Polish people largely shaped themselves.[12] Furthermore, Kolski tends to avoid images of battlefields and concentrates on the war as experienced by civilians, on their own territory.

The first chapter of what can be described as Kolski's 'war trilogy' is *Pogrzeb kartofla* (*Funeral of a Potato*, 1990). In this film, discourse on the war is linked to that of the peasants' struggle to keep their land (idealised in Polish nineteenth century literature as an effort to preserve national identity), through casting as the main character a leather worker, Mateusz Szewczyk (Franciszek Pieczka), who returns to his native village in 1946 after years spent in a concentration camp. Although he lived in the village for most of his life, he is treated as a stranger and enemy. His countrymen cannot forgive his liberation, they call him 'the Jew' and refuse to talk to him. This hatred stems from the villagers' hunger for land, particularly strong as some of them did not have even a small plot. Each expects to receive some land as a result of the division of the estate belonging to the local aristocracy; this being part of the land reform introduced by the communist authorities. Szewczyk's return means that each of them would now receive a smaller plot and they have to return his belongings they had already divided amongst themselves. Although Mateusz understands their mindset, their hostility horrifies him. In one scene he exposes himself in front of his oppressors to prove that he is not a Jew, crying 'People, are you worse than the occupiers?' This possibility was hardly considered in the films belonging to the Polish School. If they represented Poles who were worse than occupiers, they always constituted a minority, more than offset by the patriotic majority. Kolski also includes in his film a peasant who tries to persuade his girlfriend, raped and impregnated by a Nazi soldier during the war, to seduce a communist clerk. He hopes that the clerk, who will allocate the fields, will give him an extra piece as a reward for the sacrifice of his girlfriend. By including in his narrative Polish men who are using women as objects to advance their material and social positions, Kolski suggests that the war, and perhaps the whole history of regaining the country following partitions, did not inscribe in the Polish man such features as candour, courage and selflessness but thwarted his masculinity, rendering him calculating, narrow-minded and cowardly. This perception is strengthened by the fact that *Funeral of a Potato* depicts a real story – that of Kolski's uncle. The identity of the village Popielawy, in which the film is set, and the characters' names, are all authentic.

Whilst in *Funeral of a Potato* Kolski demythologises the Polish fight for land (which in Poland is a traditionally male preserve), in *Daleko od okna* (*Far from the Window*, 2000), based on the short story *Ta z Hamburga* (*The One from Hamburg*) by Hanna Krall, he strips of heroism another activity for which Poles are proud – helping the Jewish victims of Nazism. A Polish couple, Jan (Bartosz Opania), who works as a sign-maker, and his wife Barbara, on the insistence of Jan, provide refuge to an attractive Jewess named Regina. Subsequently Jan has an affair with Regina that results in her pregnancy. This event gains additional significance through Jan and Barbara's childlessness, that, before Regina's arrival, was presented as the main problem for the couple. In order to save herself and her child Regina allows Barbara to appropriate her baby, Helusia. In due course Regina leaves Helusia, most likely for the sake of the baby's safety, but after the war, when settled in Hamburg, she tries to regain her daughter. However, Jan and Barbara refuse to return the girl to her birth mother. Eventually, the adult Helusia visits Regina in Hamburg but at this stage her mother rejects her, claiming that she brings back to her the worst memories of her life.

Kolski's film intentionally leaves many questions unanswered and renders many acts ambiguous. Jan in particular does not say much and never explains his behaviour, so that we never learn why he brought Regina to his home – she appears there almost like a ghost. Moreover, despite having a family (one can even say an extended one, with two women attending his erotic needs), he strikes a solitary figure. There is also some nervousness, irrationality, even hysteria about his behaviour. For example, Jan cuts his wrist with a knife, as if he wanted to commit suicide. All these features link him to characters in Wajda's Polish School films, such as Jaś Krone and Maciek Chełmicki, who were equally lonely, reticent and nervous. However, unlike his cinematic predecessors who did not say much because their main way to communicate with the world was through fighting, Jan's silence and histrionic gestures hide his inability to act decisively and bear the consequences of his actions. At the time of his affair with Regina he behaves as if he could not commit himself either to his wife or to his lover; he is always, literally and figuratively, stuck between them or hides from both of them. It could be argued that this feature likens Jan to Polish lovers from the period of late communism and postcommunism, who in theory would like to sleep with many women but in practice could not cope with such a situation (Marszałek 2006: 164; Chapter 4). Moreover, Regina's departure, rather than liberating Jan by allowing him to be a proper husband again, devastates him and increases the crisis between him and Barbara. At the same time, he does not even try to find his lover and to start a new life with her, putting a question mark over his love for Regina. He certainly loves his daughter but again, it is a passive love. Even in relation to the teenage Helusia Jan takes the role of a child, rather than a mature parent. From a certain point Jan's reaction to the problems he himself created is to escape into alcohol. On the whole, Jan is a (pseudo)romantic hero whose romanticism is reduced to mysterious silence and empty gestures. Like Kordian he dreams about (masculine) greatness, of shedding his blood for noble causes but the only real blood shed in the film is that of the Jews killed by the Germans and that of Regina giving birth to their child. The destruction of the myth of the romantic fighter, helping his Jewish brothers and sisters, is particularly strong because Kolski uses the expressionistic visual style associated with the Polish School. The film is full of symbols, such as an unfinished picture of the Holy Mother painted by Jan, that stands for the incompleteness of his family, or Jan's finding the armband with the Star of David soaked with blood, to which he adds his own blood in his aborted or faked suicide.

Far from the Window also offers a subversive portrayal of the war because it introduces a new character to the Polish cinema – the Nazi collaborator who deserves some sympathy. This man, named Jodła (Krzysztof Pieczyński), brings food for the couple and finds work for Jan, painting signs for the Nazi offices and cleaning up after executions of Jews. By accepting such work Jan himself becomes a Nazi servant. However, while Jodła collaborates with the enemy openly and willingly, Jan does it inconspicuously and reluctantly. In one episode Jan attempts to disentangle himself from any responsibility for serving the Nazis by saying that he acts only on Jodła's order. Such an argument, however, is reminiscent of the excuses of the many Nazis who also 'acted on somebody's order'. Moreover, Jodła knows about Regina's presence in Jan and Barbara's house but does not betray them, most likely because of his secret love for Barbara. Thus, at the same time Jodła is a Nazi helper and a saviour of Jews. It could even be argued that his position as a loyal Nazi servant allows him to protect the Polish couple from possible Nazi interest.

The last film by Kolski set during the war, *Pornografia* (*Pornography*, 2003), is an adaptation of a novel by one of the most renowned and probably the most cosmopolitan Polish writer, Witold Gombrowicz. In Gombrowicz's *Pornography* the war provides only a background to the story and if it plays any ideological function, it is very indirect. In Kolski's film, by contrast, it is a crucial factor in characters' motivations and it features more widely, such as in the scenes from the Warsaw ghetto opening the film, Germans visiting the Polish village, and images of Jews harboured in a Polish manor house. Kolski himself commented on the change by saying, 'I have the impression that Gombrowicz was making sport of the war, while I would like to make things a bit more serious!' (Hollender 2002: A9). The book and the film, narrated in the first person by Witold (Adam Ferency), a middle-aged decadent man of unknown profession (who can be regarded as Gombrowicz's alter ego), casts Fryderyk (Krzysztof Majchrzak) as the main character, an equally blasé fellow of unknown background. Witold made his acquaintance in 1943, in the impoverished Warsaw literary salon. Some time later these two *culturati* go to a country estate to visit Fryderyk's gentry friend Hipolit, who is involved in the anti-Nazi resistance. Hipolit's pretty sixteen-year-old daughter Henia and Karol, a boy of her age who is a partisan fighter living on Hipolit's estate, catch the attention of the guests. Fryderyk and Witold embark on a strange game whose purpose is to stir up sparks between the teenagers by obsessively rehearsing them in a love scene for a possible movie. They also persuade them to kill a Polish officer, Colonel Siemian who, upon experiencing a nervous breakdown, deserted the Polish underground army and became a liability for the resistance movement.

Fryderyk and Witold's games prove successful but their consequences are more tragic for their 'actors', 'directors' and 'viewers' than anybody predicted. They are also very different in Kolski's film to that in Gombrowicz's novel, largely because the author of the adaptation changed Fryderyk's biography. Although in both the book and the film Fryderyk comes across as extremely cynical, even demonic, Kolski transformed this Nietzscheanian man, who lives 'beyond good and bad', into a man who entered what Primo Levi described as the Holocaust's 'grey zone' and left it completely defeated. It turns out that he had a half-Jewish daughter who was caught by the Gestapo and transported to a death camp. Fryderyk followed her and ended up in the camp, but hid from her when he saw her on the ramp. At the end of the film Fryderyk, after confessing his betrayal to Hipolit's wife (albeit indirectly, by claiming that this is his friend's story, rather than his own), commits suicide, demonstrating that his demonic masculinity was nothing more than a mask hiding his true identity as a weak man, stricken by guilt and grief. The film does not explain the connection between Fryderyk's secret and his willingness to play with the lives of the young people, but one can guess that his intention is to demonstrate to them and to himself that everybody is corruptible – human behaviour is nothing more than a reaction to a particular set of circumstances. This idea is not foreign to Gombrowicz who in his *Diaries* wrote that 'It is not in the conscience of an individual that the mechanism of human actions lie but in the relation between the individual and others' (Gombrowicz 1997: 70). Yet, in Gombrowicz's *Pornography* it is precisely individual human conscience or even abstract ideology which leads Fryderyk and Witold to behave cruelly. The emphasis put on circumstances, in this case the Holocaust, links Kolski's *Pornography* more with the work of Tadeusz Borowski, who in his short stories included a motif of parents abandoning their children in the concentration camp to avoid immediate death.

Fryderyk is not the only man in Kolski's film whose war experience strips him of his traditional masculinity. Another is Colonel Siemian. In Gombrowicz's *Pornography* he is reduced to a caricature; in Kolski's film he is a man for whom living according to Polish romantic legend proved too much of a challenge, changing him into a neurotic weakling. In the same category I will list Hipolit, who on the surface perfectly conforms to the image of a good-natured and paternalistic Polish nobleman, and most likely in the peace times would fulfil this role, but in the war makes decisions which are harmful for those whom he was meant to protect such as Karol and Henia. By including a scene in which Hipolit welcomes German soldiers visiting his estate, offering them eggs and milk, and bowing humbly, Kolski repeats the motif known from his previous film, that during the war one had sometimes to collaborate with the enemy in order to do good. A scene of killing an elderly woman by a male servant suggests that war is conducive to a certain 'killing fever' in which everybody is at risk of committing unprovoked murder. On the whole, Kolski shows that war weakened Polish males, changing them into moral wrecks. Meaningfully, it does not have the same effect on women. All the women portrayed in the film prove more resilient to the danger of moral decline than men.

The visual style of *Pornography* is a continuation of that used in *Far from the Window*. In an even more noticeable way Kolski borrows from the Polish School tradition of representing the Second World War. The manor house, placed at the centre of his microcosm, brings memories of Wajda's *Lotna* which was devoted to the bravery and futility of Polish cavalrymen. We also find here the images of white horses, another potent symbol of the Polish romantic struggle, memorable from *Ashes and Diamonds*. In many scenes the film loses colour, becoming almost black and white, again as in the Polish School films. The romantic style, as in *Far from the*

Window, underscores the gap between the noble myth of the war in which Polish men bravely fought for their motherland and the reality of the war which proved much less noble. Kolski thus suggests that if the Second World War served Polish males as a test of masculinity, they failed it abysmally.

Sinning and Forgiving: Czech Postcommunist Films

> COLLABORATOR. Historical situations, always new, unveil man's constant possibilities and allow us to name them. Thus, in the course of the war against Nazism, the word 'collaboration' took on a new meaning: putting oneself voluntarily at the service of a vile power. What a fundamental notion! How did humanity do without it until 1944? Now that the word has been found, we realise more and more that man's activity is by nature a collaboration. All those who extol the mass media din, advertising's imbecilic smile, the neglect of the natural world, indiscretion raised to the status of a virtue–they deserve to be called collaborators with the modern.
>
> (Kundera 2005: 125)

Unlike in Poland, in the Czech Republic the subject of the Second World War was appropriated by younger directors, such as Jan Svěrák (b. 1965) and Jan Hřebejk (b. 1967), who have no memory of the war and whose parents were even children at this period. This fact, in my opinion, impacts on the way war is represented in their films. In comparison with such directors as Wajda and Kolski, they are less interested in the war itself, more in its legend, and they tend to use the war more consciously and openly as a metaphor of something else: the communist past or modern condition.

Svěrák's first film on this subject, *Obecná škola* (*The Elementary School*, 1991), is set in the first postwar year in the outskirts of Prague that boasted a tightly-knit community organised around a pub and a school. The class of ten-year-old boys is so unruly that it drives their female teacher to a mental asylum. She is replaced by Mr Igor Hnízdo, a man who sports a military uniform and a small pistol and is not afraid to use corporal punishment on the boys despite the law forbidding it. The boys immediately forgive their new teacher the thrashing, mesmerised by his military style, stories from his war past and his passion for teaching. For one pupil, Eda, Mr Hnízdo serves as a litmus test to assess the war past of his own father. Although his father behaved decently or even bravely, as he listened to the outlawed radio and harboured somebody in his house (possibly a Jew), Eda finds him inferior to his teacher who fought the Nazis with guns. Only gradually Eda and other boys start to be sceptical about their teacher's heroism because his stories, that include fighting on the Eastern and Western fronts, being a parachutist and concentration camp prisoner, fail to cohere. Mr Hnízdo's war credentials are further undermined during a trip to a military bunker where the boys find a missile. Rather than disarming it himself, as the boys expect, the teacher suggests bringing sappers to dispose of it.

However, before they do so, Eda's engineer father disarms the dangerous object himself. At the same time as the heroic façade of Mr Hnízdo is being eroded, we learn about other aspect of his persona – his love of women. He has an eye for the married woman living opposite the school, as well as for Eda's mother. It turns out that he did not come to the troubled school voluntarily but as a punishment for sexual misconduct in a school for teenage girls. It looks like his career in the new school will finish in a similar way when it turns out that he had sex with, and possibly impregnated, pretty twin girls. Yet he is cleared of this charge and returns to Eda's school, to his pupils' joy. We see him for the last time when he prepares a play about the Second World War to commemorate the second anniversary of Czechoslovakia's liberation.

Being an imposter and mythmaker, who invents his whole persona as a war hero, Mr Hnízdo bears similarity with Wiktor Rawicz from Wojciech Has's *How to be Loved*, as well as to Kowalski-Malinowski in *Salto* (1965), directed by Tadeusz Konwicki; both played by Zbigniew Cybulski. However, the fate of these men are markedly different. Due to their mythmaking, Rawicz and Kowalski-Malinowski are objects of public ridicule and they end up as broken men. By contrast, Mr Hnízdo is not only forgiven by his pupils and the community at large but suffers no qualms of conscience when caught lying. His excuse for fantasising is 'young people need a model' and it hardly matters whether this model is 'real'. Mr Hnízdo's immense pedagogic successes suggest that he is right. His achievements are enlarged by the fact

Figure 2.8 In the centre Jan Tříska as Mr Hnízdo in *Obecná škola* (*The Elementary School*, 1991), directed by Jan Svěrák.

that many of his pupils lack paternal authority, such as Eda's friend whose father spends all day in a pub, drinking beer and cheating at cards. In a wider sense, the narrative of Svěrák's film points to the need for heroic legends in the upbringing of young people and building a nation. The visual style of *The Elementary School* confirms this point. Sepia dominates its palette, which creates the impression of watching not a reality but an old film, or even a new film which tries to look like an old film. It appears that in common with Mr Hnízdo, who shuns war truth in favour of a legend, Svěrák shuns reality in favour of simulacra.

The issue of legendary persona versus real man gains extra piquancy by casting in the two main roles two legends of Czechoslovak film, who bring to the screen their off-screen personas. Eda's father is played by Zdenek Svěrák, who is not only the author of the script and the father of the director of *The Elementary School*, but also one of the most successful scriptwriters and actors of the 1970s and 1980s, who specialised in the role of fathers. This position was consolidated after the collapse of communism thanks to his role as surrogate father of a little Russian boy in Oscar-winning *Kolya* (which will be discussed in the next chapter) and the protagonist of a documentary *Tatínek* (2004), both films directed by Jan Svěrák. Mr Hnízdo is played by Jan Tříska, Zdenek Svěrák's contemporary who emigrated to the US in 1977 and returned to Czechoslovakia in 1990. As Ladislav Holý maintains, upon his return to his native country Tříska was welcomed back as a returning hero. However, soon the Czechs were disappointed by him due to his unwillingness to settle in Prague, the corruption of his once beautiful Czech and the loss of his Czech cultural consciousness (Holý 1996: 68–9). The disenchantment with Tříska has much in common with the disillusionment with Mr Hnízdo portrayed by Svěrák. Likewise, as Mr Hnízdo was forgiven being a false hero, so was Tříska, who, after *The Elementary School*, continued to play in Czech films, including the main role in the immensely popular *Horem pádem* (*Up and Down*, 2004) by Jan Hřebejk. I will suggest that in *The Elementary School* Zdenek Svěrák and Jan Tříska together embody the (partly contradictory) qualities of the ideal father, one can say father as God and father as mother. At the same time as underscoring the role of fathers (real and substitute) in bringing up boys and building a nation, the Svěráks (director and scriptwriter) undermine women's role in this process. Women in *The Elementary School* come across as pathetic figures who have no interest outside sex and domestic life. Their redundancy or even damaging influence on boys is demonstrated by the character of the teacher, Mrs Maxová, whom Mr Hnízdo replaces. She is unable to interest the pupils in anything or keep discipline. Her place outside history is conveyed literaly by her teaching only biology, principally the lessons about natural reproduction, while Mr Hnízdo excels in teaching history, including the times of Jan Hus and, of course, of the Second World War. Such denigration of women can be seen as typical for postcommunist Czech cinema at large in which, as Petra Hanákova argues, national identity is epitomised mainly, if not exclusively, by male figures (Hanákova 2005a: 149).

While in *The Elementary School* Svěrák simultaneously points to the importance of war legend and shows scepticism of their adherence to reality, in *Tmavomodrý svět* (*Dark Blue World*, 2001) he proposes one that would stand the test of reality. The material for such a legend is the fate of over two thousand Czechoslovak pilots who, after their country capitulated to Germany in 1939, fled to England to join the RAF. Although their achievements constitute for Czechs probably the most heroic episode in the Second World War, this is also an episode that was suppressed during communist times. As the subtitles inform us at the beginning of the film, after the communists seized power three years after the war finished, the pilots were sent to the labour camps. The reason was the authorities fear that these brave men, contaminated by capitalism and democracy, would again fight for the freedom of their country. Svěrák follows the adventures of two military pilots, lieutenant Franta (Ondřej Vetchý), who after the communist victory was sent to a labour camp and in this grim place reminisces on his war past, and his young trainee Karel (Kryštof Hádek). They begin at the time of Czechoslovakia's capitulation, leading to the army handing their property to the German occupiers. This is a devastating moment for the pilots. Karel decides to fly to Poland, which he expects to stand up to the enemy but is prevented by his older colleague. Some time later the two men find themselves in a RAF training base and after learning English and practising their skills on bicycles with wings, they are allowed to fight the enemy planes. Both Karel and Franta prove first-class pilots but their friendship disintegrates when they fall for the same woman, Susan (Tara Fitzgerald), whom Karel encounters first when he lands near her house. Susan, however, falls for Franta who cannot face revealing their affair to his friend. Despite his broken heart, Karel saves Franta in a dog fight, paying for his bravery with his own life. When the war is over, Franta visits Susan but she, reunited with her soldier husband, treats her Czech lover as a stranger. Her rejection, although related to the nature of wartime affairs, can be seen as symbolic of the Western attitude to the Czech pilots when the war was over: showing them indifference, rather than gratitude. Back at home, Franta discovers that his old girlfriend is married to another man and has a child with him. He cannot even retrieve his old dog, as he also belongs to another family. Thus, Franta loses both his women, which can be read as losing both his countries, the old and the new one.

Dark Blue World is a rare, if not completely unique example of a Czech film that offers an image of a quintessential soldier hero. Both Franta and Karel fit this model, being brave and patriotic. Their heroism appears even stronger by the fact that both in the West and the East the flier occupies a special place in nationalistic ideologies (Paris 1995; Clark 2000: 124–9). According to the director's own words, in the earlier versions of the script his characters were even more heroic but had to be furnished with some flaws to appear more realistic (Svěrák, quoted in Chaw 2002). Ultimate proof of their patriotism and heroism is Franta's stance taken after the war. When a German doctor, who shares his life with him in the camp, asks him whether he does not regret fighting in England, knowing that it would lead to his incarceration, Fanta replies emphatically 'no', as if suggesting that heroism should not be judged from any pragmatic perspective (which is an opinion attributed to Polish Romanticism). Svěrák himself claims that in *Dark Blue World* he wanted to ask not only why his characters fought for the freedom of their country but whether they would do it again knowing that they would be punished for it–and the answer is 'yes' (ibid.).

The role of soldier is intimately connected in Svěrák's film with that of father and lover. For Karel, Franta is a father figure; the young man wants to be a good soldier largely to impress his older colleague (Prokopová 2001). Yet, Franta betrays Karel's trust when he sleeps with Karel's beloved woman. As I will try to show in the next chapter, Oedipal rivalry is a common motif in Polish and Czechoslovak cinema and surrogate fathers frequently let their sons down. There is an additional father figure in *Dark Blue World*, the English Wing Commander Bentley. Played by the charismatic Charles Dance, Bentley turns out to be a superfather, not only because he is higher up the military hierarchy than Franta and Karel, but also because in a crucial moment he is able to interfere in the Czechs' affairs and mend their friendship. Bentley's relation with the two Czech pilots can be seen as metaphorical for the relation between Britain and Czechoslovakia during the war, in which the former was militarily, politically and morally superior. Although *Dark Blue World* is a unique film in the history of Czech cinema, perhaps because it was made over half a century after the war ended and recycled hundreds of films celebrating soldiers' heroism, it comes across as old-fashioned and stereotyped. Moreover, it has a similar storyline to its more famous and expensive American contemporary, *Pearl Harbour* (2001), which makes it look like its poor relative.

For a person familiar with the Czechoslovak New Wave, *Musíme si pomáhat* (*Divided We Fall*, 2000), directed by Jan Hřebejk, looks like a palimpsest of the war films made during this period, including, to name just the most obvious 'relatives', *Diamonds of the Night*, *Closely Observed Trains* and *A Shop on the High Street*. War in Hřebejk's film is similar to that in the earlier Czechoslovak films by being fought 'at home'. Moreover, the director blurs the divisions between the hero and the traitor, and foregrounds the external circumstances as the main factor affecting human behaviour during the war.

The view that morality at the time of war is situational is proposed by the male protagonist Josef (Bolek Polívka), who says early in the film that 'it is amazing what abnormal times can do to normal people.' Josef and his wife Marie (Anna Šišková), the Jewish David Wiener (Csongor Kassai), whom they hide in their pantry after he escaped from the Terezín ghetto, and Volksdeutsche Horst (Jaroslav Dušek), are just such normal people whose war behaviour Hřebejk examines. David's arrival brings with it a plethora of practical problems and moral dilemmas for his hosts. The main issue is how to hide a Jew without arousing the suspicion of the Germans and fellow Czechs. For David and their own safety, Josef accepts Horst's offer to work for his Nazi boss, Mr Binde, and even invites his Nazi employer to his own house. Not surprisingly, the Germans and their own neighbours perceive the couple to be Nazi sympathisers. Particularly contemptuous of Josef is Mr Šimáček, who belongs to the anti-Nazi resistance, although he himself attempted to denounce David to the police when the young man asked him for shelter. The couple's situation becomes truly precarious when Horst asks them to share their flat with his Nazi employer who was evicted from his spacious villa when his youngest son deserted from the army. As housing Mr Binde will be tantamount to revealing David's presence, Marie rejects this request on the grounds of being pregnant. Such an excuse, however, forces them to get Marie pregnant and David is given the task

Figure 2.9 Bolek Polívka as Josef in *Musíme si pomáhat* (*Divided We Fall*, 2000), directed by Jan Hřebejk.

of impregnating her, as Josef is infertile. The birth of her child coincides with the liberation of Czechoslovakia. Suddenly everybody's situation changes. The Nazis are defeated, the collaborators are humiliated and imprisoned, and Josef is forced to produce a Jew to prove that he does not belong to this disgraced category. Moreover, he must find a doctor among the prisoners to help his wife to give birth. He chooses Horst, in this way saving him from likely death. Horst's salvation is sealed by successfully delivering Marie's son and David's testimony that Horst is a decent man. Neither does David reveal that Mr Šimáček tried to betray him to the Nazis.

Hřebejk compares Josef, who is a civilian, with Horst, Mr Simácek and Mr Binde, representing respectively opportunistic conformity to the authority, resistance to the Nazis and fanatic German nationalism. This comparison reveals the moral superiority of Josef and by extension, promotes a civilian outlook on life over a military one. Josef also differs from the other three men because they have large families and are physically fit, while he is a sterile invalid spending most of his time on the sofa. Yet again, even as a family man and father, Josef proves superior to them, because he loves his wife and child despite not conceiving him, as shown in the last surreal scene, when he proudly shows the boy to the passers-by. By contrast, Horst dislikes his ambitious wife who forced him to collaborate with the Nazis, and Binde loves his country more than his family, as testified by sending his three young sons to certain death in combat. Of the three men Horst is rendered the most positive thanks to lack of any fanaticism, joy in the simple pleasures of life (although it also makes him all too eager to profiteer from the Jewish misfortune), loyalty and sense of humour. The contrast between the loafing civilians who ultimately prove heroic and the disciplined military men who turn out to be cowardly or naïve bears associations with Menzel's *Closely Observed Trains*. Josef's natural decency, modesty and preoccupation with his sexuality, as demonstrated by his visit to a doctor to check if he can conceive a child, parallels that of Miloš, who also visited a doctor to check whether he is a 'true man'. Horst, on the other hand, like Tóno in *A Shop on a High Street*, is a decent but weak man, burdened with an ambitious wife who uses him as a pawn to gain social promotion. Not unlike Kadár and Klos, Hřebejk suggests that the conduct of men like Horst depends most on the situation in which they are put; even minute changes in their circumstances can make them heroes or traitors.

Paradoxically, it is Horst's very position as a loyal Nazi servant that gives him the sense of impunity when helping Josef, Marie and David. By contrast, Tóno did not enjoy such a status, therefore was more frightened to help Mrs Lautmannova and in a crucial moment gave in to panic. In the universe represented by Hřebejk, ultimately everybody is implicated in and corrupted by the immoral political order; everybody has some skeleton in his closet. According to David Paul, this overlap or blend of collaboration and resistance is specific to the Czech national character; he links it to 'Švejkism' that strongly informed Czechs' attitudes during the communist period (Paul 1979: 256). Hence, *Divided We Fall* can be read also as a parable about the lives of ordinary Czechs under socialism. Such an interpretation is facilitated by casting in the main roles Bolek Polívka and Jaroslav Dušek, who played respectively a political dissident and a 'decent conformist' in the Czechoslovakia of the 1980s, in Hřebejk's *Pupendo* (2003). Using as his mouthpiece David, the director exonerates his characters from any evil deeds, focusing on all the good acts they managed to commit in adverse times. It is worth adding in passing that such magnanimity might be partly explained by Hřebejk's relatively young age and his lack of first-hand experience of both the Second World War and the communist crimes.[13]

Apart from Czech films, *Divided We Fall* invites comparison with Kolski's *Far from the Window* (Horton 2001; Gretkowska 2002). Similarities pertain to iconography, narrative and construction of the characters. Both films include a painting of Holy Mary with Baby Jesus, to which the heroines pray, and each of the main characters in the Polish film has his/her analogue in the Czech film. However, they meet a different fate. In Hřebejk's film all the main characters are saved, literally and morally; they neither lose their lives nor their humanity. In Kolski's film, by contrast, the Nazi collaborator dies and the child born from the Polish–Jewish relationship brings misery to all three of their 'parents'. The tragedy and discord suffered by the Polish characters, compared with the happiness and harmony experienced by their Czech equivalents, can be explained by the fact that Helusia was a fruit of love, while the child of Marie was the result of a specific arrangement on which everybody concerned (except, of course, the child) was informed and consulted. It can also be viewed as pertaining to the different traditions or even sensibilities revealed in Polish and Czech war films. In Polish this sensibility is romantic, in Czech rationalistic. The critics proclaimed the superiority of the Czech film, which is also somehow validated by the international travels of *Divided We Fall* and *Far from the Window*. *Divided We Fall* was distributed worldwide and nominated for an Oscar, becoming, along with *Kolya*, the most famous Czech film post-1989. *Far from the Window*, by contrast, remained a rather parochial affair, its international career limited to a handful of festivals where it received no important awards. Andrew Horton describes the parallel between the two films as 'an unfortunate coincidence' for Kolski and claims:

> If *Musíme si pomáhat* is more successful, it's not totally without justice. Kolski tangentially raises some interesting issues about Poland coming face to face with its Jewish past, symbolically represented through the final meeting of Helusia and Regina, yet *Daleko od okna* has nothing as philosophically substantial to offer as *Musíme si pomáhat*'s exploration of the ethics of collaboration and resistance, and the murky overlap between the two. (Horton 2001)

In a similar vein Manuela Gretkowska praises Hřebejk's film while simultaneously accusing *Far from the Window* of exaggeration and pseudo-Romanticism. Although she does not state it explicitly, she suggests that as long as Romanticism reigns in Polish culture, Poles will be unable to explore the complexities of war or indeed, of any period in Polish history (Gretkowska 2002: 108).

I will close this chapter with a discussion of *Je třeba zabít Sekala* (*Sekal Has to Die*, 1998). Directed by Czech Vladimír Michálek, but with Polish actors in the main parts and co-produced by the Czech Republic, Slovakia, Poland and France, the film can be seen as symbolic for the different ways war and masculinity are treated in Polish and Czech/Czechoslovak cinema. The eponymous Sekal, the inhabitant of a fictitious Moravian village of Lakotice, uses his connections with the Nazis to extend his farm at the expense of fellow villagers, threatening them with denunciation and concentration camps. Terrorised and outraged by his greed and arrogance, the village elders decide to kill him. Rather than doing it with their own hands, they choose as an executioner a stranger, Jura Baran (Baran both in Polish and Czech means 'ram', a word bearing associations with 'goat' and 'scapegoat'), the new blacksmith, who is a Protestant and a partisan sought by the Gestapo. To convince Jura that he has no option but to give in to the villagers' demands, the elders threaten to betray him to the German authorities, which will also lead to him losing his family. Thus Jura fights and kills Sekal, and is himself seriously wounded in the duel. When he turns for help to the people who hired him, they let him die, anxious that if he survives, the Germans might learn about their role in killing Sekal. In this way they prove no better than the Nazis, as they use the same treacherous methods while preaching moral superiority.

The war is nowhere to be seen in *Sekal Has to Die*; there are no tanks or air raids, not even any Germans. However, we observe the moral devastation it causes among the civilians. In this sense, the film adheres to the dominant way the war is represented in Czechoslovak cinema, as war 'at home'. Michálek's peasants, representing the majority of society, as many of their Czech cinematic predecessors, avoid fighting and think only about their own and their families' comfort, in a way associated with women. Even the manner they excuse themselves from killing Sekal is typically ascribed to women; they claim that they are too old, too weak or too busy with their work, to fight.

Furthermore, they are sedentary figures, always occupying the closed space of a home. By contrast, Sekal and Jura are both masculine men as each of them has a military past; Jura as a partisan, Sekal as a pro-republican fighter in the Spanish civil war. These war exploits, on the one hand, testify to a certain idealism which the villagers are missing, on the other explain the brutality and disillusionment of Sekal. Similarly, Jura and Sekal like open spaces, they do not hide from the world in the cosiness of their homes, not least because they do not have cosy homes. Jura's family is far away and Sekal is a bastard renounced by his father and hated by his mother. Hence, rather than focusing on the competition between Sekal and Jura, Michálek underscores the confrontation between them as soldiers and peasants who are civilians. Such a construction of the main conflict is facilitated by the casting: the villagers are played by Czech actors while Sekal and Jura by Polish ones, respectively Bogusław Linda and Olaf Lubaszenko. This casting choice was commented on sarcastically by Petra Hanáková who noted that if the Czechs want to show 'true men' in film, they have to employ Polish actors (Hanáková 2005a: 157). The casting of Linda and Lubaszenko, the first being regarded in the 1980s and 1990s as an embodiment of Polish masculinity, can also be interpreted as symbolic of the different approach to the Second World War of Poles and Czechs – Poles were fighting in the war and bled to death, while Czechs avoided fighting but managed to reap the fruit of other nations' struggle. There is some similarity between *Sekal Has to Die* and Wajda's *The Sentence on Franciszek Kłos*, testified to even by the similar titles of the films. In both films the plot revolves around the liquidation of a Nazi collaborator who poses a serious threat to a local community. However, in the Polish film finding an executioner is not a problem; young Polish patriots are keen to do that, even more so than Maciek Chełmicki in *Ashes and Diamonds*. Moreover, there is no romantic aura about Kłos that surrounds Sekal, not least because Mirosław Baka, who plays Kłos, is most famous for his role as the murderer in Kieślowski's *Krótki film o zabijaniu* (*A Short Film about Killing*, 1987).

In common with *Divided We Fall*, *Sekal Has to Die* invites allegorical reading. Andrew Horton sees it predominantly as referring to 'contemporary Czech society as it battles with the social, political and economic traumas it has unleashed by ridding itself of communism', although he agrees that this is relevant to the histories of other countries such as Poland and Germany (Horton 1999a). As an exploration of the conflict between morality and the need to live a stable life, it can be interpreted, not unlike *Divided We Fall*, as a film about the Czech communist past, marred by opportunism.

Different Experiences, Converging Memories

To conclude, I argue that, except for the period of socialist realism where heroic images prevailed in both Polish and Czechoslovak cinema, the two countries offered rather different images of war and men during the war. Polish cinema was dominated by the romantic, idealistic fighter who, despite his bravery, is defeated; Czechoslovak by a civilian who collaborates with an enemy or accidentally becomes a hero. What both cinemas had in common, however, was their divergence from the dominant structure of representing the war that, according to Antony Easthope, includes defeat, combat, victory and comradeship (Easthope 1986: 63) by dispensing with most of these elements. The numerous films about collaborators, deserters and dodgers that dominate Czechoslovak war cinema can be seen as reflecting the largely nonheroic war and postwar history of this country. The abundance of mad patriots on the Polish screen can be interpreted as testifying to the prevalence of such attitudes among real Poles during and after the war. However, it is also possible to assess the film characters differently, regarding the lack of heroes not as a sign of Czechoslovak cowardice but rather courage, as it takes a lot of courage to expose one's own countrymen as a cowardly and selfish bunch. On the other hand, the Polish love affair with mad, idealistic patriots can be perceived as deriving from the need of the 'injured' or 'diminished' communist Polish male to look at his idealised ego at war to somehow make up for his low position in reality.

In the postcommunist period the representations of war created by Polish filmmakers on the one hand, and Czech on the other, to a large extent converged. This similarity concerns the settings, characters, and ideology. The films tend to be set away from the battlefields, in the provinces, in small, picturesque villages or on the outskirts of towns where people are familiar with each other. Such a setting underscores the theme of the impact of the war on ordinary, domestic life. The characters tend to be civilians, typically 'small people' who would rather live and love than fight for their country. Their lack of traditional heroism does not mean that they all react in the same way to the miseries, challenges and opportunities which the war brings about. On the contrary, the focus on war 'at home' allows for a subtle characterisation of different attitudes which war caused or unleashed. Paradoxically and meaningfully, it appears that after 1989 Polish filmmakers largely gave up on the heroes who populated so many films from earlier periods, and the Czechs tried to salvage some heroism from their past. Postcommunist war films can simply be treated as stories about war events, although filtered through contemporary sensibilities, or as commentaries of later times. As allegories of the postwar period, they point to the widespread pragmatism and opportunism of the generation that survived the war and those which followed them. However, rather than resolutely condemning their countrymen's willingness to collaborate with the enemy, they encourage us to look more closely into the very nature of collaboration, suggesting, as Kundera observes, that it is next to impossible to live without collaborating.

Notes

1. *The Good Soldier Švejk* was also chosen by twenty-three leading Czech literary critics as 'critics choice for best Czech novel of the century', overtaking the books by Hrabal, Škvorecký and Kundera. The results were published in *Týden* magazine in 1998 (Roberts 2005: 164).
2. Nałkowska herself was a prisoner of the concentration camp, an institution that was born out of feverish nationalism and disrespect for individual lives.

3. Mira and Antonín Liehm observe this in reference to the films of the late 1950s and early 1960s, but in my opinion it can refer to films of all periods.
4. I am omitting from this section *Eroica* partly because I analysed it elsewhere (Mazierska 2004a) and partly because I find *How to Be Loved* a more interesting polemic with the model of masculinity offered by Wajda. This also applies to *Salto* (1965) by Tadeusz Konwicki, which I have to leave out from my analysis due to lack of space. *Eroica*, in my opinion, largely conforms to Wajda's model (Werner 1987: 59–64).
5. Due to the lack of space I present very briefly the historical background of Wajda's films. More detailed analysis can be found in Paul Coates' book, *The Red and the White* (Coates 2005) and in my essay, 'Wajda on War', accompanying the DVD version of Wajda's 'war trilogy' (Mazierska 2004b), as well as in the historical books devoted to Polish history of the twentieth century, especially Norman Davies's *God's Playground* (Davies 2005: 322–66). See also Chapter 1 of this book.
6. In my opinion Cybulski's death and denigration of the films in which he played 'domesticated men' influenced negatively subsequent Polish male stardom. In particular, most Polish actors aspiring to the status of stars, including Olbrychski, Linda and Żebrowski, did not ever risk moving beyond the type of male pin-ups with hard muscles and apparent uninterest in those looking at them, as described by Richard Dyer (Dyer 1992).
7. Jackiewicz worked for some years as a film critic in *Trybuna Ludu*, the official newspaper of the Party, so it could be suggested that his political allegiance was a factor in his negative attitude to Maciek. However, I believe that his assessment of Maciek and the situation represented in Wajda's film was genuine.
8. Elsewhere I have argued that in his films Wajda is biased against working-class characters by representing them as simpletons (Mazierska 2002). This scene supports this opinion.
9. The relation between Hrabal book and Menzel's film is discussed by a number of authors, including Josef Škvorecký, Peter Hames and Jonathan Owen (Škvorecký 1982; Hames 2004; Owen 2007), therefore I am leaving it out from my discussion.
10. The literary roots and the political background of Wajda's film are discussed by Tadeusz Drewnowski (Drewnowski 1992).
11. Athough *The Ring with a Crowned Eagle* warns against and condemns serving the 'two gods' of the communist authorities and anti-communist opposition, it could be argued that such an ideological position was espoused by Aleksander Ścibor-Rylski, the author of the novel on which Wajda's film is based, and Wajda himself. Both artists were close to the establishment, playing many important roles in the official culture of People's Poland and enjoying above-average affluence, yet at the same time attempting to convey in their works criticism of the authorities, as in the famous *Człowiek z marmuru* (*Man of Marble*, 1976), which Ścibor-Rylski scripted and Wajda directed. This position of the 'double agents' is examined and maliciously ridiculed by Andrzej Horubała in an article written for the influential *Kino* magazine in 1992 (Horubała 1992). I find it interesting that an author born in 1962, who has no personal experience of the war or Stalinism, has the cheek to judge so harshly the morality of Wajda or Ścibor-Rylski.
12. Kolski's approach to Polishness and the war can be linked to the fact that he is of Jewish origin, although I try not to base too much on the filmmakers' biographies.
13. Hřebejk's forgiving attitude, to which I feel more attuned, can be contrasted with that of Andrzej Horubała, who implicitly accused Ścibor-Rylski and Wajda of being 'double agents'. It can be suggested that the former represents Czech moral minimalism, the latter Polish maximalism.

CHAPTER 3

Who Is My Father? Representation of Fathers, Sons and Family Life in Polish and Czechoslovak films

Children? Who amongst us could take responsibility for others if we hardly managed with our own lives?
(Andrzej Wajda 2000: 46)

I do not feel the need to reproduce myself. But the fact that the role of the father is missing from my life has kept me rather immature; and I am more of a failed son than a wise father.
(Jiří Menzel, quoted in Pošová 1998)

After the war, many fathers were dead. Not just one little boy sought out a father. Whole nations, countries, people created fathers, if they didn't have strong leaders. Stalin, Churchill, Roosevelt – people make fathers out of their leaders – or vice-versa?
(István Szabó, quoted in Jaehne 1978: 32)

Fatherhood in Poland and Czechoslovakia

There are several reasons to include fathers in my study. Firstly, since the 1960s the topic of fatherhood features prominently in research on men. We now find more books written about men as fathers than about men in any other role and those on men in general typically include long passages devoted to fatherhood. Consequently, writing about masculinity without mentioning fatherhood can be compared to ignoring motherhood in research on women. Secondly, in social theories, particularly Freudianism and Marxism, both drawing heavily on anthropology, the study of the family (real or mythical, current or past, civilised or primitive), with specific reference to the role of the father, provides the key to understanding society as a whole, which is one of purposes of my book. Thirdly, the experience of fatherhood in the countries of the Soviet bloc was distorted and consequently, fatherhood there gained a somewhat different meaning to that in Western societies.

According to Freudian psychoanalysis, the father enters the child's world during the stage of its development described as the Oedipus complex. At this stage the child abandons its exclusive relationship with the mother and enters into the structures of human sexuality. Confronted with the authority of the father, the child now sees the mother, formerly the repository of all identity, as lacking a phallus, as castrated, therefore a testimony only to the authority of the father. Recognition of the presence or absence of the phallus creates the child's awareness of sexual difference, and the girl's sense of lack and penis envy and, consequently, inferiority towards boys. This inferiority will last throughout her life, affecting her position within the family and society (Gay 1995: 631–45; 670–678). Freud's followers, particularly Jacques Lacan and Juliet Mitchell, argue that the Oedipus complex cannot be taken literally because it does not refer to the situation of each individual child and its relationship with its parents, but metaphorically, as a means to conceptualise how the child enters culture and acquires its heritage of ideas and laws within the unconscious mind. Thus the 'phallus' is not identical to the physical penis, but is its representation, the signifier of the laws of the social order, the Law of the Father, through which obedience to the social (and patriarchal) order is instilled. As Juliet Mitchell writes,

> The myth that Freud rewrote as the Oedipus complex and its dissolution reflects the original exogamous incest taboo, the role of the father, the exchange of women and the consequent difference between the sexes. It is *not* about the nuclear family, but about the institution of culture with the kinship structure and the exchange relationship of exogamy. It is about what Freud regarded as the order of all human culture. It is specific to nothing but patriarchy which is itself, according to Freud, specific to all human civilisation. (Mitchell 1974: 377)

Freudianism is indifferent to changes in human societies; it assumes that the Oedipus complex and the Law of the Father are eternal. This assumption was challenged by a number of thinkers, including Friedrich Engels. In *The Origin of the Family, Private Property and the State* he argued that patriarchy, understood as men's domination over women, appeared at a specific moment of cultural development, namely when the human labour force was able to produce more than was necessary for its maintenance, and wealth started to be accumulated.

> The herds and the other new objects of wealth brought about a revolution in the family. Gaining a livelihood had always been the business of the man; he produced and owned the means therefor. Hence, he owned the cattle, and the commodities and slaves obtained in exchange for them. All the surplus now resulting from production fell to the man; the woman shared in consuming it but she had no share in owning it. The 'savage' warrior and hunter had

> been content to occupy second place in the house and give precedence to the woman. The 'gentler' shepherd, presuming upon his wealth, pushed forward to first place and forced the woman into second place. And she could not complain. Division of labour in the family had regulated the distribution of property between man and wife. This division of labour remained unchanged, and yet it now put the former domestic relationship topsy-turvy simply because the division of labour outside the family had changed. The very cause that had formerly made the woman supreme in the house, namely, her being confined to domestic work, now assured supremacy in the house for the man: the woman's housework lost its significance compared with the man's work in obtaining a livelihood; the latter was everything, the former an insignificant contribution. (Engels 1972: 158)

The obvious conclusion from Engels's reasoning is that the more wealth that is accumulated in a society, the more it is 'civilised', the more patriarchal it is. As capitalism is the highest stage of wealth accumulation, it is also the stage where women are most subjugated to men. A working-class woman is exploited as an unpaid worker in the home and a wage labourer outside it, and her inferior status makes her an instrument for the intensified exploitation of the working class. At the other end of the scale, the loveless bourgeois family jealously guards its integrity and its myths, for it represents a union for the consolidation and expansion of property stolen from the workers. In this family the wife is wholly owned by her husband, and fidelity is demanded of her to insure the legitimacy of his heirs (Scott 1976: 30). However, Engels also argued that in capitalism the majority of men do not take advantage of the capitalist exploitation of women. In *The Condition of the Working Class in England* he pointed to the negative effect mothers' work outside home has on children, who feel isolated for the rest of their lives and are unable to feel at home in the families they themselves eventually set up. Engels also criticised the arrangement, not atypical for capitalism, where the wife supports the family working outside the home and the man stays at home, tends to the children, sweeps the rooms and cooks. He claimed that such an arrangement, while the other social conditions remain unchanged, undermine a working man's pride, 'virtually turning him into a eunuch' (Engels 1971: 162). On the whole, in Marxist discourse the capitalist model of the family has negative connotations, being associated with the exploitation of women,[1] a 'bourgeois mental framework' and putting private interest over the welfare of the society as a whole (Bronfenbrenner 1972). Engels did not limit himself to criticism of the status quo, but proposed a new order of things – socialism. He argued that its advent would overturn patriarchy by enabling women to take part in production equally with men, and by freeing them from domestic chores by passing them to society, as was the case in the primitive, communistic household (Scott 1976: 28–45; 138–9).

Engels and his intellectual legacy was a significant factor influencing official thinking in the Soviet bloc about the institution of the family, motherhood and fatherhood, state policy in these matters, as well as the everyday reality of millions of families living there. What was of particular importance was the assumption that the roles of mother and father should be equal or at least similar, and that this should be assured by allowing women to work outside the home and by the state looking after the children.

In Poland and in some measure in the Slovak region of Czechoslovakia, another important factor from the sphere of ideology, influencing society's ideas about family and fatherhood, and by extension, masculinity, is Catholicism, a religion that (in common with most Christian religions) is phallocentric. According to Catholic doctrine the role of the father is of utmost importance for men and society at large. This is because all men are meant to follow God the Father and Jesus Christ who are 'Fathers of the Church'. We find in the Catechism such statements as 'God's fatherhood is the source of human fatherhood', therefore a man who becomes a father becomes similar to God. Moreover, the father–son relationship is privileged over other types of relations within the family and society at large, including that between mother and her children (Adamiak 1993: 73-4). 'Father' is understood here not only as the man who conceives and brings up his children, but also as a master and leader of people who are not his biological children. A good father is one who is responsible, tender, forgiving and selfless, but also one who does not hesitate to reprimand and use physical force to make children behave well. The Catechism implies that the father's power and authority should be greater than that of the mother as, similarly, the husband should have a higher position in the home than his wife. Catholicism also tacitly assumes that the man's place is to govern both at home and in the wider world, whilst a woman should content herself with staying at home and serving her husband and children. This short description suggests that in Poland there was a conflict between the official and unofficial, albeit dominant, doctrines on the character of family and fatherhood. In reality, however, the conflict was much less because the socialist authorities failed to meet their pledges about 'liberating women' (together with the majority of their other pledges). True, women in socialist countries were allowed to work in factories and on cooperative farms, but usually in positions much lower than those occupied by men (Scott 1976; Gal and Kligman 2000). On the other hand, their domestic work did not diminish due to acute shortages of even the most basic necessities that forced them to struggle to obtain them to support their families, and the tradition created by centuries of historical development, according to which women serve their men and children (ibid.).

Czech thinking about family and fatherhood, on the other hand, is strongly influenced by the culture of Biedermeier that, according to Josef Kroutvor, was matriarchal (see Kroutvor 2001: 258). A typical Czech man does what his wife tells him both in domestic arrangements and political issues (ibid.: 257).

Another important factor shaping fatherhood in Poland and Czechoslovakia was the acute shortage of real fathers and men of fathering age after the Second World War. Fathers in the whole Eastern bloc were in short supply because of the war and its aftermath that decimated and crippled a generation of men of parenting age. They perished fighting the Nazis and in the case of Poles, as a result of being deported into the interior of the Soviet Union, following the Ribbentrop–Molotov treaty of August

1939 (Walichnowski 1989). Moreover, if they fought in Great Britain, after the war they were imprisoned in the camps for the state's enemies or sent to Siberia. This problem was particularly acute in Poland that lost six million people in the years 1939–45, the majority of them men. Moreover, many 'war children', although their biological fathers were alive, did not know them, because they were the fruit of short encounters, conceived by men who often had other families elsewhere and returned to them when the war was over. The lack of fathers put extra pressure on women and the state. Mothers of fatherless children had to fulfil the duties and combine the skills of both parents, or put up with the fact that their children lacked something important that children from 'full families' had. The state, on the other hand, had to step in financially to help the fatherless families, as well as providing role models to children, especially sons. Consequently, we could observe a relocation of fatherhood to non-fathers, such as political leaders, as mentioned by István Szabó, as well as to institutions and ideas, such as the Party or the State. Such relocation was facilitated by socialist ideology that set out to free families from some duties traditionally attached to them. The displacement of fathering functions to non-fathers was also helped by the personal ambition of certain communist leaders, especially Stalin and those who attempted to emulate him, such as Bolesław Bierut in Poland and Klement Gottwald in Czechoslovakia, to become the 'fathers of their nations'. This phenomenon can also be linked to the fact that some famous communist leaders, most importantly Lenin and Stalin, lost their fathers at an early age (Clark 2000: 134). By placing extra value on the 'surrogate father' and the 'great family' of a nation or socialist community they attempted to rationalise and soothe their pain of being orphans.

The shortage of fathers was experienced most severely soon after the war. In due course the fatherless boys matured and became parents themselves (although, it could be argued, the lack of fathers affected the way they brought up their own children)[2] and gradually the balance between the number of men and women of reproductive age was restored. Not surprisingly, the projection of fatherhood into non-fathers and national institutions pertains most to the Stalinist period. However, even when the shadows of the war and Stalinism receded, other factors remained and new factors appeared, significantly affecting men's chances of being fathers and the type of fatherhood available to them. We should list here the nationalisation of the economy, the privileging of heavy industry, the limited promotion opportunities for both men and women, the high employment rates of women, the shortage of affordable accommodation and, consequently, the small size of the average socialist apartment, as well as the relatively liberal abortion laws in the majority of the socialist countries, including Poland and Czechoslovakia. Nationalisation of industry and agriculture forced most men in socialist countries to work outside the home, in large factories where their work was unskilled, mechanical and repetitive (not unlike in capitalist factories). This situation led to the breakdown of the link between home and male work and the disappearance of opportunities for men to teach their sons professional skills and attitudes, so important, in the opinion of Robert Bly and his followers, in creating, preserving and strengthening the bond between fathers and their male offspring (Bly 1991: 96–102). Moreover, the chance to achieve higher positions in society, or even being able to earn one's living, were linked to political conformity and hypocrisy (Taborsky 1961; Paul 1979; Havel 1985; Wedel 1992; Holý 1996). This distortion of the channels of professional promotion and mechanisms of social recognition had a frustrating effect on men, sometimes leading to a sense of emasculation (Watson 1993: 471–87), or structural feminisation or infantilisation in their relations to the state (see Kligman 1994: 255; Gal and Kligman 2000: 54), which further diminished the socialist father's ability to impress and guide his children, especially his sons.

The shortage of accommodation led many adult children to live with their parents. Such a situation had its pros and cons for all concerned. On the one hand, it made grandparents in socialist countries more involved in bringing up their grandchildren than their counterparts in the West. In the absence of a parent away working long hours in a factory or on the compulsory *subbotnik*, the grandfather often took the role of surrogate father, offering the child care and entertainment that he or she otherwise would not receive. The grandparents also provided a safety net for children whose parents could not look after them at all, due to studying or living in a workers' hostel in a far-away town, as well as for busy and poor single mothers. On the other hand, sharing a small flat with their parents or parents-in-law (who typically were the owners of the apartment) led to a continuous frustration for the middle generation, and even to emasculation of the younger men, who felt responsible for 'arranging' a state or cooperative apartment. Under the wings and the watchful eyes of their elders the younger men were not able to achieve maturity and fully exercise their rights and duties as fathers and heads of the family. In a significant proportion of men the lack of their own accommodation led to a decision to postpone marriage and fatherhood. As a result, the countries of the Soviet bloc (in common with Italy which also suffered a lack of affordable accommodation for young people) developed the phenomenon of a man in his thirties or forties still living with his parents. If such a man eventually married, he tended to treat his wife as his mother, expecting from her the care he received from his own mother. Moreover, the small dimensions of the average socialist flat resulted in a shortage of personal space which reduced the scope for developing interests and indulging in hobbies that required space, such as gardening or DIY. The most common way of spending free time for men was watching television. Women, by contrast, typically spent their 'free time' cooking and cleaning. Consequently, the prevailing model of fatherhood in the Soviet bloc was that of the 'domesticated' father, derided by Bly. For a large proportion of men the only way to escape from this model was the abuse of alcohol. Alcoholism further weakened their fathering credentials because alcoholic fathers are almost by definition absent fathers or fathers unable to properly fulfil their role within the family.

The harsh living conditions, the requirement to look after one's own ageing parents, combined with the relative easiness of terminating pregnancy and, in the later period of communism, beginning in the late 1960s, the temptations of consumer goods, travelling abroad and cars, that were easier to acquire if one was childless, led to a 'neo-Malthusian prudence' on the part of both men and women.

People in socialist countries tended only to have as many children as they could afford, which meant less than they wanted. Despite the state rhetoric that promoted large families, in popular consciousness a large number of children signified recklessness and even became associated with social pathologies, such as alcoholism. As a result of these factors almost the whole of the Soviet bloc during the postwar years experienced a fertility crisis (see Scott 1976: 138–63). A relatively high proportion of men in these countries did not experience fatherhood first hand or fathered fewer children than their counterparts in the West. However, there were national variations in these phenomena. In Poland a fertility crisis struck later than in its southern neighbour, which can be attributed to the lower employment rates of women, higher proportion of people living in the countryside, and the influence of Catholicism on citizens' attitudes to reproduction. Moreover, in Poland, where a large proportion of agriculture and small businesses remained in private hands, the urban father or father working on a cooperative farm was not the only available model of fatherhood. There were also men working on their own farms or in their own factories who wanted to pass their property and skills to their offspring. On the other hand, alcoholism was more of a problem in Poland than in Czechoslovakia, therefore in this country more women were forced into single parenthood than in its southern neighbour, even if it was not reflected in the higher divorce rate.

Polish, Czech and Slovak cinema reflected both the general tendencies pertaining to fatherhood in European socialist countries and the national variations. It also reacted to the transformation of the situation of fathers stemming from the change of political, economic, social and cultural circumstances. However, it must be stressed that the reaction cannot be conceived simply as the replacement of one type of father by another in films belonging to different periods. Although in consecutive cinematic paradigms we find different types of fathers prevailing, the earlier paradigms of fatherhood return in new guises or are accompanied by a new approach from the film's author. This phenomenon can be explained by the fact that certain traits characteristic of one generation of fathers can also be found in latent form in subsequent generations. Furthermore, earlier cinematic representations of fatherhood influenced later ones. For example, the cinema created after the fall of socialist realism keeps including the figure of the 'Stalinist father', only treating him differently. For this reason, rather than using in this chapter a strictly chronological approach, I will identify certain models of fatherhood prevailing in particular historical periods of Czechoslovak and Polish cinema, but also look at how these models were used in subsequent periods and how they affected the construction of other models. Because, as I indicated, in the ideology and practice of state socialism fatherhood is particularly imbricated in such masculine roles as that of the political leader and worker, discussion of fatherhood appears to me the right place to touch upon these roles.

Non-fatherly Fathers and Fatherly Non-fathers and their Children in the Films about Stalinism

The father is like a dictator...from his voice shall depend all that is subject to him.
(Ayrault, quoted in Flandrin 1979: 130)

Stalinism and the aesthetic system it created, socialist realism, was very masculine and patriarchal (Kenez 1992; Robin 1992; Clark 2000; Tubielewicz Mattsson 2003a). Its patriarchalism did not consist only of women's subordination to men or sons to fathers, but of a rigid stratification of all relationships within the society. During this period the phenomenon of citizens' structural 'feminisation' or 'infantilisation' in their relations to the state was at its strongest. Different authors identify different principal categories of men within socialist-realistic art, but all agree that central amongst them is that of master or mentor. Stalin or other Party leaders (Bierut, Gottwald) are cast in this role or, more often, 'a sort of Stalin-to-scale, a figure with Stalin's significance but proportionate to the small world in which the action takes place' (Clark 2000: 132). He can be a Party secretary, an activist in a youth organisation, a high official in the secret service or an inventor passing his knowledge to pupils. The Party leader resembles the God-the-Father of Christianity, being utterly good, powerful and omnipresent, either appearing in person, or through his representations in monuments, pictures, sculptures, posters, or through actions of his disciples who follow his example and benefit from his actions (Tubielewicz Mattsson 2003a: 55). He is the superior or ultimate father; other men in relation to him are his sons (Clark 2000: 126–9) and can be fathers only as his deputies. Although benevolent, the leader of the Party is also a dictator – those who oppose him are by definition prodigal sons, whose actions must be corrected. This feature also likens him to the feudal monarchs and fathers in premodern societies, whose authority, as Jean-Louis Flandrin argues, included not only children and wives, but also servants, lodgers and others, and concerned such matters as the making of wills, the transfer of property, the choice of a marriage partner and the selection of an occupation. 'The authority of a king over his subject, and that of a father over his children, were of the same nature: neither authority was based on contract and both were considered "natural"' (Flandrin 1979: 1). The socialist realistic father – mentor is typically 'dressed in a semimilitary style, unencumbered by a family or love affairs, ascetic and flawless' (Kenez 1992: 158). By contrast, the son is initially allowed to be spontaneous, impulsive and to make mistakes before, as Katerina Clark puts it, 'donning the austere cloak of supreme responsibility' (Clark 2000: 133). A socialist realistic film, like a socialist realistic novel, is always a '*Bildungsroman*, that is, it is about the acquisition of consciousness. In the process of fulfilling the task, the hero, under the tutelage of a seasoned Party worker, acquires an increased understanding of himself, the world around him, the tasks of building communism, class struggle, and the need for vigilance' (Kenez 1992: 158).

The fact that the political leader in Stalinist ideology is regarded as a 'superfather' inevitably undermines the position of the biological father both within the individual family and in the society at large. Not only is he inferior in relation to the Party leader, but also to men who are above him in the political hierarchy and who encounter his children in political and professional lives, such as directors of factories, foremen or Party secretaries. Moreover, in Stalinist ideology the biological father can be a good father only through emulating Stalin in his dealings with his children. If he fails to do so, becoming, for example, an enemy of the socialist cause, he also loses any paternal rights over his offspring. Similarly, his children do not need to love or respect him any more, but could and should treat him as their enemy. In its extreme version this line of thinking requires children to denounce their parents to political authorities if they deviate from the behaviour prescribed by the Stalinist ideology. In the 1950s in the Soviet Union and other communist states camps for scouts were set up in which young people learnt how to be vigilant, even in their own homes. However, as Piotr Zwierzchowski observes, whilst in the Soviet Union it was acceptable to present as a national hero somebody like Pavlik Morozov who betrayed his own father – a saboteur – in Poland such an attitude was unacceptable (Zwierzchowski 2000: 127). Consequently, while in the Soviet Union books and operas were devoted to Morozov and the leading creator of socialist cinema, Sergei Eisenstein, made a film about him, *Bezhin Lug* (*Bezhin Meadow*, 1937), in Poland Morozov-like figures hardly found a place in literature or cinema. The closest to Morozov on the Polish screen is probably Hanka Nalepianka in Stanisław Różewicz's socialist realistic classic, *Trudna miłość* (*Difficult Love*, 1953). She denounces her father who is both a *kulak*, the murderer of the chairman of the local agricultural cooperative, a misogynist who does not allow Hanka to study and the chief obstacle against her marrying a man whom she loves. Yet, despite having so many reasons to inform on her father, Hanka is still very uneasy about doing so.

In Czechoslovakia Morozov was set up as a role model for society and was occasionally imitated. The most significant example was the son of one of the co-accused in the trial of Rudolf Slánsky, the general secretary of the Communist Party, demanding the death penalty for his own father (Taborsky 1961: 94–5). However, in Czech and Slovak cinema the motif of children denouncing their fathers, as in Polish cinema, was rare. The most memorable example of a child who declares their father to be a traitor is offered in *Žert* (*The Joke*, 1969), directed by Jaromil Jireš and based on Milan Kundera's novel that unequivocally condemns the crimes of Stalinism. Here the son, despite renouncing his father, ends up in a labour camp and is treated as a freak both by the inmates and the camp's guards.

Both in Polish and Czechoslovak films of the Stalinist period we find the figure of a fatherly man who influences or indeed, engenders a young character, a young couple and sometimes a whole group of people to achieve a goal beneficial to the cause of socialism as well as to their own happiness, on the way teaching them the principles of Marxist economics. We find a typical representation of the father figure in the Czech film *Dovolená s Andělem* (*Angel on Vacation*, 1952), directed by Bořivoj Zeman, an instalment in a popular series of films of the 1950s, featuring a zealous ticket controller Mr Anděl (Angel), played by Jaroslav Marvan. The film is set in a holiday camp for exemplary workers from all over the country and has a kind of musical structure, with several subplots and numerous characters who one by one take central stage, in due course to leave it to the next character, as well as playing ensemble. One of these subplots concerns a couple, still married, but experiencing a profound crisis, a sign of which is the wife filing for divorce. Both are dismayed to meet each other at the hotel and initially they want to return home, but the conflict around who should return and who stay, and the persuasion of the Party official, prevent their departure. They learn that their coming to this place was not a coincidence but a plot on the part of the Party organisation that wanted to offer them an opportunity for reconciliation. Indeed, exactly this then happens, as during the time they spend away from their natural environment they begin to discuss the reasons for their conflict. It turns out that the wife was frustrated by staying at home; she would like to seek fulfilment in paid employment to which her husband objected. Eventually, he understands her mindset and accepts her wish. Thus their 'adopted father', the Party secretary, and the whole political organisation he represents, succeed in two objectives at once: mending the rift between the spouses and helping the economy to overcome the problem of manpower, which at the time could be alleviated largely by mobilising women into the workforce.

By contrast to *Angel on Vacation*, in a later episode in the adventures of Mr Anděl, *Anděl na horách* (*Angel in the Mountains*, 1955), also directed by Zeman, the central role is given to a biological father – Mr Anděl himself. This time he travels to a resort in the Tatra mountains to spy on his son's fiancée and in this way to find out whether she is suitable to become young Anděl's wife. However, he mistakes the girlfriend of his son's fiancée for her and comes to the completely wrong conclusion that she

Figure 3.1 Jaroslav Marvan as Mr. Anděl in *Anděl na horách* (*Angel in the Mountains*, 1955), directed by Bořivoj Zeman.

cheats on his son with another man. As a result he even attempts to stop their wedding. Luckily, the mistake is corrected when he learns who the real fiancée is. Nevertheless, comparing these two films demonstrates that while the surrogate father who is the Party leader never makes any mistakes and acts for the good of everybody concerned, as well as for the whole country, real fathers can do much damage to the welfare of their children. The obvious conclusion is that the more fatherhood is relocated from family to respectable institutions, such as the Party, school or state, the better for everybody concerned.[3]

In Poland the fatherly non-fathers appear in such socialist-realistic films as *Opowieść Atlantycka* (*Atlantic Story*, 1954), directed by Wanda Jakubowska, *Przygoda na Mariensztacie* (*An Adventure at Marienstadt*, 1954), directed by Leonard Buczkowski, *Celuloza* (*Cellulose*, 1953) and *Pod gwiazdą frygijską* (*Under the Phrygian Star*, 1954), both directed by Jerzy Kawalerowicz, *Niedaleko Warszawy* (*Not Far From Warsaw*, 1954), directed by Maria Kaniewska, and Andrzej Wajda's *Pokolenie* (*A Generation*, 1954), in which the principles of socialist realism blend with that of the new paradigm – the Polish School. In each of these films the substitute father, typically a communist activist, takes the role of the mentor of the young person (Stachówna 1996: 21–3; Ostrowska 2005: 206). *Adventure on Marienstadt* and *Not Far From Warsaw* can be seen as Polish counterparts of *Angel on Vacation* because in these films the role of the Party secretary is to help overcome sexist prejudices predominating in factories and families. The words directed to the father of the female steelworker in Kaniewska's film perfectly capture the importance of the substitute father and the redundancy or even harmfulness of the real father: 'You think that you brought up your daughter? Wielicki [the Party secretary] brought her up, the steelworks brought her up, the working class brought her up, not you.'

I want to pay special attention to the woodcutter Blachier (Stanisław Kwaskowski) in *Atlantic Story*, despite its rather exotic setting on the Atlantic coast of France. As an uncle of a ten-year-old boy named Gaston, whose mother was killed by the police during a trade union demonstration and father was jailed for participating in the workers' movement, he is a kind of link between the real family and the communist organisation. Blachier educates his nephew in the spirit of socialism, telling him about the injustices of capitalism and imperialism. He also adopts this role in relation to Bernard, Gaston's peer, who comes to the coast on holiday with his bourgeois parents. In contrast to Blachier, Bernard's father, Doctor Oliver, is very conservative in his political views and home arrangements. He strongly rejects the idea of the French colonies gaining independence and is very strict with his son, whom he would rather see spending the whole summer in solitude than mixing with the children of the local workers. Despite his father's attitude, Bernard strikes up a secret friendship with Gaston. The boys, trying to discover who steals their fish, find in a Second World War bunker a hungry German fugitive who left the Foreign Legion because he could not accept its brutal suppressing of Indo-China's independence. At first Bernard, indoctrinated by his nationalistic father, rejects the story, claiming that the French could not do anything dishonourable, either in his own country, or abroad, but is eventually persuaded by

Gaston and his uncle to accept the soldier's version. The film ends with Bernard and his parents leaving the village. Their car is driven through a crowd of woodworkers, taking part in a protest against the employers. Among them are Gaston, his uncle and the soldier, who was given shelter by the workers. Bernard, who observes the demonstration from the window of his car, shouts to his friends that he did not betray them to anybody. Thus, Jakubowska makes us believe that the seeds of socialist ideology were planted in the young organism thanks to the 'good gardener' Blachier. In a wider sense, the film conveys the idea that good surrogate (socialist) fathers are able to overcome the influence of bad (capitalist) home.

In other films the Party secretary acts both as an educator, moulding the young person in the spirit of Marxism-Leninism and as a matchmaker, introducing him to his future girlfriend or wife. Take Sekuła (Janusz Paluszkiewicz) in *A Generation*, who explains to a young worker Stach the principles of capitalist exploitation and introduces him to the young communist Dorota who becomes his flame. It is worth adding that the woman, who is more mature than the man, if not in terms of age, then politically, also takes the role of mother. We find a similar arrangement in *Under the Phrygian Star* where a young worker Szczęsny has an older communist mentor Olejniczak (Bolesław Płotnicki) and a girlfriend who is politically more experienced than him, and therefore behaves more like his mother than his girlfriend.

Both in Czechoslovak and Polish socialist-realistic films the surrogate father is a 'mature' father, often he could be the grandfather of his adopted son or daughter. The gap in age fulfils two functions. Firstly, it endows the older man with knowledge and experience that a man twenty or so years younger might not have. It is so important because the young socialist characters tend to be impulsive and hot-tempered. Take Szczęsny in *Under the Phrygian Star* who kills a spy without consulting anybody. His act is rational but it is against Party discipline and he realises it only after a conversation with the old comrade Olejniczak. Similarly, the young conspirators in *A Generation* want to fight the Nazis immediately, without proper preparation, thus committing themselves to an inevitable defeat. Secondly, in the case of male offspring the difference in age reduces the possibility that the father might compete with the child for the commodities he is after, such as a position of power or an attractive woman. If we employ psychoanalysis, we can come to the conclusion that the construction of the substitute father as an asexual figure on the brink of retirement removes the danger of Oedipal competition between father and son. It is also worth noting that typically the substitute father does not have children of his own, or at least they are not shown in the film, to avoid any competition between two sets of children: real and adopted.

This idealised image of substitute fatherhood did not last forever. The decline of socialist realism allowed for more realistic and critical depictions of men in father-like roles, as well as a gradual shift in interest from surrogate to real fathers. However, the surrogate fathers survived both in Polish, Czech and Slovak cinema, and can be found up to the present day, although their behaviour towards their 'children' changed. In the Czechoslovak post-socialist-realistic cinema the focus is on the surrogate fathers' lack of success in moulding the young generation according to the old principles, or even simply in helping them to fulfil their most basic desires and needs. We observe this phenomenon in two films by Ladislav Helge, *Škola otců* (*School for Fathers*, 1957) and *Velká Samota* (*Great Solitude*, 1959). In the first film a middle-aged Mr Pelikán (Karel Höger), takes a post as teacher in a village school. The pupils there have very good marks but Mr Pelikán discovers that this is not thanks to their talents or hard work but due to pressure exerted by parents and the educational authorities (and in a further instance, the Party – the ultimate 'mother and father') on the teachers and the headmaster to demonstrate their achievements. Mr Pelikán opposes such an approach and for the children's good gives them worse marks than his predecessor. Although in the end he wins the children's trust and respect, as well as the heart of a young and attractive colleague, he leaves the village in disappointment.

Figure 3.2 Karel Höger as Mr Pelikán in *Škola otců* (*School for Fathers*, 1957), directed by Ladislav Helge.

In Great Solitude a young Party enthusiast brings to a degree of prosperity a foundering cooperative farm by using dictatorial methods, but in so doing loses the affection and the confidence of the people. It is worth mentioning that the characters who occupy the positions of fathers in Helge's films are significantly younger than those in socialist-realistic films and here lies part of the responsibility for their failure. Being young, they lack the experience and patience their counterparts in the earlier films revealed. Similarly, their subordinates do not treat them with the same respect which they would show if they were twenty or thirty years older.

The role of fathers, real and surrogate, was reexamined in later films that looked at Stalinism with a critical eye. Such films were made predominantly in Poland in the 1970s and early 1980s, thanks to the easing of censorship. Examples are *Wahadełko* (*Shilly, Shally*, 1981), directed by Filip Bajon, and *Człowiek z marmuru* (*Man of Marble*, 1977), directed by Andrzej Wajda, which I will discuss in detail, *Matka Królów* (*Mother of the Kings*, 1982), directed by Janusz Zaorski, *Wielki bieg* (*Big Race*, 1981), directed by Jerzy Domaradzki, *Dreszcze* (*Shivers*, 1981), directed by Wojciech Marczewski and *Niedzielne igraszki* (*Sunday Games*, 1983), directed by Robert Gliński, almost constituting a genre of its own. By contrast, the severe post-invasion regime in Czechoslovakia did not allow any frank discussion about the late 1940s and the first half of the 1950s.

Bajon's film centres on a relationship between son Michał (Janusz Gajos), and his mother (Halina Gryglaszewska) whose devotion to the cause of communism made her a shock worker, exceeding the production norms many times but at the price of neglecting her children, especially her sickly son. She did not even spare her time to visit Michał in a sanatorium and ultimately caused his mental breakdown and prolonged incapacity. The film also addresses the communist attempt to project to children the figure of a political leader as the father figure. We see it in an imaginary scene opening the film, in which small Michał enters a large hall where Christmas celebrations unfold. There a man clad as Santa Claus hands him a Christmas present. The boy, however, shouts that he is not Santa Claus and pulls the artificial beard and moustache from his face. After that the man himself removes the remaining pieces of his Christmas attire, revealing that in reality he is Stalin (whose portrait is also hanging on the wall). Subsequently the fake Father Christmas pats the boy on his shoulder in a friendly manner. In the next scene, set in the present, a man is sweating in his bed and rubbing his shoulder, at the same place he was touched by Stalin, as if he wanted to get rid of any remnants of this contact. The nightmare indicates that the boy does not want Stalin to usurp the role of Santa Claus, normally taken by biological fathers. His outrage and fear, which do not disappear even after thirty years, can also be regarded as his yearning for a real father, not one imposed on him by the state. However, unlike Michał's yearning for a proper mother, which he fully realises and articulates, his desire to have a father remains unspoken and suppressed. During the course of the film we learn that Michał knew his father but it is hinted that he was an alcoholic, marginalised in his professional and family life. We can guess that he was an absent father who had ceded his parental duties to his wife and the state. In this way he avoided his son's hatred and his bitter love, all of which was invested in his mother, testimony of which is Michał's attempt to emulate her political career in communist organisations. The ultimate proof that the Stalinist approach to bringing up children did not work is Michał and his sister's childlessness. It could be argued that the metaphorical marriage of stakhanovite mothers with their sexless, political leaders produced a generation of degenerate and sterile children. Having said that, I want to draw attention to the difference between Michał and his sister. Although she is unmarried and possibly, as her brother alleges, sexually frustrated (one sign of which is her growing of phallic cucumbers), she comes across as less traumatised by the family situation and better adapted to adult life. Thus, it could be argued, Stalinism has a particularly destructive influence on the relations between fathers/parents and sons.

The eponymous 'Man of Marble' of Wajda's film, Mateusz Birkut, a shock worker from the 1950s, is a metaphorical Stalinist son in the vein of young protagonists of socialist-realistic classics, as he faithfully follows the ideas promoted by the Party leaders. He also becomes a metaphorical father once the authorities choose him as a hero of socialist work, to be immortalised on posters and statues, and emulated by succeeding generations. Wajda focuses on various fabrications and falsifications used in the process of producing a model superson and superfather. At the same time he shows that such a fabrication destroyed Birkut's family relations, including that with his own son, Maciek Tomczyk. The fact that Maciek does not even bear his father's surname but that of his mother suggests the gap between father and son caused by subordinating family ties to political ideas in Poland of the 1950s. However, unlike Bajon, Wajda shows that despite the gap there is also real connection and closeness. It is demonstrated by the son choosing a similar career to his father as a worker and political activist fighting for a better life for ordinary people in Poland and remaining honest and true to himself. Most importantly, as Anita Skwara notes, the resemblance of father and son's biographies is conveyed by Wajda's casting in the role of father and son the same actor, Jerzy Radziwiłowicz (Skwara 2006: 322). It feels as if by such a choice he is saying that ideologies come and go, binding and dividing people, but blood ties remain.

Shilly, Shally and *Man of Marble* do not have its obvious counterpart in Czech or Slovak cinema, namely a film that would look critically at Stalinist fathers. As the closest to this model I will regard *Larks on a String* (*Skřivánci na niti*, 1969–1990), directed by Jiří Menzel, Juraj Herz's *Spalovač mrtvol* (*The Cremator*, 1968) and *Pelíšky* (*Cosy Dens*, 1999) by Jan Hřebejk, despite neither of them being set during the period of Czechoslovak Stalinism. Other films that touch upon the problem of Stalinist fathers, including Stalin himself, although more obliquely, include *Josef Kilián* (1964) by Pavel Juráček and *Farářův konec* (*End of a Priest*, 1968) by Evald Schorm.

Larks on a String, set in the late 1940s, depicts various enemies of the communist state being reeducated through work on a scrapyard, and a trade union official (Rudolf Hrušínský), who takes the role of their substitute father, as well as mentor and leader of the wider community. Superficially, he is the man who acts for the welfare of his 'children', but his interventions only worsen their situation. He is responsible for increasing the smelting quotas of the workers till they go on strike, for which they are subsequently punished. He prevents the young couple, Pavel and Jitka, from making love after their wedding, by forcing Pavel to take part in a demonstration for some elderly activist. Finally, the trade unionist turns out to be a sexual abuser of a poor Gypsy girl whom he visits in her flat under the pretext of teaching her about hygiene.

The Cremator, which is based on the novel *Spalovač mrtvol* (1967) by Ladislav Fuks, is set before the Second World War and addresses the influence of Nazism on ordinary Czechs, but can also be seen as alluding to the impact of any totalitarian ideology, including Stalinism, on family and society at large. Herz himself encouraged such reading of his film by shooting a different ending of his film that included an image of the Russian occupation tanks passing through Prague. Of course, this ending did not find its way into the final version of the film for censorship reasons (Bird 2006: 8–9). In Herz's rendering of the totalitarian reality, personal relations are subordinated to ideological directives and even closest relatives are judged according to their value or usefulness to a certain ideological project, rather than cherished because of personal ties, not unlike in the famous story of Pavlik Morozov. As a result of adapting such an approach, the protagonist, Mr Kopfrkingl kills his wife and his son because he regards them as weak, racially impure (his wife is half-Jewish, therefore his children also carry Jewish blood), effete and useless. However, by killing his son, Kopfrkingl testifies to his own deficiency as a male and father. Interestingly, although Kopfrkingl manages to murder his son, he fails to kill his daughter; she escapes from her father's crematorium. Her survival, as the survival of Michał's sister in *Shilly, Shally*, confirms the idea that Stalinism proved especially damaging to sons.

Hřebejk's film, that was made after the collapse of communism, is set in Prague during Christmas 1967 and the days leading up to the Soviet invasion of Czechoslovakia on 21 August 1968. It focuses on two families, living in the same apartment block. One is headed by Sebek (Miroslav Donutil), a high-ranking military commander who is fiercely, indeed caricaturally loyal to the communist regime; the other by Kraus (Jiří Kodet), a veteran of the anti-communist resistance. Although the men have opposing political views, they are similar in being very authoritarian toward their offspring. They expect their teenage children, respectively a son, Michal and a daughter, Jitka, to follow in their footsteps. This does not happen, but not so much due to their opposing their fathers' opinions, as because they reject their autocratic style and show little interest in politics. It could be said that Jitka and Michal's world is anti-totalitarian: softer, more feminine, tolerant and heterogeneous. Jitka is very close to her sick mother, whom the father accuses of being a hypochondriac and plotting against him; Michal dreams about trendy Western clothes which his friend wears and decorates his flat with a poster of Mick Jagger – an icon of androgyny in the 1960s. Moreover, the children are friendly with each other despite the deep antagonism between the older men.

In contrast to the appearances of toughness, the fathers turn out to be juvenile, solipsistic and misled in their views. The dissident father builds models of war memorials to Czech pilots who died in the Second World War and keeps repeating that the 'Bolsheviks will lose in one, maximum two years'. The father who is a zealous communist has a penchant for inventions in culinary equipment by scientists from neighbouring countries and predicts that socialist science and economy will soon overtake their Western counterpart. However, like Kraus, Sebek proves wrong – the East German plastic spoons he buys melt in tea and 'unbreakable' glasses from Poland break. In *Cosy Dens* we also find the familiar motif of a father who is more fatherly toward the children who are not his than to his own offspring. This is the case with Kraus – he prefers the son of his new girlfriend than his own daughter. Hřebejk's fathers are represented caustically but they never come across as truly demonic or dangerous, as did Kopfrkingl. Andrew Horton explains the 'cosiness' of *Cosy Dens* by its being produced by the state-owned Czech Television whose productions are 'Central European cinema's answer to day-time television' (Horton 1999b), namely films that are populist and 'safe' to be watched by the whole family. Indeed, one believes that a truly Stalinist father, as well as a truly Stalinist son, is a creation not fit for such audience but rather for fans of psychological thrillers and horrors.

Generational Conflict in the 1960s

In Czechoslovak films of the 1960s the figure of the father gained particular prominence. Both substitute fathers and real fathers feature extensively in the Czechoslovak New Wave films. Their strong presence, however, can be attributed not so much to their importance per se, as to the preoccupation of this paradigm with youth, especially with the difficult passage from adolescence to adulthood, often resulting from the refusal of the protagonist to grow up. This refusal, that is typically treated with sympathy by the (often young himself) director, can be regarded as a metaphor for his rejection of socialism as an ideology that requires responsibility and maturity even from the youngest members of society (Liehm 1983: 213). Similarly, the father figure who attempts to prevent or at least contain the rebellious youth is usually criticised and ridiculed, or at least represented as ineffectual. Another reason why we find so many fathers and sons in the New Wave films, as opposed to mothers and daughters, is their sheer masculinism. As Petra Hanáková argues, 'the New Wave films–more often than the movies of earlier periods–generalise the man's story as a universal human story' (Hanáková 2005b: 63).

The films of Miloš Forman are an excellent illustration of a rebellious attitude on the part of the director (Škvorecký 1971: 79; Liehm 1983). We see it first in his medium-length debut films, *Kdyby ty muziky nebyly* (*If There Were No Music*, 1963) and *Konkurs* (*Audition*, 1963). In the first film the leaders of two amateur brass bands try to give a moral lesson to two young musicians who had put the pleasure of watching a motorcycle race above a rehearsal for an annual brass band competition. As a punishment for their lack of dedication they are expelled from the bands. However, the young men easily outwit their 'fathers' by each joining the band from which the other was expelled and receiving a warm welcome there.

Forman shows that the older men are not only ineffective in their educational efforts but they have no right to preach to the youngsters about the importance of 'their' music, because the music they are playing is mediocre. In reality, there is little difference between the motorcycle race and the fireman's ball where one of the bands is playing. It can even be argued that the race is of a higher quality than the band's performance as it offers the audience more thrill. Hence, in the conflict between older and younger generations it is the former that is mistaken. Forman conveys the superiority of the 'sons' over their 'fathers' not only through the construction of the narrative, but also visually. For example, one of the band conductors (Jan Vostrčil) is overweight and when conducting perspires heavily, cutting a rather comical figure.

In *Audition* older men are juxtaposed with young women who audition for a pop group. The men are the judges and the boss of a young hairdresser who sneaks out of her work to take part in the talent competition. The majority of the girls lack talent but despite that they come across as victorious, whilst their surrogate fathers prove less impressive. This is because the girls are full of energy and enthusiasm, unlike the authoritarian and conservative men.

If There Were No Music and Audition render the spectacle as a privileged type of a relation between the men of authority and their surrogate children. Children perform for their fathers to get good marks, fathers perform for their children to convince them of their superiority and deserve their respect. There is a lack of sincerity on both parts. Ultimately, Forman shows that basing one's relationship on performance precludes partnership and true understanding between the generations. However, members of the younger generation can be excused for pretending because they did not establish the rules of the spectacle. Their elders prepared the spectacles, therefore are to blame. The show performed by the young for the elder and vice versa can be regarded as a metaphor of the mode of communication between the socialist authorities and the citizens. Neither the socialist authorities nor the citizens are sincere towards each other, but it is the authorities that are mostly to blame for the inauthenticity of their relationship.

The relation between the young person and his father and other men of authority is rendered as a performance also in the next Forman film, *Černý Petr* (*Black Peter*, 1964). Petr (Ladislav Jakim) is a supermarket apprentice surrounded by older men who try to teach him how to live. His father is an overpowering figure who feeds his son with lengthy sermons about his own achievements and values, and his plans for his son. He does not hide the fact that he wants the son to imitate him, both in his general outlook on life and in specific situations. However, his advice is either unattractive for a young person or impractical, or even contradictory, which betrays the father's lack of any morals (Świętochowska 2003: 48). For example, the father admits that he had little pleasure in his life and had to thwart his views and emotions – in short, to be a conformist and a hypocrite – in order to achieve what he achieved. He gives Petr such tips as, 'Do not interfere in anything!', 'One is lucky who is near the manger!', 'Observe and be vigilant!'. These tips are not only repulsive due to their moral viciousness but also due to their contrast with the father's modest achievements: his rather unappealing apartment, an unattractive and unsophisticated wife and a son who ignores him. Typically the father stands or walks when Petr is sitting, which gives the impression that the father is the conductor of an orchestra instructing musicians. In fact, he is a conductor in an amateur brass band and he is played by Jan Vostrčil who was also the brass band conductor in *If There Were No Music* (and who in reality was a brass band conductor). Father's educating style is so intimidating that Petr never confides in him, only reluctantly replies to his questions. The boy's lack of confidence makes his father angry and further increases the distance between them. Thus, we observe a vicious circle of the father's intimidation, the son's rebellion (albeit a rather quiet one) and his withdrawal from meaningful communication, which feeds the father's anger and exasperation.

Petr's boss, the manager of the supermarket, not unlike his father, gives Petr little opportunity to express his opinion or show initiative. He does not listen to him, only gives him orders and critically comments on his behaviour. Moreover, the manager's advice is inconsistent, which points to the same lack of morals and hypocrisy that Forman exposes in Petr's father. For example, he tells his young employee that he trusts his clients but at the same time gives him the task of spying on them, because 'some people are stealing'. He also at one point claims that working in a shop is a good job, while later admitting that this occupation has become totally feminised and only boys who are complete idiots come to work there. It is worth mentioning that for Petr's father the feminisation of the retail sector means a greater chance for his son to be promoted. He correctly assumes that where there are many women working in a particular profession, the only man among them will be their boss (Scott 1976: 117–37). Nobody in the film questions such blatant sexism, contradicting the official socialist ideology of equal opportunities for men and women. Other older men also do not miss the chance to play the role of surrogate fathers for younger men, albeit for a short time. A man at a ball, for example, noticing that Petr is smoking a cigarette, tells him that he would beat him up if he was his father. The foreman of Petr's friend Čenda so severely criticises the boy for getting drunk that he reduces the young workman to tears. On the whole, the older men have little tolerance for weaknesses of the young, although they reveal those very vices that they criticise in the younger generation.

The mentality revealed by the generation of fathers in *If There Were No Music* and, to a greater extent, in *Black Peter*, bears resemblance to the mindset described by Václav Havel in his famous essay, 'The power of the powerless' and Miroslav Kusý in 'Chartism and "real socialism"' (Havel 1985; Kusý 1985). The core of Havel's reasoning is that Czechoslovak society of the period known as real socialism (that covers the time depicted by Forman in his Czechoslovak films) is post-totalitarian. He argues that the inner aim of the post-totalitarian system is not a mere preservation of power in the hands of a ruling clique (as is the case in classical dictatorship), but making everybody in the system complicit with its aims and its functioning. Even those at the very bottom of the political hierarchy are thus both its victims and pillars by almost automatically accepting and perpetuating the rituals prescribed to them by the ideology. By pulling everyone into its power structure, the post-totalitarian system makes everyone an instrument of a mutual totality, the auto-totality of society. Kusý in his article shows how the system successfully ties people's interests to the formal acceptance of the 'as if' ideology – to a 'silent agreement' between the powerful and the powerless. In this way, they both survive. Havel and Kusý point to the dependence of the system on citizens' willingness to live a lie. Havel links this willingness to being consumption-oriented, rather than being focused on preserving one's spiritual and moral integrity. 'The post-totalitarian system has been built on foundations laid by the historical encounter between dictatorship and the consumer society' (Havel 1985: 38).

Forman shows no trust in the older generation to liberate itself from the shackles of Czechoslovak socialism because it reveals all the features that Havel identifies as demanded by post-totalitarian rule: conformity, uniformity, discipline and hypocrisy, and which other authors identify as specific to the Czech or Central European mentality (Kroutvor 2001). The marches favoured by the 'fathers' in *If there Were No Music* and *Black Peter* perfectly encapsulate the first three values. Forman shows that the 'sons' might be different because they reveal opposite characteristics to their fathers, ones that Havel regards as pertaining to the aims of life: plurality, freedom, spontaneity. Thus, what unfolds on screen can be regarded as a struggle between life itself and post-totalitarian ideology. Off-screen Forman confirms this diagnosis, claiming in an interview given in 1968 that he chooses young characters because of their nonconformity (Kopaněnová 1968: 177). However, Forman's young people come into conflict with the older men not so much because they are purposefully rebellious, as because they focus on the present day and want to enjoy their lives. They are in conflict with their elders simply because they are young. In such a positioning of young people lies both a certain pessimism and the optimism of Forman's films. They are pessimistic because they predict that when the teenage 'Peters' of the 1960s reach their fathers' age, they will become like them: opportunistic, hypocritical and consumerist; and optimistic, because they suggest that there will always be a section of the Czechoslovak population that will not succumb to the post-totalitarianism – the young generation. This ambiguity of the film's message is excellently conveyed by the ending of *Black Peter* which presents a frozen frame of Petr's preaching father: a sign of the neverending preaching of the older Czechs, but also of the chance of young Czechs to switch themselves off. From the current perspective we can say that Forman was right on both accounts. His 'Peters' created the conformist, consumerist society of the 1970s and 1980s. Yet, in the next decade this country also demonstrated its ability to break with the old ways, largely thanks to the efforts of the younger generation (Holý 1996: 145–8).

The way Forman represents young males in his first two films bears similarity to the way which, according to Laura Mulvey, women are portrayed in mainstream movies (Mulvey 1975). They are typically looked at by those in power while themselves are too shy to return their look. They are talked to, while they themselves are (almost) mute. They also remain outside the sphere of ideology and politics, perhaps because they are not aware of the advantages deriving from following certain political rules, especially from, as Kusý puts it, living 'as if'. In addition, their affinity for fresh air, for such pleasures as boating, sunbathing or even watching motorcycle races, situates them in the sphere of nature and outside culture. Hence, it could be argued that the lack of women in the New Wave films, to which Hanáková justly points, led to the young men taking women's place.

Forman's next film, *Lásky jedné plavovlásky* (*A Blonde in Love*, 1965) is set amongst the workers at a shoe factory. The very organisation of the factory attests to the patriarchal character of the socialist economy, masked by the rhetoric about championing women's cause by giving them the right to work. The factory employs hundreds of young women; only its manager (Josef Kolb) is male. Moreover, the work is manual, mechanical and low paid, and involves the uprooting and institutionalisation of its female work force; the young women live in a hostel, in cramped rooms where they are not allowed to receive male visitors. By contrast, the manager appears to come from the village where the factory is set and does not live in such conditions as his employees. Forman constructs the factory manager as a well-meaning and asexual 'father' who, unlike his socialist-realistic predecessors, does not have any ideological ambitions for 'his girls'; he simply wants them to be content, probably partly out of altruism and partly to avoid problems at work resulting from their sexual frustration. His recipe is to provide the young women with their 'mating' partners by inviting soldiers to take part in a large party. However, he finds it difficult because of the very patriarchy of which he is a beneficiary. Firstly, he has to overcome the resistance of the army representative. Played by Jan Vostrčil, who largely repeats his character from Forman's earlier films, this man personally does not want to make such a decision, but prefers his superiors to decide – which points to the widespread malaise suffered by people living under socialism: passivity and fear of responsibility. Moreover, he cannot identify with the needs of the young generation, especially anything of a sexual nature. When the manager tries to explain to him that his employees want 'what all of us need', he appears not to understand, and when he finally grasps that the director is talking about sex, he makes it clear that he regards it as something which only refers to young people. The manager finally persuades the military man, and Vostrčil's character soon disappears from the picture, but the consequences of his blunder, in which he sends army veterans, rather than young soldiers, to the village, casts a shadow on all subsequent events. As a result of the lack of young men, one of the girls, Andula, ends up with the piano player at the party, and follows him to Prague. There she encounters another father – the father of her sweetheart Milda (Josef Šebánek). Unlike Vostrčil's characters, who come across as overbearing and intolerant, or the manager of the factory, who is energetic and practical, and despite his meagre stature commands some real power, the father of the pianist is completely emasculated and powerless. Short, balding and overweight, he comes across as a couch potato totally dominated by his nagging wife. Neither does he serve as a role model for his son who earns more than him (despite only starting his adult life) and is well aware of the father's inferior position towards his mother. The father of the pianist proves better disposed to Andula than his mother who is outraged by her visit, but it can be interpreted as a sign of his powerlessness and detachment from the family problems. As a person who makes no decisions about the household, he can afford to be friendly to a stranger and his friendliness does not change Andula's situation: she has to return home.

Such a diminished father as that of Milda's dad bears associations with Bly's 'modern father'. 'When a father sits down at the table', writes Bly, 'he seems weak and insignificant, and we all sense that fathers no longer fill as large a space in the room as nineteenth-century fathers did' (Bly 1991: 98). Bly argues that the weak father creates a problem for a son: how should he imagine his own life as a man? (ibid.: 99). Forman answers this question by portraying Milda as a man who tries to be everything his father is not: promiscuous, hedonistic, outgoing, able to charm and control women, interested in live entertainment rather than sitting in front of the television. However, if Milda can be regarded as an attractive model for a young single man, we cannot regard him as a viable model of a father. His behaviour towards Andula suggests that if she became pregnant with him (as Milda's mother suspects), he would try to escape any responsibility for his child and its mother. It is worth mentioning here that such a scenario was presented in a film made in Czechoslovakia several years earlier, *Tam na konečné* (*House at the Terminus*, 1957), directed by Ján Kadár and Elmar Klos. In this film a young female student meets a charming and worldly man with a penchant for parties, who appears to fall in love with her, but abandons her when she becomes pregnant and refuses to have an abortion.

The diminishing of fathers, as represented by Forman in *A Blonde in Love*, attests not only to the actual lifestyles and positions of Czechoslovak men in the 1960s, but also indicates the weakening of patriarchy as a basis of organisation of Czechoslovak society. Other signs of its crumbling include Andula's ex-boyfriend's Tonda illegal entrance to the dormitory where Andula lives, causing almost mayhem there, and the girls' attitude to the 'sex education' offered them by their matron. Superficially they agree with her preaching, according to which girls should not cheapen themselves by going to bed with men before marriage, but in reality they, not unlike young men, want fun and do not think much about their future. The crumbling of the 'Law of the Father', as shown by Forman, might be linked to his premonition of the Prague Spring, a movement that would overcome patriarchy Czechoslovak-style by creating a more egalitarian, less puritanical and hypocritical society, albeit only for a short while.

While in *A Blonde in Love*, and earlier films by Forman, the fathers, both biological and surrogate, function predominantly as individuals, in his last Czechoslovak film, *Hoří, má panenko* (*The Firemen's Ball*, 1967) he represents older men en mass. Similarly, he shows younger people acting together, although spontaneously. This shift is significant because such a representation allows us to see not only the vertical relationships between fathers and their children, but also fathers and their children in horizontal relations between themselves. Such a portrayal affords a better insight into the workings of Czechoslovak society as a whole (Horton 2000; Hames 2005: 126). Being firemen (an occupation which bears resemblance with such professions as soldiers and policemen) involves a significant amount of masculine authority, as only men could be firemen in Czechoslovakia. The director alludes to their patriarchal power by making them organise a grand ball, which in socialist countries was the preserve of those who were in the position of political power, not least because socialist ideology was hostile towards spontaneous festivity. The ball is meant to include the presentation of a ceremonial hatchet to their retired president and a beauty contest, of course for women. Again, the character played by Vostrčil gets centre stage, being the current president of the fire brigade. This time, however, he comes across as unsure of himself and disorientated, and has little power over the other firemen who disperse during the ball, each following his own agenda. This lack of leadership, unity and order has serious repercussions for the course of the event. The hatchet disappears and the beauty contest is marred by corruption and bribery, and ends in chaos, with an old woman crowning herself queen. As Peter Hames observes, although the girls who take part in the competition lack beauty and manners, in the end they prove more dignified than the lecherous and hypocritical men who surround them. They also appear to be more in control of their lives than the men who cannot deliver what they intended (Hames 2005: 121–3). The final blow to patriarchal authority and professional competence is their failure to extinguish a real fire. Thus, if the firemen stand for the Czechoslovakian (patriarchal) state, this is a state in utter disorder and decline. We can guess that it will show little resistance to a radical change exacted from below, by those who are marginalised and silenced: the young people and women, because they are unspoilt (or at least less spoilt) by corruption, greed and hypocrisy.

From the perspective of representing father–child relationships, Forman's Czech films offer a certain trajectory. This trajectory leads from all-powerful and self-confident fathers to fathers who are weak, disoriented, ineffectual and seeking children's attention and cooperation, and from children who are sheepish and only passively resist their fathers' power to children who openly reject their authority and make the older men feel redundant. Step by step Forman strips the older men of their authority, demonstrating that they owe it to patriarchal tradition and current political culture in Czechoslovakia, as opposed to their personal achievements and charisma. Consequently, it reveals patriarchy Czechoslovak-style as vulnerable, as proved by the Czech Spring.

Whilst Forman's films focus on the relation between older men and their teenage children, a number of Czech New Wave films deal with the problems faced by young fathers. Examples are *Návrat ztraceného syna* (*Return of the Prodigal Son*, 1966), by Evald Schorm, and *Křik* (*The Cry*, 1963), directed by Jaromil Jireš. Before I move to Schorm's film, it is worth mentioning that its director combined making feature films with documentaries and devoted some of the latter ostensibly to the problem of the purpose of life, which is also a central issue in his feature films. In *Proc?* (*Why?*, 1964) Schorm asks people why they do not want more children. This question and the answers he receives point, as Jan Žalman argues, to the 'conflicts between the declared wish of society and the undeclared facts of living standards' (Žalman 1968: 66). The society, or the state, wants people to proliferate to create a larger workforce to fill factories and cooperative farms. The people, however, do not want children, because they undermine their quality of life. Moreover, they are convinced that bringing children into a world full of conflict and chaos might be not a generous act towards the future generation. The pessimism, present in *Why?*, which the director himself regards as an important feature of his cinema (Branko 1996: 69) and which we can also find in his *Každý den odvahu* (*Everyday Courage*, 1964), permeates *Return of the Prodigal Son*. At the centre Schorm situates a young engineer named Jan (Jan Kačer) who is both the real father of little Klarka and a surrogate son for a number of men (and women). Jan experiences a profound crisis that leads to his suicide attempt and hospitalisation on a psychiatric ward. This crisis has several dimensions, including his strained relationship with his wife and her parents, as well as his refusal to work. The title of the film, alluding to the Biblical story of a the prodigal son, iconography, consisting of cars and other means of transport, and the narrative form, that can be described as 'travel cinema', afford the film a metaphorical dimension. It is clear that Schorm attempts to universalise Jan's condition, seeing in it that of every

Figure 3.3 Jan Kačer as Jan and Klara Kačerová as Klarka in *Návrat ztraceného syna* (*Return of the Prodigal Son*, 1966), directed by Evald Schorm.

man. However, what is more interesting for me is not Jan as an everyman, but as a young Czech.

For Peter Hames, Jan is mostly a victim of the lack of democracy in Czechoslovakia, and of his wife, as conveyed by such a statement: 'A basic problem in his life is his relationship with his insecure and neurotic wife Jana (Jana Brejchová). She is unable to help him face reality because she is incapable of doing so herself' (Hames 2005: 90–1). Jana has an affair when Jan is in hospital but I would not regard her as neurotic or blame her for Jan's withdrawal from reality. If there is anybody to blame for this unhappy state, it is Jan himself. He comes across as an immature individual who refuses to get on with his life and places blame for his own shortcomings on others. Although he is pampered by those around him (for example, his parents-in-law offer him the best food at the table and his work-mates organise a party to welcome him back to the office), he never gives anything to anybody. Even when he accepts his responsibilities, he does not act upon them. For instance, when Jana reproaches her husband for leaving all the housework to her, he accepts her arguments, but does so absent-mindedly, as if he were bored with his wife's prosaic complaints. On the other hand, he has demands, as shown in a scene with Jana, where he asks her to prove that she loves him by standing on her head.

Jan can be regarded as a symbol of a postwar generation of Czech and Slovak men that fell victim of a socialist nanny state that, by making their life easy, disrupted their passage from boyhood to adulthood. What would happen to Jan and others like him in a different, more challenging reality? Such a speculation is encouraged by Josef Škvorecký and Peter Hames who draw attention to Schorm's interest in Jerzy

Andrzejewski's *Ashes and Diamonds* and Wajda's film based on this novel (Škvorecký 1971: 141). Hames claims that the dark glasses Jan sports make him look similar to Maciek Chełmicki in Wajda's film (Hames 2005: 94).[4] Consequently, it could be argued that *Return of the Prodigal Son* is the story of the 'Maciek Chełmicki' who never took part in the war. If so, we can conclude that for Czech mutations of Polish 'Macieks' there is no hope of happiness. If they go to war, they would be killed, and if they live in peace, they will grow frustrated and alienated from society. Never having a chance to be soldiers, they prove unable to be fathers, husbands and workers.

Jana's lover, Jiři (Jiři Menzel) is represented rather as Klarka's new father than Jana's new partner. Therefore Jana's unfaithfulness, in my opinion, testifies not to her weakness, but rather to her resourcefulness, especially her desire to ensure that her daughter has a father, at least surrogate. Jiři puts the little girl to bed, tells her a fairy-tale and gives her a dummy. In this way he appears to be a more considerate father than Jan who usually shows his daughter little attention. Another surrogate father of Klarka is Zdenek, a circus artist and Jan's homosexual friend from the mental asylum, to whom Jan and Jana entrust their daughter when they go to discuss their affairs. Again, Zdenek proves to be a good companion for the little girl, showing her various tricks and making her laugh.

Schorm also gives Jan two surrogate fathers: his father-in-law and the psychiatrist (Jan's birth father is never mentioned). The former conforms to the model of the domesticated man, whose position at home is insignificant. He has little authority over Jan and his only chance to exert any pressure on his son-in-law is through Jana. The doctor, on the other hand, has a chance to become a figure of authority for the young patient, as revealed by their discussions about the meaning of life. However, not unlike fathers in Forman's film, the psychiatrist squanders his chance by being himself thwarted and dishonest. Although he tells Jan that life is worth living, he himself lives like a zombie, experiencing no stronger emotions. Work appears to him only a matter of mechanically repeating the same prescriptions. More importantly, there is no love left in his marriage, as reflected in his wife's search for romance with his patients. The marriage is also literally sterile, as they have no children. Jan seduces the psychiatrist's wife, or more exactly allows himself to be seduced by her, not unlike the mythical Oedipus. On the whole, the figures of his father-in-law and the doctor act as a warning for Jan, showing him what might happen to him if he follows their path. Emasculation of these men might even add to Jan's depression and refusal to live.

The Cry encourages comparison with *Return of the Prodigal Son* because it also employs a narrative form of travel cinema (or, more precisely, its European version) and casts as the main character a young man separated from his wife, this time, however, due to her stay at the maternity hospital where she is giving birth to their first child. Yet, unlike Jan in *Return of the Prodigal Son*, who belongs to the intelligentsia, Slávek (Josef Abrhám) is a member of the working class: he earns his living by repairing television sets. This job is furnished with erotic undertones; television repairmen have been associated with affairs with bored housewives ready for romance. Jireš plays on these associations but only to frustrate them. During his working hours Slávek meets women willing to be seduced, but he remains faithful to his wife. Moreover, like Jan, he encounters hypocrisy and hostility 'communist style'. The former is epitomised by the meaningless jargon employed by some party dignitary in whose office he repairs a television set. The latter we see most vividly in the scene of the harassment of a young black boy. Moreover, Slávek's wandering through the city is accompanied by excerpts from newsreels, 'giving a striking impression of the chaotic, uncertain, half-mad world into which the baby is to be born' (Žalman 1968: 64). Yet, these situations do not shake his optimism or make him anxious or withdrawn, but lead Jireš's protagonist to action, for example to standing in defence of the black boy. Waiting for the birth of his child also fills Slávek with reminiscences of the happy time he spent with his wife. It appears that the main reason for bringing new life into the 'half-mad world' is to make the child part of a loving family. Slávek's honesty and simplicity make us believe that love can counterbalance the hostility and madness of the wider world. At the same time as making us enchanted with young, innocent and idealistic parents, Jireš hints at the pitfalls of family life: routine, lack of freedom, overwork, as at the scene on the maternity ward when an older mother complains to Slávek's wife Ivana that before going into hospital she had to do extra cleaning and cooking for her husband. Her complaint makes us think that to be a husband and father in Czechoslovakia is merely to fulfil a decorative function; the real work of parenting is done by women.

When Polish films from the 1960s represent the father–son axis, they depict it against the background of a love affair. Typically the father and son are interested in the same woman. Consequently, the conflict between generations comes across as more serious and difficult to overcome than in Czech films. Whilst Czech cinematic fathers act in, however misguided, good faith, trying to further the son's position in the world, with regards to Polish films this assumption cannot be made. The fathers are often their sons' worst enemies and vice versa. This rule applies mostly to films about surrogate fathers, but hostility is also present in natural families. The difference can partly be explained by different genres used by respective filmmakers. Czechoslovak directors mostly use comedy to interrogate the relationship between older and younger men; Polish ones inscribe it into the structure of thriller or psychological drama. This difference can also be attributed to political and ideological factors, namely the filmmakers' perception of different generations competing for the same goods, rather than settling for what the authorities allocate to them. This competition, which is barely present in Czechoslovak films of the 1960s, in my opinion, bears testimony to Polish society of this period being less egalitarian and more economically polarised than its southern neighbour; a feature confirmed by sociological research (Scott 1976; Holý 1996).

The first Polish film that exposes the hostility between surrogate father and son with full force is *Nóż w wodzie* (*Knife in the Water*, 1961) by Roman Polański. Andrzej (Leon Niemczyk), the middle-aged owner of the yacht where the film is set, invites a young student (Zygmunt Malanowicz) to accompany him and his wife Krystyna on a sailing expedition on the Mazurian lakes. Andrzej ascribes the guest the role of his surrogate son who should respectfully learn from his 'father'. Instead, the young man appropriates the role of an Oedipus, seducing his 'mother' and

Figure 3.4 Leon Niemczyk as Andrzej and Zygmunt Malanowicz as student in *Nóż w wodzie* (*Knife in the Water*, 1961), directed by Roman Polański.

disposing of his 'father' who is left in the deep water searching for the student whom he deems drowned (Wexman 1987: 28). This unfortunate scenario is mostly of Andrzej's own making. Contrary to the impression the older man tries to give, he does not really want to teach the student useful skills, but only to gain control over him and humiliate him in front of his wife. If he can be compared to a father at all, then only to an abusive parent who takes revenge on his children for the wounds inflicted on him by the world.

Knife in the Water was interpreted as a metaphor of a young Polish citizen's rejection of socialist authority that is paternalistic, hypocritical and inept, of a political system that pretends to have authority, whilst in reality possesses only power. However, although Polański puts greater blame on the 'father's' sins, his 'son' is also far from innocent, proving disloyal and contemptuous towards Andrzej. Moreover, there is an aggressive edge to him, signified by the knife he carries with him. Although Polański shot his film shortly before the Czech New Wave began, the living standard of his characters, marked by the Western car the couple drive to the Mazurian lakes, the yacht and its luxurious furnishings, has no equivalent in Czech films of the 1960s. Hence, it could be argued that whilst in the eyes of Czech sons their fathers are losers not worthy of emulating, for Polish sons the fathers constitute models. They must be imitated or overthrown for the young generation to gain similar prosperity and power because, as Polański points out in his film, material wealth and positions of power are very scarce in Poland. As the student notes, there are only a handful of Western cars on Warsaw streets and only one yacht on the entire Mazurian lakes.

Mój drugi ożenek (*My Second Marriage*, 1963) by Zbigniew Kuźmiński casts as the main character the farmer Marcin (Mariusz Dmochowski), with a teenage son. After the death of his wife Marcin faces the choice of marrying a poor widow or a richer, younger and more attractive woman. His son wants him to choose the older and less attractive woman, but Marcin opts for the younger girl, despite her having a bad reputation and being pregnant by another man. Although ostensibly economic factors are at the fore of Marcin's marital plans, it could be argued that his decision is imposed by his fear of being defeated by his son in the sexual game. Similarly, the son's disapproval of his father's choice of wife can be seen as deriving from the Oedipal anxiety that he will be forced to compete with his father for a woman and, whoever wins this competition, it will have deadly consequences for the father–son relationship.

'Holy Family' after the New Waves

During the period of 'normalisation' the family remained a privileged zone for Czech and Slovak filmmakers. Its significance even increased. This was partly due to heavier censorship, which prevented filmmakers from dealing openly with contentious political subjects, and partly to the character of life during this period, when the vast majority of Czechs and Slovaks withdrew from political and indeed, any communal life into the private space of their houses as the only place they perceived to be sheltered from state. Thus the chasm had grown between public and private space (Holý 1996: 16-30; Booth 2005: 43–4). The increased domesticity, encouraged by the political authority, impacted more on Czech and Slovak men than women because domestication was the accepted cultural norm for women anyway (Booth 2005: 43–4), making the men feel out of place, emasculated and powerless.

Jaroslav Papoušek's saga about the Homolkas is an important work both in terms of representing family relationships, including that between father and son, and as a bridge between the Czechoslovak New Wave and post-New Wave cinema, not least because Papoušek wrote scripts for some of the most important New Wave films, such as Forman's *Black Peter* and *A Blonde in Love* and Ivan Passer's *Intimní osvětlení* (*Intimate Lighting*, 1965) (that will be discuss in detail in Chapter 5). In *Ecce homo Homolka* (1969), Papoušek introduces us to the Homolkas, who are an extended family consisting of the grandparents (Josef Šebánek and Marie Motlová), parents Ludva and Heduš (František Husák and Helena Růžičková) and their twin sons of about six, Mata and Peta (twin sons of Miloš Forman of the same names), living in one flat in Prague. Nobody in this family has any space of their own and each member of the family has only a choice to be with different members of the family. Whilst this is not a source of conflict as such, it exacerbates all conflicts as nobody has a chance to reflect on their behaviour and cool down their emotions. The lack of personal space and claustrophobia is underscored by the motif of locking the door. First the grandfather is locked up by the grandmother as a punishment for undoing the bed in an act of anger, then the son locks himself up to detach himself from the conflict, and eventually the children lock themselves to emulate their elders.

Papoušek's film has a musical structure, with characters one by one taking central stage, as well as performing ensemble with the rest of the family. This allows more accurate presentation of the dynamics between various members of the family and the impact of performing particular roles. We learn that the Homolkas are divided along gender lines. Ludva emulates his father; Heduš, albeit to a lesser extent, her mother-in-law. The most conspicuous feature of the men is their desire to have fun together, away from women. They grow frustrated when their efforts to achieve this goal are doomed. When Heduš does not allow Ludva to see a football match because she wants the whole family to go to the horse races, he gets drunk. Similarly, the grandfather gets angry when his wife does not allow him to smoke in the bedroom. For the men, their ability to enjoy themselves is the main index of their masculine power. It could be argued that such a construction of masculinity was a consequence of the sociopolitical situation in Czechoslovakia, namely the reduction of the opportunities for self-fulfilment and participation in the public sphere. However, their efforts of male Homolkas to be 'masculine' are continuously thwarted by women. The grandmother locks her husband in the bedroom, telling him that she will only let him out after he makes the bed that he undid in an act of anger. He tries various tricks to avoid her requests, but when they fail he resigns himself to doing as she requested.

The grandfather is played by Josef Šebánek, who previously played Milda's father in *A Blonde in Love*, confirming his appearance as a man fighting against but ultimately overpowered by his wife. By extension, it corroborates the impression that Czech fathers are not patriarchs, but emasculated and domesticated men.

Figure 3.5 Helena Růžičková as Heduš and František Husák as Ludva in *Ecce homo Homolka* (1969), directed by Jaroslav Papoušek.

Domestication of Czech men does not mean, however, that they are represented as 'new men' as this concept is understood in the West, taking responsibility in equal measure for housework and bringing up children. Papoušek shows that the bulk of domestic work, including cooking, cleaning and looking after the children, is still done by women. As a result men come across as parasites or at best as trophies for which women fight among each other. We see it most acutely in the scene when the Homolka women dispute whom Ludva loves more, his wife or his mother.

Despite all the tensions and frictions and each member of the family claiming at some point that they are unhappy and their lives are wasted, the Homolkas do not come across as miserable or dysfunctional. It rather feels like their lives are a mixture of small problems and joys. Moreover, despite their lack of ambitions and achievements, they are not devoid of pride, which is located predominantly in the youngest generation; they believe they did all they could for the two small boys and the boys will make up for their shortcoming. Images of the Holy Family, decorating their house, on which they comment in the course of their conversations, suggest that the Homolkas perceive themselves as descendants of Christ's family (Waczków 1970: 8). Another source of their pride is their conviction that they are paradigmatic of Czech or even Czechoslovak society, as expressed by the grandfather who at one point says, 'I am the state'. Although this statement is treated with derision by the remaining members of the Homolka family, the director appears to endorse Mr Homolka's claim. Even the fact that he names his characters Homolka, which can be translated as Czechoslovak or Czech man, testifies to regarding them as the ultimate Czechs.

Ecce homo Homolka is a liminal film, rooted in the Czech New Wave and at the same time belonging to the cinema of 'normalisation'. The reason for its liminality is not only the date of its production but also the way it represents relations between older and younger generations, namely emptying it of any signs of the sons' rebellion against their fathers. Unlike in *A Blonde in Love* or *The Firemen's Ball* the children here do not attempt to taste freedom – they put up with their parents. It might be to do with the fact that they are older and better know their own limitations, or with the fact that the neo-Stalinist times are less conducive to rebellion. As I implied earlier, conflict between generations is largely replaced by war between the sexes. Father and son keep together, because they know that their women are against them. What also strikes one in Papoušek's film, when compared with the films of Forman or *Intimate Lighting*, is the lack of communal spirit. The Homolkas are a microcosm which does not interact with the outside world. The famous large balls where the young generation can meet their peers, assert their group identity and difference from their elders, are here replaced by domestic pleasures, most importantly watching television. Actually, the Homolkas do not watch television but not because they do not want to, but because their television set is broken. Indeed, Papoušek implies that if not for the failure of the television set, they would all be content.[5] It is worth mentioning that television had very bad connotations in Czechoslovak and Polish anti-communist discourse. It was condemned as a transmitter of lies, as in the Polish anti-communist slogan from the first period of Solidarity, 'Television lies' (which paradoxically points to the failure of communism as a means of propaganda). Television is also seen as an instrument of disintegration of identity, of changing the individual into a passive consumer, a member of a herd, easily lulled, manipulated and ultimately morally barren. The last assertion, as Robert Pynsent observes, frequently appears in Havel's writings (Pynsent 1994: 23–5). We can infer that Papoušek shares some of the criticisms Havel directs to television and consumer culture in a wider sense. For example, in the first scene of the film he alludes to the indifference and the herd mentality of Czechs by showing everyone visiting the woods running away when they hear a woman crying, possibly because she is raped. Yet, he also sees in consumer culture good points, such as providing human beings with (simple) pleasure, a value which the austere anti-communists such as Havel reject.

The two following instalments of the Homolka saga perfectly illustrate the social trends captured by *Ecce homo Homolka*, namely the relative cohesion of the average Czech family and its preoccupation with consumption. In *Hogo fogo Homolka* (1970) we encounter the Homolkas at the moment they acquire a new Skoda. This purchase, which in the 1970s testified to above-average prosperity, makes them so happy that the grandfather announces that 'from now on our life will be a fairytale'. After playing tourists for a while in Prague, visiting the Charles Bridge and the airport, and squabbling about where to go, they decide to visit the parents of Mrs Homolková (Ludva's grandparents). This visit, on the one hand, testifies to the importance of the intergenerational ties for ordinary Czechs, but on the other, to the younger generation treating their parents and grandparents as a heavy burden. When the Homolkas reach their destination, the father of Mrs Homolková is not there. He is at a hunting festival, after which he starts drinking with his friend and misses his relatives. They, annoyed by his absence, complain that their sacrifice is not appreciated and that they wasted their time that might have been spent on attending a football match. On the way home they stop to see the place where Mrs Homolková almost drowned when she was a child and one by one jump into the water. Not far from this spot the old man, exhausted from his drunken spree, collapses and probably dies without seeing his daughter. Although this conclusion is far from cheerful, *Hogo fogo Homolka*, in common with the first part in the Homolka saga, does not come across as a film about a crisis of the Czech family, but rather its strength and stability. Again, it feels as if for the Homolkas there is nothing in life but family; it is their only interest and purpose in life.

The last part of the Homolka saga, *Homolka a tobolka* (*Homolka and his Suitcase*, 1972) confirms this diagnosis. The Homolkas go on holiday to the mountains; this being their next step on the road to affluence. There two families want to exchange their rooms with them, because they were given one large room, rather than two separate ones. Although initially the Homolkas reject the offer of exchange, as the holiday gives them a chance to be together but separately and enjoy some privacy, in the end they agree, bribed with money and compliments. This exchange points to their greed, as well as to the fact that they do not need their privacy very much, they are happy together, all six of them, wives and husbands, children, parents and grandparents. The series of films about Homolka, in which little changes over a number of years apart from the growth in the living standard of the eponymous family, constitutes for me a paean to the stability and health of the average Czech family. This effect is remarkable because Papoušek does not attempt to idealise his characters but instead focuses on their shortcomings.

Polish films of the 1970s about fathers and sons (real and surrogate) are dominated by the figure of a competitive and vicious father, familiar from *Knife in the Water* (Radkiewicz 2005). We can argue that in his only 'proper' Polish film (ironically in the times of its premiere regarded as un-Polish) Polański created a genre of his own that stayed in Polish cinema for good. Not surprisingly films of this kind erupted in the period known as 'the decade of the propaganda of success', when Edward Gierek was the Party leader. In this period Poland opened itself up to Western influences and became more consumerist and less egalitarian. The old socialist principle that citizens should roughly earn and possess the same amount of material assets was practically abandoned. Especially the Party dignitaries and those close to them (*nomenklatura*), as well as the new class of private entrepreneurs, became associated with obscene wealth and consumerist pleasures unattainable to ordinary citizens, instead feeding their frustrations and anger.

The imbalance between the goods to be achieved and the number of people aspiring to them, and the widespread (and not irrational) conviction that not necessarily the best person wins in Poland, created fierce and dishonest competition. Consequently, the 1970s are perceived as a time when Poles could gain much more in material terms than in any other postwar decade, but only by paying a heavy price for their affluence in terms of morality: betraying friends, family and values. The competition took place both between peers and, more often, along the generation boundaries, leading to mutual distrust and hostility. The state aggravated the generational conflict by promoting youth in its propaganda (because old people were associated with antiquated customs and bourgeois ideas), whilst in reality positions of power were occupied by the 'fathers', of which the most striking example was the Party itself, governed by people in their fifties and sixties.

The competition between younger and older men is especially prominent in the films belonging to the Cinema of Moral Concern, the main movement in Polish cinema of the 1970s. However, before I discuss some of the examples I want to consider one of the last films of the previous decade, *Polowanie na muchy* (*Hunting Flies*, 1969), directed by Andrzej Wajda. There are several reasons to consider it here. Firstly, its subject matter, visual style and ideology bear resemblance with some examples of the Cinema of Moral Concern. Secondly, it is a rare Polish film that represents an urban multigenerational family, therefore it invites comparison with *Ecce homo Homolka* which was made the same year. Thirdly, the main role of the young husband Włodek is played by Zygmunt Malanowicz, whom Polański cast as the student in *Knife in the Water*. Włodek was Malanowicz's most important role following Polański's film and in *Hunting Flies* his character refers on many occasions to his life as a student, so one is tempted to regard Włodek as the older version of Polański's protagonist. If so, did Włodek surpass people like Andrzej? My answer is negative. Not only does Włodek not have a yacht and a foreign car, but he has no car at all, and lives with his wife, his son and his in-laws in a small apartment whose crampedness is heightened by Zygmunt Samosiuk's cinematography. He and his wife Hanka wait for a cooperative flat but it is suggested that it is the wife's parents who are paying the instalments for it. At home, unlike Ludva, for whose favours his wife and mother compete, Wajda's protagonist does not attract much affection from the women in his life. Hanka reproaches him constantly for not visiting the cooperative to push their case, as well as for not earning enough. The mother-in-law suspects him of breaking glasses and other 'petty crimes'. Moreover, the family treats him as a weakling as signified by getting vitamin injections from his wife who is a nurse. When he pulls down his pants and lies on the sofa, waiting for the injection, he seems to be totally defenceless and waiting to be castrated. At the same time, there is much less rapport between Włodek and the oldest man in the house, perhaps because Włodek is not his natural son, only son-in-law. The two men hardly speak to each other; the grandfather spends his days watching television while Włodek taps on his typewriter. The centre of everybody's attention is the youngest member of the family, Włodek and Hanka's son, whom everybody regards as exceptionally intelligent – as we might guess, in contrast to his father. For this clever child the role model is not his father but grandfather who fought in the war. He recites his war stories, and although his renditions sound slightly humorous, they convey the boy's sense of pride and identification with his grandfather. Because the younger couple wait for their own flat and have even bought some furniture for it, life with their in-laws appears very temporary and unsatisfactory, more so than the young Homolkas who have resigned themselves to living with the older generation. At the same time, Wajda is keen to emphasise that Włodek and Hanka are not very young. Włodek in particular looks as if more than eight years had passed since his younger version cruised on the Mazurian lakes in *Knife in the Water*.

Why did the student from *Knife in the Water* achieve so little in life? According to the prevailing interpretation of *Hunting Flies*, it happened because women thwarted him (see Głowacki 1969; Kajewski 1969; Chapter 4). In my opinion, however, women such as Hanka, Włodek's lover Irena and his female boss, although unsympathetic and caricatured, try to help Włodek to further his career and achieve something in life. If Włodek fails, it is not because women are standing in his way to self-fulfilment but rather because the older men do not stimulate him, and the younger regard him as a threat to their position or are too narcissistic to invest any interest in him. The second phenomenon is illustrated in an episode when Włodek approaches Irena's charismatic friend and ex-lover Ołubiec and tells him about his frustrations and ambitions, only to be told in the end to 'sod off'. The whole high society, which Włodek aspires to since befriending Irena, is depicted as utterly snobbish, mercenary and hypocritical. Nobody there is doing anything for free, all relationships are based on a precise assessment of whether the person can help in one's career. This statement refers principally to men; women ultimately prove less selfish than their partners. It even feels that they are able to sacrifice themselves to help their men, as do Irena and Hanka for Włodek. Yet Włodek rejects their sacrifice, not because he wants to achieve everything by himself but because the women's emotional investment in him lays bare his numerous inadequacies. Wajda suggests that Włodek's attitude might be widespread among men by including, in the key scene of the party for Warsaw intellectuals, snobs and noveaux riches, a male musical band who during their performance start to cry while singing 'O Mother, mother, what I am doing here?'

Films about surrogate fathers blossomed in the Cinema of Moral Concern, a movement of the second half of the 1970s, finishing symbolically in 1981, when martial law was announced. They conveyed the spirit of competition between old and young pertaining to this period and, as Dobrochna Dabert maintains, the need to find a stable value system in a world permeated by moral relativism (Dabert 2003: 107–15; see also Kornatowska 1990: 171–92). There are several types of surrogate fathers in this cinema. One is the 'perfect' surrogate father, best represented by John Lasocki (John Gielgud) in *Dyrygent* (*Conductor*, 1979), directed by Andrzej Wajda, and Karlik Habryka (Augustyn Halotta) in *Paciorki jednego różańca* (*Rosary Beads*, 1979), by Kazimierz Kutz. Lasocki is a famous Polish expatriate conductor, living in New York, who returns to Poland to guest-conduct a provincial orchestra. He immediately gains the trust of the musicians, who are inspired by his modesty and genuine love of music, contrasting with the attitude of their usual conductor for whom music is only a passport to career. Habryka is an old Silesian miner who refuses to move from his old house to a block of flats. Although, as Dabert notes, Habryka is not a role model for his own children who are very pragmatic about where they live, he represents authority for his grandson (Dabert 2003: 108). Neither Lasocki nor Habryka belong to mainstream Polish society. They normally live either outside Polish space (Lasocki) or time (Habryka) (on Kutz's character see Mazierska 2000: 184–5). Being detached from the problems of ordinary Polish people, they constitute a utopian model that cannot be emulated by their 'sons'. However, they are presented as important to them thanks to bringing moral anxiety in their lives and in this way helping them to discern between right and wrong.

The second type of surrogate father created by the Cinema of Moral Concern is a man who uses the success of his 'sons' to further his own career or substitutes their successes for his own victory. We find a paradigmatic example of such a father in *Szansa* (*Opportunity*, 1979) by Feliks Falk – a teacher of physical education named Janota (Krzysztof Zaleski) who, on being employed in a provincial college, attempts to make his subject a peak of the school curriculum. He achieves his goal but at the heavy price of forcing students to neglect other subjects, even blackmailing and tormenting them and leading one pupil to suicide, as well as antagonising other teachers, especially the gentle head of history. There is no doubt that Janota is not a man of spotless character but rather than demonising him, Falk accuses for his sins the harsh reality of the 1970s that does not allow ambitious men such as Janota flourish. There is no doubt that if the teacher used moral means to fulfil his objectives, he would be ineffectual.

The third and largest category of substitute father consists of men who are in positions of authority over younger men (or women) and are shown respect and trust by their 'children' but betray their trust. It happens because they turn out to be too selfish or weak to measure up to the expectations of a younger generation. Dabert labels men of this kind as possessing 'false authority' (Dabert 2003: 110-2). We find them in *Aktorzy prowincjonalni* (*Provincial Actors*, 1978), directed by Agnieszka Holland, *Przypadek* (*Blind Chance*, 1981), directed by Krzysztof Kieślowski, *Barwy ochronne* (*Camouflage*, 1976), directed by Krzysztof Zanussi, *Matka Królów* (*Mother of the Kings*, 1982), directed by Janusz Zaorski and *Wielki Szu* (*Big Szu*, 1982), directed by Sylwester Chęciński. The men of false authority can be further divided into two groups. In one we find the old communists, such as Werner (Tadeusz Łomnicki) in *Blind Chance*. He comes across as a decent man, bearing a resemblance with the father figures of earlier Polish films, such as Olejniczak in *Under the Phrygian Star* and Szczuka in *Ashes and Diamonds*. However, his advice to trust the Party does not do the young man any good, because the Party is disgraced; joining it equals morally polluting oneself. Consequently, the 'communist father' from the films of the 1970s and 1980s proves to be a less charismatic and sympathetic figure than his predecessor in the films made twenty or so years earlier.

The second subcategory of men of false authority is comprised of narcissistic men who use their 'sons' as pawns in advancing their careers or as a means to boost their fragile egos. Sometimes they come across as deeply ambiguous characters in which cynicism combines with yearning for the idealism and honesty which the young men epitomise and which they themselves have lost. Such an ambiguous character is Jakub Szelestowski (Zbigniew Zapasiewicz), a well-established, middle-aged academic, who takes the role of mentor of Jarosław Kruszyński (Piotr Garlicki), his much younger colleague who is only beginning his academic career. Szelestowski attempts to demonstrate to Kruszyński that Polish academia is nepotistic and corrupt and if he wants to stay there and advance on the social ladder, he has to give up his idealism. However, it is not clear whether he does it to save Kruszyński from humiliation by people who are less well-disposed to him, and in this way help him to make a less painful transition to adult life, or to impress him with his insider's knowledge of academia, or to justify his own behaviour in the eyes of the younger man and his own. It is also possible that, as Dabert argues, deep down Szelestowski remains an honest and sensitive man and only plays an opportunist to test the moral conscience of Kruszyński (ibid.: 116). All these motivations are plausible. What is beyond doubt, however, is that Szelestowski comes across as a poisonous father, who destroys his son's good opinion about the world and himself.

In the 1970s and 1980s Zanussi also became the leading film author to explore relations within real families, again focusing on the father–son relationship. In *Życie rodzinne* (*Family Life*, 1970) and *Kontrakt* (*Contract*, 1980) the main issue is the sons' right and ability to lead an independent life, away from their overbearing, but also lonely and ultimately vulnerable fathers. In *Family Life* a young engineer, Wit Braun (Daniel Olbrychski), informed that his father is dying, returns home where his father (Jan Kreczmar) lives with his sister in-law and an adult daughter, Bella. Before the war the father owned a large glass works that he inherited from his father of German origin. Now he has only a small and unprofitable workshop producing Christmas decorations that recently declined further due to an accident he caused. Bella makes clear to Wit that they survive by selling the family's possessions: antique furniture, paintings, even the garden. The decline of the Brauns' estate is matched by the decline of the family itself. The father is an alcoholic who brews alcohol illegally in his workshop, Bella is a nymphomaniac who was previously sent to jail for 'debauchery', Wit and Bella's mother left home a long time ago to live abroad and the aunt is reduced to being their servant. The father wants Wit to stay at home and take over his business, appealing to his sense of duty and luring him with the prospect of having his own car, but the son refuses and leaves his family for good, to continue his life in Chorzów, an industrial town which epitomises the success of Polish postwar industry. Yet there are ambiguities in the resolution of Wit's crisis, and the viewer cannot be sure that Wit has left his past behind completely. For example, aboard the train back to Chorzów, 'Wit is suddenly aware of an uncontrollable twitch in his eye and recognises it as a prominent physical trait of his father. Thus this determined young man who has defied his bourgeois past and put his stock in the proletarian future is nonetheless aware that his conversion to a new class identity was perhaps less than complete' (Paul and Fox 1983: 121).

Several times the characters refer to the socialist policy of nationalisation that led to the economic and moral decline of the Brauns, destroying the 'Bly paradise' where sons learnt their craft from their fathers. Beyond their garden, on the grounds that previously belonged to them, there is now a new housing complex, comprising typical socialist blocks of flats that thwart their estate and factory. However, through the mise-en-scène, Zanussi demonstrates the superiority of the new, socialist mode of living over the old, aristocratic one. In particular, Wit's friend Marek (Jan Nowicki), with whom he visits his home and who is of peasant's origin, comes across as mentally more balanced and happier than Wit. It is largely through his eyes, those of an educated parvenu, that we look at the Brauns. Moreover, whilst the Brauns appear unable to produce anything, either in the sense of material production or biological reproduction, the 'socialist classes' are represented as fertile and thriving. The construction office, where Wit and Marek work, is doing very well and even receives commissions from Indian investors that are mentioned in the television news. When Wit goes out in the evening for a walk and gazes at the windows of the flats in a block, built on the field that previously belonged to them, he sees a young family with a husband, wife and a child in a brightly lit room. There is a poignant contrast between this image and Wit's family that lurks in a shadow as a bunch of vampires. On the whole, although there is sadness about Wit's final departure, we feel that he makes the right decision.

In *Contract*, Zanussi centres on a man in his twenties named Piotr (Krzysztof Kolberger) who is getting married to a woman of his own age. Although nobody forces them to tie the knot, the young couple behave as if they are marrying to upset their parents who are affluent and influential. The peak of their rebellion is their decision to have a church wedding, although none of them is religious. This act is meant to embarrass their parents who are close to the political establishment. Although superficially the young man despises his father for corruption, snobbery and consumerism, of which the clearest sign is a spacious house near Warsaw where he lives with his second wife, a deeper motif of Piotr's resentment appears to be his conviction that without his father's help he will be unable to start an independent life. His anger, expressed by setting his father's house on fire, is thus an admission of his helplessness. If we regard *Family Life* and *Contract* not as a separate works, but as a kind of diptych representing the trajectory of a young Polish man during a different periods of socialism, then we can come to the conclusion that he had experienced infantilisation, changing from somebody able to leave his family home and take care of himself, to an individual who is incapable of leading an independent life and defines his fate and identity in relation to his father. This personal trajectory can be interpreted as a metaphor of the changing situation of young men over the decade of the propaganda of success. Ultimately, this trajectory testifies to the loss of social mobility of Poles.

In *Magnat* (*The Magnate*, 1986), Filip Bajon enters a similar territory as Zanussi in *Family Life*, representing a rich family with long traditions, led by Hans Friedrich von Teuss (Jan Nowicki), an aristocrat and industrialist, and a father of three sons, that disintegrates during the course of the twentieth century, partly because of the historical circumstances, especially the ascent of fascism, partly because of the idiosyncrasies of its members, leading to the abandonment of the traditional roles and relationships within the family. The measure of the von Teusses' transgression from the traditional model of the family is the fact that one of the sons has a quasi-Oedipal affair and later marries his father's second wife while the father is still alive. Although this event takes place before the Second World War, it can be regarded as symptomatic of Poland of the 1980s, when the hope of political and social transformation brought about by the brief victory of Solidarity was thwarted. This arguably led to the loss of any moral compass and consequently, to the breakdown of society, including the disintegration of its elementary cell – the family.

Family is also the main focus of the most famous Polish production of the 1980s, Krzysztof Kieślowski's *Dekalog* (*Decalogue*, 1988), a cycle of television films, each evoking a different commandment. This is not surprising as the purpose of most of the commandments is to regulate the private lives of believers. However, what strikes one is the level of transgression from the Christian norms that we find in the families depicted by Kieślowski. Betrayal, promiscuity, lying to one's partner and children, using members' of one's family to achieve selfish objectives, are rampant in them, not unlike in Bajon's *The Magnate*. As a result of these transgressions or, to use Christian terminology, sins, families disintegrate and fatherhood becomes problematic. For example, *Decalogue 2: Thou shalt not take the name of the Lord thy God in vain*, depicts a married woman who becomes pregnant with her lover while her husband is severely ill with cancer. She considers abortion but her decision in this matter hinges on her husband's chances of survival: she does not want to keep the baby if her husband remains alive. However, he almost miraculously recovers and becomes the father of a child who is not biologically his own. In *Decalogue 4: Honour thy father and thy mother*, a young woman, after discovering a secret letter written by her mother, begins to have doubts whether the father who brought her up single-handedly after the premature death of his wife is indeed her father. These doubts lead to an attempt to seduce her father, towards whom she had incestuous feelings even before she discovered the letter. *In Decalogue 7: Thou shalt not steal*, we find a six-year-old girl who thinks that her grandparents are her parents, and regards her biological mother as her older sister, and who does not know her biological father, who gave up on her a long time ago.

The characters in these films repeatedly ask questions such as 'Who is my father?', 'Who will be the father of my child?', 'Is the child, who thinks I am his father, really mine?', forcing the viewer to consider the very meaning of fatherhood. While mothers in these films, as Alicja Helman suggests, come across as strong and decisive, governed by their almost naked animal instinct, fathers are portrayed as weak and easily deprived of their offspring (Helman 1999: 124–5). To put it differently, Kieślowski shows that mothers always remain mothers, but fathers can stop being fathers very easily. Thus *Decalogue*, whilst establishing the ten commandments as a moral ideal towards which Polish people should strive, also demonstrates that in the apparently ultra-Catholic Poland of the 1980s the reality and even the concept of fatherhood deviated significantly from the ideas contained in the Catechism. One reason for this deviation appears to be the inhuman environment of the housing estate where Kieślowski's characters lead their lives. In such an environment human bonds disintegrate and the atmosphere of distrust and suspicion grows. Moreover, although Kieślowski does not refer directly to the martial state, his films accurately capture the stagnant atmosphere of the late 1980s, the period of one of the deepest crises in Polish society (on society after martial law see Lewenstein and Melchior 1992).

Deserters, Holy Men, Tyrants and 'Little Moles' in Postcommunist Films

The end of the communist era had a great impact both on the actual situation of men and women in Poland and Czechoslovakia, and the perception of gender roles in society. Crucially, postcommunism is associated with promoting in cultural discourses and implementing through political and legal means a conservative vision of society, in which men and women fulfil traditionally feminine and masculine roles. Most authors equate this phenomenon with the rise of masculinism in Eastern and Central Europe (Wolchik 1991; Kligman 1994; Watson 1993, 1996, 1997; Molyneux 1994, 1996; Gal and Kligman 2000; Graff 2001). For example, Peggy Watson regards this shift as a reaction to the politics and ideology of communism that was perceived as sympathetic to women and claims that it advantages men and disadvantages women.

> Traditional views of what 'normal' men and women are have acted as a vehicle for change in Eastern Europe, 'freedom' being associated with the freedom to more fully enact a traditional feminine or masculine identity, untrammelled by the constrictions of the socialist state. However, the changes which have been wrought now offer systematic advantage to men. Civil society means the empowerment of men and the enactment of masculinity on a grand scale. (Watson 1996: 217)

However, as Sharon Wolchik observes, many women in this region welcomed the return to conservative thinking about women and men's place, believing that it would help to overcome the uneven pattern of role change achieved during communist rule (Wolchik 1991: 204). My argument is that the shift towards the conventional approach to the division of labour between the genders within society did not have such a uniformly positive effect on men as Watson and others suggest. Indeed, we observe in the ex-Eastern bloc the rise of masculinism but at the same time a significant proportion of men acutely experienced the negative sides of the transformation which led them to regard the post-1989 period as worse than the times of socialism. The most negative and at the same time widespread of these side-effects was high unemployment (in Poland after 2000 in some periods exceeding twenty per cent). Unemployment affected men not less than women due to the disappearance of typically masculine jobs in heavy industry and high immigration to the West, especially after Poland, the Czech Republic and Slovakia joined the European Union. As a result of these factors 'postcommunist men' find it particularly difficult to fulfil the traditional masculine role of breadwinner, father and husband. Again, however, we should not overlook here the regional variations: the crisis of male employment was deepest in Poland, followed by Slovakia and the Czech Republic. Consequently, Poland was also most affected by mass migration in the 2000s.

While some men after 1989 have given up or postponed being fathers because they feel that they do not rise to the challenge of fatherhood on economic grounds, others have rejected it because such a role is in conflict with their chosen lifestyle of a single man, namely a man who avoids stable relationships with women. As Krzysztof Arcimowicz argues in reference to Polish postcommunist culture, the model of a single man is in vogue both among younger men and those in their thirties and forties, as it is associated with prolonged youth and complete control over one's life (Arcimowicz 2003: 212–15). The fashion for singlehood can be linked to the Westernisation of Central Europe, as suggested by adopting the term 'single' (*singiel* in Polish) to describe a man who chooses a single life. It could be argued that contemporary Polish, Czech and Slovak men are mimicking their Western colleagues by enjoying what Eve Sedgwick describes as 'ornamental culture' or even following them in rejecting patriarchy as an ideology that is more constraining than liberating (Ehrenreich 1995). Not surprisingly, men's refusal to be fathers, combined with women's anxiety about having children against the background of high unemployment, job insecurity and poverty, has led to further decline in the birth rate in Eastern Europe. After 1989, Poland and the Czech Republic were among the countries with the lowest birth rates in Europe, never exceeding 1.5 children per woman.

Polish, Czech and Slovak cinemas in the 1990s and 2000s reflect this trend of shunning fatherhood by rarely showing young fathers. Men in their twenties and thirties are usually single and they behave as if they were children themselves (see Chapter 4). We could also note an upsurge of men avoiding fatherhood in a more dangerous, even sinister way, by abandoning women who have children with them. Films including men of this kind or only alluding to them (because they are already absent when the young women count the weeks to the delivery of their babies) erupted in Poland, where the new abortion law, introduced in 1993, was particularly restrictive in comparison with the previous legislation, making abortion illegal in most circumstances (Fuszara 1993). We can list here *Wesele* (*The Wedding*, 2004), directed by Wojciech Smarzowski, *Ono* (*It*, 2004), directed by Małgorzata Szumowska, *Farba* (*Paint*, 1997), directed by Michał Rosa and *Nic* (*Nothing*, 1998), directed by Dorota Kędzierzawska. The young impregnator (Maciej Stuhr) in *The Wedding* attends the wedding of the woman who became pregnant by him, but not as the groom but only to video her wedding with another man. In *Patrzę na ciebie Marysiu* (*I Look at You, Mary*, 1999), directed by Łukasz Barczyk, a young man (Michał Bukowski), who previously appeared to be in love with his charming fiancée, becomes anxious and uncommunicative when she becomes pregnant. He has a total mental breakdown during the wedding, which can obviously be interpreted as a sign of his difficulty to reconcile the expectation of his family to behave 'decently' and his fear of fatherhood. Another young man, appropriately nicknamed 'Młody' (The Young One) (Rafał Mohr) in *Egoiści* (*The Egoists*, 2000), directed by Mariusz Treliński, gets drunk and drugged up when his fiancée is in labour, which is a sign of his neurosis caused by moving from the state of being single to becoming a father. The most drastic case of avoiding responsibilities of fatherhood is depicted in *Nothing*, in which the husband (Janusz Panasewicz) first threatens his wife that he will punish her if she does 'something stupid', and then pretends that he is unaware of his wife's pregnancy with their fourth child. The conclusion to his irresponsible behaviour is hiding when the wife gives birth in the bathroom and then kills their newly born baby.

The negative value of a child for young Polish men can also be measured by the handsome price mothers and their families have to pay men to make them agree to become fathers officially. For example, the groom in *The Wedding* marries a young woman pregnant with another man in exchange for an expensive gift of a sport's car from his wife's family. It is also suggested that 'Młody' in *The Egoists* agrees to marry his pregnant girlfriend because she has rich parents able to support his lavish lifestyle. Women must also lower their expectations when they become pregnant out of wedlock, for example by marrying the least attractive man in the neighbourhood, as was the case of the heroine of *Torowisko* (*Track-way*, 1999), directed by Urszula Urbaniak. With the exception of *Nothing*, whose author makes us aware of the presence of the absent father, so to speak, and his callous behaviour, in the remaining films the man who refuses the paternal role avoids any judgement. Consequently, the impression is given that, unlike motherhood that is a woman's duty, fatherhood is a man's right, which he can take advantage of as he wishes.

In the Czech Republic, where the abortion law did not change after the fall of communism, the motif of a man frightened of fatherhood is subdued but also present. In *Štěstí* (*Something like Happiness*, 2005), directed by Bohdan Sláma, we find Dasha, who has two small children with a man who, as her neighbour claims, abandoned her soon after the second child was born. The film starts when Dasha has an affair with another married man who, despite claiming that he loves her, does not want to take any responsibility for her and her children which leads to Dasha's mental breakdown.

When she ends up in a mental institution, pregnant with her third child, he installs in her old apartment his next, childless girlfriend. *Návrat idiota* (*Return of the Idiot*, 1999), directed by Saša Gedeon, presents the aftermath of an affair between a young woman and a man whose wife is pregnant. Although the circumstances of their encounter are not explained, one can guess that the lover gives the married man respite from the bonds of domesticity and alleviates his 'prenatal anxiety'.

Slunecní stát aneb hrdinové delnické trídy (*The City of the Sun*, 2005), directed by Martin Šulík, a Slovak director with a special interest in Czech topics, depicts four men made redundant after their factory is sold to a foreign company. Three of them have children and following their mothers' absence (one is an alcoholic, another works full time and the third one, who was previously a housewife, goes to hospital after an accident), they must look after them single-handedly. Although each man's circumstances are different, Šulík makes the point that full-time parenting does not come to them naturally; they have to overcome many external obstacles and internal barriers to reconcile themselves with this role. One of them fails, losing his sons and ending up in a psychiatric hospital. The men are best at playing with their children; providing for them, feeding them and acting as models for them proves much more difficult. Šulík makes us believe that there is a strong connection between man's general well-being and his ability to act as a father. A man 'injured' by unemployment, poverty or loss of a partner, finds it almost impossible to cope with paternity. In this respect women prove much stronger; they can better juggle many social roles.

As if to balance the number of men who do not want to or cannot be fathers present on screen and reflect the growing variety of models of family functioning in postcommunist countries (Racław-Markowska 2000), Polish and Czech cinema is awash with stories of men who become excellent surrogate fathers or single fathers. In Polish cinema we find such fathers in *Jutro będzie niebo* (*Tomorrow Will Be Heaven*, 2001), directed by Jarosław Marszewski, *Edi* (2002), directed by Piotr Trzaskalski, *Zmruż oczy* (*Squint Your Eyes*, 2003), directed by Andrzej Jakimowski, *Tato* (*Dad*, 1995), directed by Maciej Ślesicki and *Historie miłosne* (*Love Stories*, 1997), directed by Jerzy Stuhr. The number of these films appears particularly high against the background of rare movies featuring adoptive or single mothers made in a comparable period. Typically, the reason why a man is put in the position of a surrogate parent is the absence of the mother or her inability to look after her own child. In *Dad*, the father (Bogusław Linda), decides to take care of his eight-year-old daughter upon discovering that her mother is mentally ill and therefore a danger to her own child, and the girl's grandmother is a cruel monster who imprisons and abuses the child. In *Edi*, a homeless scrap dealer (Henryk Gołębiewski) is forced into single fatherhood by the brothers of a teenage girl, who became pregnant out of wedlock and concealed the true identity of her child's father, claiming that Edi impregnated her. One of several stories included in *Love Stories* depicts a priest, who decides to leave the Church when he discovers that he has a daughter in an orphanage. The ex-teacher in *Squint Your Eyes*, who left the big city to live in the provinces as a janitor, is looking after a girl who ran away from her own parents, being disgusted by their materialistic attitude to life. All the films about surrogate and adoptive fathers draw attention to the immense sacrifices made by men in order to look after their children (Mazierska 2006). Take, for example, the priest (Jerzy Stuhr) in *Love Stories*, who is faced with the choice between resuming his paternal duties, and losing his well-paid job and disgracing himself, or rejecting his daughter's plight and keeping his job. The choice is poignantly presented in his conversation with the bishop who tries to dissuade him from his decision, declaring the superiority of his duties towards God, the Church and his parishioners over the welfare of a 'bastard child'. Almost as difficult as that of the priest is the situation of Michał in *Dad*, who, despite using babysitters, still cannot reconcile parenthood with the busy schedule of a cinematographer and gradually loses job opportunities and falls into debt. Edi must look after a baby having virtually no money to live on. In cases when the man is not the biological father of a child, the directors also emphasise that the adoption is in the child's best interest. Surrogate fathers put their children first and are completely in tune with them. Neither do they grudge children for what they lost by becoming their carers. This is particularly remarkable in the case of Edi who is not only forced to take care of a child who is not his own, but is punished for the alleged 'sin' of sleeping with the baby's mother by being castrated by her brothers.

With the exception of Edi, who looks after a baby boy, all the other men care for girls aged between seven and eleven years. These men, who are usually deeply disillusioned with women, somehow project onto their 'little women' their ideals of womanhood. They want the little girls at the same time to treat them as their mentors, appreciating their intelligence and experience, and look after them. Their

Figure 3.6 Henryk Gołębiewski as Edi in *Edi* (2002), directed by Piotr Trzaskalski.

wishes are fulfilled: unlike adult women, who usually crave for themselves some independence and are more observant and critical of male vices, the 'little women' do not need any freedom and fail to notice men's weak points. In addition, thanks to being with the father, real or surrogate, they can show how mature and resourceful they are. Take, for example, the girl in *Tomorrow Will Be Heaven*, who looks after a man who literally and metaphorically got lost on the road, or Kasia in *Dad*, who cooks for her father, who is extremely clumsy in the kitchen. On the whole, the daughters of single fathers accept the place ascribed to them by Polish patriarchal tradition by becoming humble servants of men in exchange for the protection they receive from them.

The rapport between a man and a small child is often underlined by cinematic devices, especially placing the couple, consisting of a man and the child in one frame, even when they talk to each other, rather than using shot-counter-shot. There is also the tendency to poeticise their relationship by situating them against a landscape untouched by civilisation. Take, for example, the scene when Edi and the baby boy are lying near each other on the pier against the background of a pristine lake. Similarly, in *Squint Your Eyes*, the friendship between Mała and her ex-teacher develops against the beauty of picturesque lakes and forests of Suwalszczyzna region. Such use of mise-en-scène suggests the naturalness of the relationship between a man and a child and consequently, its priority over other relationships the child had in the past and might encounter later in her/his life. It feels like paradise regained.

Once the father takes an active role in taking care of a child, the mother or surrogate mother (such as the grandmother in *Dad*) must disappear from the picture. If she does not do so voluntarily, by dying of natural causes or moving to another town or country, she is annihilated. This event is represented as a positive solution to the problem, restoring the narrative equilibrium. Similarly, when the mother resumes her maternal role, the male carer of the child is required to vanish. This is the case with Edi, who is deprived of his surrogate son when his mother reveals the true identity of the child's father. However, this event is described as a heartbreaking injustice.

Surrogate fatherhood is also frequently featured in Czech cinema. The principal example of this phenomenon is *Kolya* (1996) by Jan Svěrák, which won an Oscar in 1996. Other Czech films about surrogate fatherhood include *Something Like Happiness*, Jan Hřebejk's *Divided We Fall* and *Cosy Dens*, and Svěrák's *Obecná škola* (*The Elementary School*, 1991). In *Kolya*, set in 1988, during the last months of the communist system in Czechoslovakia, the 55-year-old childless František (Zdenek Svěrák) enters into a fictitious marriage with a young Russian woman, Nadezda. When Nadezda heads for Germany and her mother dies, František is forced to look after Nadezda's five-year-old son Kolya. First he does so reluctantly, trying to pass the boy to the social services but gradually he warms to the boy and his new role as the child's stepfather. When the boy is finally reunited with his mother, who takes him to West Germany, they part as the best of friends, or like a real father and son who learnt much from each other, including some of each other's language. We even feel that the boy's place is with his surrogate father rather than his mother. As with *Edi*, the narrative is constructed in such a way that the surrogate father and natural mother cannot look

Figure 3.7 Zdenek Svěrák as František and Andrei Chalimon as Kolya in *Kolya* (1996), directed by Jan Svěrák.

after the child together; the ideal family for a child has to consist only of one parent. It appears that in order to get to grips with fatherhood, a man must do it on his own.

Kolya can be regarded simply as about 'how portentous, historical change can creep up on ordinary people with ordinary problems' (Graffy 1997: 47). It can also be seen as a metaphor for the changing positions of the occupiers and the occupied within the Eastern bloc. The Russians, who after the Second World War played the role of the fathers of the Czech nation, are now reduced to the role of the children, in need of help of the Czechs. Kolya, who is small, lost and defenceless in the unknown country, epitomises this situation, but he is not the only Russian who is reduced to such an infantile state. Another person in this position is his mother, who needs Czech documents to emigrate, as well as the Russian soldiers who nominally ensure order in Czechoslovakia but in reality come across as lost and at pains to be on good terms with Czechs. By contrast, František, who was previously thrown out of the philharmonic orchestra for anti-communist behaviour, is forced into the role of a patriarch and a guide for the young Russians lost in his country. He does so reluctantly but ultimately well. His behaviour foretells a new epoch in the Russian–Czech relationships, based on partnership between these two nations or perhaps even benevolent patriarchalism on the part of Czechs.

Against the backdrop of films previously discussed, *Something Like Happiness* is somehow different because it does not set father against mother but instead depicts the advantages for a child of having both parents or even an extended family. Toník (Pavel Liška), the surrogate father in Sláma's film, takes care of the two sons of Dasha, a mentally unstable woman who lives on the same housing estate as him. However, he does not attempt the informal adoption on his own but with a woman whom he secretly loves, Dasha's friend Monika. Caring for Dasha's children makes Monika realise how important they are for each other. When the children are taken away from them, the whole family disintegrates. We find a similar situation in Hřebejk's *Horem pádem* (*Up and Down*, 2004), in which a childless couple, Franta and Mila, who are banned from adopting due to the man's past as a football hooligan, buy a dark-skinned boy from some people-traffickers. The presence of the baby changes Franta (Jiří Macháček) immensely; he becomes a caring and proud father for whom the child's race does not matter, and he is adamant to break with his old racist acquaintances. When the parents of the boy ask for their son to be returned, Franta's marriage disintegrates and he returns to his old ways as a football hooligan. In the last scene of the film we see him shouting racist slogans when watching a football match with his old mates.

The fact that in Polish films about surrogacy the mother must disappear to allow for the father to take care of the child, whilst in Czech films it is not necessary, can be regarded as the measure of the anti-female sentiment in the respective countries after the fall of the Berlin Wall. In Poland it appears to be much deeper and widespread, even affecting thinking about the woman's role in the family (Mazierska 2006). It is worth adding that the good surrogate or single fathers are typically the creation of younger directors, who at the time of directing the films did not have children of their own. It is thus plausible to assume that such an idealistic image of fatherhood has something to do with their lack of experience of real fatherhood.

After 1989 we also notice a proliferation of 'poisonous fathers' in Polish and Czech cinema, as indeed in the films of other ex-socialist countries – overpowering, cruel or at least authoritarian men who are unable or unwilling to understand their children and who bear responsibility for their problems. In Czech cinema we find them in the previously discussed *Cosy Dens*, as well as in *Mandragora* (1997) by Wiktor Grodecki (to which I will return in Chapter 5). Grodecki's single father who works in an old-fashioned, communist-style factory in a provincial town is so entrenched in his ideas about 'decent life' and so intolerant to his son's tastes and aspirations, that he drives the boy to an escape that ends tragically. In Poland we find poisonous fathers in a number of films, including Feliks Falk's *Komornik* (*Bailiff*, 2005), but the principle example is offered in *Pręgi* (*Welts*, 2004), directed by Magdalena Piekorz and based on the script of Wojciech Kuczok, a young writer who admitted that his story has an autobiographical dimension.

Piekorz's film is set in two time planes. In the retrospective it casts as the main character a boy named Wojtek who is physically and mentally abused by his single father (Jan Frycz). The suffering inflicted by the father reflects his conviction that in order to make a 'man' of his son, he must instil in him discipline and strength, and therefore punish him for the smallest misdemeanours. Such treatment traumatises the boy and eventually causes the breakdown of their relationship. Wojtek runs away from home, leaving his father a tape on which he records his grudges. Except for his father's funeral, they never meet again. Their final exchange of news is again mediated – on the same tape on which Wojtek recorded his complaints about his father, the father records his last message to his son, telling him how sorry he was to learn about the boy's suffering. In the present time the adult Wojtek (Michał Żebrowski) reveals many of his father's traits. He lives alone and cherishes such virtues as cleanliness, discipline and endurance, and is full of contempt for people who do not adhere to his value system. However, Wojtek changes after meeting a young woman, who falls in love with him and tries to eradicate his vices inherited from his father. In the last scene he is shown awaiting the outcome of her pregnancy test. Thus, the director suggests, thanks to a woman the cycle of male loneliness and aggression might be broken.

We find a somehow different situation in *Wszyscy jesteśmy Chrystusami* (*We Are All Christs*, 2006) by Marek Koterski, largely based on the director's own life. Here the father (Andrzej Chyra and Marek Kondrat) is not cruel or authoritarian but is an alcoholic, which leads to the breakdown of his marriage and his son's continuous anxiety, shame and hatred. At one point the son even tells his father, 'I wanted you to die'. Father's alcoholism is also an important factor in the son's later drug addiction. However, unlike the authors of *Welts*, Koterski affords his characters time to mend their relationship. The film takes the form of a therapeutic session, with father and his adult son sitting next to each other and discussing their lives, complaining but also explaining themselves and asking forgiveness. Moreover, Koterski demonstrates that at certain stages of their lives father and son change their relationships: the son behaves as if he was the father, helping his father to survive a drinking binge, and the father then assists his son in his attempt to give up drugs. Thus *We Are All Christs* is perhaps the first Polish film that represents father and son as equal partners, able and willing to support each other in their everyday Golgotha.

It should be noted that the poisonous father in both Polish and Czech films is a figure firmly rooted in the communist past. This has partly to do with the fact that the young men who are in a position to judge their fathers were themselves children in the 1970s or 1980s. More importantly, however, the poisonous father reveals a socialist mindset: he is strongly attached to the values and traditions pertaining to communism and the ways 'things were always done'. The obvious conclusion is that bad parenting goes hand in hand with totalitarian ideology, therefore one can hope that fathers of the new epoch will be better.

Another type of father who harks back to the communist past is the domesticated father, overpowered by his wife and overlooked by his own children, treated as an anti-model. This type of man, familiar from the films by Forman, Menzel and Papoušek, returned in Czech cinema in the 1990s. We find him, among others, in *Return of the Idiot*, *Samotáři* (*Loners*, 2000), directed by David Ondříček, *Something Like Happiness* and *Príbehy obycejného sílenství* (*Wrong Side Up*, 2005), directed by Petr Zelenka. For example, the father (Pavel Marek) in *Return of the Idiot*, who is short, overweight and clumsy, is derided by his daughters who nickname him 'Little Mole'.[6] He even searches at night for food, as did some older men in earlier Czechoslovak films–their appetite for food being a metaphor of their lack of any erotic fulfilment and domestic power, and a means to compensate for this deprivation. Hanka's father (František Němec) in *Loners* is so thwarted by his wife that he cannot even express his own sentiments. It is the wife who tells him that he is happy – although he feels that he is not. Similarly, the father (Miroslav Krobot) in *Wrong Side Up* is regarded by his wife as a retard whose place should be in a mental asylum. Men in these films openly express nostalgia for the communist past and disappointment with the present. We find the clearest example of this attitude in *Wrong Side Up* where the father, who for several decades had worked as a reader on newsreels, is unable to free himself from the propagandist texts which he used to read. The father in *Something Like Happiness* betrays his mental belonging to the earlier epoch by advising his daughter, whose boyfriend left Prague for the US, that she should give up on him and enjoy her modest life in Prague. Interestingly, in the end the older men prove more in tune with times than their more 'progressive' spouses. For example, the father in *Wrong Side Up* turns out to be healthier than his wife who ends up in a mental hospital.

In Polish films, such as *Amok* (*Stupor*, 1998), directed by Natalia Koryncka-Gruz and *Dług* (*Debt*, 1999), by Krzysztof Krauze, the fathers come across as less senile and domesticated, but equally locked in the past and ineffective in their dealings with their adult children. In *Debt*, father's attachment to tradition is conveyed by him reciting verses from the Polish national poem *Pan Tadeusz*, in *Stupor* – by renovating religious sculptures. Their relatively slow pace of life and their lack of interest in consumerist pleasures is contrasted with their sons' desire to become rich virtually overnight. In both cases the fathers and, by extension, the generation of fathers, whom the sons scorn for their apparent naivete and backwardness, are vindicated. The sons lose morally and financially on their way to quick wealth and freedom. However, their ruin gives their fathers no comfort; it is a mutual loss for fathers and sons.

Sometimes it is Easier to See a UFO than One's Own Father: the Role of the Father in Polish, Czech and Slovak Film

I borrowed the title of the concluding section of this chapter from *Loners*. The words, 'Sometimes it is easier to see a UFO than one's own father', are uttered by Vesna, an immigrant from Macedonia who comes to Prague to look for her father whom she never met. Although they refer to her specific situation, they also ring true in relation to a large proportion of children in Polish and Czechoslovak films. They do not know their fathers; often they never met them or are not sure whether the men whom they address as fathers conceived them. On other occasions the fathers disappoint them so much that they hate them and are reluctant to call them by this title. Fathers and sons often compete with each other, as do the men of different generations; much more rarely do sons try to emulate their fathers and other elders. Yet even an absent or inadequate father proves very important for his child, especially for his son, because his lack or his failures influence the child's identity and his future behaviour. It can happen through allowing other men or institutions to fill the gap the father left, or through forcing the child to construct his identity in opposition to the missing or bad father, which typically leads to perpetuating the father's vices. Moreover, sometimes the gap is never filled; the child of the missing father feels a nobody.

Another important feature of the father, as represented in Polish and Czechoslovak films, is his position not next to, but against the mother. Rather than supporting his child's bearer and equally sharing the burden of parenthood, the father either withdraws completely from active parenting, or opposes the mother and usurps her place, becoming a single father. It feels like the father can spread his wings only when he has no competition from a woman. By and large, neither Polish nor Czechoslovak cinema propose a heartening image of fatherhood, whilst acknowledging the significance of this role for family and society at large. If we regard this assessment as true in relationship to the outside world, then in it we find an important reason why men in these countries avoid fatherhood more than their Western counterparts. The consequences of failure to be a good father are dire while any advantages are problematic.

Notes

1. Engels emphasised the enslavement embodied in the family by noting that the word 'familia' originally referred to the total number of slaves belonging to one man (Engels 1972: 121).
2. The idea that 'it is a man who engenders man' has a long tradition, beginning with Aristotle (Badinter 1995: 67–95).
3. Unlike biological fathers, mothers are represented in Czechoslovak socialist realistic films as useful, but marginal – literally and metaphorically relegated to the kitchen.
4. A connection between Schorm's protagonist, again played by Kačer, and Maciek Chełmicki is also noticeable in *Everyday Courage*. Schorm himself in an interview mentions Jerzy Andrzejewski as an important source of inspiration (Branko 1996: 69).
5. The importance of the television in Papoušek's narrative is openly pronounced by the Polish title of his film, *Straszne skutki awarii telewizora* (*The Horrendous Consequences of the Television Failure*).
6. Most likely the origin of this nickname is the popular Czechoslovak animated series, *Krtek* (*Little Mole*), beginning in the 1950s. Little Mole, being small, peaceful and shy, but resourceful, became one of the symbols of postwar Czechoslovakia.

CHAPTER 4

Larks on a String, or Men in Love

No love is possible in an unhappy world.
(Raoul Vaneigem 2001: 41)

Romantic Love and its Discontents

In its singlemindedness, love is weakness, melodrama, a need to suffer.
(Bataille, quoted in Botting and Wilson 1997: 44)

This chapter will analyse the love life of Polish and Czechoslovak men as represented in film. Yet 'love' means different things to different people, as well as in different periods and cultural contexts; therefore it is useful to map out the territory to be explored. Denis de Rougemont notes that, 'Classical Greek used at least sixteen terms to designate love in all its forms: *erōs* for physical love, *agapē* for altruistic love, *philia* for tender or erotic feelings, etc.' (de Rougemont 1983: 5). I will compare all types of loving relationships with 'romantic love', because I believe that this is a model of love that the majority of contemporary viewers have in mind when assessing the attitudes and behaviour of characters in films. Although 'romantic love' is by no means a straightforward concept, I will regard as its crucial component the conviction that love is the highest value in human life. As Susan and Clyde Hendrick put it:

> The romantic focus was on love itself, love as the valued ideal, and one that sometimes seemed almost objectless. Religious thinking of the Middle Ages developed the view that 'God is love'. Romanticism stood that concept on its head and evolved as a philosophy that 'love is God'. Romantic love further developed the concept of sexual love as an ideal toward which all men and women could strive for fulfilment. (Hendrick and Hendrick 1992: 39)

Sex is usually regarded as a component of romantic love, as 'sex with love yields both pleasure and meaning' (ibid.:114), but it is possible to love somebody romantically without having a sexual relationship with this person. Indeed, some authors argue that romantic love is more an attitude, a disposition, than an act (Wasylewski, quoted in Piwińska 1984: 520–1), or that romance finishes when it is consummated (de Rougemont 1983: 15–102). Equally, it is possible to have sex with somebody without loving this person. Most authors regard loveless sex as a poor substitute for sex with love or even love without sex, as it is associated with such negatively viewed behaviour as exploitation, domination, cruelty and humiliation. However, others maintain that 'pure sex' is best because, unlike in loving relationships, nothing stands in the way of achieving sexual satisfaction (Vannoy, quoted in Hendrick and Hendrick 1992: 24).

The very term 'romantic love' suggests that this concept emerged at a specific moment in (Western) history, that of Romanticism, although its roots are found in the twelfth century legend of Tristan and Iseult (or Isolde) (de Rougemont 1983: 15–55). It appears that to experience romantic love requires a prior sense of the self as a distinct individual agent, which emerged at this point in history. One author states that: 'Romantic love is possible only in a society that strongly emphasises individuality and self-identity, along with the associated concepts of independence and social mobility. In such a society with "atomistic individuals" romantic love can be thought of functionally as "an attachment device that brings people together into mating pairs"' (Solomon, quoted in Hendrick and Hendrick 1992: 21). Other authors argue that romantic love is itself a powerful force in the growth of individualism. Marta Piwińska claims that thanks to romantic love a person is able to discern their unique fate and reject social authorities and conventions (Piwińska 1984: 525). Karen Lystra maintains that there was a connection between the emergence of the concept of romantic love and the expansion of individualism in America (Lystra, quoted in Hendrick and Hendrick 1992: 23). However, individuality in Romanticism was granted almost exclusively to men. As Friedrich Kittler observes, Romanticism construed woman as a passive and silent recipient of male attention and affection, as a narcissistic support for the formation of male identity. Romantic discourse effectively subsumed women under the idealised one Woman whose silence was productive of male poetic speech (Kittler 1990: 124–173).

Apart from extremity and individualism, romantic love is known for its tragedy and masochism. As Denis de Rougemont puts it, 'Happy love has no history' (de Rougemont 1983: 15). Romantic love does not promise a happy end on this earth; on the contrary, it is expected to bring danger, suffering, despair, madness and death to a man. It has to be such if it is to bring a human transcendence, to show him a different life to that which people are living (Piwińska 1984: 527–8).

In this chapter I want to focus on men both in love and making love; those who love and have sex, those who love without having sex and those who have sex without love. I am interested most in the 'styles of love' dominating particular periods of Czechoslovak and Polish history and factors affecting these styles. Yet, before I begin delving into men's love life, as manifested in Polish and Czechoslovak films, it is worth sketching the role of love in the respective cinemas and wider culture.

Love in Polish, Czech and Slovak Culture

Sestřičky (*Nurses*, 1983), by Karel Kachyňa begins with the scene of a male hospital patient approaching an auxiliary nurse who is mopping the floor, in order to slap her bottom. As the film credits unfold on screen, this scene (which the British viewer might associate with *Carry On* films) is repeated several times, drawing attention to the artificial character of the presented occurrence. Accordingly, we can regard this episode as a key to capture film eroticism Czechoslovak or Czech style – it is naughty and crude, initiated by men and serving male pleasure, and does not lead to any real intimacy between men and women. The idea that love 'Czechoslovak style' equals bottom-slapping is also suggested by Jan Hřebejk, who meaningfully named one of his films *Pupendo* (2003) (*pupa* means bottom). Hřebejk even claims that not only love but everything in Czechoslovakia finished as *pupendo* – a trivial and farcical pursuit. Love and sex in Czechoslovak cinema cannot be reduced to childish games, but they constitute a large enough proportion of screen eroticism to serve as a basis of popular assessment of how this phenomenon is treated by Czech and Slovak filmmakers.

While the episode from Kachyňa's film and the title of Hřebejk's film capture the dominant image of Czech and Slovak screen eroticism, the alleged specificity of the Polish one is excellently conveyed by a rude anecdote, told by the leading jester among Polish film critics, Zygmunt Kałużyński. He claimed that when a Polish man in a film undoes his fly, bullets from a rifle fall to the ground. This anecdote illuminates the sheer inability of Polish male characters to enjoy eroticism and points to the reason for this situation – love in Poland is sacrificed to the demands of war and, in a wider sense, to the service of one's country. Consequently, when Polish filmmakers do overcome their fear of eroticism and show naked bodies and sexual intercourse, in Kałużyński's opinion 'they are so sad, so simply without heart, that they fail to arouse the viewer' (Kałużyński 1976: 184). He summarises his argument by saying that there is 'no erotic climate in Polish films' (ibid.). Kałużyński's assessment about the character of love in Polish film is shared by the chief Polish specialist on melodrama, Maria Kornatowska, who maintains that it typically takes the form of an impossible love or, as she puts it, 'nonlove' (Kornatowska 1975: 42). This Polish inclination to 'nonlove' is excellently conveyed by the titles of many Polish films such as *Lekarstwo na miłość* (*Medicine for Love*), *Trudna miłość* (*Difficult Love*), *Niekochana* (*Unloved*) or *Trzeba zabić tę miłość* (*To Kill this Love*), especially when compared with such love-affirming titles of Czech and Slovak films as *Lásky jedné plavovlásky* (*A Blonde in Love*), *Touha zvaná Anada* (*Desire Called Anada*) or *Ja milujem, ty miluješ* (*I Love, You Love*). The difference in the erotic standards of Czechs and Slovaks on the one hand and Poles on the other is also symbolised by the Polish translation of a relatively recent Czech film, *Nuda v Brně* (*Boredom in Brno*) as *Sex in Brno*. We could deduce that what for Czechs is an ordinary, mundane activity, for Poles is out of the ordinary and highly arousing. It is also worth adding that in two Polish films titled *Porno* and *Pornografia* (*Pornography*) there is no pornography worthy of its name. To summarise, according to popular perception, in Czechoslovak cinema love fails because it begins too early and is conducted too hastily and physically, without due attention to feelings. In

Polish film it never properly starts as other goals come between man and woman's erotic joy. However, although there is a kernel of truth in such statements, we should treat them with care, because they are very general and insensitive to the changes occurring in cinema and in society at large.

By contrast to Kornatowska and Kałużyński, who purported to capture the essence of Polish screen love, Jerzy Krysiak in his article *Romans z władzą* (*Romance with an authority*) and Rafał Marszałek in *Krótka historia ciała* (*Short Story of a Body*) attempt to present Polish film eroticism diachronically, focusing on the changes that took place during the forty years between the end of the Second World War and the end of communism (Krysiak 1990; Marszałek 2006). Krysiak's main argument, as the title of his essay suggests, is that love in Polish film has reflected the relationship between filmmakers and viewers on the one hand, and political authority on the other. After the war, political authority in Poland became communist and communism is in principle anti-love and even more anti-eroticism; therefore images of love in Polish film were unsatisfactory, confirming the previously quoted opinions of Kałużyński and Kornatowska. As he puts it with some derision, the typical image of 'communist love' in film is that of two people who look straight ahead. 'They do not look at each other as lovers normally do, they are not interested in each other but in their glorious future' (Krysiak 1990: 17). Yet, this image could not be sustained for very long, because communist ideology was almost from the very beginning challenged by the people who were either dissatisfied with its content or implementation. Consequently, after the demise of Stalinism viewers demanded bolder images of love, and decade after decade various previously forbidden aspects of eroticism, such as nakedness, sexual intercourse, pornography, sadism, etc., were 'released' and offered for mass consumption (ibid). It would be wrong to assume that the changes in representation of eroticism reflected only the pressure of 'the sexually hungry Polish masses' on the filmmakers and censors to give them more and more sex. Screen eroticism was also deployed 'positively', so to speak, by politically obedient filmmakers, as a way to glorify the sociopolitical system. Conversely, anti-communist filmmakers used eroticism subversively, to tackle obliquely political issues and criticise the state and the Party.

Krysiak can be criticised for overestimating one element, namely politics, in the creation of a complex image, but no doubt he picked an important factor. Moreover, his analysis has much validity also for films of other countries of the Soviet bloc, including Czechoslovakia. From the fact that communism is anti-eroticism, we should not, however, conclude that anti-communist discourse is pro-eroticism. There are writers whose works are both hostile to communism and erotic, such as Marek Hłasko in Poland and Milan Kundera in Czechoslovakia. Yet a significant part of anti-communist literature is not erotic or even hostile to eroticism. For example, in Václav Havel's writing, such as in the plays *Spiklenci* (*The Conspirators*, 1974) and *Vernisáž* (*Private View*, 1976), as Robert Pynsent observes, sex is described as a banal and vulgar pursuit which, instead of liberating man, increases his imprisonment and stress. Moreover, it is regarded as a form of consumerism to which Havel is particularly badly disposed. It is worth noting that in Havel's work it is typically men who consume, while women are passive objects of consumption (Pynsent 1994: 27–8). Similarly, in Tadeusz Konwicki's *Mała apokalipsa* (*Small Apocalypse*, 1979), sex is presented as part of the vulgar lifestyle of those possessing political power. In other important Polish anti-communist works, such as Ryszard Bugajski's *Przesłuchanie* (*Interrogation*, 1981) (which functions both as a novel and as a film), enforced sex is construed as a form of political oppression. It is also worth adding that anti-communist opposition in Poland in the 1970s was fuelled by stories of the excessively consumerist and lecherous behaviour of communist dignitaries and their families, such as the playboy son of the Prime Minister Jaroszewicz. In Poland anti-communist hostility to eroticism was also connected with the fact that democratic opposition in this country was close to the Catholic Church, which regards erotic pleasure not as a goal in itself but only as a tool of procreation, and strongly condemns love outside marriage and any form of erotic experimentation.

Other factors affecting the representation of love in Polish and Czechoslovak films are the prewar literary and artistic traditions of these countries. In their histories we can identify a movement in which love took central stage: the Decadence, the period between Romanticism and modernism, marked by pessimism and heavy use of symbols. However, in Czech and Slovak culture this paradigm lasted longer than in Poland – for the whole of the second half of the nineteenth century and early twentieth century – and was of greater importance than to its neighbour. The main Czech decadent poets, such as Jiří Karásek and Ladislav Klíma, are regarded as national poets; their works contributed in a major way to Czech renewal in the nineteenth century and impacted on Czech self-perception (Pynsent 1989, 1994). Decadent art influenced Czechoslovak film largely by foregrounding the pleasures of the body and the link between Eros and Thanatos, consisting of the conviction that 'sexuality was delightful but sullying, and woman comprised the desire to sully man, that is spoil his classical bourgeois beauty or offend his aspirations to other beauty' (Pynsent 1989: 179).

The period of Decadence cannot be overestimated for the development of the Polish art of representing love, be it in poetry, prose or plastic arts. Tomasz Gryglewicz goes as far as arguing that no earlier paradigm introduced eroticism to Polish art (Gryglewicz 2004: 19). However, in Poland the Decadence, which lasted from about 1890 till 1918, was only a subcurrent in a larger movement known as Młoda Polska (Young Poland) rather than a dominant strand. Its leading figure, playwright, poet, novelist and philosopher, Stanisław Przybyszewski, travelled widely through Europe and influenced the erotic ideas of some of the greatest artists of the nineteenth and twentieth century, such as August Strindberg and Edvard Munch. However, in Poland he never achieved the status of a national poet. On the contrary, he became marginalised within Polish literary discourse, regarded as a foreign body within Polish literature – not least because he wrote in Polish and German, and his wife, Dagny Juel, was Norwegian – and he was treated with derision.[1] In addition, the contribution of other writers of Young Poland to the development of Polish erotic literature, such as Stefan Żeromski, is somehow overlooked in the critical discourse. This is because Polish critics tend to privilege the literary discourses on the nation over those on private lives. The Decadence did influence Polish screen love but its impact is largely limited to prewar cinema, when four films were based on Przybyszewski's work. On the whole, the part of Young Poland's literature that focused on love did not reach a wider audience and in due course was forgotten (Piwińska 1984: 520). On the other hand, in the literary movement regarded as crucial for Polish self-perception, that of Romanticism, unlike in its Western counterparts, erotic liaisons are overshadowed by and subordinated to men and women's relations with the Patria (see Chapter 2). The previously quoted Piwińska, pointing to the relatively low status of those romantic works which are concerned with love, such as Adam Mickiewicz's Part IV of *Dziady* (*Forefathers' Eve*, 1820–3) or Zygmunt Krasiński's *Listy do Delfiny* (*Letters to Delfina*, 1846–48), concludes: 'Polish culture does not know and does not like romantic love'.

In contrast to Polish literature, in Czech and Slovak Romanticism love is an important motif. The principal example is the contemplative epic with a strong Oedipal subtext, *Máj* (*May*, 1836) by Karel Hynek Mácha, which inspired Czech and Slovak writers throughout the nineteenth and twentieth century (Pynsent 1993: 241). Its protagonist, an Italian bandit, falls in love with a woman who has been seduced by an older man whom the hero kills. The man turns out to be his father. The hero is executed and the woman drowns herself.

After the First World War, love in Czech and Slovak literature became a constant theme in surrealist literature, represented by such authors as Vítězslav Nezval and Bohumil Hrabal. Their work accentuates the importance of sensual pleasures and the impact of the unconscious on people's erotic behaviour. In Polish literature of the same period, love is associated predominantly with two authors, Jarosław Iwaszkiewicz and Helena Mniszkówna. Iwaszkiewicz is inscribed into the tradition of 'high modernity', in which love is often unspoken and sublimated into pure intellectual pursuit or artistic creativity.[2] Iwaszkiewicz also foregrounds the connection between Eros and Thanatos, which links his work with the decadent and surrealist traditions. However, unlike surrealists, Iwaszkiewicz's style is realistic, albeit not free from metaphors. Mniszkówna is an author of probably the most popular Polish melodrama: *Trędowata* (*The Leper*, 1909). Not only is *The Leper* the most popular Polish novel about love; it is also the most derided Polish book ever written, equated with cheap sentimentality and kitschy exaggeration, testifying to Polish difficulty in coping with the subject of love.

Polish, Czech and Slovak cinema fed on the work of Nezval, Hrabal, Mniszkówna and Iwaszkiewicz. Hrabal is the most screened author in Czechoslovakia, with over ten films being adapted from his novels and short stories; Iwaszkiewicz is in this respect Hrabal's Polish counterpart, with over twenty films and television series being based on his works. Also both Hrabal and Iwaszkiewicz were actively involved in cinema, writing scripts for films. Needless to add that a large proportion of films based on their work include love stories. Mniszkówna was one of the most adapted Polish authors in prewar years, with four of her books being screened, and *The Leper* was again filmed in the 1970s. Nezval's writing served as the source of some of the most erotic (and most famous) Czechoslovak films: *Ekstase*

(*Ecstasy*, 1933), directed by Gustav Machatý and *Valerie a týden divů* (*Valerie and Her Week of Wonders*, 1970), directed by Jaromil Jireš. However, in my study I will refer only to screenings of Hrabal and Iwaszkiewicz's work, because they foreground the male perspective on love.

Of course, love life as depicted in Polish, Czech and Slovak cinema was also affected by the styles of love of real Poles, Czechs and Slovaks. Unfortunately, until the 1990s sociological studies of the sexual behaviour of people living in these countries practically did not exist. However, it is safe to assume that sex and especially erotic experimentation was a preserve of young and unmarried people, most prone to 'romantic accidents'. Overwork, difficult housing conditions, often forcing young couples to live with their parents, poor access to contraceptives and, in Poland, Catholic teaching of sex as a sinful activity unless it leads to conception, did not help romantic love to flourish (Gal and Kligman 2000). This opinion is partly confirmed by empirical studies conducted in Poland in the late 1990s that suggest that, for the majority of Poles, sex on the one hand and marriage and having children on the other are separate spheres of human life (Duch-Krzysztoszek 1998). As if to confirm this assessment, there are practically no Polish and Czechoslovak films about love between spouses. If marriage appears in these films, it is typically represented as love's graveyard; a place where the partners either put up with their mutual indifference or hostility, or try to alleviate them by engaging in extra-marital sex. It is even less likely to find a film presenting love between older people: those in their fifties or sixties. If it happens at all, it is an unequal love, in which an older man offers money and experience, and the younger woman freshness and beauty. Finally, the way love and sex have been portrayed in Polish and Czechoslovak cinema was also affected by the conventions of representing eroticism in Western film (Marszałek 2006: 154–6). The growing openness in depicting sex in the West helped to ease erotic censorship and self-censorship in the East. I will even argue that after the end of socialist realism, Czechoslovak cinema was barely behind the rest of Europe in this matter and Polish cinema in the 1970s was also fast catching up.

The negative attitude to love, especially love that is autonomous and sexualised, has impacted on the way love films are treated in Polish and Czechoslovak critical discourse and film history. In Poland the films that put male–female relationships at the centre of the narrative and represented sex graphically were relegated to the margin of national cinema as kitschy, populist or as 'women's cinema'. Similarly, the filmmakers specialising in films about love did not gain the same status as directors making films about 'national pursuits'. I have here in mind Janusz Morgenstern, in my opinion a director of equal talent to that of Wajda who, however, was never regarded as Wajda's equal. It is also telling that the most 'erotic' filmmaker to come from Polish soil, Walerian Borowczyk, director of such films as *Contes immoraux* (1974) and *Emmanuelle V* (1987), made the vast majority of his films in France, the proverbial European 'capital of love'. We could also observe a tendency to downplay eroticism in critical discourse on film or regard love as a metaphor of something else. While I disagree with the opinion that Polish love films are bad, it is true that the majority of them are focused on women. However, in this respect Polish cinema is not unique; John Cawelti goes as far as proclaim that there is a basic affinity between romance and the female sex (Cawelti 1976: 41).

In Czechoslovakia the importance of screen love was also downplayed, but not to the same extent as in Poland, most likely because eroticism constitutes a more respected tradition in Czech and Slovak cultures than in Polish. Prewar love films, particularly Machatý's *Ecstasy*, are a pride of Czech cinema. It can also be argued that Czechs, unlike Poles, admit enjoying pleasures of the body. 'Devotion to pleasure of sensuous enjoyment' was listed among the traits most often mentioned by Czechs in a sociological survey of stereotypes of Czech character conducted in 1992 (Holý 1996: 75). Czech and Slovak love cinema is also more balanced from the perspective of gender; even the majority of protagonists of Czechoslovak melodramas are men. Yet this feature might be connected with the special interest granted to men in the most important paradigms of Czech and Slovak film – that of the New Waves (Hanáková 2005b: 63).

Love in a Shadow of War

I would like to devote the first part of my analysis to ex-soldiers and other men whose love life is shaped by the war even after the war is finished. The theme of 'war scars' is an enduring motif in Polish cinema, although it most affected films made in the 1950s and 1960s, such Andrzej Wajda's *Ashes and Diamonds*, *Ostatni dzień lata* (*The Last Day of Summer*, 1958) by Tadeusz Konwicki and *Powrót na ziemię* (*Return to Earth*, 1966), directed by Stanisław Jędryka. In Czechoslovak cinema this motif is more subdued but we also find it in films of a similar period, examples are *Král Šumavy* (*Smugglers of Death*, 1959), directed by Karel Kachyňa and *Adelheid* (1969), directed by František Vláčil. All these films, paradoxically, at the same time as proclaiming the need for love as a means to overcome war trauma, convey the idea that for people who went through the war love is not a viable option. The principal differences between them concern the reasons why war survivors cannot love happily.

In *Ashes and Diamonds* it is the war itself, unfinished for Maciek, that renders love impossible (see Chapter 2). Stefan (Stanisław Mikulski), the male and possibly Jewish protagonist of *Return to Earth*, a handsome doctor working in hospital, avoids close contact with women because of his war memories that awaken guilt in him. In Berlin, together with his wife Wanda (Ewa Krzyżewska), he escaped from the transport to a concentration camp. Seeing no chance to save their lives, the couple decided to commit suicide by jumping into the river from a bridge. Wanda did jump but Stefan was prevented by a Polish worker who found him on the bridge. After the war Stefan keeps mistaking women whom he meets by chance for his wife, which signifies both his yearning for Wanda and his fear of meeting her, until one day she truly does reappear in his life. It turns out that she was rescued by some slave workers who fished her from the river. Stefan tries to explain to Wanda the circumstances of his survival, but he fails to convince her and perhaps even himself, that he did the right thing. The couple spend a night together in a room that Stefan rents and part in the morning.

Wanda leaves Stefan, unable to forgive him and resume their life together. For Stefan her departure means returning to his solitary life, led in a flat that does not belong to him, filled with work and devoid of any lasting attachments, be it a person or any material possession. The director makes us believe that this sole war episode, when Stefan somehow failed as a husband and a man, destroyed his chance for love and meaningful existence. Yet it is not really Stefan who is to blame for his failure and his subsequent anguish, but the war itself that put him through such a cruel test. This idea is reinforced by the construction of the secondary characters, such as Stefan's landlady, whose husband was fighting on a submarine. Although his ship sunk, she still hopes that one day he will return home, or at least while she has no proof that he died she dos not want to look for another man. On the other hand, Jędryka shows that not everybody lives in the past. Many people around Stefan enjoy their lives; the whole country is recovering from the war's destruction, as signified by crowded and buzzing cafés, new shops with luxurious goods, as well as a political campaign marked by demonstrations and political slogans.

In *The Last Day of Summer*, love is rendered impossible because the woman (Irena Laskowska) still waits for her pilot fiancé who went to Britain during the war to fight the Nazis and never returned. We can guess that this prolonged waiting caused a kind of emotional atrophy in her. She refers to this state in an internal monologue, saying, 'When the friend offers me a hand, I hide from him as if he was to attack me, I protect myself from any tender gesture'. As in *Return to Earth*, the woman's difficulty in coming to terms with the war loss affects her potential partner, a mysterious young man (Jan Machulski) who secretly accompanies her on holiday to a lonely beach. Despite finding him attractive, she rejects his affection. Yet when he eventually disappears in the sea, probably to commit suicide, she is devastated, knowing that she destroyed the young man, as well as squandering her last chance of happiness. The tragedy of the mysterious outsider is magnified by the appearance, acting style and costume of Machulski. In his simple black trousers and jumper he epitomises the 'generation of Bim-Bom'[3] of young people who wanted to forget about the war and start their lives afresh, be creative and have fun.[4] Moreover, he bears resemblance to Konwicki himself (Lubelski 1996: 65–8). Thus, showing Machulski's character as sentenced to unfulfilled love and death, Konwicki metaphorically depicts himself and his generation as doomed. The ominous music, bearing association with the soundtrack of Wajda's *A Generation*, underscores the motif of impossible love – love that was dead even before it blossomed.

In *Smugglers of Death* and *Adelheid*, love has no future because the male protagonists choose the wrong women, who are too entangled with enemies of the state to be able to begin new lives with the 'right' men. The main character of *Smugglers of Death*, set in the border region of the Šumava Mountains in 1948, is the border guard Karel (Jiří Vala). He casts his eyes on the attractive shopkeeper Marie (Jiřina Švorcová), who is married to a man who left the village to escape punishment for accidentally killing a child. It turns out that Marie's husband is still alive but lives now in Bavaria, and is involved in smuggling people and goods over the border to Germany. One day he steals into Marie's flat and asks her to follow him abroad, but she refuses out of disdain for his cowardice and due to her loyalty to Karel. On his next visit the husband forces Marie to accompany him through the swampland of Šumava on his last illegal trip abroad, in which both of them lose their lives. Marie drowns in a bog when trying to escape her husband; the husband is shot by their guide, when the border guards are about to catch him.

Marie's death is a tragedy for Karel but it is also a conclusion which accords with the logic of the times. As a woman contaminated by liaison with a traitor, she has little chance of a 'decent' life in the new Czechoslovakia. Karel's commander Kot assumes Karel and Marie's incompatibility from the beginning and tries to prevent their meetings and Karel's leaving Šumava on Marie's request. Marie must also die because as a woman she poses a threat to the 'moral purity' and professionalism of the border guards, who cannot have any distractions in the service of their country. Kot, for example, admits to being separated from his wife and shows no interest in the opposite sex. The message that woman equals danger is made clear in an episode when Karel leaves his duty in order to meet Marie, risking court martial and, more importantly, increasing the danger of smugglers crossing the border. Marie's unsuitability for a soldier and a 'new man' of the socialist era is also conveyed by her eroticism; she is a pretty woman who goes to work through the puddles in high heels and wears close-fitting dresses. As if to confirm the opinion that fighting the enemies of the state is irreconcilable with pursuing private pleasure, another man in Karel's team who is in love, Ciganek (and who misses his fiancée so much that he writes her a letter every day), is killed during the course of the narrative. In the last scene of *Smugglers of Death* all Kot's men gather around him and offer him a light for his cigarette, as if he was their adored woman. Among them is Karel who uses the last match for Kot and has none left for his own cigarette, so that his commander passes the light from his cigarette to Karel's in a gesture confirming their friendship and intimacy.

Adelheid (1969) casts Victor (Petr Čepek) as the main character, a Czech officer who returns home after serving in the British army. His new home becomes a manor that previously belonged to a rich German industrialist and Nazi activist named Heldemann who now awaits trial. Heldemann's daughter Adelheid (Emma Černá) lives in an internment camp for Germans and works as Victor's maid. As Miloš Fiala observes, Victor and Adelheid's past and present, which construes any intimate relationship between a Czech and German as betrayal, divides them. They are only linked by coincidence, finding themselves in the same place (Fiala 1969: 644). Despite these obstacles they become lovers. However, their affair ends tragically, when it turns out that the woman shelters her brother who did not surrender his weapons to the victorious forces. Rather than disown her family, Adelheid commits suicide.

The title of Vláčil's film suggests Adelheid's centrality but the director presents the events from Victor's perspective. In due course we realise that Victor has only partial knowledge of Adelheid and his interpretation of their relationship might be very different from that of the woman. Most importantly, what for him appears to be finding a sisterly soul and comforting each other in their misery and solitude, from Adelheid's perspective might be taking advantage of her vulnerability and abusing her position as a member of the defeated nation. The silence and impassivity,

Figure 4.1 Petr Čepek as Victor and Emma Černá as Adelheid in *Adelheid* (1969), directed by František Vláčil.

excellently conveyed by Emma Černá (ibid.: 645), make Adelheid particularly attractive for Victor, rendering her as an ideal recipient of male romantic attention and affection (on woman's passivity in romantic discourse see Kittler 1990: 124–173). However, Adelheid's silence also make it almost impossible to guess whether she sleeps with Victor with pleasure or with disgust. Similarly, one is not sure about the cause of Adelheid's suicide. It might result from her sadness about losing her family and her guilt that she was not able to save her brother, or might signify her rejection of Victor and the future he can offer her. Ultimately, Vláčil poses the question whether eroticism is the right method to bring reconciliation between former enemies, or is it a means to humiliate the loser and aggravate the war wounds.

In summary I want to emphasise that, paradoxically, 'love in the shadow of war' is the only type of screen love where man's happiness depends mostly on a woman. Although a woman does not choose her partner, she has the right to reject him and exercises this right to the man's disadvantage. It appears as women, who are normally excluded from any decisions of military nature but have to endure their discomforts, consciously or subconsciously punish men for their unfortunate position by rejecting their need for love when the war is over. Men's misfortune is particularly deep as they need love badly, being deprived of it in time of war. However, this very deprivation might be partly responsible for their bad choice of women or their inability to gain or regain woman's heart.

Larks on a String, or Love under Stalinism

> *I will not vouch for the men who run after every petticoat and let themselves in with every young female. No, no, that does not go well with revolution.*
> (V.I. Lenin 1972: 104)

For the classics of Marxism the ideal love is the union between a man and a woman, in which neither side is coerced into sex and both are equal partners. However, this ideal could not be fulfilled under the conditions of capitalism. There was little scope for love in bourgeois marriage, because it was only an instrument for the preservation and expansion of property stolen from the workers. The husband owned his wife and demanded fidelity from her to ensure the legitimacy of his heirs. He, on the other hand, freely indulged in extra-marital affairs and prostitution. In such circumstances the myth of romantic love was promulgated to obscure the true function of marriage as an economic institution. By contrast, money was no consideration for members of the working class, who therefore could marry from and for love. However, due to extreme poverty the life of the proletariat was reduced to animal-like conditions and there was little opportunity for love pleasures of a higher order. Instead, its members indulged in the immediate gratification of sex, knowing that there would be no future happiness. Moreover, some of the workers, particularly young women, were forced to sell their bodies in order to survive, often to members of the higher classes (Engels 1971: 144--5). This despicable situation was meant to change under socialism. The bourgeois marriage was predicted to die away as it would not be able to sustain its principal function: to perpetuate property and power. On the other hand, the improvement in the living condition of the working class would allow their members to develop their erotic life by moving beyond the simple pleasures of hasty sex. Principally, there should be no need for marriage, as true love does not need to be institutionalised. Yet although there were experiments in the abolition of marriage in the Soviet Union immediately after the October Revolution, in the 1930s the Soviet state returned to the concept of conventional morality and marriage, reintroducing restrictions on abortion and divorce (Scott 1976: 43). Thus, the ideal of socialist love as proposed by Engels, if not altogether abandoned, was at least temporarily sacrificed to the political goals of the day, such as the requirements to increase the population, resist external aggressors and fulfil ambitious production plans. To capture the approach to love in Stalinist ideology (and any totalitarian system), Jonathan Owen refers to Georges Bataille's opposition between the homogenous and heterogeneous, in terms of economic and political organisation.

> Social homogeneity consists in the reduction of human individuals to a mere exchange value, to instruments of production and social advancement deprived of any self-sufficient meaning. The heterogeneous, by contrast, is defined in terms of those experiences and activities that resist assimilation into a socioeconomic order dependent upon functionality and usefulness.

> Heterogeneous activities represent 'unproductive expenditures', instances of profligate, deliberate waste. Bataille identifies the realm of the heterogeneous, though not exclusively, with the realm of eroticism, insofar as eroticism (which Bataille distinguishes from sexuality in its functional, i.e. procreative guise) is characterised by its utterly gratuitous waste of energy and its rupture of the limits of self. (Owen 2007)

By advocating total social homogeneity (Robin 1992; Clark 2000), Stalinism has to condemn all eroticism that is not functional as wasteful and dangerous, and approve only that which helps to create a socialist society. Because of this instrumental approach, love in the Stalinist world lacks the dignity with which it is endowed in Western culture. It is less important than, for example, work and friendship between men (Szczepańska 2006). In no circumstances can it be romantic because romantic love assumes the primacy of love over other values. The romantic concept of love, or more accurately the sentimental idea of love presented in the socialist-realistic discourse as romantic, was derided (ibid.: 67-8).

The subjugation of love to the pursuits of socialist goals impacted on the assessment of erotic relationships in socialist-realistic films. The most important criterion in establishing whether love is good or bad is the social composition of the loving couple. The rule is that if the couple belongs to the working class, their relationship is blessed within the film's diegesis, because together they will work most effectively for the victory of socialism. If one part belongs to the proletariat, the other to the 'exploiting' class such as the bourgeoisie or *kulaks*, then love becomes 'difficult' and a happy ending is possible only if the latter renounces his or her class allegiance. Finally, a relationship between members of the exploiting classes is condemned as acting against socialist goals. To help the viewer make the right judgement in whom to invest sympathy, the filmmakers typically provide non-proletariat lovers with such unappealing features as promiscuity, obscenity or violence.

The instrumental treatment of love and the outright condemnation of 'nonsocialist romance' in due course became contested by filmmakers. Therefore it is worth dividing the films depicting love under Stalinism into two groups: those made according to the principles of socialist realism, predominantly in the late 1940s and the first half of the 1950s, and those produced in the later periods that criticised the state as a regulator of the erotic activities of their citizens. Films of the first type often focus on the difficulty of love among the members of the working classes under capitalism, and conversely the blossoming of love under socialism. They also show that 'socialist love' liberates woman and in this way makes the whole couple happy, whilst a relationship organised along the bourgeois ideas of marriage, even if it takes place in a socialist country, fails.

In Czechoslovakia we find a model of this approach in *Chceme žít* (*We Want to Live*, 1949), directed by Emil František Burian, whom Mira and Antonín Liehm described as the 'most notable member of the prewar theatrical avantgarde, who really believed in the "truth" of Stalinism' (Liehm and Liehm 1977: 102). The main part of the film is set during the economic crisis of 1933. A young seamstress from

Prague, Marie (Jaroslava Adamová), visits her home village, where she meets her childhood friend, glass blower Josef (Gustav Heverle). He proposes to her but she refuses, regarding the time as too difficult to set up a family. Soon Josef loses his job and moves to Prague, trying to find both employment and Marie. He gets work on a building site and finds Marie in a hospital, recovering after a botched abortion of their child. Subsequently they struggle to make ends meet, always on the verge of destitution and unable to afford a child. Josef joins a communist organisation and participates in anti-capitalist demonstrations which costs him his job. Their situation, however, changes dramatically after the war, when socialism wins and Josef becomes a member of the People's Militia. At this stage they also have a child, a symbol of their personal triumph over the adverse circumstances and of the victory of socialism over capitalism.

Although Marie proves more mature than her partner, both politically and in other aspects of life, he has a dominant position in their home, and he is the one who is involved in frontline politics. She only supports him in his efforts to fight for a better society. In accordance with the rules of socialist realism (Krzywicka 1956: 1–2; Fast 2003: 215; Szczepańska 2006: 71), the love of Josef and Marie is represented as very chaste, more like an intense friendship and cooperation than romantic, passionate love – *agapē* rather than *erōs*. Similarly, their union comes across as a marriage of economic positions and adherent ideologies, not of bodies searching for intimacy. Images of intimacy are avoided and the characters talk more about politics and economy than

Figure 4.2 Gustav Heverle as Josef and Jaroslava Adamová as Marie in *Chceme žít* (*We Want to Live*, 1949), directed by Emil František Burian.

their personal lives, typically staying some distance from each other, so that their bodies cannot meet. The chastity of Josef and Maria is signified by their names. Like the biblical Joseph and Mary who were parents of the founder of the new religion, Burian's Josef and Marie give life to a man whose birth marks the beginning of the new, communist Czechoslovakia. Also, like the biblical parents, they do not live for themselves, for their own pleasure (even when the principal goal of their lives is achieved) but for the future – for the happiness of their children and grandchildren.

I would like to compare *We Want to Live* with Jerzy Kawalerowicz's *Celuloza* (*Cellulose*, 1953) and *Pod gwiazdą frygijską* (*Under the Phrygian Star*, 1954), based on the popular novel by Igor Newerly, *Pamiątka z celulozy* (*A Souvenir from Cellulose*, 1952). The diptych, set in the 1930s in the industrial town of Włocławek (known before the war as 'America' because of its excellent employment opportunities) and Warsaw, presents the history of the Polish communist movement as seen through the eyes of a young working-class man Szczęsny (Józef Nowak). Not unlike in *We Want to Live*, the political maturation of Kawalerowicz's protagonist goes hand in hand with his gaining erotic experiences. Szczęsny's first affair is in Warsaw, with the wife of his boss, owner of a joinery workshop. This relationship is marred by incompatibilities between the lovers. Not only is Szczęsny's flame, Czerwiaczkowa, married and significantly older than her lover, but she also comes from a different social background of petite bourgeoisie, and she is very sexual, domineering and greedy. Because of these traits she constitutes a danger to a man's dominant position

Figure 4.3 Józef Nowak as Szczęsny and Lucyna Winnicka as Magda in *Celuloza* (*Cellulose*, 1953), directed by Jerzy Kawalerowicz.

in the relationship, which is tacitly assumed by socialist realism. She also breaks with the socialist-realistic prudishness and rejection of hedonism (Zwierzchowski 2005: 88–9). To become a socialist-realistic hero, Szczęsny has to abandon her. His next love is Magda (Lucyna Winnicka), a young woman met in Włocławek who turns out to be a communist activist. First Szczęsny is quite dismissive of her, regarding her as superstitious and backward, following her reading his hand and telling him that he was born 'under the Phrygian star'. Yet Magda's fortune-telling is in reality a joke as there are no Phrygian stars, there were only Phrygian caps worn by the participants of the Paris Commune, the first communist revolution. By pronouncing the Phrygian star as his sign, Magda foretells his future as an ardent communist.

Szczęsny again makes a mistake when he becomes jealous of a mysterious 'comrade Julian', with whom Magda appears to be in love. It turns out that Julian is only a printing machine, used by Magda for producing anti-capitalist leaflets. However, in his jealousy Szczęsny is not irrational, because Magda's affection, which is normally located in the opposite sex, is indeed displaced to the machine and, in a wider sense, to the communist cause. Her sexless devotion becomes an obstacle in her romance with Szczęsny. When the young man proposes to her, she rejects him, explaining that a communist fighter (especially a female one) should remain unattached to a family. Otherwise a conflict arises between her loyalty to her family on the one hand, and the party on the other. Szczęsny accepts her argument and they both give up on private happiness, to devote their time and energy to collective goals (Rek 2005: 276). Of course, the conflict between private fulfilment and public duty only refers to the places and times where capitalists have an upper hand. Magda believes and infects Szczęsny with her conviction that when communism will win, love will win too. In *Under the Phrygian Star* it does not happen, though. Magda is arrested in Włocławek during a general strike and in the last scene Szczęsny leaves for Spain, to fight in the Spanish Civil War. We can only guess that if Szczęsny's story is continued after the war; he might marry Magda and have a child with her, not unlike Josef and Marie in *We Want to Live*.

Unlike his liaison with Czerwiaczkowa, Szczęsny's relationship with Magda is chaste; the couple are tender towards each other but it is shown by very subtle gestures or even only by gazes. Often when we expect that they will embrace each other, they only shake hands as communist comrades do. Piotr Zwierzchowski observes that although in the Party hierarchy Szczęsny is below Magda, in their relationship she plays the role of an obedient wife, cooking and caring for him. In this way, unlike Czerwiaczkowa, she does not threaten his dominant position and the patriarchal order in a wider sense (Zwierzchowski 2005: 89).

In the films that are set after the communist victory, love is represented as advantageous, viable or even real, presuming that it is the 'right' type of love. Perfect examples are the comedy with Mr Angel, *Angel on Vacation* and *Adventure at Marienstadt* (both discussed in the previous chapter). In these films a young couple are brought together by working for the common good. In *Angel on Vacation* a young worker gains the heart of a kindergarten teacher by renovating a building where a group of orphans are spending their summer; in *Adventure at Marienstadt* a man and a woman come together by building together an estate for working class people. Similarly in both films, overcoming the obstacles related to work brings the young people together. These people have no problems that are strictly personal, deriving, for example, from a difference in tastes or interests. This is understandable as they represent the class of working people that is rendered homogenous. Moreover, their stories finish before their love is tested by living together and having children, when putting extra hours of work for any selfless goal, such as building a nursery, might be at the expense of time spent with one's own children. As combining work and child-rearing was the greatest challenge for the citizens of socialist countries (Scott 1976), the problem of love within a marriage in socialist realism is avoided.

The sexless nature of the male–female relationship affected the way bodies are represented in socialist-realistic films. There is a tendency to monumentalise male bodies (Tubielewicz Mattsson 2003b; Skwara 2006) by choosing actors with young, athletic, lithe and flawless bodies, one can say 'superbodies', and accentuate these qualities by such means as lighting and camera angles. However, this tendency is stronger in Polish than Czechoslovak films. For example, in comparison with the athletic builders in *Adventure at Marienstadt*, men in *Angel on Vacation* come across as rather average in terms of musculature, which can be explained by the fact that even in the period of socialist realism the Czechoslovak filmmakers cared about realism more than their Polish counterparts.

In the films made in the second half of the 1950s, when Stalinism and socialist realism had been rejected but socialism itself was not yet questioned, love is rendered as difficult to reach due to the conflict between man's duty towards the communist cause and his private happiness, that did not end even after the victory of socialism. A principal Czechoslovak example of this approach is *Velká Samota* (*Great Solitude*, 1959), directed by Ladislav Helge. Its main character Martin (Július Pántik) returns from Prague, where he works in the ministry, to his home village of Velká Samota, where some years earlier he was involved in setting up a cooperative farm. His purpose is to marry his sweetheart Anna (Blanka Bohdanová), who is the daughter of the only remaining smallholder in the village. After their wedding they are to go together to Prague. Yet Martin changes his mind when he notes that the cooperative is in a state of disrepair. Such a state can be attributed to the failure of the very idea of the collectivisation of the countryside, but Helge explains it by the farmers' weaknesses: their laziness, selfishness and drunkenness. Martin decides to postpone his marriage and takes the post of cooperative chairman. In due course he succeeds but at the price of alienating the farmers, his fiancée and his own mental and physical wellbeing. The film, however, finishes on an optimistic note, suggesting that the people of Velká Samota might warm to Martin.

The way Helge constructs Martin bears comparison to the portrayal of young communists in Burian and Kawalerowicz's films; for all of these men love is a luxury that cannot be consummated until more basic goals (professional and political) are achieved. This association of love with luxury is suggested in an episode when Anna invites Martin to her house. She hopes to impress him by a large collection of dresses which she plans to wear once they move to Prague. However, the dresses and the whole affluence and order of her bourgeois world only annoy Martin, as they poignantly contrast with the poverty and chaos he just witnessed on the cooperative farm.

The years that passed since the demise of socialist realism added erotic dimension to the female–male relationship, as represented in *Great Solitude*. There is a palpable desire in Martin and Anna; when they meet, they throw themselves in each others arms and even when they part, they cuddle and have tears in their eyes, being overwhelmed by emotions. Yet the love and desire filling Helge's characters only underscore the harshness of the reality in which Martin operates, and the magnitude of his task that must be completed before he can start looking after his personal life.

In periods of political 'thaw' we find films criticising the Stalinist state for interfering too much in the private lives of its citizens. One such film, *Larks on a String* by Jiři Menzel, was completed when the thaw of the Prague Spring was already over and the old regime had returned. Consequently, it awaited its premiere till the victory of the Velvet Revolution in 1990. The main subject of Menzel's film, set in the early 1950s, is the difficulty of pursuing romance in a totalitarian state, but also the need of love to survive in it. The main characters in the films, Pavel and Jitka, played by Václav Neckář and Jitka Zelenohorská, both familiar from *Closely Observed Trains*, meet, as was also the norm in socialist-realistic films, at work. However, this time it is not work on which they embark voluntarily, although it is represented as such to the outside world, but labour imposed on them as a punishment for their transgressions against the communist rules. At the time of their meeting Jitka is a prisoner, accused of trying to flee Czechoslovakia; Pavel works as a cook in a nearby scrapyard, where various types of 'bourgeois elements' are reeducated. Pavel and Jitka fall in love when posing for a propaganda film about Czechoslovak solidarity with North Korea. For the purpose of shooting an idyllic scene is created, in which Pavel and Jitka hold each other's hands and look into each other's eyes, when the voice of the commentator pronounces that they are the new, young and beautiful people who will work, love and raise their children in a perfect world of lasting peace. It is worth noting here that the message conveyed in this fake documentary conforms to the socialist-realistic rule that pleasure is always postponed, always in (somebody else's) future; the everyday, ordinary present matters only as much as it paves the way to a future utopia (Clark 2000: 39-40).

In due course Pavel and Jitka get married, each using a proxy, Pavel his own aunt, Jitka her prison guard. They hope to consummate their love when Jitka finishes her sentence but it does not happen, because in the meantime Pavel is sent to prison. The title of Menzel's film hardly requires explaining – the eponymous larks are the couple whose love life is organised and controlled by the political authorities and, by extension, all people living under totalitarian rule. According to the rule that there is no proper Czech film about love without some bottom-slapping, Menzel saturates *Larks on a String* with images of male erotic games, such as dazzling with a mirror and spying on women when they are undressing. However, on this occasion they do not signify man's sexist attitude to a woman but rather the difficulty of both sexes to lead a normal erotic life under communism and the inventiveness of people in finding ways to overcome it. It is worth noting that there is symmetry in the situation of men and women in Menzel's film, pointing to their harsh but ultimately equal treatment by the communist authority.

Pavel and Jitka's romance is juxtaposed with the family life of the male guard in the female prison and his Gypsy wife. Although, unlike Pavel and Jitka, they do not experience any political difficulties, they are less happy than the prisoners. The reason is the cultural differences between the couple; the husband does not understands the Gypsy rituals and gets upset when his wife is soaked in wine by the members of a Gypsy band playing at their wedding. She, on the other hand, feels completely alienated in their new but sterile flat, and hides from her husband. Another person whose erotic life is contrasted with Pavel and Jitka's is the trade union representative who supervises the work at the scrapyard. This man, who boasts that he is the only genuinely working class person in a company of the relics of the imperialist system, periodically visits the slums inhabited by the Gypsies. Ostensibly he does so to teach the Gypsy children about the advantages of cleanliness but in reality he uses his position of power to sexually abuse an adolescent Gypsy girl. By and large, Menzel undermines the official images of 'socialist love' as love between members of the working classes that involves no coercion, and in which no other differences between the individuals (such as ethnicity and religion) matter. As if to make a mockery of this image, his ideal love is a disgraced love between the enemies of socialism.

Andrzej Wajda's *Człowiek z marmuru* (*Man of Marble*, 1977) appears to be a good analogue to *Larks on a String* as it is also set in a similar time (early 1950s), against the backdrop of steelworks, and includes a young man and a woman, Mateusz and Hanka, who are represented as a perfect couple for communist propaganda. Not only do they pose for posters, photographs and fake documentaries but even take part in a fake wedding. Although the story of their relationship is overshadowed by the narrative of Mateusz's rise to fame as a 'man of marble' and his subsequent fall, and is somehow rendered obscure by the narration of Wajda's film, we get some clues as to why Mateusz and Hanka eventually split up. It transpires that part of their problem was the pressure to play for the camera and the lack of privacy resulting from being a state property. Living in a staged, socialist-realistic world also made Mateusz and Hanka feel 'socrealistic' – unrealistic and fake. It could be argued that their eventual separation testified to their rebellion against Stalinism.

The stories of these two couples demonstrate the failure of the socialist state to produce a happy society where couples are as united by love as they are by their service to the communist cause. Menzel and Wajda show that love cannot be imposed on people from the top. However, whilst Wajda depicts Stalinism as a system in which love is impossible because all human relations are subordinated to the person's relationship with the state, Menzel renders love possible in such circumstances and necessary for surviving it. The difference in Menzel and Wajda's attitude can be attributed to their outlook on life. Menzel, as he himself confessed more than once, is always trying to include optimistic messages in his films (see, for example, Buchar 2004: 38–48). Wajda's *Weltanschauung*, on the other hand, is tragic (Woroszylski 1993: 11; Nurczyńska-Fidelska 1995). These attitudes, in the last instance, we can regard as pertaining to Czech and Polish national characters respectively.

The type of love promoted in Polish socialist-realistic film we find in some later films. The most prominent example is *Człowiek z żelaza* (*Man of Iron*, 1981) by Andrzej Wajda, in which the main characters, Agnieszka and Maciek, fall in love with each other mostly because they share the same political ideas. It could be argued that their relationship is the kind of intensified comradeship we found earlier in *Under the Phrygian Star*, except that, paradoxically, we find more erotic passion between Szczęsny and Magda than between Maciek and Agnieszka. This sexlessness of Wajda's film might be explained by the fact that political cinema (a genre to which both Kawalerowicz's dylogy and *Man of Iron* belong) tend to adapt the same clichés, even if for different political objectives (Zwierzchowski 2000: 153). It is also plausible that Wajda consciously emptied Maciek and Agnieszka's relationship of sex as a way to oppose the 'wave of sex' that flooded the Polish screen in the 1970s and 1980s (Zięba, quoted in Szyma 1988).

The 1960s: Feelings are now Fashionable

While in the period of socialist realism and the so called Czechoslovak 'first wave', as well as in films set shortly after the war, love is represented as determined by the political and economic situation of the characters, in films of the 1960s it gains more autonomy. I will argue that in this decade love is important as was never before and as it never will be again in Polish, Czech and Slovak cinema – the 1960s are the true 'decade of love'. Filmmakers in this period convey love's autonomy in two intertwined ways. Firstly, erotic relationships appear divorced from the social and political context, or are only influenced by it in a minor way. Secondly, when politics and the economy bear a great significance on the situation of the characters, even their very ability to find a sexual partner, they fight for their right to love rather than accepting its impossibility. However, as a result of their determination to love whatever the circumstances, we find in films of this period a large number of erotic and psychological mismatches and misalliances, and characters who suffer 'romantic fever'. They are willing to fall in love, prepare themselves for this occurrence or are limerent: have all the symptoms of being in love without having its real object (Hendrick and Hendrick 1992: 59–60; Tennov 1999). Typically women initiate and perpetuate the romantic fever. Men either resist it or give into it passively, or take advantage of their partner's desire to love by using women solely as erotic objects. Because of the lack of compatibility, happy love is a rarity. In a number of films love, especially when experienced by a young person, is presented as a means of self-exploration, of learning about one's identity and discerning oneself from the crowd.

Although the relation between feelings and the material and political circumstances of the characters' lives is pushed to the background, the general situation of the 1960s is largely responsible for love taking the central stage. In the Western world the 1960s come across as a decade of free love, where the previous rules governing erotic behaviour crumbled, and when political radicalism went hand in hand with erotic radicalism (Roszak 1995). In Poland and Czechoslovakia, the 1960s, up to their culmination in 1968, was a period of relative prosperity and stability, when after the sacrifices of the austere 1950s, citizens could at last think about themselves and their happiness, be more individuals than members of the collective. In 1960s Prague, writes French:

> Popular culture flourished, and for a brief spell it became known as the Hippie capital of Europe. The American off-beat poet Ginsberg was crowned King of the student festival – then he was arrested on a narcotics charge and deported. Tourism from Western Europe was booming, and it became a two-way process. In 1965 the Czech Parliament had affirmed the right of Czechoslovak citizens to a passport for foreign travel. (French 1982: 218)

This image is confirmed by Carlos Fuentes, who in his autobiography, *Myself with Others*, reminisces on his trip to Prague, undertaken in 1968 with fellow Latin American writers, Julio Cortázar and Gabriel García Márquez (Fuentes 1988: 160–79).

Warsaw in this period did not have such a happy and cosmopolitan atmosphere as Prague. In Poland, the 1960s, when Władysław Gomułka was the Party leader, was rather contemptuously labelled 'small stabilisation'; a term which awakens associations with relative prosperity and boredom (not unlike 'normalisation', used to describe Czechoslovakia post-1968). However, as the motto for this chapter suggests, love needs a certain prosperity and stabilisation to be born. Moreover, I argue that in Polish cinema love was given the role of destabilising the 'small stabilisation'. Following the division between heterogeneous and homogenous society, proposed by Bataille, we can argue that both in Poland and Czechoslovakia the 1960s became more heterogeneous, thanks to which carefree libidinal expenditure became permitted.

I will regard as the paradigmatic example of 'romantic fever' in Polish cinema *Pociąg* (*Night Train*, 1959) by Jerzy Kawalerowicz, from which I borrowed the title of this section. The man who says 'Feelings are now fashionable' suggests that previously feelings were not in vogue in Poland, which can be read as a clear allusion to the period of Stalinism. He, an advocate specialising in financial affairs, is rather contemptuous about the shift towards feelings and especially the fact that these days they seem to explain everything, overshadowing other values and motives. His own wife who is half his age does not share his attitude – she is utterly bored with him and desperately looking for romance. Kawalerowicz presents a number of characters, each consumed by their own unresolved personal crises and their hunger for feelings. At the centre of the narrative is a young woman, Marta (Lucyna Winnicka), who buys a ticket for a sleeping compartment from an unknown man and boards a train from Łódź to Hel at the seaside. She is followed by a young man, Staszek (Zbigniew Cybulski), with whom she had an affair. This affair did not matter much for Marta but for him proved very important, as demonstrated by his love letters in which he threatens to derail the train if she continues to ignore him. Marta's fellow passenger is an attractive, middle-aged man, Jerzy (Leon Niemczyk), a surgeon who initially seems to be indifferent or even hostile towards her, but in due course shows her understanding and becomes affectionate. Marta tells him that she was once with a man whom she loved, but their affection did not lead anywhere as he used her only as a mirror to admire himself. It appears that Jerzy might be different but their possible romance does not materialise either, as his wife is waiting for him at the station. The end of the journey finds Marta completely lonely and desperate, as Staszek eventually gives up on her, and her previous flame whom she hoped to meet at the station does not turn up.

The psychological complications are played against the criminal story of a murderer hiding on the train, who sold Marta her ticket. This man also turns out to be the victim of a romantic fever, as he is accused of killing his own wife. The melancholy jazz score of Andrzej Trzaskowski, based on *Moon Ray* by Artie Shaw, underscores the impossibility of love, of its being condemned to failure even before it properly begins. Although there is no reference in Kawalerowicz's film to the sociopolitical situation in Poland, one wonders whether the romantic fever and complete ineptitude his characters betray in matters of the heart is not a consequence of the sterility of the previous period, as well as a legacy of war. Can the romantic fever be treated as making up for the times when citizens had to love their country and political leaders, rather than their girlfriends and spouses? Zygmunt Kałużyński suggests such an answer, regarding *Night Train* as a subtle investigation of the problems of people who attempt to rebuild a normal emotional life after historical cataclysms (Kałużyński 1959).

Kawalerowicz's next film, *Matka Joanna od Aniołów* (*Mother Joan of the Angels*, 1960), although set in the eighteenth century in the distant Smoleńsk region, can be interpreted as pertaining to the times in which the film was shot, because it also represents a 'romantic fever' that cannot be suppressed by any ideology or social rules. In such fever pure desire is more important than its object; it can remain even when its object perishes. The main male character in the film, Father Józef Suryn (Mieczysław Voit), goes to a monastery where allegedly Satan possessed the nuns. The most affected is Mother Joan (Lucyna Winnicka), therefore the priest has to take special care of her, holding private sessions of exorcisms. However, in due course he falls in love with Joan, and in order to save her from her demons, himself commits hideous crimes, murdering two innocent men. Kawalerowicz makes it clear that the demons possessing the characters are born inside them; they derive from the conflict between a religious dogma that does not allow them to have erotic feelings and their need for such a love. In director's own words, 'The devils that possess these people are the external manifestations of their repressed love. It is as if the devils give the man and the woman an excuse for their human love. Because of the excuse, they are able to love' (Privett 2001). Love is able to fill the emptiness in their souls that religion cannot replenish and give them a sense of individuality, of being different from others of that kind, that living in a convent obliterated. Mother Joan admits that she prefers to be possessed by demons, to be a great sinner, than one of a crowd of anonymous nuns. The desire for a distinct identity is underscored by the nuns' standardised, plain clothes. Under their white habits they all look the same and they merge with the background of white walls of the nunnery, therefore only their excessive behaviour furnishes them with uniqueness. Religion constitutes the chief obstacle for experiencing love and acquiring individuality, but it can be regarded as a metonymy of any totalitarian ideology, including the communist one. In *Mother Joan of the Angels* both women and men give in to their erotic needs, but it is a woman, Mother Joan, who instigates the erotic game and is more single-minded in obeying its rules. Father Suryn, as with his predecessor who was burnt at the stake, only allows himself to be led by temptation. Such a construction of love adheres to the biblical image of Adam, who is lured and ruined by Eve, but contradicts the Polish tradition of romantic love, in which woman remains a passive object of male desire. Kawalerowicz's Father Suryn is thus a 'lark on a string' pulled by a strong, determined and clever female.

While in the two films by Kawalerowicz love is depicted as excess, hysteria, madness, something for which the characters are prepared to die, in Wajda's *Niewinni czarodzieje* (*Innocent Sorcerers*, 1960), as well as in Janusz Morgenstern's *Do widzenia, do jutra* (*See You Tomorrow*, 1960) and *Jowita* (1967), its role is reduced to a social game. The male protagonist of *Innocent Scorcerers*, who is a doctor and amateur jazz musician, meets a beautiful girl in a fashionable student club. He invites her to his flat, but instead of expressing their mutual attraction by going to bed with each other, the two characters have a long talk, in which they experiment with various identities, as demonstrated by introducing each other as Bazyli and Pelagia, which are not their true names. They also play a real game, where the reward is the other taking off one piece of clothing. When the woman is about to lose her last garments, the man stops the game and they put their clothes back on, thus rejecting the chance of sexual fulfilment. Although both the man and the woman withhold their true feelings, it is mainly the man's fault that they stop half way, because in Polish culture of the time, even in the progressive students' subculture, it was a man's privilege and responsibility to lead erotic play. Yet, for Wajda's male protagonist, whose true passion is jazz, relationships with women is like playing jazz; it is a matter of repeating the same theme in different variations without reaching a definite conclusion – the climax. Moreover, for 'Bazyli' love, like jazz, must be cool: one has to avoid pathos and exaggeration, to underplay it rather than overplay. However, Wajda also shows that underplaying love means missing the opportunity to truly experience it. On the whole, *Innocent Scorcerers* demonstrates that for Poles love is impossible even when it is possible, so to speak, namely when they have all the required means to enjoy it (peace, money, their own space, and its perfect object). Maybe this is because they want to enjoy its very possibility, without spoiling it by too early consummation. Or, perhaps, they lack the required 'erotic culture' to reap the fruits of love.

Jowita, directed by Janusz Morgenstern, an adaptation of Stanisław Dygat's novel *Disneyland* and one of the few Polish films that seem to be inspired by the French New Wave (a movement in which a troubled love is a constant motif), develops the theme of love as a social play indulged in by the Polish upper classes. A large part of the film is set in the public spaces frequented by the young and fashionable, including a concert hall, a gallery and a sports club which also serves as a venue for balls and parties. Here would-be lovers meet and exchange gazes, as does the architect and sportsman Marek Arens (Daniel Olbrychski), who at a costume ball casts his eye on a beautiful woman in the guise of a Muslim woman (Barbara Kwiatkowska) with her nose and mouth covered by a black veil. She introduces herself as Jowita and he immediately falls in love with her. Subsequently, he tries to meet her and encounters a beautiful art student called Agnieszka. She looks like Jowita but claims that she is only her best friend. Marek and Agnieszka become lovers but neither of them is able to commit to their partner. They have affairs with

Figure 4.4 Barbara Kwiatkowska as Agnieszka/Jowita and Daniel Olbrychski as Marek Arens in *Jowita* (1967), directed by Janusz Morgenstern.

other people and eventually split up. In the last scene Agnieszka tells Marek that she is about to marry Marek's friend and that in fact she was Jowita.

Why did Agnieszka hide herself under the disguise of a mysterious 'foreigner'? Perhaps she enjoyed having a double persona or wanted to test Marek's true interest in her. If the latter, then Marek failed the test as he did not stop thinking about, searching for, and comparing Agnieszka to his memory of the girl from the ball. Marek preferred an imaginary (limerent) object of desire over a real woman or even over several women with whom he had affairs and, ultimately, he chose nonlove. This choice was noted by Zygmunt Kałużyński, who gave the title 'The Pole still cannot succeed in love' (Polakowi wciąż miłość nie wychodzi) to his review of Morgenstern's film (see Kałużyński 1967). I will point to two likely reasons why Morgenstern's hero shuns 'ordinary' love. The first reason, spelt out by Marek, is his conviction that love should only be a minor pursuit in man's life, something not worth dying or even living for, unlike such 'noble affairs' as fighting in a war or winning a sporting contest. From this perspective Marek comes across as a typical Polish romantic, which is emphasised by casting in his role Daniel Olbrychski, an actor specialising in the roles of virile heroes (see Chapter 2). The second reason is Marek's fear of 'giving in' to women and domesticity, fuelled by his observation of the miserable fate of the two men closest to him – his previous and current coach. The first man became so infatuated with some 'whore' that he committed suicide. The second became the plump, domesticated husband of a bored and unfaithful woman, spending his afternoons washing underwear in a small bathroom. His demise is conveyed by casting in this role Zbigniew Cybulski, who a decade earlier played Maciek Chełmicki in *Ashes and Diamonds*. It could be argued that by showing Cybulski in 'old slippers', as Krzysztof Kornacki puts is (Kornacki 1996: 80), Morgenstern warns Polish men against the dangers of 'normal' love.

In Czechoslovakia in the 1960s we also find a number of films about 'romantic fever'. One is *Return of the Prodigal Son* (discussed in Chapter 3), in which a number of characters are consumed by their desire of love, including Jan (Jan Kačer), whom we can regard as Marek Arens's analogue, because for both men love is a poor substitute for something else – a noble cause, perhaps fighting in a war. Romantic fever also affects characters in *Rozmarné léto* (*Capricious Summer*, 1967). This film is based on the novel by Vladislav Vančura and directed by Jiří Menzel, who deserves the title of the master of 'melodrama Czech style', directing many of the finest Czech films devoted to love. In *Capricious Summer* love is only an ideal – respected and cherished but hardly searched for in real life by the male characters. The three pillars of a provincial society: Antonín (Rudolf Hrušínský), the proprietor of the river bath huts; Canon Roch (František Řehák); and Major Hugo (Vlastimil Brodský), represent respectively commerce, the Church and the army. They lead a static life in which eroticism is at best the topic of conversation. Even Antonín, the only one of the three friends who is married, stopped having sex with his wife Kateřina a long time ago, much to her disappointment. Their life temporarily changes when an itinerant conjurer Ernie (Jiří Menzel) and his beautiful assistant Anna visit their village. Anna, according to Peter Hames, 'is a vision that recalls their youth and the possibility of attaining a romantic dream' (Hames 2005: 161).

However, they fail to fulfil their dream despite Anna's willingness to be seduced and her surprising patience with their clumsiness and even impotence. Hames explains this failure by the age and social position of the three would-be lovers: 'As inactive pillars of a static society, they have lost the capacity to act and can only fantasise and talk' (ibid: 162). I will agree with this explanation but would add another factor contributing to their inactivity in erotic matters, which is prioritising friendship over other relationships. Having each other's company and support, Antonín, Roch and Hugo do not need anybody else. This self-sufficiency of the three men is also the reason why Kateřina, who feels romantically unfulfilled in her marriage, grasps the opportunity of changing her love life with greater courage than her husband and his friends. Unlike Antonín, who meets Anna secretly, Kateřina openly moves into Ernie's caravan and adopts the role of his lover and companion, even trying to force Anna out of the magician's life. Yet, her attempt to change her life also ends in failure when Ernie injures his back in one of his performances; his injury symbolising his erotic ineptitude and impotence. Disappointed, Kateřina returns to her loveless marriage, as perhaps returned the psychiatrist's wife in *Return of the Prodigal Son* and many other women portrayed in Czech films. These are women whose immense erotic energy, their need to give and receive love, finds no permanent home, only a temporarily 'safety valve'.

Menzel not only excelled in directing films about love but also (both in films he directed and those of other directors) specialised in the roles of men who help forlorn women and men to cope with their rejection, solitude and sexual problems. For example, in *Return of the Prodigal Son* he plays Jana's lover, in *Capricious Summer* Ernie, in *Closely Observed Trains* a doctor, helping Miloš to overcome his sexual problems. Taking into account that Menzel is not an ordinary actor, but an actor–director, the 'face of Czech cinema' and for several decades a symbol of its continuity, it could be suggested that his appearances symbolise the role of cinema in the romantic life of the viewers. This role is therapeutic – it can alleviate the problems of the viewers by giving them direction and offering a substitute for romantic love, but cannot overcome them.

In *Slnko v sieti* (*Sunshine in the Net*, 1962) by Slovak director Štefan Uher, the erotic life of a teenage inhabitant of Bratislava, nicknamed Fajolo (Marián Bielik), takes central stage. The teenager discusses his state through an internal monologue, giving us direct access to his subjectivity. Fajolo is enchanted by his peer, a fair-haired Bela (Jana Beláková), but their relationship is a chain of frustrations and disappointments. At first, Bela wants Fajolo to show her more interest, most importantly, talk to her rather than being immersed in his own thoughts. When in an act of frustration she destroys his precious transistor radio, he gets angry and their relationship is strained. Later the boy, encouraged by his father, takes up voluntarily work on a cooperative farm. There he meets a dark-haired girl from Bratislava and has sex with her. At the same time, this encounter makes him realise how much he cares for Bela. He writes long and poetic letters to her, which she reads aloud lying on a raft on a river with her new boyfriend, who makes fun of Fajolo's lofty literary style. When Fajolo returns from the farm, their love rekindles, but the boy breaks up with Bela when he accidentally learns that she showed his letter to another man.

Uher's film suits the model of a story about 'puppy love': first feelings, mismatches and mistakes made by young people. Yet the rich background, against which Fajolo and Bela's relationship develops, and the elaborate metaphors used by the director, also makes *Sunshine in the Net* a universal story about the value of love in human life, as well as a subtle commentary on the erotic life of Slovak people. Fajolo and Bela live with their parents but we get the impression that there is little love between members of the older generation, confirming the opinion that for East Europeans marriage is a grave of love. Fajolo's mother works so much (as indeed, did the whole generation of Czechoslovak women in this period), that she hardly sees her family. The only sign of her presence are meals that she leaves in the fridge for Fajolo and his father. Bela's mother is blind and she spends whole days at home. Her continuous presence is a burden for her husband, who complains that due to her incapacity, he has to work more. We learn that her blindness was the result of a suicide attempt, precipitated by her husband's infidelity. When she learnt that he had an affair, she swallowed a large quantity of pills and was saved by Bela, who asked her for bread, making her change her mind. Ten years later Bela's mother regrets her 'stupid revenge', regarding her husband as unworthy of such a reaction and feeling guilty towards her children, who must now take care of her. The story of Bela's mother thus testifies to the dangers of believing in the romantic life and, especially, of putting it above maternal love. In the context of Fajolo and Bela's romance, on the other hand, it shows how dangerous unfaithfulness can be. However, it is mainly women who pay for their own mistakes, as well as for those committed by men. Men tend to forget about their flaws and move on.

Figure 4.5 Marián Bielik as Fajolo and Jana Beláková as Bela in *Slnko v sieti* (*Sunshine in the Net*, 1962), directed by Štefan Uher.

Sunshine in the Net has an almost magic quality, resulting from its skilful use of symbolism, especially the motifs of water and sun, frequently combined in one scene. The young characters often recline and kiss on an abandoned boat or near the water. The water underscores their budding sexuality, as well as the uncertainty and fluidity of their future. In the proximity of water they gain and lose their love. The film begins during the day of a total sun eclipse, an event that happens only once every hundred and twenty years. This rare phenomenon is compared to the moment of total happiness that also happens rarely and can be missed or blind the person who experiences it. It can be argued that love was like an eclipse for Fajolo and Bela, as well as for Bela's mother. The sun also appears in a bottle in a net over the water (that gives the film its title). Again, it is as elusive and immaterial a phenomenon, as the happiness of first love.

Miloš Forman's characters in *Black Peter* and *A Blonde in Love* are about the same age as those of Uher and they experience similar desires but different dilemmas. Their main problem is simply to find the partner and 'do it', which is not easy if one is shy or lives in a provincial town where there are not many people of one's own age and of the opposite sex. For the main character in *Black Peter* (Ladislav Jakim) the main issue is to learn the alphabet of an erotic game: to know how to approach a girl and show interest in her. Petr and other boys from his surroundings, such as Čenda who gets drunk at a party instead of chatting up an all-too-eager girl, fail, but the director suggests that their failure is not ultimate – it is a necessary stage to learning how to deal with women and succeed with them. This diagnosis is confirmed in *A*

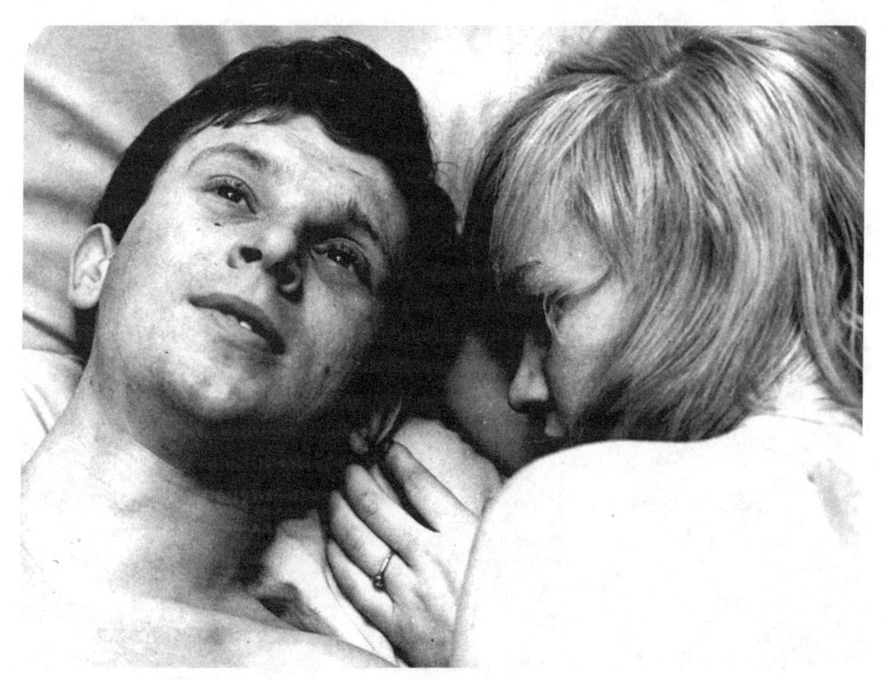

Figure 4.6 Vladimír Pucholt as Milda and Hana Brejchová as Andula in *Lásky jedné plavovlásky* (*A Blonde in Love*, 1965), directed by Miloš Forman.

Blonde in Love, where Milda, played by Vladimír Pucholt, whose earlier incarnations were an epitome of clumsiness in erotic circumstances, comes across as an expert lover, able to seduce any girl he encounters, including the eponymous blonde Andula. Forman shows that it is the girls who have to pay with their broken hearts for Milda playing a Casanova. Girls love, men seduce – this is the rule governing the behaviour of women and men in *A Blonde in Love*. However, instead of mourning this phenomenon or interrogating its origins, Forman treats it as a law of nature.

In all the films discussed in this section eroticism is suggested rather than shown, with nudity still being a taboo. Amos Vogel claims that the East's first nude scene is in *A Blonde in Love* (Vogel 1974: 220). This statement is rather problematic, as it depends on the definition of 'nudity'. However, what is beyond doubt is a tendency to poeticise or romanticise the bodies of lovers, even if they are placed in not a very poetic setting, as in Forman's film. Such a tendency, in my opinion, points to the fact that in the 1960s erotic love was still regarded as something outside the ordinary which required, if not a special place, at least a special attitude.

I shall close my discussion of the 1960s with *Vtačkovia, siroty a blázni* (*Birds, Orphans and Fools*, 1969) by the Slovak director Juraj Jakubisko. His style is often compared to that of Federico Fellini but for me bears more similarity with that of Polish director, Andrzej Żuławski. Surreal, complex, saturated with references to Slovak history, politics and mythology, self-referential and fragmented, with many scenes that seem to be included solely for their symbolic and visual potential (Liehm and Liehm 1977: 298–300; Hames 2005: 212–23; Kaňuch 2004), Jakubisko's film does not easily lend itself to a psychological interpretation. However, somehow against the grain, I shall offer it, as it appears to me that ascribing to the characters clear motives and ideas, especially specific ideas of love and happiness, allows us to find an overall meaning in this fragmented film and to decipher a large part of the film's symbolism. I will also suggest that such an interpretation is encouraged by the director himself, who announced *Birds, Orphans and Fools* as the first part of his 'Trilogy of Happiness', thus suggesting that happiness is its main topic. Like François Truffaut in *Jules et Jim* (1962), Jakubisko presents the birth and disintegration of a ménage à trois, consisting of three Bohemians or drop-outs: Slovak Yorick (Jiří Sýkora), Polish Andrzej (Philippe Avron) and Jewish Marta (Magda Vášáyrová). The difference in their nationalities, again as in *Jules et Jim*, does not drive the wedge in their relationship but rather brings them closer. The fact that the parents of Yorick, Andrzej and Marta killed each other, makes them aware of the brutality and madness resulting from nationalism. As orphans, they want to give each other love, warmth and shelter from the outside world. However, while initially it suffices to keep them together, in due course the differences between them become stronger or more transparent, making life together impossible.

The film's true protagonist is Yorick. We first meet him at some seedy party, invited by a stranger and attended by homosexuals and transsexuals. There Yorick embraces a young person of androgynous appearance. He asks about his sex, only to dismiss his question immediately by saying that 'It does not matter'. I will regard this sentence as key to Yorick's attitude to eroticism: he does not mind with whom he goes to bed, even whether it is a man or a woman, as long as it is 'fun'. Sex, along with playing, clowning, fooling around, are for him only a means to distract him temporarily from the hopelessness, despair and madness of the 'normal life' that he cannot bear. This normal life is encapsulated by the dilapidated houses and orphanages, as well as by police patrols and continuous shoot-outs on the streets, although the Second World War ended twenty years earlier, as one of the character in the film points out. At the party Yorick also meets Marta. With very short hair and old clothes, she also at first looks more like a boy than a girl (or an androgynous concentration camp inmate). Marta's presence first upsets Andrzej who wants Yorick to get rid of her, but when she becomes ill Andrzej warms to her and the three friends engage in a masquerade, often inviting their elderly landlord to keep them company. Eventually Marta and Andrzej become lovers. Yorick does not mind their intimacy; he even asks Marta to go to bed with his Polish friend, telling her that Andrzej never had a woman in his life. In fact, it is Marta who gets upset when Yorick offers her as a present to Andrzej. She asks him with dismay how he could tell her that he loved her if he wanted her to have sex with Andrzej. Such a question suggests that her idea of love is different to that of Yorick who appears to embrace Guy Hocquenghem's concept of love as a blind, animal-like force (Hocquenghem 1993; Chapter 5). Marta, by contrast, believes in romantic love that demands eternal devotion and exclusiveness. When Yorick is away for a year, arrested by the police and sent to prison for fooling around, Marta becomes pregnant by Andrzej. The couple welcome Yorick back home, and for a while all of them again wear silly hats and run madly through their enormous half-ruined house, but life does not return to its old crazy ways favoured by Yorick. During his absence Marta and Andrzej became an almost conventional couple, reconciled with the outside world. Yorick cannot accept their ordinariness, especially Marta's embracing of the future and domesticity. The ultimate manifestation of Yorick's disappointment with his friends and of his rejection of the path they had taken is the triple murder he commits of Marta, her unborn child and himself.

In comparison with the films discussed in this section, *Birds, Orphans and Fools* is very daring in representing the physical dimension of love. Particularly worthy of attention is Jakubisko's focus on the male body, normally treated with utmost discretion by male directors of this period. This literal baring of the male has to do with Marta's willingness and ability to enjoy the male body, which in this case is a consequence of her position as an owner of a small 'male harem'. Especially memorable is an episode in which Andrzej and Yorick say that they want to see Marta naked and she agrees but asks them to strip first. They remove their clothes, but Marta remains covered.

Birds, Orphans and Fools deserves to close this part of my discussion about lovers in Polish and Czechoslovak cinema, as it is a borderline film from the perspective applied in this chapter. Its atmosphere of romantic fever, even madness, searching for a limerent object, links it with the 1960s. On the other hand, its focus on pure sex, nudity and brutality, points to the more 'pornographic' 1970s. Most importantly, Jakubisko's film can be seen as liminal because it explores the failure of the 1960s utopian lifestyle, if not everywhere, at least in the socialist East.

The 1970s and 1980s: Sex is Now Fashionable

In Jerzy Krysiak's periodisation, the 1970s and 1980s are marked by increased sexualisation of female–male relationships in film. During this period it became acceptable to show female and male genitals and sexual intercourse. Indeed, Krysiak argues that the image of unconsummated erotic passion practically disappeared from the screen. Other features pertaining to these two decades are a more active role in sex for female characters and the use of eroticism as a commodity that can be exchanged for more tangible goods such as money or career, and as a means to deprive and humiliate the partner. In Czechoslovakia sexualisation of cinema, following the overturning of the Prague Spring, can be explained by the strengthening of political censorship and the promotion of consumerist and hedonistic attitudes by the state, as a way to lull citizens into political inactivity (see Chapter 3). Consequently, love became a popular theme for filmmakers as an alternative to representing on screen explicitly political and social issues. In Poland in the 1970s and early 1980s sex was not so much a 'substitute theme' for subjects such as political and social pathologies (because filmmakers in this period were relatively unbound by political censorship), as a way to denounce them. Accordingly, in the films of this period traditional eroticism was replaced by pathological sex: brutality, sadomasochism and (as I will argue in the next chapter) homosexuality. The last statement is particularly true in relation to Polish cinema after the introduction of martial law in 1981. In a significant proportion of cases, putting more sex into a film was a response to the state's demand to make more commercial, popular films. It was assumed that nakedness and sex sell films, therefore films should be saturated with them (Szyma 1988).

To illustrate the trends pertaining to Czech cinema I choose to discuss the films of Jiří Menzel and Zdeněk Troška. Although the former is associated with high-brow cinema and the latter with low-brow, the films of both of them testify to the shifting conventions of representing eroticism in film, as well as to the changing attitude of society to this aspect of human life. *Postřižiny* (*Cutting It Short*, 1981), Menzel's best-known film from his post-Soviet invasion period, based on a novella by his regular collaborator, Bohumil Hrabal, is set at the beginning of the twentieth century and focuses on the relationship of a brewery's manager, Francin (Jiří Schmitzer), with his wife Maryška (Magda Vášáyrová).

As Peter Hames observes, the film focuses on Maryška as a 'personification of female sexuality' (Hames 1989: 117). Maryška's eroticism, despite her classic Slavic beauty and extremely long fair hair, does not conform to the Slavic model of female behaviour because rather than being a passive object of male erotic pursuits, she follows her own instincts and controls male interest in her. Her appetite for sex is conveyed by her appetite for food; she indulges in meat and beer, eating two pork chops for breakfast with a large glass of beer, which is a diet associated with working-class men. She is also responsible in her household for pig slaughtering and preparing the meat. While Maryška's tastes are masculine, Francin's are feminine. For breakfast he drinks black coffee and bread, and avoids contact with raw meat. He even faints when faced with challenging situations, like the heroines of sentimental novels. Moreover, we never see him drinking alcohol, although inspecting the quality of beer in pubs and hotels is part of his job. The power of Maryška's sexuality is metaphorically represented in a scene when (together with Francin's eccentric brother) she climbs a high chimney. Filmed from the ground, which is also the position taken by Francin and various passers-by, she looks as if sitting on an enormous penis.

Francin is uncomfortable with Maryška's energy that leads to her usurping the masculine role within the house and her exuberant sexuality, making her the object of attention and affection of the men folk in their entire town. He is happiest when his wife injures her ankle and must stay in bed for some weeks. During this time he takes the role of the head of the family, containing her in a small area of bed, doing all the jobs that previously were Maryška's responsibility and protecting her from the gazes of other men (except from the doctor who examines her chest with utter delectation). However, when she recovers, she again reveals energy, power and independence that overwhelms and threatens Francin, as revealed in her decision to cut her long hair. This is, however, the last act in which she exerts such control over her sexuality, as she is severely punished by her husband who publicly slaps her. Francin's is probably the harshest 'tender slapping' ever recorded in Czech cinema, in which, as I mentioned earlier, this form of 'caress' is a trademark. It is worth bearing in mind this episode when looking at other screen lovers jokingly pinching or slapping women's bottoms. Although these acts might appear innocent enough, they are not innocent as they can give way to more barbaric behaviour that will go unpunished. In *Cutting It Short* Maryška's public chastisement is followed by her revealing to her husband that she is pregnant. Thus, it could be predicted, her sexual power would be eventually contained, confirming the view that motherhood in Czech and Polish cinema is hardly compatible with sexual allure.

While Menzel is master of 'arthouse' love, we can regard Zdeněk Troška as the main specialist in explicitly erotic cinema. In the period between early 1980s and early 1990s he shot three films set in his home village of Hoštica u Volne that focus on the Škopek family, that can be regarded as the rural equivalent of the Homolka family discussed in the previous chapter. The titles of all of them begin with 'sun, hay', which alludes to their rustic and mildly erotic climate. They are *Slunce, seno, jahody* (*Sun, Hay and Strawberries*, 1984), *Slunce, seno a pár facek* (*Sun, Hay and a Couple of Slaps*, 1989) and *Slunce, seno, erotika* (*Sun, Hay and Eroticism*, 1991). Needless to say, the title of the last film, made after the Velvet Revolution, rather than only alluding to the film's erotic plot, pronounces it openly.

Of particular interest to me is the first part of the Škopek's saga, as it captures the sexual mores of a Czech village during the period of late socialism, as well as the relationship between sex and (local) politics. The main characters in the film are four young people. They are Škopek's young daughter Blažena, her boyfriend Jirka, Mila, a girl of Blažena's age who is erotically interested in Jirka, and Simon, a newcomer from the town. Simon gets a work placement in the local cooperative, testing his theory of the influence of the cultural environment on cow's milk, and becomes

Škopeks' lodger. Initially Simon's ideas about exposing cows to music during milking are scorned by the villagers, but when it turns out that Simon has the same surname as a dignitary who is about to inspect the cooperative, their attitude changes. The cooperative's management goes to great lengths to implement his agricultural theories (that awake associations with the Russian experiments in farming of the 1930s) and Blažena is given the role of finding out what he is up to and making him well disposed to the people of the village. Although it is never spelled out, we can guess that she is encouraged to seduce Simon. Her excessive interest in the guest angers Jirka, who regards her as a tart and seeks solace in Mila's arms. Their intimacy, on the other hand, makes Blažena jealous. The situation gets serious when Blažena discovers that she is pregnant and Jirka rejects her on the grounds that the child she is carrying is Simon's. Luckily for Blažena and everybody involved, Simon is not interested in her erotically, as he has a girlfriend in Prague. Armed with a document confirming that Blažena became pregnant before she met him, Simon manages to convince Jirka that he poses no threat to their relationship and the film ends happily.

As this synopsis suggests, Troška employs a well-known plot of romantic comedy, in which someone in love mistakenly believes that the object of his or her affection is unfaithful, and becomes erotically involved with another person. However, he firmly situates this scheme in the Czechoslovak political, social and economic circumstances, foregrounding consumerism, hedonism and the corruption of the inhabitants of a village. Eroticism is an index of their hedonism and corruption – wherever we look, we see people indulging in extra-marital sex. It is not only Jirka and Blažena but also Mila, who in the period of only a couple of days gets laid with Jirka and with a truck driver who brings supplies for her shop, and Evička, the secretary in the cooperative farm who behaves in a provocative way in the presence of men, exposing her legs and cleavage and giggling when a man slaps her bottom. On the whole, Troška's women do not need to be seduced by men as they are able to take the initiative. Blažena's power to seduce Simon is also used to increase the material well-being of the village. It is assumed that if Simon's assessment of the village is positive, so will his high-ranking father's, and their good disposition, rather than any real achievements of the cooperative, will ensure their good publicity and financial bonuses. Troška also demonstrates that erotic relationships are the preserve of young and unmarried people. There is no place for them in the family, as demonstrated by the behaviour of Blažena's parents, who do not treat each other with even the slightest affection but only irritation and contempt. As for Mrs Škopkova, however, this does not mean that she gave up on love completely, as she projects her romantic dreams into heroines watched on television. Tellingly, her enjoyment in watching melodrama on the screen is disturbed by her husband's snoring. As for him, he prefers to watch children's cartoons.

In Polish cinema of the 1970s and 1980s we also observe a proliferation of sexual images. Within this general tendency we can identify two approaches. One focuses on the conflict between love and other values, such as money, career or peace of mind, as well as the welfare of one's own family. Often sex is used by characters as a commodity which can be exchanged for more tangible goods such as money or access to important information. In this type of film men more often than women engage in selling love, becoming pimps or prostitutes. Films of this kind are typically set in contemporary Poland, examples are *Polowanie na muchy* (*Hunting Flies*, 1969), directed by Andrzej Wajda, *Trzeba zabić tę miłość* (*To Kill this Love*, 1972), directed by Janusz Morgenstern and *Wodzirej* (*Dance Leader*, 1977), directed by Feliks Falk. The other type of film foregrounds the sheer power of erotic attraction, both for men and for women, particularly its ability to destroy human beings, as in *Thais* (1983), directed by Ryszard Ber, *Szkoda twoich łez* (*Tears Won't Help*, 1983), directed by Stanisław Lenartowicz, *Łuk Erosa* (*Cupid's Bow*, 1987), directed by Jerzy Domaradzki and, most importantly, *Dzieje grzechu* (*Story of a Sin*, 1975), directed by Walerian Borowczyk, which I will discuss in detail. These films are set in the past, most often in Poland before the Second World War.

Andrzej Wajda's *Hunting Flies* was made in 1969 but I regard it as being ahead of its time, pointing more to the materialistic 1970s than the romantic 1960s. Its main character Włodek (Zygmunt Malanowicz) is a weak man surrounded by strong women who ensnare him as fly-paper ensnares flies. Particularly effective is Włodek's girlfriend Irena who dominates his life virtually from the first day they meet. She arranges their dates, initiates lovemaking and tries to organise Włodek's social life and his career. She takes him to a fashionable party where she introduces him to her influential friends. Among them is the wife of an editor of a popular journal whom Irena wants Włodek to seduce 'for the sake of both of them', as she puts it. Włodek reluctantly agrees but his encounter with the editor's wife ends in disaster. First he behaves as if he wanted to escape from her room, and then he takes off his shirt and tells the woman to 'take him' as if he were a prostitute. Such blunt behaviour, however, puts off his lover-to-be so much that she throws him out of her room, saying that 'Nobody here will rape you'. After this failure Włodek retires to the point from which he started his journey into high society: that of an 'invisible man', content with his low position at home and at work.

Hunting Flies was criticised for conveying men's fear of women (see Kajewski 1969), which even the author of the script, Janusz Głowacki, acknowledges (Głowacki 1969). It is true that women in this film are hardly positive heroines, being materialistic, career-oriented, ruthless and pretentious (see Chapter 2). However, I will argue that the author's main target are men who not only stopped being romantic, but are even unable to play romantic or find any other strategy to conquer women. Włodek's blunder with the editor's wife is the ultimate proof of it. On the whole, if Włodek eventually fails, both as a lover and a career man, it is not because of women's conspiracy against him but due to his own shortcomings: laziness, lack of charm and general mediocrity.

The critics acknowledged Głowacki's immense influence on the ideology and general atmosphere of Wajda's film, which is cynical. *To Kill this Love* was also scripted by Głowacki and pertains to the same phenomenon as *Hunting Flies*, namely the end of romantic attitudes to love among Poles. It depicts the trials and tribulations of a young couple who are about to start an independent life after their first major failure. Magda (Jadwiga Jankowska-Cieślak) did not pass competitive entrance exams to medical school, Andrzej (Andrzej Malec) failed to obtain a place in an engineering college. Before they try again to win a place at the university, they have to find jobs that will help them to gain extra points in their next application, as well as earn enough money to rent a flat. These goals prove difficult to achieve, as flats in Warsaw are expensive. In order to solve this problem, Andrzej becomes a rent boy for the wife of a wealthy garage owner and he steals a precious ornament from their apartment to pay the deposit for a flat. When his act is discovered, he steals money from Magda, to compensate for the loss of his boss and his wife. Magda learns about Andrzej's infidelity and his financial misdemeanours, and rejects him, despite his protesting that he committed all the crimes for their future happiness. The director makes us share in Magda's distaste and contempt for Andrzej, and reveals facts that further undermine his moral standing. We learn that Andrzej goes to bed with his boss's wife without any hesitation or soul-searching, and he prostitutes himself largely for the pleasure of receiving the attention of an older and rich woman. Neither does he suffer any qualms of conscience when Magda discovers him in bed with his lover. Instead he mocks her naivety. Although Magda is also in a position to 'siphon' money from an older man, a doctor in the hospital where she works as an auxiliary nurse, she rejects this opportunity. In her last dialogue with the doctor the heroine admits that it would be very convenient for her to fall in love with him but she cannot do it; love is for her a value that cannot be exchanged for anything. Andrzej, on the other hand, seems to be incapable of any deeper reflection on the nature of his feelings.

The title of Morgenstern's film suggests that Magda's and Andrzej's love, or more precisely, the romantic love they share at the beginning of their relationship, is dangerous and unwelcome to society, like a virus that needs to be eradicated. Such an interpretation is corroborated by the behaviour of Andrzej's flatmate Staszek (Tomasz Lengren), whose main goal in life is to have as many lovers as possible, and Magda's father's second wife Dzidzia, who treats her relationship with Magda's father solely as an economic arrangement. Dzidzia admits that she lost faith in romantic love because younger men tended to use and discard her. The advantage of Magda's father is, paradoxically, his limited opportunities for romance. Dzidzia even admits that she enjoys the fact that her husband is most of the time impotent; his shame at not being able to sexually satisfy his young wife gives her immense power over him. Andrzej's married lover and her husband also prove to be very cynical about love. Their marriage is a mockery of the idea of a monogamous union; each of them has affairs with younger people, with the full knowledge of the spouse. They behave like vampires who suck the blood of their young victims and discard them when they cease to be attractive. Although all these people have an air of self-confidence, they are less happy than they admit.

Magda and Andrzej's relationship also parallels the story of a janitor and his dog. The dog does not allow the janitor's 'customers' to steal the building materials he is watching, therefore the master uses all possible tricks to get rid of his companion, but the faithful dog always returns. Finally, the janitor ties up the dog and attaches explosives to the animal, but the dog frees himself and returns to the shed where the janitor is staying, blowing up himself and his master. The obvious moral of this story is that by destroying the love that binds us together we also destroy ourselves. The idea of a strong connection between love and personal identity is obviously romantic. Hence, *To Kill this Love* is ultimately a romantic film. In this respect it is different to *Hunting Flies* which offers no alternative to a cynical attitude to love. Zygmunt Kałużyński links the ultimately optimistic tone of this film to the influence of Janusz Morgenstern on Głowacki's text, whom he regards as a filmmaker 'with feelings'. In his opinion Morgenstern allowed us to see that behind Głowacki's cynicism and irony there is an anger at his generation and a desire to waken his peers, to show them the possibility of a different, less materialistic life (Kałużyński 1973).

In comparison with *Hunting Flies* and *To Kill this Love*, *Dance Leader* represents a further step towards commodification of love because for the eponymous dance leader, Lutek Danielak (Jerzy Stuhr), nothing about love remains sacred. Or, to put it differently, he is no longer capable of love and, indeed, any other selfless feelings, because he thinks only about his career. To climb the social ladder he is prepared to sell himself and those closest to him. We see him prostituting himself with an older ex-colleague, in order to find out embarrassing details about a competitor for a prestigious assignment, and he tries to exchange his girlfriend for a favour that can help him to eliminate another competitor. What strikes us most is how much Lutek will sacrifice in terms of personal cost to gain some uncertain material and social advantages. The doubtfulness of what he will achieve by his cynical exchanges diminishes the value of love, as well as of personal unity. Falk not only underscores Lutek's extreme careerism and selfishness but also his erotic ineptitude. His dealings with his older lover and his girlfriend are ultimate proof of his erotic incompetence, as both women eventually give up on him. Erotic incompetence or plain impotence is also a motif of many other films of Moral Concern, for example Wajda's *Dyrygent* (*The Conductor*, 1980). Men's impotence was interpreted by critics as a metaphor of men's political helplessness. Such reading is plausible, but the very fact that men's sexual failures are used to illustrate their political failures is also meaningful, pointing to the 'real' problems of these men. On the whole, judging by the films discussed in this part, Polish men can rarely be genuinely romantic in love and playing romantic is even a more difficult task for them.

Kieślowski's *Krótki film o miłości* (*A Short Film about Love*, 1988), probably the most famous Polish film about love ever to come out of Poland, summarises many of the tendencies discernible in the earlier films, but also introduces a new motif. It tells the story of a young male, a boy really, a postal worker named Tomek (Olaf Lubaszenko), who falls in love with an older woman named Magda (Grażyna Szapołowska). To learn about her life Tomek steals her letters and spies on her from his window using a telescope. When he eventually confesses his infatuation to her, he is severely punished. First Magda's lover beats him up, then she humiliates him in her home, arousing him and causing premature ejaculation. The shame of being unable to sustain excitement is so great that Tomek leaves Magda's flat and attempts suicide. After this incidents their roles change; Magda starts to spy on Tomek and visits the places where he can be found, although without success. The film has two endings. In the television version Magda eventually meets Tomek in the post office but he treats her coolly. In the cinema version, they are united in an imaginary scene, but its dreamy character only underlines the failure of their romance.

A Short Film about Love is typical for Polish cinema of the 1970s and 1980s, because it depicts a strong, seductive and promiscuous woman and a young man who falls under her spell. It is worth mentioning that Olaf Lubaszenko played a role similar to that of Tomek in a film made a year earlier, Domaradzki's *Cupid's Bow*. Moreover, although Kieślowski avoids graphic sex, he conveys the idea that sex is the main component of the lives of his characters. Magda, her numerous lovers, even Tomek and his friend who first drew his attention to Magda, are all obsessed with sex. On the other hand, the film's author points to the difference between love and sex, and attempts to restore the former its rightful place in human life. He subjects both Tomek and Magda to this love education. Through meeting Magda and experiencing her cruelty, Tomek learns how costly love can be – it almost destroys his life. Perhaps thanks to her he also abandons his romantic illusions as indicated by telling Magda at the end of the television version of the story, 'I do not spy on you any more'. Magda also learns that there is more to relationships with men than purely physical attraction and expert handling of 'romantic situations' (such as holding hands in a café), and starts to yearn for real love. After her final encounter with Tomek she shuns her previous lovers. When one of them knocks on her door, she says 'I am not here' and cuts short her telephone conversation with another lover. *A Short Film about Love* alludes to the sixth commandment, but it condemns promiscuity less than cynicism understood as the lack of faith in real love, although

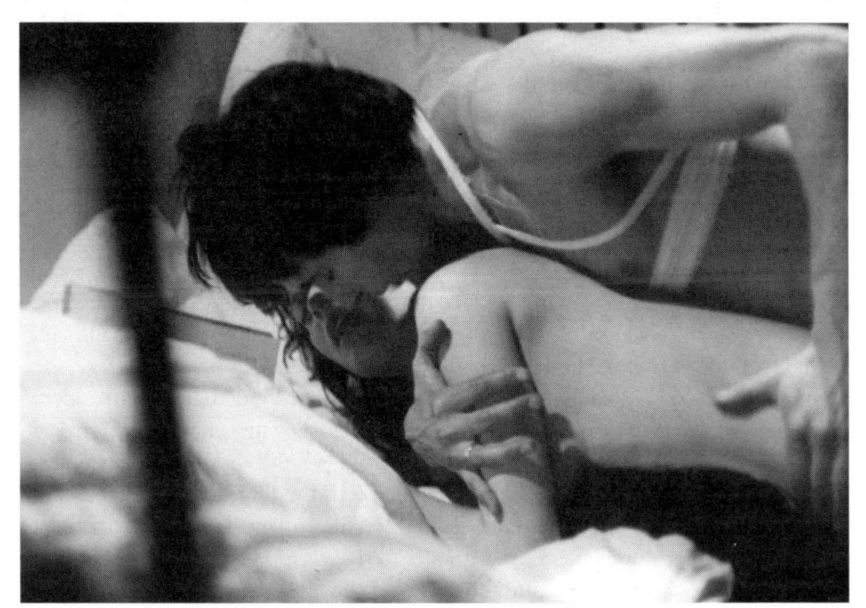

Figure 4.7 Grażyna Długołęcka as Ewa Pobratyńska and Jerzy Zelnik as Łukasz Niepołomski in *Dzieje grzechu* (*Story of a Sin*, 1975), directed by Walerian Borowczyk.

it can be argued that promiscuity leads to cynicism. There is also a motif in *A Short Film about Love*, which at the time of the film's premiere might appear marginal but seems to be important from the post-1989 perspective, namely of the right match between a man and a woman. It is introduced when Magda visits Tomek's landlady and the elderly woman tells Magda, 'You were a bad match for him.' Magda agrees with this statement and we have to agree too – if Tomek had met a less experienced woman, perhaps a girl of his age, he might have retain his romantic ideals.[5]

Story of a Sin is set at the turn of the nineteenth century, but it pertains to the time it was made, as indicated by the interest it attracted from critics and ordinary viewers. To shoot it, one of the most famous Polish emigrant filmmakers, Walerian Borowczyk, returned to Poland. His decision to make a film in his native country was understandable as *Story of a Sin* is an adaptation of the novel by Stefan Żeromski of the same title. Although published in 1909, it remains one of the most erotic books ever written in Polish. Borowczyk's choice of literary source is not surprising because his trademark from the very beginning of his career was to clash extreme emotions with utter stylisation, or monstrosity with decorum (Kałużyński 1975: 12). Such a clash was already included in Żeromski's work; the challenge was to convey it cinematically. The book focuses on a beautiful woman, named Ewa Pobratyńska (Grażyna Długołęcka), from an impoverished noble family, who reaches the bottom of moral and social decline. She has an affair with a married man Łukasz Niepołomski (Jerzy Zelnik), becomes pregnant by him and kills their child. After that, blackmailed by a shady man named Pochroń (Roman Wilhelmi), who knows about her infanticide, she becomes a prostitute and kills her rich lover Zygmunt Szczerbic (Olgierd Łukaszewicz). Finally, she loses her own life trying to save her first lover Łukasz.

Borowczyk's film, as its literary original, is also a story of a sin, or even of multiple sins, committed by Ewa. More importantly, however, it is a story of a deep love on the part of the heroine that never dies or withers. In this respect, as Stefan Morawski notes, the film significantly departs from its literary source, in which Ewa is more led by her senses than by love, and becomes sexually attracted not only to Łukasz but to other men as well, including her oppressor Pochroń (Morawski 1975). *Story of a Sin* is also a persuasive portrayal of the fin-de-siécle reality with its moral and social contradictions. On the one hand, it is a harsh and trivial world, in which most people must work very hard seven days a week to earn their living, divorce is difficult to obtain, abortion is illegal and having children out of wedlock brings disgrace. On the other hand, the inhabitants of this world are surrounded by the decadent atmosphere of cabarets, casinos and art exhibitions showing canvasses of naked women, which suggest that (sexual) love is everything (Kałużyński 1975; Marszałek 1975). We could see how the three main characters in the film, Ewa and her lovers, Łukasz Niepołomski and Zygmunt Szczerbic, are infected by the decadent atmosphere that surrounds them. Ewa decides to risk everything, including her own life, to be with her lover. Niepołomski teaches her the art of (sexual) love from some foreign manual and writes her 'ornamental' letters. Szczerbic sells his estate and follows Ewa with a sack full of money, and is killed by her during their lovemaking.

Women are the main victims of the gap between the trivial and oppressive reality and the lofty ideal of love as the god, conveyed by art and literature. Men (as Engels noted several decades before Żeromski published his novel), are able to find a compromise between reality and ideal. Prostitution and extra-marital sex is such a solution to their problems. The fissure between the trivial and oppressive everyday reality and the atmosphere of erotic fever, which ultimately points to the hypocrisy of Polish society, is excellently created by the cinematography of Zygmunt Samosiuk, who renders the characters as if they were locked in small interiors, always oppressed and hunted. If we return to Bataille's dichotomy of homogenous/heterogeneous society, then we can argue that Borowczyk represents the homogenous capitalist world about to implode due to erotic energy collected over the years, and the external stimuli, such as art, that help to release it from the human souls. Yet, we should not conclude that either Żeromski or Borowczyk (or Bataille for that matter) postulate that people should wholeheartedly give in to their erotic desires. In fact, *Story of a Sin* focuses on the tragic consequences of following one's heart and, in this way, paradoxically, validates the instrumental attitude to love prevailing in the films of the 1970s and 1980s.

To conclude, sex was in vogue in the 1970s and 1980s because romantic love became outdated. This end of romanticism is sometimes the result of the attitudes of the new, 'liberated' women. More often, however, the lack of romanticism is due to men who discovered that sex could be a commodity. Its particular usefulness as an object of exchange had to do with the fact that, as with other goods in a socialist country, its value was vague and flexible. One can get a lot for selling one's own body or those of one's family or friends, or pay nothing for sex, pretending the service was for free. Interestingly, whilst in films set in the past we find professional pimps and prostitutes, in the films set in the present they are virtually absent, which can be explained by the fact that almost everybody was willing to partake in sexual exchange.

The focus on sex in the films of the 1970s and 1980s inevitably led to a new way of representing the male body. In contrast to socialist-realistic films, where bodies tended to be monumentalised, or to the New Wave films, where they were poeticised, in the 1970s and 1980s they appear material, physical, biological. Unlike men in the previous period, men in these films often work on their bodies and are not shy to display the results of their efforts. Take, for example, Francin building his muscles in *Cutting It Short*, or Staszek in *To Kill this Love* proudly displaying his physique in the hope that Magda will fall for him. We are also acutely aware of the physicality of male bodies because they are often unattractive: plump or withered, old or deformed, which in the Polish films of the 1970s largely results from avoiding stars, and instead using less known, more average-looking actors or even using non-professionals (Kornatowska 1990: 61–106). Such representation of the male bodies underscores the message that while sex is available to everybody, love is the privilege of a few.

Postcommunist Times: How to Find the Right Match

The 1990s and 2000s are similar to the 1960s in showing great interest in love. This interest can be attributed to the end of communism and with it, greater privatisation of the lives of East Europeans, and the unprecedented commercial pressures exerted on filmmakers, who have to search for subjects able to attract a large number of viewers. Love is, of course, one such subject. Yet, as before, interest in love does not go hand in hand with seeing it on the street, so to speak. The characters of the films of the 1990s and 2000s have as many problems in their erotic lives as their cinematic fathers and grandfathers, if not more.

Because of its liminality, I would like to begin with *Porno* by Marek Koterski. It was produced in 1989, the year communism collapsed in the large part of the Eastern bloc. More importantly, it looks at love from the perspective of a man who carries into the new Poland his outmoded ideas about love, while simultaneously acknowledging that the world around him has changed. In addition, the film itself offers a diagnosis of the position and state of a 'love film' in Polish cinema. The narrative of *Porno* is simple. To overcome insomnia, Michał Miauczyński (Zbigniew Rola) counts all the women with whom he had sex in his life. There were plenty, but he was only in love with his first girlfriend Asia. He hoped to steal her virginity when they went camping together, but failed because the girl promised her parents to 'behave herself'. Later in his life Michał meets Asia again but for various reasons their paths part and eventually he sees her married and pregnant by another man. Michał also gets married. According to the unwritten rule that marriage in Poland is only for procreation and fulfilling social expectations, he does not love his wife. Bespectacled and plump, she is the least attractive woman Michał has had sex with.

Miauczyński is the first Polish screen lover who in matters of the heart behaves as an ardent consumer. He shops for women as others shop for socks and ties, although he deludes himself that in the depth of his heart he has remained a romantic. Unfortunately for him, other men (as well as women) also have consumerist attitudes to love – all look for the best available 'product'. This is the reason that Asia is picked by somebody more attractive than Michał and he ends up with Marta; their mutual lack of attractiveness brings them together. Unfortunately, while Marta is prepared to put up with Michał's weaknesses, he continues dreaming about his perfect match. As we might learn in the following instalments of Miauczyński's adventures, *Nic śmiesznego* (*Nothing Funny*, 1995) and *Ajlawju* (1999), this dissatisfaction will eventually lead to the break-up of his marriage (Mazierska 2004c).

The provocative title of Koterski's work encourages us to regard *Porno* not only as a story about Miauczyński but also as a self-conscious meta-film. This reading is also invited by an episode in the earlier film by Koterski, *Życie wewnętrzne* (*Inner Life*, 1986), in which the wife of the main character, while filling in a questionnaire in a magazine, asks him what kind of film he would like to watch in the cinema. From a number of available options he chooses a 'film about love and sexual intercourse'. No doubt *Porno* is such a film in which the sexual sphere dominates over other aspects of man's life and is excluded from a wider social context. As if to validate Koterski's opinion that a 'film about love and sexual intercourse' is what the average Pole wants to see, *Porno* was the biggest Polish box office success in 1990. However, the critics did not share the viewers' enthusiasm, accusing the film of either providing cheap entertainment, or of being somehow 'broken' by neither fitting the model of artistic nor commercial cinema.

In sexual matters Miauczyński behaves as a consumer but one who is naive and amateurish, as testified by repeatedly catching venereal diseases. In contrast, in a film made a decade after *Porno*'s success, *Zakochani* (*The Loving Ones*, 2000) by Piotr Wereśniak, erotic consumption is utterly professional. The film's main characters, Mateusz (Bartosz Opania) and Zosia (Magdalena Cielecka), earn their living by making rich men and women fall in love with them, and giving them expensive gifts. Their methods hardly differ; she uses her feminine charm, he his masculine magic, to attract their victims, or clients, depending how one looks at their erotic relationships. Eventually Zosia and Mateusz fall in love with each other but this does not make them give up their professions. They even decide to join forces and strengthen their business. As the reviewers noted, Wereśniak's film testifies to the greater equality between men and women in the erotic sphere, or at least as far as affluent men and women are concerned. At the same time, it points to the end of romantic love as experienced by Polish postcommunist youth (Chyb 2000; Janicka 2000). Does Mateusz really love Zosia? Does she love him? We really do not know and do not care. Whilst for Miauczyński romantic love is still his ideal, Mateusz and Zosia do not know what there is to yearn for.

If there is anybody in *The Loving Ones* who knows anything about love, they are members of the older generation, especially Mateusz's ex-lover played by Katarzyna Figura, the greatest female star of the 1980s, specialising in playing dumb blondes. Her final confrontation with Mateusz shows how empty the lives of young Poles are. For a moment Mateusz is ashamed but he easily puts up with embarrassment when more tangible benefits are at stake. The same rule applies to other male lovers in Polish films, such as Piotr in *Ławeczka* (*The Bench*, 2004), directed by Maciej Żak. All of them are consumption-oriented and regard love as a minor value, below such assets as money and career.

At the opposite end of Polish postcommunist love films we find movies that return to the idea of love as a romantic fever, elaborated in the 1960s. This trend is exemplified by *Egoiści* (*The Egoists*, 2000) by Mariusz Treliński and *Przemiany* (*Transformations*, 2003) by Mateusz Barczyk. However, whilst in the first film it is only the woman who herself burns in an unfulfilled desire and the man comes across as resigned and suicidal, in the second film the man takes an active (and traditional) role of somebody who awakens erotic passions. He, named Adrian Snaut (Jacek Poniedziałek), one day comes to the house of his fiancée, where he also meets her two sisters and their mother. In a short period of time Snaut forces the three women, as Bożena Janicka puts it, 'to look at their libido' (Janicka 2003: 51). Snaut has affairs with all the sisters, causing in the oldest, who suffers from diabetes, an acute attack which kills her, impregnating the youngest sister (whose husband is impotent) and driving the middle one, his own fiancée, to a nervous breakdown. The extreme character of his intervention provokes one critic to compare him to the characters in Przybyszewski's novels (Janicka 2003). Indeed, the man's only purpose of action appears to be sex, which brings as much pleasure to himself as to his lovers. When Snaut tells his female hostesses that they are lying, this means that they do not live in tune with their sexual desire but instead conform to some oppressive bourgeois standards of decency. However, the origin of Snaut in Przybyszewski's writing might pass by younger and less educated viewers. For the majority he has more in common with Brazilian soap operas that dominated Polish television a decade previously. Barczyk himself is well aware of the danger of comparing his film with this widely derided product, and he tries to prevent it by making one sister comment on their situation, 'This is like in a Brazilian soap opera'. Such a meta-cinematic moment saves Barczyk's film from ridicule but does not add much credibility to the main character. Snaut, whose name sounds rather foreign to the Polish ear, comes across as completely divorced from present-day Poland. Perhaps this was Barczyk's objective – by demonstrating the strangeness of Snaut, he wanted to make a point about the lack of sexual passion in the lives of his male compatriots.

Between *Porno* and *The Loving Ones* on the one hand, and *The Egoists* and *Transformations* on the other, there is not much to be found, as far as love is concerned. In particular, there are not many films in which love is neither solely an article for sale nor is reduced to fulfilling purely sexual desire but, instead, is marked by such features as commitment and loyalty. If it appears at all, it is typically in films made from the perspective of a woman looking for such qualities in men, such as *Nigdy w życiu!* (*Never in My Life!*, 2004), directed by Ryszard Zatorski and *The Bench*. I would also like to mention *Dług* (*Debt*, 1999), directed by Krzysztof Krauze, one of the most awarded and discussed Polish films of the last two decades, although hardly analysed from the perspective of the representation of love. Nevertheless, *Debt* is important as it endows (marital) love with the status of the highest value in one's life. Neglecting it brings tragic consequences for the main protagonist and rediscovering it can redeem an otherwise destroyed life.

After the fall of the Berlin Wall, Czech and Slovak filmmakers also acknowledged the consumerist aspect of erotic relationships between men and women, although they avoided the extremes in representing love that is a norm in Polish films. This difference partly results from the fact that their works derive from different traditions to the Polish films, mainly from the Czechoslovak New Wave. I will focus on *Jízda* (*The Ride*, 1994), directed by Jan Svěrák, *Samotáři* (*Loners*, 2000), directed by David Ondříček, *Návrat idiota* (*Return of the Idiot*, 1999), directed by Saša Gedeon and *Nuda v Brně* (*Boredom in Brno*, 2003), directed by Vladimír Morávek, because they perfectly capture the new approach to love among young Czechs. It is also worth adding that these films were popular in Poland, largely because they filled a gap in the market left by Polish filmmakers, being intelligent, but not too 'arty', rooted in everyday reality and concerning young ex-communists. Ondříček's film especially tapped into the need of young Poles to see themselves on screen (Gretkowska 2002).

The main male characters in *The Ride* are two men in their twenties, Radek (Radek Pastrňák) and Franta (Jakub Špalek), who leave Prague in a dilapidated secondhand convertible for a ride through the countryside. Their aim is to find adventure and joy, especially of a sexual nature. In an early conversation they mention the advantages of foreign prostitutes, who are cheaper than local girls and, because of the language barrier, cannot complain if something goes wrong. However, their consumerist expectations are upset by a young woman named Anna (Aňa Geislerová), whom they meet on their journey. They find her, like a prostitute, by the side of the road, with no possessions, but unlike a prostitute, she sits and examines her shoes as if unconcerned whether anybody will notice her presence, and she is not foreign but Czech. More importantly, instead of allowing Radek and Franta to treat her as a sexual object, she manipulates them for her own goals, namely to play a game on her rich boyfriend Honzik from whom she ran away. Honzik also owns a Western car but much newer and more expensive than Radek and Franta's convertible, which undermines the friends' consumerist power and forces them to prove their masculinity in a competition with him. To add to their frustration, Honzik persistently attempts to track Anna down, appearing in the same towns and villages which the three travellers visit, and trying to stop their car. Besieged by a powerful competitor, Radek and Franta not only fail to take sexual advantage of the girl, but go to great lengths to impress her. They get Anna her favourite food, alcohol and share their supply of marihuana with her, and despite their modest financial resources they book into a cheap hotel to secure a comfortable night for her. In the end, anxious that she might abandon them, they even offer her a lift to anywhere in the country she wishes to go. However, rather than show the boys some gratitude, Anna only teases them, disappearing and reappearing, and removing and replacing

Figure 4.8 Aňa Geislerová as Anna, Radek Pastrňák as Radek and Jakub Špalek as Franta in *Jízda* (*The Ride*, 1994), directed by Jan Svěrák.

her underwear. Moreover, she is not shy to strip them of their masculine power, as when she ties Radek up or when, after a bathe in the lake, she gazes at and comments on his penis that shrank in cold water. Anna's gaze in this scene is not reciprocated: the friends do not see her naked, as she swims some distance from them. In the end Anna leaves the two friends and returns to her boyfriend, leaving Radek devastated. Radek and Franta's last encounter with the girl takes place when they attend the scene of a car accident, whose dead victims are Anna and Honzik. Although Honzik was behind the steering wheel, Anna caused the crash, performing the same trick with the car key which she had attempted earlier with the old convertible. The accident demonstrated that Anna did not allow men to decide if and where to go and when to stop, but shaped her own as well as their itinerary. What was meant to be an exercise in careless sexual consumption on the part of men, turned out to be a real love story of men emotionally consumed by their feelings.

Loners is set in contemporary Prague and represents a number of young men and women of different backgrounds, jobs, even nationalities. Among them are a student, a presenter from a radio station, an immigrant from Macedonia working in a bar, a driver of a removal van, a neurosurgeon and two employees of a tourist agency (a man and a woman), specialising in serving Japanese tourists. As the title of the film suggest, they are all loners, although not in the sense of having nobody to talk to and suffering deeply due to this state, but rather in shunning deep engagement. Paradoxically, the greatest loner of them all is the greatest playboy, who excels in seducing barwomen and confesses to using prostitutes while in Thailand. This man rejects commitment, because only sex matters to him, and being relatively affluent he does not need a woman to cater for his day-to-day needs. However, he gets tired of his erotic life and buys himself a dog. A different case is the couple who have lived together for some years but decided to split up because they were not sure whether their partner was the best one for them, and kept looking for somebody else. As one of them says, 'We are looking for somebody who will not look for somebody else'. Another character is a married neurosurgeon who, using various disguises, stalks another woman, hoping to impress her with his professional achievements. Finally, there is a van driver who has smoked so much cannabis that he has forgotten that he has a girlfriend and has embarked on an affair with another woman, until a friend reminded him that his girlfriend is about to return from abroad. The only exception from this lifestyle of neverending shopping for a partner that involves betrayal, envy and disappointment, is the wife of the neurosurgeon, who does not look for any extra-marital affair and forgives her husband his infatuation with another woman, regarding it a sign of his transvestite tendencies. Although both Ondříček's men and women are young and unsettled, this state has a different effect on them, endowing women with extra maturity and dignity, and changing men into eternal Peter Pans, who behave as if they were on permanent vacation, clowning and playing with toys (principally video cameras). In this respect *Loners* is similar to Jakubisko's *Birds, Orphans and Fools*, where men also did not know when to stop their games.

For the young characters in *Return of the Idiot*, not unlike *Loners*, love also appears to be a matter of consumption, of using another person until it stops offering them pleasure. This attitude is openly expressed by Anna (Aňa Geislerová), who tells the mother of her boyfriend that she stays with somebody as long as their relationship has something to offer her. This selfish approach dismays the elderly woman so much that she asks Anna angrily what she herself has to offer. In another scene, perfectly illustrating the hedonistic approach to love of the young Czechs, we find a young woman, Olga, asking Emil (Jiří Langmajer), with whom she spent their last night, whether he wanted to get rid of her because he was afraid she might expect or demand something from him. He asks rhetorically, 'What on Earth could you expect from me?' This answer can be understood in two ways: as an acknowledgement that in the contemporary world men do not pay women for sexual services (unless they are professional prostitutes) because women, like men, go to bed for their own pleasure. However, it can also be regarded as the man's rejection of any responsibility and commitment, suggesting that for him sex is not an index of deeper feelings. This is the meaning that Olga appears to derive from Emil's utterance and finds it very upsetting. The measure of characters' hedonism is the fact that in their pursuit of sexual pleasure they betray those closest to them – their own family. Anna has an affair with the married brother of her boyfriend Emil, and Emil sleeps with Anna's sister Olga when Anna is away. Although there is a balance between the number of betrayals committed by Gedeon's characters, testifying to erotic consumerism adopted by both sexes, their betrayals are not of the same gravity. Only unmarried women commit adulteries in *Return of the Idiot*, while one of the male characters betrays his pregnant wife. Moreover, the sisters eventually confess to each other their transgressions, while men are prepared to play the cheating game as long as possible. When their lie is eventually exposed, Emil is not angry at himself but at an innocent man whom he accuses of disclosing his transgression. We can guess that after learning their lesson Gedeon's women will be more wary of purely hedonistic eroticism, while men will carry on as before.

The theme of searching for a right match is most openly explored in *Boredom in Brno*. This film presents the various ways contemporary Czechs search for love or perhaps only sexual fulfilment. Some do it through hanging out in cafés; others arrange meetings by correspondence and prepare themselves solemnly for their first sexual encounter as if it were an important exam. Some succeed, others fail. The key to success appears to be compatibility: it is easier to find the right match for an 'idiot', who limits his search to a pool of 'not-so-clever' women, than for married men looking for young girls. Yet, as if to contradict this opinion, other Czech films are awash with young women casting their eyes on older men. We find them, for example, in *Příběhy obyčejného šílenství* (*Wrong Side Up*, 2005), directed by Petr Zelenka, *Horem pádem* (*Up and Down*, 2004), directed by Jan Hřebejk and in *Román pro ženy* (*From Subway with Love*, 2005) by Filip Renč. In the last film the main female character falls in love with a man whom her own mother left many years ago, disgusted by his coarseness and bad manners. Perhaps the young's woman infatuation suggests that, although 'communist men' were 'larks on a string', they were still better lovers than their free sons. Or, maybe, the older men succeed in love because they have had more time to learn from their mistakes and appreciate the significance of love.

Neglected Love

In conclusion I want to return to the main question posed by this chapter: did Polish, Czech and Slovak men, as represented on screen, love romantically? My answer is that most of the time they not. Life was too harsh for them to waste energy on love or, deprived of many basic goods, they treated sex as a way to achieve them, in this way denying themselves the experience of true love. Moreover, if they approached the romantic ideal, it was typically thanks to women who showed them that it is worth living, if not dying, for love. Yet because there were so many 'strings' attached to men willing to fall in love – the requirement to work for their country, to make a career or simply to survive – films with a motif of love are an excellent litmus test of men's freedom in communist Poland and Czechoslovakia. After the collapse of communism there are less obstacles for love but romantic love is again a rarity in Polish, Czech and Slovak cinema. Now it seldom befalls men because there are too many ways to achieve satisfaction (if not happiness) without being madly in love. In my opinion the conditions most conducive for love existed in the 1960s; in other periods men were either too oppressed or too distracted to see this elusive entity.

Notes

1. A sign of this derision is the term 'Przybyszewszczyzna' used to describe too 'ornamental' or simply kitschy descriptions of erotic states.
2. I will return to Iwaszkiewicz in the following chapter, because he is also the leading Polish writer to tackle homosexuality. Homosexuality is also an important reason why love in his work demands sublimation.
3. Bim-Bom was a Sopot students' theatre, where their talents presented stars of the cinema of the Polish School, such as Zbigniew Cybulski and Bogumił Kobiela, whose performances at the time attracted the artistic cream from all over Poland.
4. A thorough analysis of the type of character, played by Machulski, is offered by Iwona Kurz (Kurz 2005: 74–95).
5. As Paul Coates notes, Tomek's slashed wrists recall Miloš in Jiři Menzel's *Closely Observed Trains* (Coates 1999: 111). However, Miloš attempts suicide after an encounter with a woman his age, while Tomek with a woman much older than him. Perhaps this suggests that in romantic matters age is a secondary factor.

CHAPTER 5

You Will Not Find Much? Construction of Men's 'Other Sexualities' in Polish and Czechoslovak Cinema

'Condemned, condemned is my fate!' But soon, raising his hands to heaven, he shouted shrilly, 'Blessed is my fate, Oh, how sweet, wonderful is my fate and I do not wish any other!'
(Witold Gombrowicz, *Trans-Atlantyk*)

Seeing what is Hidden or Creating the Object of Vision?

The first part of the title of this chapter, 'You will not find much', is borrowed from an article by the Swiss Slavist, Rolf Simmen. Simmen received this discouraging answer from an employee of the Czech film archive when he visited the institution to identify Czechoslovak films with homosexual motifs (Simmen 2006). My aim in this chapter is similar to Simmen's but I include Polish films. Neither is the answer that I receive substantially different from his, although my Polish colleagues are able to provide me with two or three titles of Polish films about homosexuals, whilst their Czech and Slovak counterparts find it more difficult to list even one Czech or Slovak film on the subject. When they can, the only title offered to me is *Mandragora* (2003), which is a Czech film, but directed by the Polish filmmaker, Wiktor Grodecki, which can be interpreted as a sign that if Czechoslovak cinema wants to discuss homosexuality, it has to learn from its northern neighbour. Much less known is the fact that Polish cinema was also inspired in this matter by its neighbour, as demonstrated by the film *Wśród nocnej ciszy* (*In the Silence of the Night*, 1978), directed by Tadeusz Chmielewski, which is an adaptation of a book by the Czech writer, Ladislav Fuks, *Příběh kriminálního rady* (*The Case of the Criminal Investigation Counsel*, 1971).

For the whole of the communist period male homosexuality on screen, along with other types of sexual otherness, remained practically unspoken in critical

Figure 5. 1 Piotr Łysak as Wiktor and Mirosław Konarowski as Bernard in *Wśród nocnej ciszy* (*In the Silence of the Night*, 1978), directed by Tadeusz Chmielewski.

discourse in both countries (Strohlein 1999), which is particularly striking in Poland, where there are more movies that lend themselves to an analysis foregrounding homosexual issues than in Czechoslovakia. One critic mentions as many as thirty-five gay men present in Polish postwar films (Jagielski 2004: 68). As Elżbieta Ostrowska and Michael Stevenson observe, when this issue was considered in Poland, it was usually tackled in relation to Western European and American cinema. This attitude prevailed well into the postcommunist period. For example, in an issue of the alternative film periodical *Easy Rider*, entitled *Kino gejowskie* (*Gay Cinema*), published in 1996 (*Kino gejowskie* 1996), there was not a single word on homosexuality in Poland or in relation to Polish cinema, except for some observations written by Derek Jarman in his diary, when he visited Poland in 1990. Moreover, when critics tackled Polish films with strong homosexual motifs, they either overlooked them and focused on other aspects of the movie, or considered homosexuality as a metaphor of something else. 'One gets the impression', argue Ostrowska and Stevenson, 'that homosexuality itself can never be elaborated into an artistic form and so it is necessary to "enrich" it with some universal meaning to produce a real piece of cinema' (Ostrowska and Stevenson 2000). Their analysis points to the need to change the old attitude, although they offer little insight into how this goal should be achieved.

We can note a striking similarity in the way male homosexuality was treated in film criticism during communism to how it was treated in literary criticism – in both areas homosexual motifs were either ignored or regarded as metaphors. Moreover, in

Poland the 'queer taboo' survived in literature in the first years after the fall of the Berlin Wall. Błażej Warkocki confirms its existence by examining the critical reception of *W ptaszarni* (*In the Birdhouse*) by Grzegorz Musiał. This novel, published in 1989, the symbolic transition from totalitarianism to liberal democracy, constitutes for Warkocki the first contemporary Polish 'gay novel' (Warkocki 2002: 52). However, he observes that it only attracted a few reviews, and although mostly positive, they overlooked or sidelined the homosexual identity of the main character and the gay aesthetics employed by the author. In contrast, Warkocki proposes using 'gay sensitivity' as the main prism to analyse the content and form of *In the Birdhouse* and, by extension, many other works, old and new, in which homosexual motifs were previously ignored.

The programme outlined by Warkocki, that he himself describes as 'opening the closet', eventually began to be realised in Poland, the Czech Republic and Slovakia, in literature (Ritz 2002; Tomasik 2005; Dunin 2005; Warkocki 2005; Warkocki 2006), in film (see Sadowska and Żurawiecki 2004; Jagielski 2004; Simmen 2006; Moss 2006) and in other areas of cultural production. This new critical strategy can be regarded as progressive because it makes up for the times when homosexuality was a taboo, opening up the discourse on homosexuality and championing the gay cause. However, I also find it risky and even potentially regressive on several accounts. First, privileging homosexuality as the main lens to look at a text brings with it the danger of reducing the work of art to the emanation of queer sensibility, and of seeing in its characters people who only play homosexual roles, as opposed to being individuals with a plethora of traits and even facets. It is worth recollecting here the words of Pedro Almodóvar who once said that 'I am gay, but my films are not gay' (Almodóvar, quoted in Murphy 1990: 39). That could be interpreted as a sign of Almodóvar's rejection of privileging queer analysis as the main way to interpret his oeuvre. Secondly, inscribing homosexual motifs into texts produced in the past might lead to projecting contemporary understanding of homosexuality onto cultures whose members might have engaged in same-sex relations but ascribed to them very different meanings (Foucault 1998; Marshall 1981; Weeks 1981). Thirdly, attributing to somebody a clear homosexual identity assumes the existence of such a rigid identity and the right of anyone to attribute it from outside, not only of the people who have this orientation. This is contested by authors who study modern 'identity', such as Stuart Hall and Slavoj Žižek, and specifically those who explore the identities of sexual minorities, such as Michel Foucault, Mary McIntosh and Kenneth Plummer. Hall, by claiming that 'rather than speaking of identity as a finished thing, we should speak of *identification*, and see it as an on-going process' (Hall 1992: 287–8), rejects the concept of stable identity as discordant with personal experience. Foucault and McIntosh reject the concept of 'homosexual' on moral grounds, arguing that the imposition of identity can be seen as a tactic of power, designed to obscure real human diversity with the strict categorisations of uniformity and, hence, a mechanism for labelling and ghettoising homosexuals, as well as controlling and blackmailing the rest of society (Foucault 1998: 99–102; McIntosh 1981). Jeffrey Weeks claims that using unambiguous sexual categories brings both advantages and disadvantages. The reason for that lies in the paradox inherent in the politics of sexual identity resulting, as he puts it, from the conflict between, on the one hand, our awareness that 'sexuality is about flux and change' and, on the other, our 'striving to fix it, stabilise it, say who we are by telling of our sex' (Weeks 1985: 188). Weeks himself rejects the temptation to fix a sexual identity by referring to Foucault's edition of the tragic memoirs of the mid-nineteenth-century hermaphrodite, Herculin Barbin, which is a 'gentle hymn to the happy limbo of non-identity and a warning of the dire consequences of insisting upon a true identity hidden behind the ambiguities of outward appearance' (ibid.: 187).

In this chapter I am trying to take Weeks's and Foucault's warnings to heart. Thus, although I use here the term 'homosexual' to describe a person who engages in same-sex sexual activity or has a sexual attraction towards a person of the same sex, I am doing so aware of the problems embedded in the term.[1] However, in most cases discussed in this chapter I find the word 'homosexual' the most appropriate and certainly more suitable than 'gay', which is a self-label, therefore should not be applied to men who do not wish to be addressed this way. Hence, whilst my purpose is to identify examples of homosexual behaviour and homosexual form in films, as well as other examples of 'non-straight' sexualities,[2] I will try to fulfil this purpose with an awareness that I will be creating a discourse, rather than uncovering what exists objectively.[3]

Homosexuality in Poland and Czechoslovakia

Before I focus on cinematic texts, it is worth referring briefly to the relationship between homosexuality and nationalism and socialism, and summarising the situation of homosexuals in Poland and Czechoslovakia. Andrew Parker et al., citing George Mosse and Benedict Anderson, argue that nationalism favours a distinctly homosocial form of male bonding, but finds itself compelled to distinguish its 'proper' homosociality from more explicitly sexualised male–male relations, a compulsion that requires identification, isolation and containment of male homosexuality (Parker et al. 1992: 6).

Following this line of reasoning we can expect that nations that are less nationalist and less prone to engage in military action would show greater tolerance for homosexuality. This issue is explored in Witold Gombrowicz's *Trans-Atlantyk* (1952), a novel compared to Mickiewicz's *Pan Tadeusz* (1834), because it can be read as a polemic with the concept of patriotism Mickiewicz offers in his romantic epic. As Ewa Płonowska Ziarek notes,

> In *Pan Tadeusz*, the patriotic motif of the political struggle for national independence is so fully harmonised with the heterosexual romance that the heterosexual couple, Tadeusz and Zosia, embodies the spirit of national union and the promise of national freedom. The happiness of the couple becomes the figure of hope for the future independence of the partitioned nation. By

> contrast, Gombrowicz not only removes any traces of heterosexual romance from *Trans-Atlantyk* (to the effect that the female characters are conspicuously absent in the narrative) but also coordinates the struggle against the dangers of nationalism with the sexualisation of male bonds. (Płonowska Ziarek 1998: 230)

Amongst Gombrowicz's characters we find Ignacy, a young Pole from a family with patriotic traditions, and Gonzalo, a rich homosexual whose mother is Turkish and father Portuguese. Gonzalo and Ignacy's father, the Major, fight each other for Ignacy's body and soul; the former wants to seduce him, the latter to force him to defend Poland against Germany. At the crucial moment of the narrative Ignacy's father challenges Gonzalo to a duel, in which he can either be killed as a 'proper man' or be shot as a homosexual. As Płonowska Ziarek notes, Gombrowicz warns us that nationalism is a homophobic force – one can be a citizen only to the extent one is a heterosexual man (ibid: 229–32).

In its criticism of patriotism and specifically patriotism equated with military action, *Trans-Atlantyk* comes close to *The Good Soldier Švejk* by Jaroslav Hašek who, like Gombrowicz, was a homosexual (Steiner 2000: 26). Although Švejk himself is not, during his military peregrinations he is often dealt with not very differently to the way homosexuals are treated in nationalistic discourses: as an incomplete, defective man. Much of his misfortune during the war results from the fact that he does not conform to the ideal of a soldier as a fit, young and unreflective man, being an old invalid who approaches everything that happens to him with philosophical detachment. It is also worth noting that Hašek questions the idea of the nation at war as a male fraternity. We find little genuine fraternity amongst the Emperor's soldiers, because in their desperate attempts to survive they are prepared to betray everyone. Similarly, those in power, although they might use nationalistic rhetoric in official propaganda, in day-to-day business appeal not to soldiers' patriotism but to their fear (see Chapter 2). I will argue that by ridiculing the concept of war patriotism and challenging the very idea of the nation as Anderson's 'deep, horizontal comradeship', making it possible for millions of people to die willingly (Anderson 1991: 7), Hašek rejects the homophobic arguments used by nationalists. As far as he is concerned, there is little difference between the homosexual and heterosexual man in relation to the Patria; most men behave as the stereotyped homosexual, putting their private welfare over the good of their country.

Trans-Atlantyk and *The Good Soldier Švejk* are both now widely regarded as masterpieces, but they occupy different positions within the Polish and Czech literary canons. *Trans-Atlantyk* is regarded only as a polemic with the dominant vision of Polishness and so far it failed to replace *Pan Tadeusz* or the works of Sienkiewicz in national history and consciousness. *The Good Soldier Švejk*, on the other hand, is regarded as a 'national novel'. The rejection of militarism, nationalism and any form of subordination of the individual to the community and the forces of history, advocated by Hašek, is widely regarded as constituting the core of Czech national character (see Chapters 1 and 2).

It is also worth mentioning another pertinent aspect of Czech literature and art: the works of Czech Decadents, such as Jiří Karásek ze Lvovic, Otokar Březina, Julius Zeyer, Miroslav Rutte and Jaroslav Maria. Karásek wrote man-loving verse and described homosexual coition in his work, produced in the end of nineteenth century. Rutte and Maria portrayed female homosexuality in their plays from the early 1900s. Although in the works of others we do not find explicit references to homosexual characters and acts, the themes, motifs and styles they employed, as well as the ideas they used, bear a strong resemblance to the works of such authors as Oscar Wilde, Friedrich Nietzsche and Marcel Proust. In their works we find such figures as the dandy, the idea of a fluid, fragmented or multiple self, the polymorphous desire that can be directed both to men and women (later theorised and elaborated by Guy Hocquenghem in his *Homesexual Desire*) and the cult of beauty and youth. Moreover, they were hostile to or at least distrustful of official nationalism, regarding it as constraining the individual (Pynsent 1994: 101–146). Consequently, we can argue that a part of the Czech literary and artistic canon includes ideas that are sympathetic to homosexuality, even promoting it.

If nationalism favours heterosexuality, the relationship between socialism and homosexuality is more complex. As Jeffrey Weeks observes: 'Homosexuality has no particular political belonging. Authoritarian regimes of both left and right have at times reviled it and at other times tolerated it' (Weeks 1989a). Weeks, however, also points out that the first country to remove all penal sanctions on homosexual activities (along with reforming the laws concerning abortion, contraception and marriage), was Soviet Russia, the first modern country that eschewed nationalism, privileging a community based on a common set of values. 'For a while in the 1920s, the Soviet moral code was seen as an enlightened model for the rest of the world. While the left remained committed to informed debate and justice for all citizens, the rights of homosexuals were, to a degree, affirmed and protected' (ibid). Yet the next decade brought a significant change in this respect in the Soviet Union that coincided with the persecution of homosexuals in Nazi Germany. 'Ironically, at the same time as homosexuals were being denounced as degenerates by fascists, the communists under Stalin were denouncing them as the product of "decadence in the bourgeois sector of society" and a "fascist perversion"' (ibid.). Homosexuals were labelled counter-revolutionaries, demoralising young workers and students and attempting to penetrate the army and navy (Healey 2001: 181–204). In March 1934 homosexuality once again became a criminal offence in the USSR and the communist movements of the rest of the world soon followed suit in labelling homosexuality 'unsocialist'. As Weeks put it, the 'liberation of human personality and potential for all, including homosexuals, that pioneering socialists had offered as a vision, was buried beneath the grim realities of the 1930s' (Weeks 1989a).

The association of homosexuality with bourgeois decadence remained an element of the communist mindset throughout the history of authoritarian socialist countries (Healey 2001) and even beyond socialism. However, it must be remembered that Poland and Czechoslovakia were not in the socialist camp before the Second World War, therefore the views of Stalin or Lenin did not significantly affect their attitude to this issue. In fact, Poland proved to have a relatively liberal attitude to homosexuality over most of its history as an independent country. Homosexual practices were legalised there from 1932 and were never criminalised. Consequently, although there were periods when the police persecuted homosexuals, as during the years 1985–87, when the infamous operation 'Hiacynt' (Hyacinth) took place, which led to the compiling of over 10,000 files on homosexuals, on the whole Polish communist authorities were less interfering in sexual matters than in the majority of remaining socialist countries. An indicator of this freedom was the existence of official gay and lesbian organisations even before the collapse of communism.

Postwar Czechoslovakia, as the majority of East and Central European countries, had a less liberal attitude to homosexuality. Until 1950 homosexual acts were 'crimes against nature', and from 1950 to 1961 they were crimes against society that were 'incompatible with the morality of a socialist society' (Sokolová 2001: 278). In 1961 homosexuality was decriminalised by a new law, which legalised homosexual acts under specific conditions. However, as Věra Sokolová points out,

> Despite the decriminalisation of homosexuality in the early 1960s, the police throughout the communist period compiled detailed records of fingerprints and photos evidencing Czechoslovak gays. Gay social and cultural institutions served as convenient sites where these lists could be brought up to date and gays reminded how vulnerable they were if they refused to cooperate with the police. It is not an exaggeration to say that during the communist period homosexuals, and gays especially, lived under constant pressure and potential social and emotional blackmail. (ibid.: 277)

Only in 1990, after the collapse of communism, was the homophobic §241 removed in its entirety from the criminal code of Czechoslovakia. In 1993, when the World Health Organisation officially removed homosexuality from its list of illnesses, SOHO (Association of Organisations of Homosexual Citizens) managed to ratify the removal of this in the Czech Republic (Sokolová 2004: 260–1).

Needless to say, the differences in the way homosexuality was treated by law had a major impact on the lives of homosexuals in Poland and Czechoslovakia, and in further instances on the way homosexuality was represented in cultural texts, especially films, whose production needed state funding. Yet, as Jeffrey Weeks observes, the criminal law is only one index of a society's attitude towards homosexuality. Another important factor is religion – its power to shape people's preconceptions about what is correct sexual behaviour. In Czechoslovakia after the Second World War, largely thanks to the state's success in suppressing religious institutions, neither the Catholic Church nor indeed any other Church played a major role in influencing citizens' opinions about sexuality. In Poland, on the other hand, the Church's role in this matter was always significant. It is suggested that it was and still is the single most important factor affecting the way 'the average man on the street' thinks about homosexuals (Sypniewski and Warkocki 2004). The Church's attitude to homosexuality has been uniformly negative; in its teaching homosexual behaviour is equated with sin and pathology, undermining the holy institution of marriage and polluting society as a whole. Priests have also perpetuated such opinions as, for example, that most homosexual sex involves the corruption of boys by older men and involves the exchange of money.[4] After 1989 the Church's interest in and opposition to homosexuality appears to be on the increase. Signs of this phenomenon are the openly homophobic utterances of some prominent priests and the promotion of such radically anti-homosexual policies as isolating homosexuals, whom the Church accuses of spreading AIDS, from the heterosexual majority (Biedroń 2004: 222). The importance of the Church in this matter cannot be overestimated because, as was stated earlier in this book, Catholicism is widely perceived as being at the core of the Polish national character.

At the same time, it could be argued that the Church's uncompromisingly negative attitude to homosexuality during communist times helped Polish homosexuals in their relationship with the state. They enjoyed relative freedom and resisted the temptation of criticising the communist authorities. The state, on the other hand, was aware that it would not gain much by declaring war on sexual minorities; by doing so it would be seen to share the same moral platform as its chief foe. Equally, by its relatively tolerant attitude to homosexuality it could gain some allies. Indeed, among the highest-profile supporters of communism in the field of culture we find a surprisingly high proportion of homosexual men, including a number of prominent writers like Jerzy Andrzejewski and Jarosław Iwaszkiewicz. The latter in particular enjoyed the status of informal spokesperson for the communist regime – socialist Poland's 'national writer'. His complete political loyalty was also convenient for the authorities because he was one of the greatest writers of prewar Poland and one of the main representatives of Polish modernism. Consequently, he epitomised the continuity of Polish literature and culture as a whole from the First World War to the communist period.

Can Andrzejewski's and Iwaszkiewicz's oeuvre, as well as of those of other prominent Polish homosexuals, such as Witold Gombrowicz, Jan Lechoń, Tadeusz Breza and Miron Białoszewski, be labelled 'homosexual'? And hence, did homosexual literature exist in communist Poland? Usually we receive a positive answer to this question but the answer is qualified: it did exist, but had to hide its homosexual dimension by using elaborate metaphors and referring to what cannot be verbalised. Typically, the homosexual was encoded as an artist or a connoisseur of art. As Bartosz Warkocki argues, 'One could talk in Poland about homosexuality by talking about art' (Warkocki 2006). Moreover, a large part of this literature was homophobic, suggesting that the authors themselves internalised the heterosexist norms of mainstream society. Discretion and guilt about the character's and one's own sexual tastes, however, allowed the authors of this literature to enter the literary canon to a greater extent than in any comparable national literature. Thus, paradoxically, homosexuality is both at the centre of Polish literature and, because of its low visibility, on its margin. Whilst these 'discreet' Polish homosexual writers were able to enter the canon, those who talked about homosexuality in unambiguous terms, and who usually published their work towards the end of the communist period, such as Marian Pankowski, the author of *Rudolf* (1980), were criticised for their explicitness and bad taste, and in this way relegated to the periphery of literature (Ritz 2002; Warkocki 2005; Dunin 2005). It is worth adding that some famous homosexual writers like Gombrowicz and Lechoń were émigrés, but enough authors worked in Poland to reject a claim that Polish homosexual literature was displaced abroad.

In postwar Czechoslovakia homosexual literature was more on the edge of the canon or even outside it than in Poland. Those authors who themselves had homosexual tendencies and wanted to convey them in their work, had to hide them. This applies, for example, to the author of children's books, Jaroslav Foglar, whose work contains hints of homosexual feelings towards young boys. Hidden homosexuality can also be identified in the work of Ladislav Fuks,[5] the best known homosexual author living in Czechoslovakia, especially renowned for his depiction of the impact of the Shoah on the individual. These authors, however, did not achieve a position in national literature comparable to that of Iwaszkiewicz and Andrzejewski. Moreover, those who were bolder in revealing their interest in homosexuality, such as Václav Jamek (known also as Eberhardt Hauptbanhof) had to emigrate.

Another factor that separates Poland and Czechoslovakia and partly explains the harsh attitude towards homosexual men in the latter country, is the inclusion of homosexuality in the discourse on male prostitution. Being the most Western (geographically and culturally) Eastern European country, Czechoslovakia, and especially Prague, was treated by a number of foreign, especially German and Austrian homosexuals, as a place where they could find cheap 'rent boys' and indulge in acts with them that would be unacceptable in their native countries. The authorities were particularly wary of such practices, as they highlighted not only Czechoslovak decadence but also the inferiority of this country compared to the West, and its accessibility to foreign penetration and exploitation.

Whilst for most of the communist period homosexuality was rendered invisible in Polish and Czechoslovak culture, in the final period of communist rule and after 1989 it gained significantly in visibility. This happened, on the one hand, thanks to homosexuals' new courage to reveal their orientation and to demand they be treated equally with heterosexual citizens, including having the right to have their partnerships registered and to adopt children. On the other hand, in Poland, homosexuality became more widely discussed due to the homophobic backlash to these demands conducted and encouraged by groups close to right-wing political parties and the Catholic Church. In the Czech Republic we observe the mushrooming of homosexual organisations, the most prominent being the previously mentioned SOHO, the proliferation of gay clubs (in Prague alone there are over thirty of them), and the presence of gays on national television. While homosexuals were initially content with their new liberty and enjoyed it amongst themselves, later their strategy was to enter a dialogue with the heterosexual section of the population and take advantage of the democratic parties seeking their support, in short, to become a political lobby. Sokolová argues that 'homosexuality has been such a popular topic of debate that some politicians have used it to promote themselves and their programmes rather than contributing to the issue itself. Through discussions in the media, the public often learned about the sexual orientation of political representatives and candidates; this type of information is now an integral aspect of political discourse' (Sokolová 2004: 260).

Likewise, in Poland the late 1980s and the 1990s witnessed a proliferation of homosexual organisations, periodicals and clubs. In the 2000s Polish gays extended their activities to drawing the attention of society at large to their existence and the inequalities they suffer, and in this way advancing their struggle for equal rights. One of the elements of this strategy was the action 'Let them see us', organised by the 'Anti-Homophobic Campaign' (Kampania Przeciw Homofobii), which lasted for three months during 2003. It included an exhibition of a series of photographs taken by Karolina Breguła, depicting fifteen gay and fifteen lesbian couples. This exhibition travelled to several Polish towns, causing controversy in all of them. Later the organisers attempted to put the photographs on billboards, but they succeeded only in Warsaw and Cracow, and even there the billboards were vandalised (Sypniewski and Warkocki 2004: 9–10). We should also list demonstrations and marches against homophobia, as well as some demonstrations that were planned but did not take place due to political opposition against them. However, even the failed actions or, perhaps, especially the failed actions proved successful as they illustrated the point that Polish homosexuals were deprived of rights that heterosexuals take for granted. Despite these campaigns, the majority of Czechs, Slovaks and Poles have remained blind to 'other sexualities'. According to a study conducted recently by the Czech Sexological Institute, more than half of the country's population claimed that they had never met a homosexual (Sokolová 2004: 260). In Poland this percentage is even higher – 90 percent of Poles claim that they do not know any lesbian or gay person (Sypniewski and Warkocki 2004: 10).

In Western scholarship the opinion now prevails that sexualities are socially and culturally constructed discourses (Foucault 1998; Weeks 1981; 1989b; 1991; Marshall 1981) and even that we should talk about homosexualities rather than homosexuality as a single category (Weeks 1981: 81). On the other hand, the bulk of Polish and Czech homosexuals, and certainly those whose voices reach the heterosexual majority, argue that homosexuality is an inborn and essential trait of an individual (Sokolová 2004: 261–2). Katarzyna Gawlicz and Marcin Starnawski explain the Polish homosexuals' attachment to the rather outdated genetic/biological/psychiatric concept of sexuality by the sociocultural context in which Polish (and by extension, all East European) homosexuals live, especially the type of arguments used by their political opponents. Polish homophobes claim that homosexual identity emerges as a result of being seduced by an older and wealthier homosexual, often a paedophile, and is facilitated by the permissiveness of some cultures, such as, for instance, the postcommunist. Thus, by claiming that homosexuals play a part in choosing their identity they will only encourage their opponents to regard them as corrupters of children and as decadent, taking advantage of society's tolerance (Gawlicz and Starnawski 2004: 42).

If we reject the way Polish, Czech and Slovak homosexuals describe the aetiology of their sexual identity and instead foreground social and cultural factors, then we shall also concur that certain cultures and social environments are more conducive to creating homosexual identities than others. Polish culture, because it extols certain masculine environments and activities, such as fighting wars, partaking in uprisings and drinking vodka,[6] is more conducive to homosocial behaviour than Czech culture, with its less enthusiastic attitude towards military life and penchant for weaker alcohol. Equally, as it was established earlier, extreme homosocial pressure is usually accompanied by homophobia to compensate for the danger of the emergence of homosexuality. Hence, what in Polish culture constitutes 'normal' masculine behaviour, in Czech culture might be regarded as deviation from the heterosexual norm. Similarly, a personal trait or manner of behaviour that in a particular moment in history can be regarded as straight, might be given a 'queer interpretation' later, and vice versa. As Jeffrey Weeks observes, 'In different cultures (and at different historical moments or conjunctures within the same culture) very different meanings are given to same sex activity both by society at large and by the individual participants. The physical acts might be similar but the social construction of meanings around them are profoundly different' (Weeks 1981: 81).

These differences should be taken into account when interpreting films from these two and later three countries. The most significant 'cult scene' in a Polish film: an episode in Andrzej Wajda's *Ashes and Diamonds*, in which Maciek Chełmicki burns spirit in glasses, reminiscing about his friends who perished in war, is regarded as epitomising Polish romantic and virile masculinity. As if to confirm that interpretation, the film also contains an episode of heterosexual lovemaking. However, if we would move this scene to a Czech film and take it out of its heterosexual context, we might conclude that the characters are closet homosexuals. Similarly, the previously mentioned difference in the level of openness with which Polish and Czech artists in the communist period tackled 'non-straight' sexualities in their work requires a different level of awareness to the signs of the homosexual messages included in them. Again, what in Polish film is regarded as 'straight', in Czechoslovak film might invite interpretation in 'queer mode' and vice versa. This difference also points to the problem of studying a specific gay culture by a person who does not belong to this culture. This difficulty was recognised by Richard Dyer who wrote in the introduction to his book on gay films: 'The specificity of the idea of "being" lesbian or gay means that the very different way same-sex relations are constructed and experienced in Japan or Third World countries does not come into my purview' (Dyer 1990: 2–3). In regard to Czech and Slovak films with a homosexual theme this problem is exacerbated for me, because I have neither first-hand experience of Czech and Slovak cultures, nor of homosexual life, being myself Polish, heterosexual and female. For this reason, in this chapter, more than in others parts of my book, I rely on the insights of my colleagues and friends.

Uranians and Ordinary Men in Polish and Czechoslovak Films of the Communist Period

As was previously mentioned, few male homosexuals were depicted in Czechoslovak cinema in the years 1945–1989. There were even fewer films in which this type of sexuality was named or discussed, and I could not find even one film that depicts a homosexual act. Hence, it was up to the viewer to decode a certain character or situation as 'queer'. Josef Škvorecký claims that homosexual motifs were discovered in the films of Václav Krška, especially *Stříbrný vítr* (*The Silver Wind*, 1954) (Škvorecký 1971: 39). Krška's film, which is set in the second half of the nineteenth century, tackles only heterosexual love, namely the trials and tribulations of the fifth-former Jan Ratkin who simultaneously falls in love with several different women. However, the way the film depicts love deviates from the puritanical sexual morality of the time it was made, especially in relation to the representation of the male body. It could be guessed that such images as those of naked boys swimming in a river or visiting a brothel, and being observed by a religion teacher, were produced for the delectation of a male homosexual audience, including Krška himself, who was a well-known homosexual. The actor Eduard Cupák, who played Jan Ratkin, as well as main parts in other films by Krška, was also homosexual. It could be argued that the director and his star created a special style of romance, in which the man's feelings mattered more than those of the women, and which could be interpreted by the viewer as homosexual emotions. Moreover, an atmosphere of hysteria permeating *The Silver Wind*, as well as a visual, 'decadent' richness and stylisation, that poignantly contrast with the austerity of socialist realism, are typical characteristics of queer aesthetics. One can risk the statement that *The Silver Wind* is the first example of a socialist camp film.[7]

There was no overt homosexuality in socialist realism but homosocial behaviour was common among male protagonists of socialist-realist novels and books. In particular, relationships between men were often rendered more important than those between a man and a woman. Moreover, between master and his pupil or two comrades working in the same production plant or on a building site we often find tenderness that is lacking in male–female relationships (see Chapter 4). Consequently, I will suggest that contemporary viewers can decode a large part of socialist-realist cinema as conveying repressed homosexuality.

We find more open references to homosexuality in the New Wave; the best example being *Return of the Prodigal Son* (1966) by Evald Schorm (referred to in the previous chapters). Zdeněk (Jiří Kilian), the dancer who is a patient in a psychiatric hospital, is recognised as a homosexual because he fits perfectly the stereotype of the feminine man, the 'invert', the 'Uranian' or, more crudely, the 'pansy'. Not only is his occupation 'queer' (theatres, operas and ballets were regarded as places where homosexual subcultures flourished), but even in the asylum he occupies himself with dancing and acrobatics, wearing make-up and a tight costume that accentuates his slender, rather feminine body. Moreover, he completely shuns female company and directs all his attention to his room-mate Jan. His attention to Jan is tender and physical; Zdeněk cries in his presence but also attempts to console his new friend by talking to him and touching him. He helps Jan to overcome his mental crisis and even at times he makes him happy.

Representing a homosexual man in a psychiatric hospital inevitably brings to mind the concept of homosexuality as a psychiatric illness that had dominated discourses on homosexuality for a large part of the twentieth century. However, Schorm does not subscribe to such an oppressive definition, but opposes it by showing that through labelling and locking up Zdeněk society changes him into a sick man rather than curing him from his alleged 'condition'. Zdeněk commits suicide shortly after a man calls him a 'pederast'. The proximity of these two events suggests that such a labelling is the main reason why the dancer decides to take his life, by making him aware that even in a mental hospital there is no refuge for him and others like him. Although Schorm constructs Zdeněk as different from the heterosexual men who surround him, including Jan, he also shows that these two men have more in common than the homophobes are prepared to grant them. Particularly touching episodes show Zdeněk teaching Jan how to jump and dance, and him looking after Klárka, Jan's little daughter who visits her father in hospital with her mother.[8] Jan, on the other hand, acts as Zdeněk's protector: he chases and beats the man who denounced the dancer as a 'pederast'. This scene is in fact the only one in the entire film in which Jan acts with passion. Similarly, his friendship with Zdeněk is the only relationship Jan enters that is not tainted by his disappointment, boredom or lack of commitment. On the whole, *Return of the Prodigal Son* concerns the dangers of various social boundaries, including the boundary between heterosexual and homosexual people, or that between people who are mentally healthy and those who are ill, as obstacles preventing individuals from enriching their personality and achieving inner harmony.

Critics discussing the representation of homosexuality in socialist cinema point out that it uses homosexuality as a metaphor for something else, especially various aspects of politics (Ostrowska and Stevenson 2000; Moss 2006). It could be argued that the same strategy is applied by Schorm. Thus, if we regard the psychiatric ward as a metaphor for a socialist country that in reality is totalitarian, then the figure of Zdeněk can be regarded as a metaphor of a man who does not fit into such a country – a political dissident. A dissident has to conceal his identity in the same way as a homosexual; both have to live in the closet or risk perishing.

Black Peter by Miloš Forman is not renowned for breaking the 'queer taboo' in Czech culture. However, we can attribute a homosexual desire to Lada (Pavel Sedláček), the friend of Petr's macho 'acquaintance' Čenda. The suggestion that Lada is a homosexual is conveyed by his tender attachment to Čenda, his complete lack of interest in girls (which is an oddity among teenage boys who appear to think only about the opposite sex), and by his shy attempts to sabotage Čenda's attempts to find a girlfriend. When Petr tells Čenda and Lada that he saw them with 'their girls', he insists, 'They were not our girls', and a while later pulls down his shorts, which results in both boys being excluded from the conversation with Petr and his female friend Petra. Although Lada protests to Čenda that his striptease was an accident, his friend does not believe him, perhaps because he had dealt with such incidents before. As if to confirm that Čenda and Lada do not fit the heterosexual norm, Petr and Petra comment that the couple look 'queer' and Petra admits that neither of them could ever be her boyfriend. If Lada is indeed a homosexual, he is also a member of a rare species: a homosexual who is only himself rather than serving as a metaphor of something else; he is neither a victim nor oppressor, nor an artist or an intellectual but (contrary to Petr and Petra's pronouncement) is utterly ordinary.

Zdeněk Troška, popular director of the 'normalisation' period and the director of the series of three comedies about the erotic trials and tribulations of the inhabitants of a small village: *Sun, Hay and Strawberries* (1984), *Sun, Hay and a Couple of Slaps* (1989) and *Sun, Hay and Eroticism* (1991) (see Chapter 4), like Forman, does not openly pronounce one of his characters, a local priest (Luděk Kopřiva), to be homosexual. However, he constructs this character in such a way as to encourage viewers to decode him as a homosexual; the priest is clumsy and effeminate, often sporting a female covering on his head. Moreover, one can meet him secretly stalking in a wood, in a manner associated with homosexuals searching for their prey in parks.

As I mentioned earlier, during socialist times there were significantly more films showing homosexuals in Polish than in Czechoslovak films. However, Polish viewers had to wait much longer for such a sympathetic and deep portrayal of a homosexual as that offered by Schorm. It can be said that the quantity of homosexuals on screen was not accompanied by the quality in their representation. Probably the first Polish film to include a homosexual character was the comedy *Ojciec* (*Father*, 1967) by Jerzy Hoffman. Here the role of the homosexual is episodic; he is only a man met by

Figure 5.2 Luděk Kopřiva as priest in *Slunce, seno, jahody* (*Sun, Hay and Strawberries*, 1984), directed by Zdeněk Troška.

the main character in a park, looking for 'casual' sex. However, from my perspective this film is important as it provided a matrix for the way homosexual characters were cast in the Polish films of the next two decades. They appeared either in comedies or were meant to add a comic dimension to the narrative, usually were represented as men hungry for sex and they were reduced to episodic or at best secondary characters. This was the case, amongst others, in *Motylem jestem* (*I'm a Butterfly*, 1976) directed by Jerzy Gruza and *Zaklęte rewiry* (*Hotel Pacific*, 1975) by Janusz Majewski (which was a Polish–Czechoslovak coproduction). In the first film the homosexual is a ballet dancer; in the second an ageing effeminate man who is falling for a young, straight man. In Polish jargon this type is called *ciotka* or *ciota* (*auntie*).[9] At least half the remaining homosexual characters in the films of the 1970s and 1980s were either ballet dancers (or representatives of similar occupations, such as circus performers) or older noblemen. By themselves such stereotypes are not homophobic; after all, theatres and operas were frequent sites of homosexual subcultures. Yet in the context of postwar Polish culture they were, because noblemen and artists represented the sections of Polish society that communist authorities barely tolerated. The Polish aristocracy was a remnant of the old, overthrown class system; artists were parasites taking advantage of the working classes, and both were associated with decadence and self-indulgence. Moreover, in the films featuring them a style of acting was employed to distance the viewer from the homosexual character. For example, the gestures of the ballet dancer in *I'm a Butterfly* are extremely mannered and his voice, as Maciej Maniewski puts it, is the 'voice of an eunuch' (Maniewski 1994: 88). It is clear that the actor, Bogdan Łazuka, creates a caricature of the familiar 'boy from the ballet' stereotype, rather than trying to represent such a figure realistically. By contrast, Czesław Wołłejko (an actor who specialised in the roles of aristocrats and was never shy about revealing the feminine side of his characters), playing Baron Humaniewski in *Hotel Pacific*, perhaps against the director's intentions, crosses the boundaries of caricature and turns out to be tragic rather than funny.

Camerawork and the mise-en-scène are another means of creating distance between the homosexual and heterosexual characters in the film, and by extension, between the homosexual on screen and the heterosexual audience in the cinema. *Kontrakt* (*Contract*, 1980), by Krzysztof Zanussi, provides a model example of such a strategy. Here we find an effeminate ballet dancer taking part in a conversation with a famous French ex-ballerina who pays a visit to the Polish opera. This man, played by Eugeniusz Priweziencew, who specialises in the roles of eccentric and emotionally unbalanced men, is objectified by the camera. We look at him from a distance and do not hear what he says, since his voice disappears amongst the many voices uttered by the dancers and other opera sounds. He is the only man in a company of female dancers, which underscores his position as a 'queen'. Moreover, he is looked at by a young woman who does not know much about ballet conventions, therefore is embarrassed by his demeanour, and her embarrassment adds to the impression of the strangeness created by his costume and mannerisms. He, on the other hand, is unable to return her gaze and to force her to question her appearance and to feel strange in her heterosexuality. The otherness of the dancer is strengthened by his proximity to the French ex-ballerina, who is portrayed by Zanussi as snobbish and fake, complete with miniature dog, smuggled from Paris in her handbag.

In the 1970s and 1980s Polish filmmakers even succeeded in laughing at homosexuals without showing them, as in *Dzięcioł* (*The Woodpecker*, 1970) by Jerzy Gruza. Here a middle-aged man (Wiesław Gołas), whose wife, a famous sportswoman, has left him for three days to take part in a sports championship, embarks on an affair with another woman. In order to have an empty house to win her heart, he takes his ten-year-old son to the theatre, where he leaves him on his own. When he returns, saying 'I came to collect my boy', he is informed by the porter, 'The entrance to the ballet is from the other side'. It is worth noting that this apparently innocent joke plays on a couple of not-so-innocent associations, including the link between homosexuality and power (the boy is to be collected by an older man, as a slave or servant by his master) and homosexuality and paedophilia (the object of affection is a child).

In the bulk of Polish films of the 1970s and 1980s, the homosexual category is defined less by the sexual preferences of its members and more by their gender identities. Here the homosexual is the 'invert' – the possessor of a feminine soul enclosed in a male body. As John Marshall maintains, such a concept prevailed in Western discourses on homosexuality in the nineteenth century and the first decades of the twentieth, to be gradually replaced by the conception of a homosexual as being attracted to the same sex (Marshall 1981). We may deduce that the way Polish cinema in the 1970s and 1980s constructed homosexuals testifies to the fact that Poles are in this matter something like twenty to thirty years behind the West. The proliferation of 'pansies' or home-grown *cioty* used for comic effect in the 1970s can also be explained by the rise of popular or populist cinema in this period – the final period of socialism in Poland. As comedies constituted a large part of the diet offered to viewers at the time, there was a need to find new objects to make viewers laugh. Homosexuals were well suited to this purpose because, unlike politicians or policemen, they did not constitute a powerful group, therefore laughing at them proved cheap and the filmmakers could take for granted that the laughter would be shared by the vast majority of the audience.

In *Ziemia obiecana* (*The Promised Land*, 1975), directed by Andrzej Wajda, the discourse on sexuality is intertwined with a discourse on ethnicity. Based on the novel of the same title by Władysław Reymont about the growth of capitalism in Łódź during the nineteenth century, Wajda's film focuses on three male characters, an impoverished Polish noble Karol Borowiecki, a Jew Moryc Welt and a German Maks Baum, who cooperate to build a factory that is supposed to make them a fortune. Through the narrative, the mise-en-scène and casting (Karol is played by Daniel Olbrychski who was the sex symbol of the 1970s) Wajda constructs a sexual hierarchy of his male characters and, by extension, of the nations to which they belong. Thus, Karol is at the top of the hierarchy, having a Polish fiancée who is utterly devoted to him, a Jewish lover and eventually a rich German wife. Below him is Maks who lusts after Karol's Polish fiancée, but fails to seduce her. At the very bottom is Jewish Moryc (Wojciech Pszoniak), who is unhappily in love with Karol, as demonstrated by the photo of Karol that he carries with him (and once loses, to the embarrassment of his friends), and his exaggerated gestures and mannerisms. Thus, Wajda uses sexual stereotypes to elevate Poles over other nationalities and ethnicities. I regard such representation as compensatory; it betrays Wajda's willingness to flatter his male compatriots who might feel inferior towards nations more successful than Poles or even his own sense of being a powerless and emasculated Pole.

It is worth noting that in Reymont's novel Moryc is a heterosexual man, unhappily in love with a young woman. He also proves treacherous in his business dealings with Karol, and his disloyalty is one of the reasons for Karol's bankruptcy and subsequent moral fall, whereas in the film this disaster is presented as a result of Karol's love affair with a married Jewish woman. Ostrowska and Stevenson argue that Wajda removed any taint of treachery from Moryc's character to avoid the accusation of anti-Semitism (Ostrowska and Stevenson 2000). In my opinion, by moving the blame for Karol's downfall from a Jewish man to a Jewish woman (who is, besides, portrayed by Wajda as a dangerously sensual creature, not unlike Jewish women in Nazi propaganda), the film did not become less anti-Semitic. On the other hand, through linking Jewishness with homosexuality (both validated negatively by the majority of Poles), the director played into the hands of those who regard homosexuality as an 'imported illness', alien to the Polish national character. It could be argued that by rejecting the stereotype of the 'ballet boy' and instead, showing him as a man engaged in the 'serious' activities of setting up his own business Wajda offers us a more progressive vision of a homosexual man than in the Polish films previously discussed. However, at the same time he suggests that in Poland a homosexual can only be treated seriously if his interests, habits and values are in accordance with those of straight men; he cannot enter 'polite society' on his own terms.

Let me now turn to Chmielewski's *In the Silence of the Night*, an accomplished film practically overlooked by Polish film critics and historians, perhaps because of the director's courage in tackling homosexuality in a way that was new at the time in Poland. Set in the 1920s, in the part of Poland that previously belonged to Germany, it focuses on the relationship between the teenage Wiktor, who reveals a homosexual tendency and his father, Teofil Herman, a police officer searching for a paedophile killer of small boys. Wiktor's interest in the same sex is presented by Chmielewski not as a dangerous aberration but as the source of the boy's noblest deeds and purest joy, even the core of his very humanity. The sensitive teenager's tender attachment to his school friend Bernard allows him to survive life with his authoritarian father and the loss of his mother. Banned by the father from seeing Bernard, Wiktor grows even more distant to his parent and begins acting irrationally, which leads to a double tragedy for father and son, culminating in the father killing his own son. This very act renders the father cruel and mad, and positions the son as an innocent victim. Such an impression is reinforced by acting and make-up. Tomasz Zaliwski, playing

Teofil, comes across as cold, intolerant, selfish and preoccupied only with his work – an archetypal follower of 'Prussian drill'. Moreover, his small moustache and his command of German evoke associations with Hitler. By contrast, Piotr Łysak's blond Wiktor, with his fascination for exotic places and ship journeys, comes across as an archetypal Polish romantic.

Despite this atypical rendering of the homosexual in *In the Silence of the Night*, the first film that attempts to 'make a modern homosexual' (to use Kenneth Plummer's phrase) on the Polish screen is widely regarded as *Zygfryd* (1987), by Andrzej Domalik. Based on a short story of Jarosław Iwaszkiewicz and set in 1934 in a sleepy village in the south of Poland, it depicts the fascination of Stefan Drawicz, an elderly art connoisseur and philosopher, for a young acrobat from an itinerant circus, the eponymous Zygfryd. After seeing the young man's performance, Drawicz invites Zygfryd to his home and gradually draws him into his world of art, literature and philosophy that he presents to him as full of spiritual beauty. Moreover, he pampers the teenager, offering him fine alcohol and buying him expensive clothes. As a result of this exposure to art and luxury, Zygfryd begins to feel out of place in the circus and shows contempt for his colleagues, who now appear to him crude. His distance from the old company is increased by a rivalry between himself and a number of other men, including the circus manager Waldo, for the sexual favours of the most attractive woman in the circus, Waldo's wife Maria. Having to choose between Drawicz who appears always to be accessible, and Maria whose interest in him is flimsy, Zygfryd gravitates towards the former. Yet he becomes repelled by the old man when, posing naked for his portrait as a beautiful Greek male, Drawicz touches him on the arm (that may be a prelude to more intimate caresses). Zygfryd abruptly rejects this intimate gesture, hits Stefan and runs off, convinced that he killed his patron. When, the same evening, during his trapeze performance, he sees Drawicz in his usual place in the audience, he is convinced that he is seeing a ghost. He loses his balance, falls from the ladder and is subsequently paralysed. As an invalid, he has no value for the circus, which leaves him behind and travels on. He moves into the house of Drawicz but by this stage the old aesthete has no interest in him.

The relationship between the elderly aristocrat and the young artist conforms to the stereotype of the same-sex liaison. Yet in other aspects Domalik breaks with the homophobic cliché. His Zygfryd reminds us less of an 'invert', more of a 'new man', who rejects macho masculinity not because he feels too weak to be macho, but because he regards such a model, encapsulated in the film by Waldo, as outdated, even ridiculous. His dismissive attitude towards Waldo is most clearly revealed in a scene when Zygfryd refuses to be the target in Waldo's knife-throwing act, showing his boss that he is above his masculine games. Similarly, Domalik leaves no doubt that although Drawicz's sexual behaviour is homosexual, his gender identity is male and his gender role is masculine. Everyone around him treats him as a 'proper' male whilst being aware of his sexual preferences. The casting and acting confirm the 'manliness' of both Stefan and Zygfryd. Drawicz is played by Gustaw Holoubek, a well-known (heterosexual) actor who himself specialised in the roles of mature intellectuals, and so brings to his character the seriousness and dignity of his earlier roles. Zygfryd, played by Tomasz Hudziec, who was earlier cast as a child actor in a number of films, accentuates the adolescence of his character, his openness to new experiences.

Ostrowska and Stevenson note that in the Polish press *Zygfryd* was considered to be a film in which homosexual attraction epitomises a 'purely intellectual yearning for perfect beauty' (Ostrowska and Stevenson 2000). In my opinion, however, the opposite is true; following Iwaszkiewicz, Domalik unmasks such an 'intellectual yearning' as hiding a purely physical passion for a perfect body of an adolescent male. Drawicz is quite frank with Zygfryd that his collection of pictures, dominated by portraits of naked young men, pales into insignificance in comparison with the beauty of young flesh. Accordingly, his passion for collecting art and his attempts at sketching portraits of young men, and his own self-portraits as an attractive youth, are poor substitutes for physical contact with another man, and the way to come to terms with his own ageing and loneliness. Consequently, Drawicz's later rejection of Zygfryd is a logical development of his mindset. Once the young body is broken, the attractiveness to an older man also evaporates and the boy is discarded like an old toy. It could be argued that the fate of Zygfryd epitomises the predicament of young men who sell their bodies to older men. Although at one point they might appear to be in a position of power over those who pay them, this position is only temporary, if not illusionary.

For me *Zygfryd* produces an autobiographical effect – I cannot help but see in the figure of the ageing aesthete lusting after the young boy Iwaszkiewicz himself. If this effect was intended by the writer, he offered us a sombre, if not masochistic diagnosis of homosexual relations, based on inequalities and destined to fail. Perhaps, as some critics argue, such a construction of homosexual love is the price writers and filmmakers have to pay to be able to represent it at all, because happy homosexual love would be unpalatable to Polish audiences (Maniewski 1994; Kot 2006). It must be stressed that representing a homosexual as an unhappy person, a victim or a sad young man, was also the norm in Western cinema (Dyer 1993). Yet it could be argued that this tradition is gradually being superseded by a new approach of depicting homosexuals as happy or at least not less content than the population average. Thus the emphasis on sadness and tragedy might be viewed as a measure of Polish cinema's backwardness in tackling homosexual issues.

Magnat (*The Magnate*, 1987) by Filip Bajon, released in the same year as *Zygfryd*, invites comparison with Wajda's *The Promised Land*, because in it homosexuality is also inscribed in the discourse on Polishness. Bajon depicts the history of the fictitious noble Silesian von Teuss family (modelled on the real von Plesses of Pszczyna), during the first half of the twentieth century. The patriarch of the family, Hans Heinrich von Teuss (Jan Nowicki), is a virile man who was married twice and fathered four children, including three sons with his first wife Daisy. Moreover, for most of his life he successfully inhabited the geographical and cultural boundaries spanning Poland and Germany. Nationality was never a problem for him; he happily served the Kaiser but also employed a Polish engineer to manage his coalmines. He could be described as a quintessential Central European. By comparison, his sons prove unable either to emulate their father's potency or balance their multicultural heritage. Franzel, the eldest son, who comes across as cold, asexual and domineering, becomes a Nazi collaborator, and is involved in the abduction of his youngest brother Bolko by the Nazis. Bolko, on the other hand, is a compulsive gambler and womaniser who spends most of his life in the casinos of Nice and Monte Carlo, and eventually marries his stepmother when his father is still alive, causing a major scandal in the whole region. Finally, the middle son Conrad is a homosexual. His homosexuality is construed by Bajon as one of many flaws suffered by the younger von Teuss generation, which together mark the family's decadence and decline, not unlike Luchino Visconti's *The Damned* (*La Caduta degli Dei*, 1969). However, against the backdrop of his brothers' extreme behaviour, Conrad comes across as moderate. He neither squanders the family fortune, nor becomes possessed by a dangerous ideology. In his pragmatism and 'ideological sobriety' he proves closest to his father, who eventually chooses him as his heir. Conrad is also the only one of the brothers to embrace his Polishness, as signified by his conversion to Catholicism, having a Polish lover (who is the son of the manager of his father's coalmining business) and moving to Warsaw. Furthermore, Conrad is the only one of the sons and, indeed, the only member of the von Teuss clan, who survives the political storms of the 1930s and 1940s, and after the Second World War returns to the family country house, albeit only as a tourist. The style of acting of Jan Englert, playing Conrad, contrasting with the histrionic performance of Bogusław Linda as Bolko and 'cold madness' of Olgierd Łukaszewicz's Franzel, underscores his character's normality. On the whole, whilst Bajon succumbs to the homophobic view that homosexuality is a deviation from the norm, he also stresses that it is a minor aberration, that might even save a person from more dangerous pathologies such as political fanaticism. It is worth adding that in the television version of *The Magnate*, entitled *Biała wizytówka* (*A White Visiting Card*, 1989), another homosexual character, Conrad's lover Jurek Zbierski (played by homosexual actor Marek Barbasiewicz), gains a prominent role. As Ewelina Nurczyńska-Fidelska notes, this character bears a similarity to Witold Gombrowicz and is the only character in the film who understands the position of other characters in relation to history (Nurczyńska-Fidelska 2003: 119–120), not unlike the narrator of *Trans-Atlantyk*, significantly enough named 'Witold Gombrowicz'. It appears that both for Gombrowicz and Bajon the position of the Polish homosexual is to be outside history. However, as history turns out to be cruel and mad, this is might be the only place worth occupying.

The construction of Conrad suggests that in contrast to Wajda, for Bajon homosexuality is compatible with Polishness, although not with the type of Polishness exalted by Polish romantics. The difference in this respect between these two directors reflects the wider variations in the way they construct Polishness. Wajda focuses on the dominant discourses of Polishness; the Polishness of his central (male) characters is beyond any doubt. I will argue that this is the reason that, as was established on many occasions (see, for example, Meller 1992), Wajda is the ultimate Polish national director. Bajon, on the other hand, searches for liminal identities, often suggesting that for people who lived on the margins of Poland, national identity was a question of pragmatic choice, not patriotism.

Jonathan Katz, the author of *Gay American History* (1976), claims that 'all homosexuality is situational' (Katz, quoted in Weeks 1981: 79). For Polish filmmakers the situation most conducive to the emergence of homosexual tendencies is a state of extreme oppression caused by political circumstances. Such an approach to homosexuality construes it, to use Guy Hocquenghem's phrase, as 'poor man's sexuality'. One example is *Kornblumenblau* (1988), directed by Leszek Wosiewicz and based on the war memoirs of Kazimierz Tymiński, where a homosexual relationship develops in a concentration camp between the German *kapo* (Krzysztof Kolberger) and a Polish prisoner Tadek (Adam Kamień), a young married man, who was sent to the camp as punishment for an anti-Nazi conspiracy. The German saves Tadek's life through giving him special patronage that remains even after the *kapo* is transferred to the frontline. As in *The Promised Land*, the motif of homosexual relation has been added by the director in the process of adapting a literary work (Wróbel 2000: 100). According to Ostrowska and Stevenson, this change adds a sexual dimension to the totalitarian relationship between the two main characters, confirming the 'slave' status of the Polish man towards his German 'master' (Ostrowska and Stevenson 2000). I disagree with such a reading ; in my opinion the homosexual relationship is represented here as a non-totalitarian element in a totalitarian world. Testimony to that is the way the homosexual *kapo* treats Tadek. Although he does not regard him as his equal, he shows him loyalty and care that is normally absent in relations between prisoners and their oppressors. Moreover, homosexual undertones pervade not only the relationship between ordinary prisoners and those in positions of authority, but also amongst the prisoners themselves, as we see in the scene when the prisoners, cramped on the floor of an overcrowded barrack, cling to each other's backs and move their bodies as if they are having homosexual intercourse. The director leaves the viewer to decide if the incarcerated men are hugging each other, trembling with cold or looking for comfort derived from sexual activity. Similarly, the cruel treatment pertaining to the concentration camp is to an extent balanced by acts of generosity between men that sometimes go beyond ordinary friendship and might suggest erotic affection. Tadek's friend, in particular, behaves as if he were jealous of the favours Tadek receives from his German masters, in a similar way to a man or woman's jealousy of his or her lover's attachment to someone else.

The shift in the representation of the homosexual from the 'invert' to the ordinary male who simply happens to be sexually attracted to persons of the same sex, as well as greater courage in depicting homosexual love, took place in Polish cinema in the late 1980s, shortly before the collapse of communism. Ostrowska and Stevenson perceive this shift as an element of the increased 'sexualisation' of love in Polish film, of which other features are brutality and an abundance of images of sadomasochism on screen (Ostrowska and Stevenson 2000). Depending on the axiological position, this sexualisation can be seen as a sign of the moral decadence of the late-communist period or of its liberalisation.

Close Friends

In psychoanalytical discourse male friendship and comradeship are regarded as the sublimation of homosexual tendencies (Freud 1963: 160–170; Hocquenghem 1993: 55–61). Such a sublimation can be regarded as a product of society's fear and rejection of homosexuality. If we adopt this reading, then we should conclude that the representation of intense male friendship might in fact be a depiction of repressed homosexual desire. This interpretation seems even more plausible in relation to the products of cultures that are particularly puritanical in sexual matters, as were Polish and Czechoslovak during the socialist period. A different meaning to male comradeship is offered by Michel Foucault who suggests that the emergence of homosexuality as a distinct category is historically linked to the disappearance of male friendship (Foucault 1998). This statement can be regarded as an assessment of the oppressive character of cultures that adopted the concept of 'homosexuality' and as a directive not to read too much into male bonds, but instead to see male friendship simply as male friendship.

Rather than opting for one of these positions as truthful, I treat them simply as methodological directives that might be useful in different contexts. Accordingly, in this part I am using a Freudian reading of male friendship to look at two films, one Czechoslovak, *Intimní osvětlení* (*Intimate Lighting*, 1965), directed by Ivan Passer, and one Polish, *Barwy ochronne* (*Camouflage*, 1977) by Krzysztof Zanussi, a director with a sustained interest in men who do not suit the heterosexual norm (Sadowska and Żurawiecki 2004). Lets begin with their titles, which suggest hiding, masking (Zanussi's film) and the need to use special circumstances to achieve intimacy and privacy (Passer's film). These titles bear associations with political dissidence and with the homosexual closet, both features, as Kevin Moss observes, pertaining to the communist regimes (Moss 1995).

Passer depicts the weekend visit of Petr (Zdenek Bezusek), a musician from the city, and his girlfriend, to a village where his old friend nicknamed Bambas (Karel Blažek) lives with his extended family that comprises his wife, their three children and his parents-in-law. Although both men have women by their side, one gets the impression that their friendship matters more to them than their relationships with the opposite sex. Both men reject the erotic advances of their women as if they were utterly bored with them. Neither do they want to talk to the members of the opposite sex. Bambas specially feels trapped by his provincial life and large family, although it is only Petr's arrival that makes him aware how tedious his life is and how heavy the burden of his numerous relatives, as if confirming the words of André Morali-Danninos: 'Were homosexuality to receive a show of approval, we would soon arrive at the abolition of the heterosexual couple and of the family, which are the foundations of the Western society in which we live' (Morali-Danninos, quoted in Hocquenghem 1993: 60).

The special significance of the male bond is poignantly revealed when the men get drunk together on slivovitz. Alcohol, especially a strong one, loosens various cultural taboos, including the prohibition of touching and kissing a member of the same sex.

Accordingly, during their drinking session Petr and Bambas embrace each other and cuddle. They also reminisce about their past and talk about how their lives would look if Bambas had not migrated to the provinces. At one point Bambas encourages Petr to set off with him into the world outside, to start anew, as itinerant musicians. But, as Philip Bergson observes, 'On the brow of the hill, car-lights remind us that Petr is still wearing his pyjamas, and there is no escape' (Bergson 2005) – no escape from socialism, provinciality and, one is tempted to add, from the strict heterosexism imposed on Czechoslovak men by folk tradition and socialist rules. The special relationship between men is also signified by the mise-en-scène, including the 'intimate lighting', in which Petr and Bambas can hide from reality and be themselves, albeit for a short time, as the daylight destroys the male idyll. Another enclave is provided by music; only men in the film are able to play instruments and when they play, they occupy space that is unavailable to women and that comes across as superior over any female zone. However, one can be an artist only from time to time; usually one is not. The male universe remains a paradise that can be inhabited only briefly.

Camouflage by Krzysztof Zanussi focuses on the relationship between two single academics of different generations at a camp for academics and students: a young lecturer Jarosław Kruszyński (Piotr Garlicki) and the mature professor Jakub Szelestowski (Zbigniew Zapasiewicz). Superficially, both conform to the heterosexual norm. Jarosław has an English girlfriend Nelly, and Jakub shows interest in a maid to whom he eventually offers payment for sexual services. However, Zanussi renders these interests insincere and lacking in passion, and overshadowed by the platonic relationship between the two men. Rather than trying to seduce Nelly, Jarosław only allows this sexually liberated woman to accompany him, as a kind of proof that he is a 'normal' man. Moreover, at a crucial moment when Nelly offers to 'massage' him to relieve some tension in his body, which is meant to lead on to greater intimacy, he abruptly withdraws from her erotic game. Not surprisingly, in due course Nelly settles for an Italian man at the camp who provides a marked contrast to the young Pole. Jakub, on the other hand, negotiates a price for sex with the maid in such a way that his negotiations are clearly visible to Jarosław; he even looks discreetly at him while talking to the woman. It seems as if Jakub wanted to provoke the younger man to jealousy. Moreover, the film is full of episodes associated with homosexual activity, for example Jakub is often peeping at young campers with his long-lens camera, ostensibly used for photographing birds. He spies on both men and women but the focus of the camera on male genitals leaves little doubt that it is men who attract his attention. Moreover, at one point the students find his camera and take pictures of each other's bottoms, most likely to disgrace him in his workplace, as he will use the university's photographic lab to process the incriminating material. Thus we can guess that within academia Jakub has the reputation of being interested in men. Finally, the professor has a penchant for rough games with men; we see him wrestling with Jarosław and pretending that he accidentally killed him, only to continue their game.

Zanussi not only hints at the presence of homosexual desire amongst the Polish intelligentsia but also points to the reasons that such desire must remain hidden. He does so by showing that patriarchy and heterosexism in Poland constitute norms that nobody dares question. Men there have a much higher position than women and married people a higher position than those who are single. The vice-chancellor of the university where Jakub and Jarosław work is married to a woman much younger than himself and the couple have a small child. Virility constitutes an important part of the vice-chancellor's charisma. Revealing oneself as homosexual in this society where 'Oedipus reigns' brings the danger of finding oneself not only below heterosexual men, but even below women – sinking to the very bottom of the social hierarchy.

Total Abstainers

The next category I will consider comprises films about men who reveal pathological sexuality, and in a wider sense, a pathological mentality. I would include here *The Cremator* (*Spalovač mrtvol*, 1968) by Juraj Herz and *Za ścianą* (*Behind the Wall*, 1971) by Krzysztof Zanussi, films that despite belonging to different genres reveal important common traits.

Herz's work, which is based on a novel *Spalovač mrtvol* (1967) by Ladislav Fuks, is set shortly before the outbreak of the Second World War and focuses on Karel Kopfrkingl (Rudolf Hrušínský), the eponymous cremator who is manager of a funeral service. Testimony to his pathological mentality is his killing of his own wife, his son, and eventually his attempt to murder his daughter. These extreme acts can be seen as a consequence of Kopfrkingl's adoption of the Nazi ideology that requires the annihilation of Jewish members of society – his wife is Jewish and so are their children, or at least Kopfrkingl's Nazi friend convinces him that his family belongs to the inferior race. Whilst I am not discarding this interpretation, I will also link Kopfrkingl's killings to his sexual identity. Herz questions whether Kopfrkingl ever truly loved his family, by suggesting in the first scene that his marriage was a strictly economic arrangement. In this episode the cremator admits that they owe their comfortable life to his wife's dowry and the financial help they received from her aunt. The extra opportunities for cremation and thus earning additional income, brought by the Nazis, make the financial help from his wife's family redundant. By ridding himself of his wife and children, Kopfrkingl can devote his whole attention to himself, be in love with himself alone. He conveys his narcissism by his favourite gesture or, indeed, his favourite activity of combing his hair. He also frequently looks in a mirror and when he talks to others, it is clear that he is self-conscious, as if he were seeing himself in their eyes. At one point he also imagines splitting himself into two; his second, imaginary persona being that of the Dalai Lhama.

Kopfrkingl's murderous activities can also be explained by his attraction to death itself, as indicated by his occupation. Although Herz does not present Kopfrkingl as an ordinary necrophiliac, he points to his character's attraction to corpses. For example, the cremator likes to open coffins, touch the bodies of his clients and comb their hair, and typically does so after tending to his own hair. In this way he establishes an imaginary connection between himself and the corpses, as if they belonged to the same secret society of 'death lovers'. He also comments on the beauty of the dead exceeding that of living people. Kopfrkingl's favourite topic of conversation is serious illness in other people as if he cannot wait to see them in coffins. Even his pet name for his wife, 'angel', signifies not his affection for her but rather seeing her as a future corpse. Furthermore, the cremator is attracted to images of death. At a funfair to which he takes his wife and children, he interrupts their pleasure in watching acrobatics and takes them to a 'theatre of death'. Here a master of ceremonies tells stories of serial killers and their victims. These stories are presented by actors whose movements are mechanical and who look like waxworks. After the end of the show the audience are directed by a waxwork dwarf (who proved to be a real dwarf) to a room full of jars containing abnormal foetuses and diseased body parts preserved in formalin. Whilst for Kopfrkingl's family the spectacle is horrifying, he enjoys it immensely. It could be said that what interests him in living people are signs of their decay and imminent death, whilst death appears to him full of life and promise.

At several points in the narrative the cremator says, 'I am a total abstainer'. Although these words are his response to questions whether he smokes or drinks alcohol, it can also refer to his whole attitude to people: he abstains from any meaningful contact with them. The energy he saves by avoiding fellow humans he invests in self-love and his attraction to death. Perhaps his very conversion to Nazism is rooted in his necrophiliac tendencies. This opinion is confirmed by the fact that he embarks on his task to annihilate Jews not so much from his hatred of them (though he shares the anti-Semitic view that Jews are weak and effeminate), as from his desire to liberate them from suffering. His fascination with Buddhism and imagining himself as the Dalai Lhama testify to his wish to alleviate human suffering.

Jan (Zbigniew Zapasiewicz) in *Behind the Wall* does not come across as so extreme in his erotic tastes as Kopfrkingl, which can be explained by the difference in genre used by Zanussi. However, he shares with Herz's character some important traits. Jan is an academic (a profession frequently featured in Zanussi's films), devoted to his work in the lab. Like Kopfrkingl, he is also very clean, pedantic and self-centred. Moreover, his work involves killing, although only animals used in biochemical experiments and, like Kopfrkingl, Jan appears to be very concerned for their welfare, reproaching his assistants for causing a laboratory rat any unnecessary suffering. He is also, perhaps even more so than the cremator, 'a total abstainer', since he is childless and single, and of course he does not smoke. His settled existence is disrupted by his female neighbour (Maja Komorowska), who is also a scientist, but less successful. She invites him to her flat, puts on music and in her shy way attempts to seduce him but without success. Jan runs away, as if frightened that somebody might disrupt his sterile existence.[10] He carries on as before even when his neighbour attempts to commit suicide, although his encounter with her makes him realise that there is little joy and purpose in his life.

The question arises, what would the sexual identity of these men be in a different, more tolerant culture? With regards to Kopfrkingl the critics' answer is 'Not very different'. He is a madman whose condition is only exacerbated or laid bare by certain social circumstances, namely Nazism or totalitarianism in a wider sense (Wilson 1971; Hames 2005: 225; Bird 2006). As for Jan (and some other male characters in Zanussi's films), Sadowska and Żurawiecki suggest that they might be homosexual; the suppression of homosexual desire changed them into physical and emotional impotents (Sadowska and Żurawiecki 2004). By claiming that 'the eye of the camera looks at them [Zanussi's handsome male protagonists] with a distinctive, albeit discreet enchantment' (ibid.: 120), they also allude to the idea that Zanussi's films are the product of suppressed homosexual desire on the part of their author. However, they do not articulate this conclusion, most likely out of concern that attributing homosexual tendencies to the married director regarded as a stalwart of Catholicism in Polish cinema will be an anathema inviting libel action. Hence, according to this interpretation, *Behind the Wall*, as well as many other films by Zanussi, and the discourse formulated around them, is a product of multi-layered censorship. The films cast as the main characters men who suppress their homosexual identity till it disappears, making them impotent. The representation of the suppression of homosexual identity is itself timid, testifying to the self-censorship of the filmmaker, who must bow to the requirements of Polish culture which is distinctly homophobic. Finally, the critics who detect homosexual sensitivity on the part of the director 'behind the wall' of his prudishness and homophobia, lack the courage to attribute a homosexual identity to him, confirming the claim that concealment and secrecy are the crucial characteristics of homosexual discourse in East European culture (Moss 1995; Ritz 2002; Warkocki 2006).

'Non-straight' Sexualities in Postcommunist Cinema

Films about homosexuality and other alternative sexualities erupted after 1989 both in Poland, Czechoslovakia and its succession states. More homosexuals were seen on Polish, Czech and Slovak screens after 1989 than in the entire communist period. Moreover, members of sexual minorities in the films made after the collapse of communism represent a wider social spectrum than before and they receive more prominent parts than they did in films made under socialism. This proliferation is typically attributed to Westernisation of the ex-socialist East. Showing homosexual men and women on film, as in other media, is, in the opinion of the majority of critics, a sign of a new openness and acceptance of plurality of lifestyles and ideological positions brought about by the return of democracy and a market economy (Sokolová 2004; Kot 2006). In this respect postcommunist Polish, Czech and Slovak cinema can be compared to Spanish cinema after Franco when the affirmation of the new national identity manifested itself through an upsurge in images of homosexual, transvestite and transsexual men and women. However, we must be careful not to push this analogy too far, for whilst in post-Franco Spain representatives of 'non-straight' sexualities were brought to the screen chiefly by Pedro Almodóvar, who shared his homosexual characters' attitudes and was not shy to show himself amongst them, in Polish, Czech and Slovak cinema a large gulf has remained between the author and subject of the film. After 1989, as before, films about homosexual characters are usually made by straight directors or at least by those who do not admit to being homosexual. Moreover, the old homophobic stereotypes, that began to be challenged in the Polish cinema of the 1980s, did not die after 1989 but erupted with a vengeance, although they are now accompanied by representations of new types.

In the majority of Polish postcommunist films homosexual men are still seen through the hostile eyes of heterosexual characters and directors. Moreover, homosexuality, even more than during the communist period, is linked to inequality and oppression, and serves as an indicator of other types of negatively valued otherness such as the decadent nobility. *Zakład* (*The Reformatory*, 1990) by Teresa Kotlarczyk and *Urok wszeteczny* (*Devilish Charm*, 1996) by Krzysztof Zanussi (both directors renowned for their solemn films, devoted to Catholic figures), illustrate this trend. Kotlarczyk's film depicts a reformatory for young men from a young woman's perspective that can be equated with the point of view of the director herself. She is making a documentary about 'the human being in extreme circumstances' and its extremity can be equated with totalitarianism. The hierarchy of the totalitarian system is maintained through sexuality; homosexuality is both the result of a totalitarian system and its pillar (Ostrowska and Stevenson 2000). Such a representation contrasts with that offered in *Kornblumenblau* where homosexuality was presented as a force civilising a totalitarian universe, and testifies to the homophobia on the part of the director of *The Reformatory*.

Zanussi casts as the main character a rich old aristocrat who uses his position to humiliate and sexually exploit younger men. The narrative focuses on his attempt to corrupt a young married academic Karol, who because of financial problems begins to work as his assistant. However, the ageing homosexual fails to pervert the young man and ends up disgracing himself. It is worth mentioning that the homosexual is played by Zbigniew Zapasiewicz, who previously played such sexually ambiguous characters in Zanussi's films as Jakub in *Camouflage* and Jan in *Behind the Wall*. The fact that in this film his character comes out, encourages us to treat the earlier incarnations of Zapasiewicz as homosexuals also, thus confirming the interpretation offered by Sadowska and Żurawiecki that Zanussi films represent and are product of suppressed homosexuality. Zapasiewicz's roles in these three Zanussi's films can even be treated as the trajectory of a Polish homosexual: from total sexual abstinence in *Behind the Wall*, through timid attempts to enter into a relationship with other men in *Camouflage*, to openly homosexual behaviour in *Devilish Charm*. Unfortunately, by the time 'Zanussi/Zapasiewicz's homosexual' is able to declare his sexual preferences and act upon them, he is too old and bitter to build a lasting partnership with another man. Thus, paradoxically, despite the open homophobia conveyed by Zanussi in his last film on this subject, the film points to the damage caused by the atmosphere of sexual intolerance to the well-being of individuals who do not fit into mainstream society.

Ogniem i mieczem (*With Fire and Sword*, 1999), directed by Jerzy Hoffman, one of the principal examples of Polish heritage cinema, in a way reminiscent of Wajda's *The Promised Land*, uses homosexuality as a means to mark the difference between

Poles and other nations. The film depicts Polish–Ukrainian conflict in the seventeenth century and represents the leader of the non-Christian Tatars, who help the Ukrainians to fight the Poles, with his effeminate male lover, whom he feeds with sweetmeats. Such an image poignantly contrasts with the portrayal of the 'Spartan' Poles, who do not have time for any frivolities and whose sole affection is directed either at their fiancées waiting for them in remote villages or to the Virgin Mary. Hence, not unlike Wajda's film, homosexuality here equals foreignness and weakness.

In the film by Marek Koterski, *Dzień świra* (*Day of the Wacko*, 2002), the homosexual neighbour of the main character, Adam Miauczyński, conforms to the stereotype familiar from Polish films of the 1970s of an ageing, effeminate *ciota* with aristocratic pretensions, conveyed by body language and a particular way of pronouncing 'r'. Miauczyński, who dreams of romantic greatness, is full of contempt for this man. At the same time, his failure in the traditional roles of father and lover makes him worried that something important links him with his neighbour, as revealed in his internal monologue, 'What does he sense in me? Maybe he wants to fuck me?' Miauczyński's anxiety confirms the opinion that the 'homosexual' label serves not only to control and punish 'non-straight' sexual behaviour, but also to define and maintain appropriate definitions of masculine and feminine behaviour. In other words, Koterski shows that the behaviour of a homosexual man serves as a litmus test of Miauczyński's own maleness. It should be mentioned that *Day of the Wacko* is the first Polish film in which the proximity of a homosexual man awakens in a heterosexual man such anxiety, which might be attributed to the crisis of masculinity experienced by Polish men after 1989 (Mazierska 2003).

Whilst the aforementioned films are made from a distinctively homophobic perspective and depict a homosexual as a social outsider, *Egoiści* (*The Egoists*, 2000) by Mariusz Treliński treats him with some sympathy and situates him at the centre of society. Despite that, I would describe it as a 'middle-of-the-road film' that slips into the familiar stereotypes. The main character, the homosexual Filip (Jan Frycz), is a famous architect in his forties who lives in a tasteful house and socialises with Warsaw *glitterati* and yuppies. He does not look any different from his heterosexual male friends, even appears more 'cool' and macho than they, as testified by a female prostitute who takes him for a potential client. However, as time passes, the masks of his success, macho masculinity and belonging to the mainstream society drop, and Filip reveals the familiar face (and body) of a Polish *ciota*. His literal and metaphorical striptease takes place in his own house where we find him first pleading with his young soldier lover to stay with him, and when he refuses, dancing with a doll and crying. The doll is a sign of his effeminacy and, in his own words, plays the role of his adopted child and, therefore, a symbol of his aborted effort to create a family with his lover. Needless to say, such an image perfectly fits the opinion, typical of the Polish Church but also famously expressed by Margaret Thatcher, that homosexuals only pretend to have families. The final stage of Filip's demise is his committing suicide by setting fire to himself in his own house. In this scene Treliński's protagonist takes off his clothes, including a tight, female corset that he wears under his masculine clothes–the symbol of his 'uranian' personality and his closet.

Figure 5.3 Jan Frycz as Filip in *Egoiści* (*The Egoists*, 2000), directed by Mariusz Treliński.

The Egoists is set in 2000 – the last year of the century and the millennium, regarded as the peak of decadence and the expected end of the world. Treliński plays on these associations, presenting Warsaw in 2000 as a contemporary inferno where people are desecrating religious and national symbols and nothing is sacred any more. In this world a homosexual is not an outsider but a leader. The gap between the homosexuals and straight people is closing because heterosexual society has adopted what was previously identified as homosexual lifestyles, becoming self-centred, hedonistic, sick and sterile. Treliński does not accuse Filip and others of his kind for depraving 'healthy' youth; the young engage in illicit pleasures on their own initiative. However, for the homophobic critic the very proximity between the homosexual and the hedonistic, immoral youth might be enough to attribute to the former full responsibility for corrupting the latter. It is worth remembering that such scapegoating was a common feature of a large period of the communist history of Russia (Healey 2001).

Parę osób, mały czas (*Few People, Small Time*, 2005) by Andrzej Barański can be regarded as another step towards making homosexuals more important in the narrative, as well as more complex and dignified, although again, not free from clichés. The main character is the poet and novelist, Miron Białoszewski (1922–83) (played by Andrzej Hudziak). Barański's film acknowledges Białoszewski's homosexual identity but focuses on the period of his life when he 'did not practise' sex, following his separation from his long-term lover. During this time Białoszewski met a blind woman with artistic interests, Jadwiga Stańczakowa (Krystyna Janda), who was married and still lived with her philandering husband, but was emotionally separated from him. Despite her disability, she took the role of Białoszewski's secretary and personal assistant, succeeding in organising the practical side of his life. He, on the other hand, helped her to battle with her depression and encouraged her to follow her artistic ambitions. During the time of their friendship, Stańczakowa wrote a diary, documenting their lives. This diary provided the source of the film.

As a result of choosing the period of Białoszewski's life dominated by the female presence, homosexuality in *Few People, Small Time* is rendered as sublimated into a certain sensibility conducive to artistic creativity – as was also the case of homosexuals depicted in Polish postwar literature (Warkocki 2005, 2006). It is linked to the poet's famous role as a socialite (his flat used to be an important literary salon in the 1960s and 1970s), his disdain for material possessions, his insistence on *carpe diem*, rather than making long-term plans, as well as his experience of being an outsider in socialist Poland. I will argue that this sublimation and consequently, avoiding the question of homosexual desire as sexual desire, is the chief reason that Barański's film was well received by the Polish critics (see, for example, Felis 2006). It allowed viewers who regard themselves as liberal and who are often 'closet homophobes' to enjoy the feeling that they are sympathetic to the plight of Polish homosexuals without really challenging their values and tastes. Whilst in this respect I regard Barański's film as conservative or at least timid, in another I see it as courageous and pioneering in Polish cinema, thanks to representing relationships that do not adhere to the conventional, Catholic definitions of the 'family' but function well, giving love and support to its members and even providing a good environment for bringing up children (Sobolewski 2005). Hence, *Few People, Small Time* has the potential to open a debate about the meaning of 'family' in the new postcommunist Poland. Finally, Barański's film deserves special attention and praise for documenting the cultural history of Polish homosexuals which, as Błażej Warkocki observes, is largely unwritten (Warkocki 2005).

The last Polish film I want to discuss here is *Kochankowie z Marony* (*Lovers from Marona*, 2005) by Izabella Cywińska. Cywińska's work is a remake of the film made almost forty years earlier by Andrzej Zarzycki, both being based on Jarosław Iwaszkiewicz's novella of the same title. Comparison of these two adaptations can thus serve as a litmus test of the change in the attitudes to homosexuality that occurred in Poland over the period. Both films depict love between Ola, a young unmarried village teacher, and Janek, a married patient from a sanatorium who is dying of consumption. However, Zarzycki makes their affair the kernel of the story; the tragedy in the film results from society's intolerance towards heterosexual promiscuity. Ola is spurned by the village community and, despite Janek's affection, has to give way to his wife. In Cywińska's version, on the other hand, the situation is more complex, since Janek (Krzysztof Zawadzki) is also romantically involved with another man named Arek (Łukasz Simlat). The director reveals sympathy towards all characters, irrespective of their gender and sexual orientation. The reason for that, according to Cywińska's own words, is her respect for love as the strongest and purest of human emotions, able to overcome death, and her conviction that love (or desire) is essentially the same in heterosexuals and homosexuals (Pawłowski 2006).[11] However, of all the loves depicted in *Lovers from Marona*, the noblest is that between Ola and Janek. Ola also suffers most when in the final moments of her lover's life she must step aside, to make way for Janek's wife. Nevertheless, the addition of a homosexual liaison and the way it is represented obviously testifies to the greater openness with which homosexuality can be treated in Poland a decade and a half after the fall of communism. It is worth adding that this openness was unattainable for Iwaszkiewicz himself. Although *Lovers from Marona* alludes to the greatest love of his life, for a man called Jurek Błeszyński, Iwaszkiewicz, who co-wrote the script of Zarzycki's film, ensured that the narrative of the cinematic *Lovers from Marona* was free of any traces of homosexual behaviour (ibid.: 13).

In common with Poland, in the Czech Republic and Slovakia we also observe after 1989 an increase in films with homosexual characters and they receive more important roles than in the films made during socialism. Moreover, their identity is less problematic; the viewer does not need to decide whether the character is homosexual by deciphering some subtle clues but is informed through his sexual behaviour and dialogue. Also, not unlike in Poland, most of them I will describe as regressive although their homophobia is not as blatant as in some of the Polish films. However, despite these similarities there are also distinctive differences in the approach to homosexuality in the respective cinemas. In Polish films we typically find homosexuals who are older and lonely. Moreover, even the characters living in contemporary Poland can be transported to the period before the fall of communism without dramatically changing their lifestyle, mindset and the attitude of others to them. By contrast, in the Czech and Slovak films homosexual men are usually young and belong to a specific subculture – we are thus justified in calling them 'gay'. Moreover, they are very much a feature of the contemporary cultural landscape. Consequently, we cannot imagine them living the way they live twenty or thirty years earlier. I will risk the statement that the gay figure in Czech and Slovak films stands for the 'new Central Europe' which is sexually liberated and Westernised. Thus the discourse on homosexuality is frequently inscribed into a debate about the changes experienced by Czech and Slovak society after the Velvet Revolution. However, such a treatment does not guarantee a sympathetic attitude to the homosexuals. On the contrary, as the majority of filmmakers reveal a negative attitude to the changes affecting their countries, they also tend to show a negative disposition to the homosexuals. Two principal examples of this trend are *Šeptej* (*Whisper*, 1996), directed by David Ondříček and the previously mentioned *Mandragora*. However, let me first refer briefly to *Pelíšky* (*Cosy Dens*, 1999) by Jan Hřebejk, since it provides an excellent background to the films of Ondříček and Grodecki. Although set in 1967–68 and containing no homosexual characters (see Chapter 2), it includes a scene in which a teenage boy, Eilen, is accused of being homosexual on the grounds of wearing 'feminine' clothes. Whether his clothes are indeed feminine is debatable, but what is beyond doubt is that they came from the West and are very fashionable, as are his hairstyle, his collection of records and films, and the decoration of his room. His whole appearance sets him apart from his peers, which is not surprising since Eilen's parents had emigrated to New York. Hence, what Hřebejk conveys is that in the Czechoslovakia of the 1960s and in the whole postwar period homosexuality was equated with Western decadence. There was also a perception that a link existed between lack of parental control and 'going queer'. Representatives of the older generation suggested that Eilen behaves in a 'queer' manner (which means feminine, eccentric and in defiance of socialist morality) because he has no parents to oversee his behaviour. However, whilst Hřebejk uses the character of Eilen to ridicule 1960s ideas about morality and sexuality, the directors of *Whisper* and *Mandragora* endorse them.

In *Whisper*, a sixteen-year-old provincial Anna (Tatiana Vilhelmová) runs away from home and hitchhikes to Prague. There she befriends a group of trendy twenty-somethings and falls in love with one of them, Filip (Jan P. Muchow), who is homosexual, and has a boyfriend nicknamed Kytka (Flower) (Martin Myšička). Kytka earns his living prostituting himself with older German men whom he picks up at Prague's main railway station. Anna thus has to compete with Kytka for Filip's attention and affection. Eventually, she succeeds in gaining Filip's heart and 'converting' him to heterosexuality, leaving Kytka devastated. Filip's change of heart marks the film's happy ending – it is equated with his return to normality and the reinstatement of the narrative's equilibrium. However, whilst for Filip there has been a chance of conversion, Kytka has gone too far on his way to corruption to have any chance of redeeming his behaviour. It is suggested that whilst Filip will return to normal society, Kytka will sink further and further into the criminal underworld. By structuring his film this way, as well as by presenting Filip as an attractive man, and Kytka as emotionally unstable and physically unattractive, Ondříček clearly positions heterosexuality as a biological and moral norm, and homosexuality as an aberration. Andrew Horton and Kazi Štastná rightly point out that

> *Šeptej*'s depiction of homosexuality is reduced to tired old clichés: gay men are promiscuous and hang around railway stations trying to pick up other men,

Figure 5.4 On the left Miroslav Caslavka as Marek in *Mandragora* (2003), directed by Wiktor Grodecki.

> and homosexual men don't *really* enjoy other men anyway – they just haven't found the right woman to make them realise they are actually straight. All this suggests that beneath the thin veneer of rebellion, Prague's acid-dropping youth have nothing real to offer which could potentially challenge some of the attitudes of the society in which they live and are merely tomorrow's conservative middle class in waiting. (Horton and Štastná 1999)

The main character in *Mandragora*, Marek (Miroslav Caslavka), is a fifteen-year-old boy who runs away to Prague from his home, where he is bullied by his single father, from his technical school, where he is training to be a welder, and from his provincial town of Ústí nad Labem. Before his escape he smashes the window of an elegant shop with Western clothes, stealing a fashionable leather jacket and a pair of shoes. Only hours after his arrival in the Czech capital he is stripped of these symbols of affluence and fashion by a gang of teenage boys. Having no money, nowhere to stay and even nothing to walk about in, he agrees to be taken home by a pimp, who drugs him and allows his business partner to sexually abuse him. From there on his life deteriorates. He is used and abused by a series of pimps and clients. Although at the beginning he only drinks soft drinks, soon he gets used to alcohol and later drugs, and then he dies. It all happens within a very short distance of his father, who comes to Prague to find his son and bring him home.

Before directing *Mandragora*, Grodecki made two documentaries about young male prostitutes living in Prague, *Andělé nejsou andělé* (*Not Angels, but Angels*, 1994) and *Tělo bez duše* (*Body without Soul*, 1996). As a follow-up to Grodecki's documentary films and a product of his collaboration with the ex-prostitute David Švec, *Mandragora* was heralded as an 'authentic' film. For example, on the cover of the DVD version of the film, produced by Millivres Multimedia, we can read that '*Mandragora* is Wiktor Grodecki's compelling dramatisation of his documentaries'. It is indeed close to Grodecki's documentaries in its daring depiction of homosexual relationships and male bodies. However, it is also deeply biased against homosexual men and homosexuality as a lifestyle. In particular, Grodecki espouses the opinion that there is a link between homosexuality and a lack of parental authority. A poster of the pop group 'Queen' decorates Marek's bedroom, but this sign of his possible homosexual inclination is only shown for a short while, and might even slip the attention of the viewer. We are to believe that if Marek had stayed with his stern, but ultimately loving father, he would still be alive and healthy. Moreover, the director perpetuates the opinion that homosexual identity emerges as a result of being forced into homosexual relations by older homosexuals. Furthermore, the most fertile environment for homosexual identities to emerge is urban decadence. A decadent culture flourishes in Prague, while the Czech provinces remain unspoilt. As Kevin Moss observes

> Both Marek and his father are shown fresh from the provinces, and the camera focuses on their faces as they watch in puzzled shock the excesses of Prague: a drag queen singing, boys dancing with each other, two boys kissing! Perhaps the father's most shocking voyeuristic moment comes in a bar brawl, when he pulls down the curtain of the darkroom to reveal what looks like an orgy, with everyone naked and oblivious to the absence of the curtain. (Moss 2006)

Moreover, as the province is represented as the place where time stands still, whilst Prague experienced a profound transformation thanks to Western influence, the film tacitly condemns the path the Czech Republic took in the 1990s. Homosexuality itself is represented by Grodecki as a kind of infectious disease which came from the West (the railway station where clients rent the boys is a potent symbol of this route), spreads from the old to the young, and leads to accelerated ageing and death. Of course, such a portrayal reinforces the association of homosexuality with AIDS that is also made explicitly in the film by making Marek die of this disease. As Moss argues, Marek's clients 'are all bizarre, ugly, criminal and Western' (ibid.). Grodecki contrasts Marek with these men when he was fresh from the province. However, early on he suggests that soon Marek will lose his freshness by including boys not much older than him whom nobody wants any more. Although reviewers note that *Mandragora* is artistically a mediocre film because of its heavy-handed preaching, sentimentality and the lack of originality in visual style (Horton and Štastná 1999), its significance as a portrayal of homosexuality in the Czech Republic cannot be overestimated because, as I mentioned at the beginning, it is the best-known film about homosexuals made in the country.

It is worth mentioning in passing that after completing *Mandragora* Grodecki returned to his native Poland to direct *Nienasycenie* (*Insatiability*, 2003), with David Švec as an assistant director. Although the film is based on the novel by Stanisław Ignacy Witkiewicz and set in Poland, in terms of representing masculinity it has much in common with Grodecki's Czech films. Again homosexuality in a young man emerges as the result of a seduction by an old man, who is obnoxious and insatiable in his lust, is facilitated by parental neglect and thrives on the general climate of decadence, in this case related to the demise of Polish noble culture. Unlike *Mandragora*, *Insatiability* failed to be treated seriously as a statement on (homo)sexuality, but was rather regarded as an unsuccessful film trying to make capital on cheap thrills (see, for example, Maniewski 2004).

Hana a její bratři (*Hannah and Her Brothers*, 2001) by the openly homosexual Slovak director Vladimír Adásek shares with *Mandragora* a similar character: a teenage boy from a dysfunctional family searching for his identity. However, in its ideology and visual style it is markedly different from Grodecki's film. Whilst in *Mandragora* Marek's 'homosexualisation' marks his demise, in Adásek's film it leads to Martin's liberation. Moreover, Adásek refrains from the old communist cliché that homosexuality came to the pure East from the decadent West. Instead, it represents it as firmly rooted in Slovak society and even Slovak family life. Stylistically, *Hannah and Her Brothers* moves away from the classical narrative which dominates in the films discussed in this chapter, and it draws on a number of films that invite queer reading, such as Bob Fosse's *Cabaret* (1972), not least because it is partly set in a cabaret. However, unlike Grodecki's film that reduces contemporary Czech urban culture to a handful of features, all borrowed from the West, Adásek's camp is very Slovak. I will argue that it is the first film from Eastern Europe employing distinctively camp aesthetics, as well as the first film where the representation of homosexuality is not subordinated to other discourses.

By contrast to Adásek's film, in Vladimír Morávek's *Nuda v Brně* (*Boredom in Brno*, 2003) homosexual romance constitutes only a minor subplot, overshadowed by the heterosexual relationship between two mentally impaired characters. However, the mode of representing the homosexual relationship as liberating young men, who are unsure about whether they fit into society or are even normal, bringing them a sense of belonging, conforms to the way offered by Adásek. For both Adásek and Morávek, coming out, or even not entering the closet in the first place, is a path to happiness and self-fulfilment.

From Homosexual to Gay

In conclusion I would like to reiterate my opinion that in Polish and Czechoslovak cinema during the communist period homosexuality and other 'non-straight' sexualities were typically used as metaphors for something else, and incorporated into wider discourses: of personal and political oppression/freedom, and nationality and foreignness. The most common representation of the homosexual was that of the (effeminate) invert. However, gradually he has been replaced by a man who in terms of his appearance does not stand out from the crowd, only reveals different sexual preferences. Homosexuals in the films made prior to 1989 are rarely cast in leading roles and they are treated with derision or with compassion by the films' authors. Their stories end tragically which, on the one hand, points to the difficult situation of Polish and Czechoslovak homosexuals and, on the other, to the homophobia or at least to the timidity of the filmmakers who are afraid to challenge the audience's conceptions by showing homosexuals who are better off than the society average. I will argue that neither Polish nor Czechoslovak postwar cinema developed a 'queer aesthetics' worthy of this name.

In postcommunist times the majority of films with homosexual men conform to the same characteristics, but they are accompanied by films in which homosexuality is regarded as a phenomenon in its own right. We also encounter films with reasonably happy homosexuals. As for the prospects of homosexuals in Polish, Czech and Slovak films, I will link them to the attitude to homosexuality in their countries. So far Polish, Czech and Slovak homosexual directors are reluctant to leave the closet. The cloud of homophobia is still too heavy in their countries to risk one's career in an attempt to break it.

Notes

1. Guy Hocquenghem describes homosexuality as a 'manufactured product of capitalist society' and a 'psychologically repressive category' (Hocquenghem 1993: 50–1).
2. In its embracing the sensibilities of closet and repressed homosexuals, and bisexuals, and other people who do not fit these categories, my essay can be regarded as contributing to 'queer studies', as defined by Harry Benshoff and Sean Griffin (Benshoff and Griffin 2004: 2). However, as queer analysis typically foregrounds 'gay aesthetics', to which I devote relatively little attention in my study, I am also refraining from applying the term 'queer', unless there is a serious reason for using it.
3. This leads me to consider in this chapter a film whose characters I regard here as homosexual, although elsewhere in this book I described the two males as being in a surrogate father – surrogate son relationship.
4. It should also be acknowledged that the Church's arguments against homosexuality are not confined to the Polish environment, but cut across many cultures. Gayle Rubin's diagram, which shows how the sexual value system operates in Western traditions, demonstrates that what the Polish Church describes as 'bad sex' is also regarded as bad in the West (Rubin 1993).
5. Fuks's best known novel, *Pan Theodor Mundstock*, was adapted by the Polish director, Waldemar Dziki as *Kartka z podróży* (*Postcard from a Journey*, 1993). Other films based on his works include *The Cremator* and *Tajemství zlatého Buddhy* (*Mysteries of a Golden Buddha*, 1973), directed by Dušan Klein.
6. The connection between vodka culture and homosexuality was also noted in Russian culture (Healey 2002).
7. For an extended discussion of the term 'camp' and its application to different forms of cultural production see Sontag 1994 and Meyer 1994.

8. It is worth noting that the scene when Zdeněk, clad in a clown's costume, shows little Klárka various tricks, that in Schorm's film, is completely innocent in the current context can be interpreted as having paedophilic undertones.
9. This term bears similarity to the Russian *tetka*, a word used to describe older homosexuals in Russian (Healey 2002). This similarity suggests that in both countries subcultures were created around these characters. This is certainly true as confirmed by a number of Polish novels about the lives of the Polish homosexuals such as *Czeska biżuteria* (*Czech Jewellery*, 1983) by Grzegorz Musiał, *Rudolf* (1980) by Marian Pankowski and *Lubiewo* (2005) by Michał Witkowski.
10. In the opinion of Sadowska and Żurawiecki, Jan's neighbour stands not for a physical woman (since she looks and behaves as if she came from a 'different world') but Jan's displaced or repressed sexuality which frightens him as it makes him realise that he is in conflict with his true identity, that he has lost something important and precious (Sadowska and Żurawiecki 2004).
11. The terms in which Cywińska discusses homosexual love in the interviews, given in relation to *Lovers from Marona*, reminds me of Guy Hocquenghem's famously saying that 'There is no subdivision of desire into homosexuality and heterosexuality. Properly speaking, desire is no more homosexual than heterosexual. Just like heterosexual desire, homosexual desire is an arbitrary frozen frame in an unbroken and polyvocal flux' (Hocquenghem 1993: 49–50).

CONCLUSIONS

Between Fate and Emptiness

In conclusion I want to look again at men in Polish, Czech and Slovak films from a bird's eye view, asking about what affected their lives and identities most and whether they were happy?' My answer is that the majority of them came across more as products of history and ideology or, more exactly, histories and ideologies, than as independent agents. Sometimes the male characters gave in unreflectively to circumstances, as if oblivious to the alternative values and lifestyles of those they chose. On other occasions, they were aware of them and even tried to take advantage of them, but in the end succumbed to what looked to them as the power of 'fate'. As emblematic examples we can regard Maciek Chełmicki in Andrzej Wajda's *Ashes and Diamonds*, Wiktor Rawicz in Wojciech Has's *How to Be Loved*, Miloš Hrma in Jiří Menzel's *Closely Observed Trains* or the males in the Homolkas saga, directed by Jaroslav Papoušek.

These ideologies which shaped men's lives, among which both socialism and Catholicism have a special position, are patriarchal; they overtly or covertly favour men, granting them privileges of action, power and often a place on a pedestal, if they fulfil their destiny. However, by and large, they did not make them happy for at least three intertwined reasons. Firstly, because with privileges came expectations and duties, which proved difficult or even impossible to fulfil. The hardest of all was most likely fighting in a war. Every war is extremely traumatic, but it could be argued that for Poles, Czechs and Slavs, squeezed between more powerful neighbours, their usual aggressors, it was especially so, as it offered little hope of victory. For this reason Polish war cinema abounds with mad patriots, whilst Czech and Slovak cinema with collaborators and deserters.

The second reason why patriarchal ideologies, promoted and implemented in Poland and Czechoslovakia, did not grant men fulfilment, even less happiness, was them being simultaneously a source of acute inequalities and conflict between men. The most obvious victims of patriarchal order are homosexual men. In the films discussed by me they often function as less than complete humans and negative models, showing heterosexual men what they should avoid in their lives. Moreover, homosexual men are not only victimised by heterosexual men and social institutions, but often act as their own oppressors, testifying to the their identification with patriarchal norms.

Some of the most visible and painful conflicts observed in the films are between fathers or men in paternal positions, and their sons. It could be argued that whole movements or 'schools', such as the Czech New Wave and Polish Cinema of Moral Concern, were built around the theme of the Oedipal rivalry. From these films come such memorable images as that of the preaching father which ends *Black Peter*, of Andrzej and the Student fighting over a knife in Roman Polański's *Knife in the Water* or of the eponymous 'cremator' in Juraj Herz's film killing his own son. Paradoxically, although socialist ideology was oriented to the future, regarding the prosperity of incoming generations as more important than of the current one, children, especially sons, typically turned out to be unhappy, and fathers frustrated and unfulfilled. Having said that, it should be mentioned, however, that by and large, the family as represented in Czechoslovak films, tended to be the location of both greater crimes and greater pleasures than its Polish equivalent. This imbalance might be explained by, on the one hand, the influence of Romanticism and, on the other, of Catholic teaching, on the behaviour of Polish men. Romanticism rendered public life more important than private; Catholicism demanded love and respect for one's parents.

Thirdly, patriarchy injured, rather than helped men, because it led to their antagonism with women or at least to a misunderstanding between women and men. Polish and Czechoslovak films time and again reveal how little the two sexes have in common, how much time and energy both men and women devote to fighting with each other or suppressing their affection, which could be used more profitably on working for the common good, such as, for example, improving one's economic situation or raising children. Patriarchal values and traditions are chiefly responsible for the failure of Polish, Czech and Slovak men as lovers. Even women's acceptance of patriarchy, which was not an uncommon position in the respective realities and respective cinemas, did not guarantee that the opposite sexes would create a happy team. On the contrary, on such occasions women often rejected men or men withdrew from the relationship with them, because men could not match the minimum standard women applied to them. This trend is excellently reflected in the erotic failures of characters such as Włodek in *Hunting Flies*, Marek in *Jowita* or Jan in *Return of the Prodigal Son*. Having said that, I must add that the gap between men and women appears to me larger in Polish films than in their Czechoslovak counterparts, again because the double forces of Romanticism and Catholicism in Poland chiselled a male ideal which was especially difficult for real men to match.

Although patriarchal ideologies encouraged men to act together with other men, as well as join forces with women, men in the films discussed in this book, typically come across as lonely figures, who must take their most important decisions single-handedly and live or die unhappily with their consequences. By and large, Polish, Czech and Slovak cinema, perhaps with the exception of socialist realism (whose representation are hardly convincing anyway) is populated by defeated men. I will even suggest that the image of a defeated man is more common in them than of a defeated woman. Failure or at least a lack of straightforward success is most clearly conveyed by the male stars of the postwar period. In particular, Zbigniew Cybulski and Jan Kačer personify men who are in conflict with their surroundings and with themselves. The actors appear always to be on the move, always chasing something, but the object of their pursuit proves unattainable, as the trains which Cybulski's characters fail to catch.

A clear indication of the dominance of injured or defeated masculinity is the way male bodies are represented in the respective cinemas. Their authors rarely allow the viewers to enjoy the view of a naked man and when it happens, the spectacle is dismal. Take, for example, the bathing men in Menzel's *Capricious Summer*, Włodek's aborted striptease in *Hunting Flies* or the sexual antics of the protagonist of *Porno*. Irrespective of whether the men in the films discussed by me are 'objectively' handsome or not, they tend to play men whose bodies do not arouse their female partners. The fact that men's, often prolonged, death, is such a common motif in many of them, adds to the impression that men in the films and, by extension, Polish, Czech and Slovak men, are unattractive. The only exception are those characters who are very young, in their teens and early twenties; their puppiness still hiding their future, unappetising physique.

The fall of communism to a large extent abolished the ideological, political, economic and social framework in which men operate. It also dramatically changed the conditions of filmmaking. It is suggested that postcommunist society is a-ideological or at least ideology plays a minor role in the lives of the real members of ex-Soviet bloc. Consequently, men as the film characters, as well as the creators of their images and their consumers now enjoy freedom as never before. However, the change in representation is smaller than one might expect, judging from the scale of changes that took place during this period. Still the prevailing image of a man is of a defeated or unfulfilled individual, although the nature of his failure differs from those during the communist period. If he fails now, it is almost exclusively due to his own shortcomings, rather than those of the system and he fails as a private man, father, lover, provider for his family or entrepreneur, not as bearer of a specific ideology. Men's lack of fulfilment is typically due to their disorientation and the sense of emptiness. It appears that when the male characters have no 'fate' to succumb to or fight against, they do not know how to shape their identity and enjoy themselves. This situation, at least as far as Polish cinema is concerned, reminds me somewhat of the 1960s, when political stabilisation and improvement in material conditions made male characters feel marginal, useless and full of envy for their elders who went through the experiences of the Second World War and Stalinism.

In this period we also find more men who are self-content and at peace with themselves than in previous epochs, but if it happens, usually it is at the price of somebody else's misfortune. A case in point are the frequent examples of young businessmen or men in position of authority, who confirm their masculinity by crushing the men and women over whom they have power. Young entrepreneurs in Feliks Falk's *Bailiff*, *Stupor*, directed by Natalia Koryncka-Gruz, Jan Svěrák's *The Ride* and *Loners*, directed by David Ondříček, perfectly illustrate this trend. They come across as selfish, shallow and generally unpleasant.

Not surprisingly, Polish, Czech and Slovak postcommunist cinema abounds in narratives that convey nostalgia for old heroes. This nostalgia is reflected in and fed by the fashion for war films, which, almost by definition, present men who are very different from those living today. Yet, even in contemporary films young men and women often look at older, 'communist' men as unattainable models. These older men appear to know better what is important in life, they do not fall prey to various traps capitalist reality lays for them, they understand women better and find rapport with their children. This nostalgia for communist heroes is reflected in the continuing strong presence in leading roles of actors, who began their careers in the communist period, such as Zdenek Svěrák, Bolek Polívka, Jan Tříska, Jiří Menzel, Bogusław Linda or Daniel Olbrychski. Rather than being disconcerted by the proximity of younger men, it affords them extra virility. As with all types of nostalgia, I find the yearning for the 'communist man' regressive and hope that with the passage of time it will disappear rather than thwarting the efforts to create a 'new men' who will be neither tragically heroic nor empty.

I want to reiterate, however, that my conclusions are not a product of an objective, impartial study, but a result of creating a discourse: choosing certain examples, at the expense of others, as well as of using certain methods. In particular, throughout my research I privileged better known films, and deliberately I focused on their overt content, albeit trying to account for some of the symbols and meanings hidden in the text. Of course, there are many more films with male characters which await interpretation, often lending themselves to different tools than those used in this book. As examples can serve the comedies of Stanisław Bareja, regarded nowadays as the most popular films in the history of People's Poland, the films Wojciech Has made after *How to Be Loved*, perhaps the most talented filmmaker to originate from the Polish soil who, yet, has been regarded as idiosyncratic or even somehow 'un-Polish', the surrealist films of Jan Švankmajer that mix live action with animation or the immensely popular crazy Czech comedies and spoofs of 1970s and 1980s. Other fascinating examples are the films of female directors with feminist concerns, such as Věra Chytilová or Barbara Sass, and the works of the directors who emigrated to the West.

Discussing the less mainstream films considered in this book, as well as other examples from outside the cannon, usually confirm my suspicion that employing looser narratives is usually accompanied by subverting or questioning patriarchal assumptions and including somewhat less stereotyped male characters than those populated in mainstream films. However, it should not be taken for granted that freeing a narrative automatically liberates its characters. Rather such an assumption should be carefully tested by analysing the numerous Polish, Czech and Slovak films awaiting discovery. I hope that my book will encourage readers to embark on this task.

Bibliography

Adamiak, Elżbieta (1993). 'O co chodzi w teologii feministycznej', *Więź*, 1, pp. 68–77.

Anderson, Benedict (1991). *Imagined Communities*, second edition (London: Verso).

Arcimowicz, Krzysztof (2003). *Obraz mężczyzny w polskich mediach: Prawda Fałsz Stereotyp* (Gdańsk: Gdańskie Wydawnictwo Psychologiczne).

Badinter, Elisabeth (1995). *XY: On Masculine Identity*, trans. from French by Lydia Davis (New York: Columbia University Press).

Benshoff, Harry and Sean Griffin (eds). (2004). *Queer Cinema: The Film Reader* (London: Routledge).

Bergson, Phillip (2005). 'Intimate Lighting/Intimní osvětlení' (Essay accompanying the DVD version of Ivan Passer's film) (London: Second Run DVD).

Bhabha, Homi K. (ed.). (1990). *Nation and Narration* (London: Routledge).

Biedroń, Robert (2004). '"Nieerotyczny dotyk": O hipokryzji i homofobii Kościoła katolickiego w Polsce', in Zbyszek Sypniewski i Błażej Warkocki (eds), *Homofobia po polsku* (Warszawa: Sic!), pp. 201–26.

Bird, Daniel (2006). 'The Cremator/Spalovač mrtvol' (Essay accompanying the DVD version of Juraj Herz's film) (London: Second Run DVD).

Biró, Yvette (1983). 'Pathos and Irony in East European Films', in David W. Paul (ed.), *Politics, Art and Commitment in the East European Cinema* (London: Macmillan), pp. 28–48.

Bly, Robert (1991). *Iron John: A Book About Men* (Shaftesbury: Element).

Booth, Stephenie (2005). 'Looking-glass women? A comparative analysis of gender and nation in Britain and the Czech Republic', in Vera Tolz and Stephenie Booth (eds), *Nation and Gender in Contemporary Europe* (Manchester: Manchester University Press), pp. 38–52.

Borowski, Tadeusz (1992). *This Way for the Gas, Ladies and Gentlemen*, trans. from Polish by Michael Kandel (London: Penguin).

Botting, Fred and Scott Wilson (1997). *The Bataille Reader* (Oxford: Blackwell).

Bradley, J.F.N. (1971). *Czechoslovakia: A Short History* (Edinburgh: Edinburgh University Press).

Branko, Pavel (1996). 'Zrcadlení?: Rozhovor s Evaldem Schormem', in Stanislav Ulver (ed.) *Film a doba: Antologie textu z let 1962–1970* (Prague: FaD), pp. 66–9.

Bronfenbrenner, Urie (1972). 'The Changing Soviet Family', in Michael Gordon (ed.), *The Nuclear Family in Crisis: The Search for an Alternative* (New York: Harper & Row), pp. 119–42.

Buchar, Robert (2004). *Czech New Wave Filmmakers in Interviews* (Jefferson: McFarland).

Cawelti, John G. (1976). *Adventure, Mystery, and Romance* (Chicago: The University of Chicago Press).

Chaw, Walter (2002). 'Dark Victory: Film Freak Central Interviews Dark Blue World Director Jan Svěrák', *Film Freak Central*, http://www.filmfreakcentral.net/notes/darkvictory.htm.

Chyb, Manana (2000). 'Bujać to my…', *Film*, 1, p. 52.

Cieslar, Jiří (2004). 'Daleká cesta/Distant Journey', in Peter Hames (ed.), *The Cinema of Central Europe* (London: Wallflower Press), pp. 45–52.

Clark, Katerina (2000). *The Soviet Novel: History as Ritual*, third edition (Bloomington: Indiana University Press).

Coates, Paul (1999). 'The curse of the law: *The Decalogue*', in Paul Coates (ed.), *Lucid Dreams: The Films of Krzysztof Kieślowski* (Trowbridge: Flicks Books), pp. 94–115.

————. (2002). 'Observing the Observer: Andrzej Wajda's *Holy Week* (1995)', *Canadian Slavonic Papers*, 1–2, pp. 25–33.

————. (2005). *The Red and the White: The Cinema of People's Poland* (London: Wallflower Press).

Cohan, Steven and Ina Rae Hark (eds). (1993). *Screening the Male: Exploring Masculinities in Hollywood Cinema* (London: Routledge).

Cohen, David (1990). *Being a Man* (London: Routledge).

Comolli, Jean Luc and Narboni, Jean (1992). 'Cinema/Ideology/Criticism', in Gerald Mast et al. (eds), *Film Theory and Criticism*, fourth edition (Oxford: Oxford University Press), pp. 682–9.

Černý, Václav (2001). 'Europejskie źródła czeskiej kultury', in Jacek Baluch (ed.), *Hrabal, Kundera, Havel…: Antologia czeskiego eseju* (Kraków: Universitas), pp. 169–222.

Dabert, Dobrochna (2003). *Kino moralnego niepokoju: Wokół wybranych problemów poetyki i etyki* (Poznań: Wydawnictwo Naukowe Uniwersytetu im. Adama Mickiewicza).

Daniel, František (1983). 'The Czech Difference', in David W. Paul (ed.), *Politics, Art and Commitment in the East European Cinema* (London: Macmillan), pp. 49–56.

Davies, Norman (2005). *God's Playground: A History of Poland*, vol. II, second edition (Oxford: Oxford University Press).

Dawson, Graham (1994). *Soldier Heroes: British Adventure, Empire and the Imagining of Masculinities* (London: Routledge).

Deleuze, Gilles and Guattari, Felix (2000). *Kafka: Toward a Minor Literature*, trans. from French by Dana Polan (Minneapolis: University of Minnesota Press).

Dowling, Maria (2002). *Czechoslovakia* (London: Arnold).

Drewnowski, Tadeusz (1992). 'Drugie życie Ścibora', *Kino*, 9, pp. 14–8.

Duch-Krzysztoszek, Danuta (1998). *Małżeństwo, seks, prokreacja: Analiza socjologiczna* (Warszawa: Wydawnictwo IFiS PAN).

Dunin, Kinga (2004). 'Fałszywi przyjaciele. Pożądana asymilacja czy asymilacja pożądania?', in Zbyszek Sypniewski and Błażej Warkocki (eds), *Homofobia po polsku* (Warszawa: Sic!), pp. 17–26.

———. (2005). 'Polska homoliteracka', *Gazeta Wyborcza*, 17/12, pp. 12–3.

Dyer, Richard (1990). *Now You See It: Studies on Lesbian and Gay Film* (London: Routledge).

———. (1992). 'Don't look now: The male pin-up', in *The Sexual Subject: A Screen Reader in Sexuality* (London: Routledge), pp. 265–76.

———. (1993). *The Matter of Images: Essays on Representations* (London: Routledge).

Easthope, Antony (1986). *What a Man's Gotta Do: The Masculine Myth in Popular Culture* (London: Paladin).

Eberharadt, Konrad (1982). *Konrad Eberhardt o polskich filmach* (Warszawa: Wydawnictwa Artystyczne i Filmowe).

Effenberger, Vratislav (1996). 'Obraz člověka v českém filmu', in Stanislav Ulver (ed.), *Film a doba: Antologie textu z let 1962–1970* (Prague: FaD), pp. 164–75.

Ehrenreich, Barbara (1995). 'The Decline of Patriarchy', in Maurice Berger et al. (eds), *Constructing Masculinity* (London: Routledge), pp. 284–90.

Engels, F. (1971). *The Condition of the Working Class in England* (Oxford: Basil Blackwell).

———. (1972). *The Origin of the Family, Private Property and the State* (London: Lawrence & Wishart).

Falkowska, Janina (2004). 'Popiół i diament/Ashes and Diamonds', in Peter Hames (ed.), *The Cinema of Central Europe* (London: Wallflower Press), pp. 65–74.

Fast, Piotr (2003). *Realizm socjalistyczny w literaturze rosyjskiej* (Kraków: Universitas).

Fiala, Miloš (1969). 'Vláčil. Körner. *Adelheid*', *Film a Doba*, 12, pp. 642–5.

Felis, Paweł T. (2006). 'Mały wielki film Barańskiego', *Gazeta Wyborcza*, 06/07, p. 13.

Filipowicz, Marcin (2005). 'Poglądy Tomasza Garrigue'a Masaryka na emancypację kobiet i ich wpływ na kształt ruchu kobiecego w I Republice Czechosłowackiej', in Elżbieta Durys i Elżbieta Ostrowska (eds), *Gender: Wizerunki kobiet i mężczyzn w kulturze* (Kraków: Rabid), pp. 311–23.

Flandrin, Jean-Louis (1979). *Families in Former Times: Kinship, Household and Sexuality* (Cambridge: Cambridge University Press).

Foucault, Michel (1986). 'What is an author?', in John Caughie (ed.), *Theories of Authorship* (London: Routledge), pp. 282–91.

———. (1998). *The History of Sexuality, vol. 1: The Will to Knowledge*, trans. from French by Robert Hurley (London: Penguin).

French A. (1982). *Czech Writers and Politics 1945–1969* (New York: Columbia University Press).

Freud, Sigmund (1963). *Sexuality and the Psychology of Love* (New York: Macmillan).

Fuentes, Carlos (1988). *Myself with Others* (London: Picador).

Fuszara, Małgorzata (1993). 'Abortion and the Formation of the Public Sphere in Poland', in Nanette Funk and Magda Mueller (eds), *Gender Politics and Post-Communism* (London: Routledge), pp. 240–52.

Gal, Susan and Gail Kligman (2000). *The Politics of Gender after Socialism: A Comparative-Historical Essay* (Princeton: Princeton University Press).

Gay, Peter (ed.) (1995). *The Freud Reader* (London: Vintage).

Gawlicz, Katarzyna and Starnawski Marcin (2004). 'Budzenie dyskursu: analiza debaty o prawach gejów i lesbijek na internetowym forum *Gazety Wyborczej*', in Zbyszek Sypniewski i Błażej Warkocki (eds), *Homofobia po polsku* (Warszawa: Sic!), pp. 27–52.

Głowacki, Janusz (1969). 'Zmowa pań', *Panorama*, 44, p. 7.

Gombrowicz, Witold (1997). *Dziennik 1953–1956* (Kraków: Wydawnictwo Literackie).

———. (2005). *Trans-Atlantyk* (Kraków: Wydawnictwo Literackie).

Graff, Agnieszka (2001). *Świat bez kobiet* (Warszawa: W.A.B).

Graffy, Julian (1997). 'Kolya', *Sight and Sound*, 5, pp. 46–7.

Gretkowska, Manuela (2002). 'Scheda', *Wprost*, 1007, p. 108.

Gryglewicz, Tomasz (2004). *Erotyzm w sztuce polskiej* (Wrocław: Wydawnictwo Dolnośląskie).

Haltof, Marek (2002). *Polish National Cinema* (Oxford: Berghahn Books).

Hall, Stuart (1992). 'The Question of Cultural Identity', in Stuart Hall et al. (eds), *Modernity and its Futures* (Cambridge: Polity Press), pp. 273–325.

Hames, Peter (1989). 'Czechoslovakia: After the Spring', in Daniel J. Goulding (ed.), *Post New Wave Cinema in the Soviet Union and Eastern Europe* (Bloomington: Indiana University Press), pp. 102–42.

———. (2000). 'The Good Soldier Švejk and after: the comic tradition in Czech film', in Diana Holmes and Alison Smith (eds), *100 Years of European Cinema* (Manchester: Manchester University Press).

———. (2004). 'Ostře sledované vlaky /Closely Observed Trains', in Peter Hames (ed.), *The Cinema of Central Europe* (London: Wallflower Press), pp. 117–27.

———. (2005). *The Czechoslovak New Wave*, second edition (London: Wallflower Press).

Hanáková, Petra (2005a). 'The Construction of Normality: The Lineage of Male Figures in Contemporary Czech Cinema', in Uta Röhrborn (ed.), *Mediale Welten in Tschechien nach 1898: Genderkonstructionen und Codes des Plebejismus* (München: Kubon and Sagner), pp. 149–59.

———. (2005b). 'Voices from another world: Feminine space and masculine intrusion in *Sedmikrásky* and *Vražda ing. Čerta*', in Anikó Imre (ed.), *East European Cinemas* (London: Routledge), pp. 63–77.

———. (2007). '"The Films We are Ashamed of": Czech Crazy Comedy of the 1970s and 1980s', paper presented at the conference 'Via Transversa: Lost Cinema of the Former Eastern Bloc', Art Museum of Estonia, Tallinn, October 2007.

Hašek, Jaroslav (1973). *The Good Soldier Švejk and his Fortunes in the World War, trans. from Czech by Cecil Parrott* (London: Penguin).

Havel, Václav (1985). 'The Power of the Powerless', in John Keane (ed.), *The Power of the Powerless* (London: Hutchinson), pp. 23–96.

Haynes, John (2003). *New Soviet Man: Gender and Masculinity in Stalinist Soviet Cinema* (Manchester: Manchester University Press).

Healey, Dan (2001). *Homosexual Desire in Revolutionary Russia: The Regulation of Sexual and Gender Dissent* (Chicago: University of Chicago Press).

———. (2002). 'The Disappearance of the Russian Queen, or How the Soviet Closet Was Born', in Barbara Evans Clements et al. (eds), *Russian Masculinities in History and Culture* (Basingstoke: Palgrave), pp. 152–71.

Helman, Alicja (1999). 'Women in Kieślowski's late films', in Paul Coates (ed.), *Lucid Dreams: The Films of Krzysztof Kieślowski* (Trowbridge: Flicks Books), pp. 116–35.

Hendrick, Susan S. and Clyde Hendrick (1992). *Romantic Love* (London: Sage).

Hocquenghem, Guy (1993). *Homosexual Desire*, second edition, trans. from French by Daniella Dangoor (Durham: Duke University Press).

Hollender, Barbara (2002). 'Siedem lat starań, trzy scenariusze', *Rzeczpospolita*, 201, p. A9.

Holý, Ladislav (1996). *The Little Czech and the Great Czech Nation* (Cambridge: Cambridge University Press).

Horrocks, Roger (1994). *Masculinity in Crisis* (Houndmills: Basingstoke).

Horton, Andrew J. (1999a). 'For a Fistful of Korunas: Vladimír Michálek's *Je třeba zabít Sekala*', *Kinoeye*, 18, http://www.ce-review.org/kinoeye/kinoeye15old3.html.

———. (1999b). 'Summer of Discontent: Jan Hrebejk's *Pelisky*', *Kinoeye*, 10, http://www.ce-review.org/99/10/kinoeye10_horton1.html.

———. (2000). 'A Nation of Thieves: Miloš Forman's *Hoří, má panenko, Kinoeye*, 5, http://www.ce-review.org/00/5/kinoeye5_horton.html.

———. (2001). 'Karlovy Vary: Concern for the Devil', *Kinoeye*, 3, http://www.kinoeye.org/01/03/horton03.php.

———. (2000-1). 'Just who owns the Shop: Identity and nationality in *Obchod na korze*', *Senses of Cinema*, 11, http://www.sensesofcinema.com/contents/00/11/shop.html.

Horton, Andrew J. and Kazi Štastná (1999). 'The Straight and Narrow Path: David Ondricek's *Septej*', *Kinoeye*, 7, http://www.ce-review.org/99/7/kinoeye7_horton2.html.

Horubała, Andrzej (1992). 'Stan lekkiego oszołomienia', *Kino*, 9, p. 19.

Iordanova, Dina (2003). *Cinema of the Other Europe* (London: Wallflower Press).

———. (2005). 'The Cinema of Eastern Europe: Strained loyalties, elusive clusters', in Anikó Imre (ed.), *East European Cinemas* (London: Routledge), pp. 229–49.

Jackiewicz, Aleksander (1968). *Film jako powieść XX wieku* (Warszawa: Wydawnictwa Artystyczne i Filmowe).

———. (1975). *Antropologia filmu* (Kraków: Wydawnictwo Literackie).

———. (1983). *Moja filmoteka: Kino polskie* (Warszawa: Wydawnictwa Artystyczne i Filmowe).

———. (1989). *Moja filmoteka: Film w kulturze* (Warszawa: Wydawnictwa Artystyczne i Filmowe).

Jaehne, Karen (1978). 'István Szabó: Dreams of Memories', *Film Quarterly*, 1, pp. 30–41.

Jagielski, Sebastian (2004). 'Daleko od nieba – czyli gej w polskim kinie', *Panoptikum*, 3, pp. 68–74.

Janicka, Bożena (1993). 'Kula w łeb', *Film*, 16, pp. 12–3.

———. (2000). 'Polowanie na jelenia', *Kino*, 1, p. 61.

———. (2003). 'Naga dusza', *Kino*, 11, pp. 51–2.

Janion, Maria (1998). *Płacz generała: Eseje o wojnie* (Warszawa: Sic!).

———. (1989). *Wobec zła* (Chotomów: Verba).

Janowska, Katarzyna (2005). 'Bohater naszych czasów', *Dialog*, 9, pp. 93–8.

Kajewski, Piotr (1969). 'Żart entomologiczny', *Odra*, 11, pp. 15–8.

Kałużyński, Zygmunt (1959). 'Pociąg z Warszawy czyli satyra na niemożność miłości', *Polityka*, 39, pp. 16–7.

———. (1967). 'Polakowi wciąż miłość nie wychodzi', *Polityka*, 38, pp. 16–7.

———. (1973). 'Tej miłości zabić się nie da', *Polityka*, 1, p. 8.

———. (1975). 'Bibeloty oskarżają', *Polityka*, p. 12–3.

———. (1976). *Wenus automobilowa: Obyczaje współczesne na ekranie* (Warszawa: Państwowy Instytut Wydawniczy).

Kaňuch, Martin (2004). 'Vtačkovia, siroty a blázni/Birds, Orphans and Fools', in Peter Hames (ed.), *The Cinema of Central Europe* (London: Wallflower Press), pp. 163–71.

Kenez, Peter (1992). *Cinema and Soviet Society* (Cambridge: Cambridge University Press).

Kino gejowskie (1996). *Easy Rider*, 8–9.

Kittler, Friedrich A. (1990). *Discourse Networks 1800/1900*, trans. from German by Michael Metteer (Stanford: Stanford University Press).

Kligman, Gail (1994). 'The social legacy of communism: women, children, and the feminisation of poverty', in James R. Millar and Sharon L. Wolchik (eds), *The Social Legacy of Communism* (Cambridge: Woodrow Wilson Centre Press and Cambridge University Press), pp. 252–70.

Kopaněnová, Galina (1968). 'Dvě hodiny s Milošem Formanem', *Film a doba*, pp. 399–405.

Kornacki, Krzysztof (1996). 'Bohater w przydeptanych kapciach: Zbigniew Cybulski w kinie "małej stabilizacji"', in Mariola Jankun-Dopartowa i Mirosław Przylipiak (eds), *Człowiek z ekranu: Z antropologii postaci filmowej* (Kraków: Arcana), pp. 73–88.

Kornatowska, Maria (1975). *Filmy o miłości* (Warszawa: Wydawnictwa Artystyczne i Filmowe).

———. (1990). *Wodzireje i amatorzy* (Warszawa: Wydawnictwa Artystyczne i Filmowe).

———. 1995). '"...Yet We Do Not Know What Will Become of Us". On the Artistic Output of Wojciech Jerzy Has', in Ewelina Nurczyńska-Fidelska and Zbigniew Batko (eds), *Polish Cinema in Ten Takes* (Łódź: Łódzkie Towarzystwo Naukowe), pp. 39–49.

Kostková, Pavlina (2001). 'A Small Stone in a Big Mosaic: Arnošt Lustig on why he is more than just a writer on the Holocaust', *Central Europe Review*, 28, http://www.ce-review.org/01/28/kostkova28.html.

Kot, Wiesław (2006). 'Kino gejowskiego niepokoju', *Wprost*, 1209, pp. 96–9.

Král, Petr (1983). 'Być Czechem', *Zeszyty Literackie*, 2, pp. 45–9.

Kroh, Antoni (1992). *O Szwejku i o nas* (Nowy Sącz: Sądecka Oficyna Wydawnicza).

Kroutvor, Josef (2001). 'Europa Środkowa: anegdota i historia', in Jacek Baluch (ed.), *Hrabal, Kundera, Havel...: Antologia czeskiego eseju* (Kraków: Universitas), pp. 223–89.

Krutnik, Frank (1991). *In a Lonely Street: Film Noir, Genre, Masculinity* (London: Routledge).

Krysiak, Jerzy (1990). 'Romans z władzą', *Kino*, 8, p.16–9.

Krzemiński, Adam (1991). 'Zmiana kodu: Rozmowa z Marią Janion', *Polityka*, 48, pp. 17–8.

Krzywicka, Irena (1956). 'Współczesna miłość', *Nowa Kultura*, 6, pp. 1–2.

Kundera, Milan (1981). 'The Czech Wager', *New York Review of Books*, 21/01, pp. 21–2.

———. (2005). *The Art of the Novel*, trans. from French by Linda Asher (London: Faber and Faber).

Kurz, Iwona (2005). *Twarze w tłumie: Wizerunki bohaterów wyobraźni zbiorowej w kulturze polskiej lat 1955–1969* (Izabelin: Świat Literacki).

Kusý, Miroslav (1985). 'Chartism and "real socialism"', in John Keane (ed.), *The Power of the Powerless* (London: Hutchinson), pp. 152–77.

Lenin, V.I. (1972). *On the Emancipation of Women* (Moscow: Progress Publishers).

Levi, Primo (1988). *The Drowned and the Saved*, trans. from Italian by Raymond Rosenthal (London: Michael Joseph).

Lewenstein, Barbara and Małgorzata Melchior (1992). 'Escape to the Community', in Janine R. Wedel (ed.), *The Unplanned Society: Poland During and After Communism* (New York: Columbia University Press), pp. 173–80.

Liehm, Antonín (1983). 'Miloš Forman: the Style and the Man', in David W. Paul (ed.), *Politics, Art and Commitment in the East European Cinema* (London: Macmillan), pp. 211–24.

Liehm, Mira and Antonín Liehm (1977). *The Most Important Art: Soviet and Eastern European Film after 1945* (University of California Press).

L.K. (1965). 'The Shop on the High Street', *Films and Filming*, 6, pp. 43 and 53.

Lubelski, Tadeusz (1992a). *Strategie autorskie w polskim filmie fabularnym lat 1945–1961* (Kraków: Wydawnictwo Uniwersytetu Jagiellońskiego).

———. (1992b). '*Popiół i diament* (Polskie filmy kultowe)', *Kino*, 9, pp. 20–3 and 44–6.

———. (1996). 'Bohater Konwickiego', in Mariola Jankun-Dopartowa i Mirosław Przylipiak (eds), *Człowiek z ekranu: Z antropologii postaci filmowej* (Kraków: Arcana), pp.63–71.

Lukowski, Jerzy and Hubert Zawadzki (2001). *A Concise History of Poland* (Cambridge: Cambridge University Press).

MacKinnon, Kenneth (2003). *Representing Men: Maleness and Masculinity in the Media* (London: Arnold).
Malečková, Jitka (1996). 'Gender, Nation and Scholarship: Reflections on Gender/Women's Studies in the Czech Republic', in Mary Maynard and June Purvis (eds), *New Frontiers in Women's Studies: Knowledge, Identity and Nationalism* (London: Taylor and Francis), pp. 96–112.
Maniewski, Maciej (1994). 'Zakazane rewiry?', *Film*, 5, pp. 88–9.
———. (2004). 'Przesycenie', *Kino*, 1, p. 51.
Marshall, John (1981). 'Pansies, perverts and macho men: changing conceptions of male masculinity', in Kenneth Plummer (ed.), *The Making of the Modern Homosexual* (London: Hutchinson), pp. 133–54.
Marszałek, Rafał (2006). *Kino rzeczy znalezionych* (Gdańsk: Słowo/ Obraz Terytoria).
Mazierska, Ewa (2000). 'Life and work in Silesia according to Kazimierz Kutz', in Valerie Mainz and Griselda Pollock (eds), *Work and the Image: Work, Craft and Labour* (Aldershot: Ashgate), pp. 177–92.
———. (2002). 'The Exclusive Pleasures of Being a Second Generation Inteligent: Representation of social class in the films of Andrzej Wajda', *Canadian Slavonic Papers*, 3–4, pp. 233–49.
———. (2003). 'The redundant male: representation of masculinity in Polish postcommunist cinema', *Journal of Film and Video*, 2–3, pp. 29–43.
———. (2004a). 'Eroica', in Peter Hames (ed.), *The Cinema of Central Europe* (London: Wallflower Press), pp. 55–63.
———. (2004b). 'Wajda on War' (Essay accompanying the DVD version of Andrzej Wajda's *A Generation*) (New York: Criterion).
———. (2004c). 'Domesticating madness, revisiting Polishness: the cinema of Marek Koterski', *Journal of Film and Video*, 3, pp. 20–34.
———. (2006). 'In the name of absent fathers and other men: Representation of motherhood in the Polish postcommunist cinema', *Feminist Media Studies*, 1, pp. 67–83.
McIntosh, Mary (1981). 'The homosexual role', in Kenneth Plummer (ed.), *The Making of the Modern Homosexual* (London: Hutchinson), pp. 30–49.
Meller, Stefan (1992). 'Wajda: historiozof, a może medium?', *Dialog*, 6, pp. 86–91.
Merz, Irena (1954). *O filmie czechosłowackim* (Warszawa: Filmowa Agencja Wydawnicza).
Messner, Michael A. (1997). *Politics of Masculinities: Men in Movements* (London: Sage).
Meyer, Moe (ed.). (1994). *The Politics and Poetics of Camp* (London: Routledge).
Michałek, Bolesław (1973). *The Cinema of Andrzej Wajda*, trans. from Polish by Edward Rothert (London: The Tantivy Press).
———. (2002). 'Has, Brandys, Krafftówna. "Nowa Kultura" 1963, nr 4, s. 8', in Bożena Janicka i Andrzej Kołodyński (eds), *Bolesław Michałek: Ambasador polskiego kina* (Kraków: Rabid), pp. 132–4.
Michałek, Bolesław and Turaj, Frank (1988). *The Modern Cinema of Poland* (Bloomington: Indiana University Press).

Mistríková, Lubica (2004). 'Obchod na korze/A Shop on the High Street', in Peter Hames (ed.), *The Cinema of Central Europe* (London: Wallflower Press), pp. 97–105.

Mitchell, Juliet (1974). *Psychoanalysis and Feminism* (London: Allen Lane).

Molyneux, Maxine (1994). 'The "Woman Question" in the Age of Communism's Collapse', in Mary Evans (ed.), *The Woman Question* (London: Sage), pp. 303–30.

———. (1996). 'Women's Rights and the International Context in the Post-Communist States', in Monica Threlfall (ed.), *Mapping the Women's Movement: Feminist Politics and Social Transformation in the North* (London: Verso), pp. 232–59.

Morawski, Stefan (1975). 'Czy *Dzieje grzechu* są szmirą?', *Literatura*, 27, pp. 6–7.

Moss, Kevin (1995). 'The Underground Closet: Political and Sexual Dissidence in Eastern Europe', in Ellen E. Berry (ed.), *Postcommunism and the Body Politic* (New York: New York University Press), pp. 229–51.

———. (2006). 'Who's Renting These Boys?: Wiktor Grodecki's Czech Hustler Documentaries', *InterAlia*, 1, http://www.interalia.org.pl/numery.php?nid=1&aid=9.

Mosse, George L. (1985). *Nationalism and Sexuality: Middle-Class Morality and Sexual Norms in Modern Europe* (Madison: University of Wisconsin Press).

Mulvey, Laura (1975). 'Visual Pleasure and Narrative Cinema', in Gerald Mast et al. (eds), *Film Theory and Criticism* (Oxford: Oxford University Press), pp. 746–57.

Murphy, Ryan (1990). 'A Spanish Fly in the Hollywood Ointment: Gay Director Pedro Almodóvar Refuses to Be Tied Up by Censorship', *The Advocate*, 19/06, p. 39.

Murray, Raymond (1998). *Images in the Dark: An Encyclopedia of Gay and Lesbian Film and Video* (London: Titan).

Nurczyńska-Fidelska, Ewelina (1982). *Andrzej Munk* (Kraków: Wydawnictwo Literackie).

———. (1995). 'Romanticism and History: A Sketch of the Creative Output of Andrzej Wajda', in Ewelina Nurczyńska-Fidelska and Zbigniew Batko (eds), *Polish Cinema in Ten Takes* (Łódź: Łódzkie Towarzystwo Naukowe), pp. 7–19.

———. (2003). *Czas i przesłona: O Filipie Bajonie i jego twórczości* (Kraków: Rabid).

Ostrowska, Elżbieta (2004). 'Landscape and lost time: Ethnoscape in the work of Andrzej Wajda', *Kinoeye*, 5, http://www.kinoeye.org/04/05/ostrowska05.php.

———. (2005). 'Socrealistyczne maskarady patriarchatu', in Małgorzata Jakubowska et al. (eds), *Między słowem a obrazem* (Kraków: Rabid), pp. 205–12.

Ostrowska Elżbieta and Michael Stevenson (2000). 'Other Sexualities in Polish Cinema', paper presented at the conference 'Marginality and Representations in European Cinema', Kingston University, London, December 2000.

Owen, Jonathan (2007). 'The Avant-Garde Tradition in Czech New Wave Cinema', Ph.D dissertation (Manchester: University of Manchester).

Ozimek, Stanisław (1980). 'Film fabularny', in Jerzy Toeplitz (ed.), *Historia filmu polskiego*, vol. 4 (Warszawa: Wydawnictwa Artystyczne i Filmowe), pp. 11–209.

Paris, Michael (1995). *From the Wright Brothers to Top Gun: Aviation and Popular Cinema* (Manchester: Manchester University Press).
Parker, Andrew et al. (1992). 'Introduction', in Andrew Parker et al. (eds) *Nationalisms and Sexualities* (London: Routledge), pp. 1–18.
Parker, Andrew et al. (eds). (1992). *Nationalisms and Sexualities* (London: Routledge).
Paul, David W. (1979). *The Cultural Limits of Revolutionary Politics: Change and Continuity in Socialist Czechoslovakia* (New York: East European Quarterly).
Paul, David W. and Rebecca Fox (1983). 'The Fickle Dialectic: Realism and the Cinematic Hero in Films from Socialist Europe', in David W. Paul (ed.), *Politics, Art and Commitment in the East European* Cinema (London: Macmillan), pp. 100–30.
Pawłowski, Roman (2006). 'Jestem łże-elita: Z Izabellą Cywińską rozmawia Roman Pawłowski', *Wysokie Obcasy* (Supplement to *Gazeta Wyborcza*), 25, pp. 11–4.
Piotrowska, Anita (2001). 'Przeszłość jako teraźniejszość', *Kino*, 3, pp. 19–20.
Piwińska, Marta (1973). *Legenda romantyczna i szydercy* (Warszawa: PIW).
———. (1984). *Miłość romantyczna* (Kraków: Wydawnictwo Literackie).
Płonowska Ziarek, Ewa (1998). 'The Scar of the Foreigner and the Fold of the Baroque: National Affiliations and Homosexuality in Gombrowicz's *Trans-Atlantyk*', in Ewa Płonowska Ziarek (ed.), *Gombrowicz's Grimaces* (Albany: State University of New York Press), pp. 213–44.
Pošová Katerina (1998). 'We ought to have a Ministry for the Moral-Intellectual Environment: An interview with Jirí Menzel', *Filmkultura*, 5, http://www.filmkultura.iif.hu:8080/articles/profiles/menz2.en.html.
Powrie, Phil, Ann Davies and Bruce Babington (eds). (2004). *The Trouble With Men: Masculinities in European and Hollywood Cinema* (London: Wallflower Press).
Privett, Ray (2001). 'God and country (or maybe not): Jerzy Kawalerowicz interviewed', *Kinoeye*, 7, http://www.kinoeye.org/01/07/privett07.php.
Prokopová, Alena (2001). 'Tmavomodrý svět', *Cinema*, 5, pp. 34–40.
Pynsent, Robert B. (1989). 'Conclusory Essay: Decadence, Decay and Innovation', in Robert Pynsent (ed.), *Decadence and Innovation: Austro-Hungarian Life and Art at the Turn of the Century* (London: Weidenfeld and Nicolson), pp. 111–248.
———. (1994). *Questions of Identity: Czech and Slovak Ideas of Nationality and Personality* (London: Central European University Press).
———. (ed.) (1993). *The Everyman Companion to East European Literature* (London: J.M. Dent).
Racław-Markowska, Mariola (2000). 'Od jednorodności do różnorodności; modernizacja rodzin w Polsce', *Problemy rodziny*, 2–3, pp. 22–9.
Radkiewicz, Małgorzata (2005). 'XY–tożsamość mężczyzny w polskich filmach fabularnych', in Elżbieta Durys i Elżbieta Ostrowska (eds), *Gender: Wizerunki kobiet i mężczyzn w kulturze* (Kraków: Rabid), pp. 259–68.
Rek, Jan (2005). 'W cieniu socrealizmu: wczesne filmy Jerzego Kawalerowicza', in Małgorzata Jakubowska et al. (eds), *Między słowem a obrazem* (Kraków: Rabid), pp. 263–84.
Ritz, German (2002). *Gender i płeć w literaturze polskiej od romantyzmu do postmodernizmu* (Warszawa: Wiedza Powszechna).

Roberts, Andrew (2005). *From Good King Wenceslas to the Good Soldier Švejk: A Dictionary of Czech Popular Culture* (Budapest: Central European University Press).

Robin, Régine (1992). *Socialist Realism: An Impossible Aesthetic*, trans. from French by Catherine Porter (Stanford: Stanford University Press).

Roszak, Theodore (1995). *The Making of Counter Culture* (Berkeley: University of California Press).

Rougemont, Denis de (1983). *Love in the Western World*, trans. from French by Montgomery Belgion (Princeton: Princeton University Press).

Rubin, Gayle S. (1993). 'Thinking Sex', in Henry Abelove et al. (eds), *The Lesbian and Gay Studies Reader* (New York: Routledge), pp. 3–44.

Sadowska Małgorzata i Bartosz Żurawiecki (2004). 'Barwy ochronne, czyli kino seksualnego niepokoju', *Dialog*, 6, pp. 118–20.

Sayer, Derek (2000). *The Coasts of Bohemia: A Czech History* (Princeton: Princeton University Press).

Scott, Hilda (1976). *Women and Socialism: Experiences from Eastern Europe* (London: Alison and Busby).

Segal, Lynne (1997). *Slow Motion: Changing Masculinities, Changing Men*, second edition (London: Virago).

Simmen, Rolf (2006). 'Moc toho nenajdete…', *CinePur*, 45, http://www.cinepur.cz/article.php?article=971.

Siwicka, Dorota (2002). *Romantyzm 1822–1863* (Warszawa: Wydawnictwo Naukowe PWN).

Skwara, Anita (2006). 'Film socrealistyczny – ciało ekranowe jako inskrypcja ideologii', in Krzysztof Stępnik i Magdalena Piechota (eds), *Socrealizm: Fabuły-komunikaty-ikony* (Lublin: Wydawnictwo Uniwersytetu Marii Curie-Skłodowskiej), pp. 315–23.

Slater, Thomas J. (ed.). (1992). *Handbook of Soviet and East European Films and Filmmakers* (London: Greenwood Press).

Sobolewski, Tadeusz (1993). 'Andrzej Wajda: Pojedynek z dniem dzisiejszym', *Kino*, 4, pp. 4–8.

———. (2005). 'Dziwna rodzina', *Kino*, 10, p. 94.

Sokolová, Věra (2001). 'Representations of Homosexuality and the Separation of Gender and Sexuality in the Czech Republic Before and After 1989', in Ann Katherine Isaacs (ed.), *Political Systems and Definitions of Gender Roles* (Pisa: Edizioni Plus, Universita di Pisa), pp. 273–88.

———. (2004). '"Don't Get Pricked!": Representation and the Politics of Sexuality in the Czech Republic', in Sibelan Forrester et al. (eds), *Over the Wall/After the Fall: Post-totalitarian Cultures through an East-West Gaze* (Bloomington: Indiana University Press), pp. 251–67.

Sontag, Susan (1994). 'Notes on Camp', in her *Against Interpretation* (London: Vintage), pp. 275–92.

Spicer, Andrew (2004). 'The "other war": subversive images of the Second World War in service comedies', in Stephen Caunce et al. (eds), *Relocating Britishness* (Manchester: Manchester University Press), pp. 167–82.

Stachówna, Grażyna (1996). 'Równanie szeregów: Bohaterowie filmów socjalistycznych 1949p-1955)', in Mariola Jankun-Dopartowa i Mirosław Przylipiak (eds), *Człowiek z ekranu: Z antropologii postaci filmowej* (Kraków: Arcana), pp. 7–25.

Steiner, Peter (2000). *The Deserts of Bohemia: Czech Fiction and its Social Context* (Ithaca: Cornell University Press).

Stern, J.P. (1992). *The Heart of Europe: Essays on Literature and Ideology* (Oxford: Blackwell).

Strohlein, Andrew (1999). 'A Queer Taboo', *Central Europe Review*, 7, http://www.ce-review.org/99/7/theissue7.html.

Studlar, Gaylyn (1996). *This Mad Masquerade: Stardom and Masculinity in the Jazz Age* (Chichester, NY: Columbia University Press).

Sypniewski, Zbyszek and Błażej Warkocki (eds). (2004). *Homofobia po polsku* (Warszawa: Sic!).

Szczepańska, Anna (2006). 'Miłość erotyczna w polskiej prozie produkcyjnej', in Krzysztof Stępnik i Magdalena Piechota (eds), *Socrealizm: Fabuły-komunikaty-ikony* (Lublin: Wydawnictwo Uniwersytetu Marii Curie-Skłodowskiej), pp. 67–79.

Szyma, Tadeusz (1988). 'Na marginesie *Łuku Erosa*', *Tygodnik Powszechny*, 19, p. 12.

Škvorecký, Josef (1971). *All the Bright Young Men and Women: A Personal History of the Czech Cinema*, trans. from Czech by Michael Schonberg (Toronto: Peter Martin).

———. (1982). *Jiří Menzel and the History of the Closely Watched Trains* (New York: East European Monographs).

Świętochowska, Grażyna (2003). 'Szkic o Czarnym Piotrusiu Miloša Formana', *Panoptikum*, 1, pp. 46–8.

Taborsky, Edward (1961). *Communism in Czechoslovakia 1948–1960* (Princeton: Princeton University Press).

Tennov, Dorothy (1999). *Love and Limerence: the Experience of Being in Love* (New York: Scarborough House).

Tomasik, Krzysztof (2005). 'Szuflada z podwójnym dnem', *Krytyka Polityczna*, 9\10, pp. 56–60.

Trzaska, Paweł (1992). 'Koniec starych czasów: Rozmowa z Jiřím Menzlem', *Kino*, 3, pp. 10–3.

Tubielewicz Mattsson, Dorota (2003a). 'Mężczyzna w nieludzkim świecie: Wizerunki mężczyzny w poezji polskiego socrealizmu', in Ewa Teodorowicz-Hellman and Dorota Tubielewicz Mattsson (eds), *Wizerunki mężczyzny w języku i literaturze polskiej* (Stockholm: Stockholms Universitet), pp. 53–66.

———. (2003b). 'Mężczyzna w nieludzkim świecie: Wizerunki mężczyzny w poezji i plastyce polskiego socrealizmu', *Blok*, pp. 90–116.

Vaneigem, Raoul (2001). *The Revolution of Everyday Life*, trans. from French by Donald Nicholson-Smith (London: Rebel Press).

Vogel, Amos (1974). *Film as a Subversive Art* (London: Weidenfeld and Nicolson).

Voráč, Jiří (1997). 'Czech Film after 1989: The Wave of the Young Newcomers', *Kinema*, Spring, pp. 5–12.

Waczków, Józef (1970). 'Ecce Homo', *Ekran*, 42, p. 8.
Wajda, Andrzej (2000). *Kino i reszta świata* (Kraków: Znak).
Walichnowski, Tadeusz (ed.). (1989). *Deportacje i przemieszczenia ludności polskiej w głąb ZSRR 1939–1945: Przegląd piśmiennictwa* (Warszawa: Państwowe Wydawnictwo Naukowe).
Warkocki, Błażej (2002). 'Otwieranie toalety', *Res Publica Nowa*, 9, pp. 52–7.
———. (2005). 'Skradziony list, czyli homoseksualna tajemnica wobec kanonu literatury polskiej', in Tatiana Czerska and Inga Iwasiów (eds), *Kanon i obrzeża* (Kraków: Universitas), pp. 295–307.
———. (2006). Tożsamość Innego: Dyskurs płci i konstruowanie odmienności w prozie najnowszej, Ph.D dissertation (Poznań: University of Adam Mickiewicz).
Watson, Peggy (1993). 'Eastern Europe's Silent Revolution: Gender', *Sociology*, 3: 471–87.
———. (1996). 'The Rise of Masculinism in Eastern Europe', in Monica Threlfall (ed.), *Mapping the Women's Movement: Feminist Politics and Social Transformation in the North* (London: Verso), pp. 216–31.
———. (1997). '(Anti)feminism after Communism', in Ann Oakley and Juliet Mitchell (eds.) *Who's Afraid of Feminism?* (London: Hamish Hamilton), pp. 144–61.
Wedel, Janine R. (ed.). (1992). *The Unplanned Society: Poland During and After Communism* (New York: Columbia University Press).
Weeks, Jeffrey (1981). 'Discourse, desire and sexual deviance: some problems in a history of homosexuality', in Kenneth Plummer (ed.) *The Making of the Modern Homosexual* (London: Hutchinson), pp. 76–111.
———. (1985). *Sexuality and its Discontents: Meanings, Myths and Modern Sexualities* (London: Routledge and Kegan Paul).
———. (1989a). 'Sexual Politics', *New Internationalist*, 201, http://www.newint.org/issue201/politics.htm.
———. (1989b). *Sex, Politics and Society: The Regulation of Sexuality since 1800*, second edition (London: Longman).
Werner, Andrzej (1987). *Polskie, arcypolskie...* (Warszawa: Niezależna Oficyna Wydawnicza).
Wexman, Virginia Wright (1987). *Roman Polanski* (London: Columbus Books).
Wilson, David (1971). 'The Cremator', *Monthly Film Bulletin*, 452, 184–5.
Wolchik, Sharon L. (1991). *Czechoslovakia in Transition: Politics, Economics and Society* (London: Pinter Publishers).
Woroszylski, Wiktor (1993). 'Pierścionek ze znakiem zapytania', *Kino*, 4, pp. 9–11.
Wróbel, Marta (2000). 'Metaforyzacja rzeczywistości lagrowej w filmie *Kornblumenblau* Leszka Wosiewicza', *Kwartalnik Filmowy*, 29-30, pp. 96–112.
Zwierzchowski, Piotr (2000). *Zapomniani bohaterowie: O bohaterach filmowych polskiego socrealizmu* (Warszawa: Trio).
———. (2005). *Pęknięty monolit: Koteksty polskiego kina socrealistycznego* (Bydgoszcz: Wydawnictwo Uniwersytetu Kazimierza Wielkiego).
Žalman, Jan (1968). *Films and Filmmakers in Czechoslovakia* (Prague: Orbis).

Index